GREAT ROCK MUSICALS

GREAT

ROCK MUSICALS

Edited, with an introduction and notes
on the plays, authors, and composers,
by

STANLEY RICHARDS

STEIN AND DAY/*Publishers*/New York

Copyright © 1979 by Stanley Richards
All rights reserved
Designed by Ed Kaplin
Printed in the United States of America
Stein and Day/*Publishers*/Scarborough House
Briarcliff Manor, N.Y. 10510

Library of Congress Cataloging in Publication Data

Main entry under title:

Great rock musicals.

    Librettos.
    1.   Musical revues, comedies, etc.—Librettos.
I.   Richards, Stanley
ML48.G7   782.8′1′2   78-7005
ISBN 0-8128-2509-8

for
MARILYN PHILLIPS

CONTENTS

INTRODUCTION

Although rock 'n' roll began to make inroads on the popular music scene in the middle fifties, it didn't invade the legitimate theatre until the late sixties. The breakthrough came with the enormous success of *Hair* and was followed almost immediately by *Your Own Thing,* which made history of its own by becoming the first Off-Broadway show to win the New York Drama Critics' Circle Award for the season's best musical.

In the 1960s the great blossoming of the counterculture, the protest pageants, the be-ins, sit-ins and happenings, inspired any number of rock musicals, particularly in the Off-Broadway sector. Its impact was such that Otis L. Guernsey, Jr., editor of the distinguished theatre yearbook, wrote in *The Best Plays of 1969–1970:*

> The rock lyric is a literary form developed in this decade; as different from the June-moon cadences of our rose-colored memory as the Beatles from the Lombardo brothers; a pounding, psychedelic, powerful and versatile new word style to match the new music, expressive of any feeling from despair to ecstasy, of any social comment . . . This season, the rock lyric was so prominent a part of the musical scene, particularly Off-Broadway, that it would be inappropriate to close a section of 1969-70 "bests" without citing it high up among the most exciting elements of the contemporary stage.

While the rock musical was nurtured in the environs of Off-Broadway, it soon moved uptown to more affluent Broadway, where it was enthusiastically greeted with cheers and huge patronage by the theatregoing public. To consider some figures: seven of the musicals included in this volume totaled 8,050 performances in their initial engagements. (Two—*The Wiz* and *Grease,* as of this writing—are still playing to packed houses and are approaching long-run records.) What went beyond—with countless revivals, road, stock, concert, and amateur performances—only God and the musicals' copyright holders can determine.

How does the rock musical differ from the traditional musical? It is more freewheeling, less confined, and even when set in a specific period, manages to evoke an expressive topicality, an implied contemporaneousness. Frequently, it is also more generous in its utilization of lights and audiovisuals and, of course, there is the beat and the amplified sound. (It might be of interest to point out here that even in the more traditional musicals and revivals produced today, the amplification is souped-up to give them a more modern sound.)

While some professional theatrical observers and score-keepers initially considered the rock musical as merely a trend that would not last out the decade, it has been proven otherwise. Its box-office potency remains high, and it has lost none of its sheen or theatrical effectiveness. Surely it is no idle coincidence that three major motion pictures based on rock musicals represented in this collection—*The Wiz, Grease,* and *Hair*—were released in 1978 and in their cinematic transformations will now be seen by many millions of moviegoers throughout the world.

Now, too, these eight exceptional rock musicals are appearing together in an anthology for the first time. One—*The Wiz*—has never been published before; and the others, with the exception of *Grease,* are making their literary debuts between hard covers. It is the hope of this editor that they will now delight and entertain readers as they have countless numbers of theatregoers.

—Stanley Richards
New York, New York

GREAT ROCK MUSICALS

THE WIZ

(Adapted from The Wonderful Wizard of Oz

by L. Frank Baum)

Book by William F. Brown

Music and Lyrics by Charlie Smalls

EDITOR'S NOTES

On the night of January 5, 1975, a tornado hit the Broadway stage in the form of a marvelously energetic, spectacularly colorful and thoroughly entertaining rock musical, *The Wiz*. Based on L. Frank Baum's ageless *The Wonderful Wizard of Oz*, which initially began to entrance readers and, subsequently, theatregoers in the early part of this century, it retains the characters and structure of the original but also manages, with considerable cheerfulness, to absorb facets of the contemporary black experience. As Jack Kroll imparted to his *Newsweek* readers:

> American blacks have been moving down a yellow brick road (badly in need of repair) for a long time, looking for Oz or the Emerald City or some other dream deferred, so the idea of an all-black version of *The Wizard of Oz* makes perfect sense. And happily *The Wiz* is more than that; it's also perfect nonsense and one of the most cyclonic blasts of high energy to hit Broadway in a long time. Only a wicked witch or a pooped-out drama critic could remain unmoved by *The Wiz*'s blazing high spirits, its piping-hot servings of soul and its sly sagacity about the pleasures and perils of fantasy.

Richard Watts, Jr. of the *New York Post* lauded the production as "An enchanting show! The new black musical version of *The Wizard of Oz* is picturesque, vivid, exotic and charming, and it moves with dynamic speed and humor."

Clive Barnes stated in *The New York Times*: "With a musical mixture of rock, gospel and soul music, written by Charlie Smalls, who provided both score and lyrics, *The Wiz* is a new kind of fantasy, colorful, mysterious, opulent and fanciful." And according to Howard Kissel of *Women's Wear Daily*: "The book by William F. Brown gives *The Wiz* a sassy archness . . . the tone is self-mockery with a satiric bite, L. Frank Baum out for a night at the Cotton Club, sometimes marvelously outrageous, sometimes hip, always fun."

The Wiz immediately became a "hot" ticket and, more than

three years after its opening, is still playing to huge audiences both on Broadway and on tour, leaving box-office records in its wake as it joyfully continues to "ease on down the road."

The presentation collected seven Antoinette Perry (Tony) Awards, including one for best musical of the season. As this is being written, *The Wiz* is being filmed under the direction of Sidney Lumet with a cast headed by Diana Ross, Richard Pryor, Lena Horne, and Nipsey Russell.

William F. Brown, author of the book for *The Wiz*, was represented earlier on Broadway with his comedy, *The Girl in the Freudian Slip*, which starred Alan Young and Marjorie Lord, and was a contributor to *New Faces of 1968*. He also wrote the book for the Off-Broadway musical success, *How to Steal an Election*.

Mr. Brown's sketches and lyrics have enhanced many Julius Monk revues at Plaza 9 and Upstairs at the Downstairs. He has fashioned material for almost a dozen leading nightclub performers. Active in television as well as in the theatre and postprandial divertissements, he has written for scores of television programs including "Love American Style," "That Was the Week That Was," "The Jackie Gleason Show," and a number of Max Liebman specials.

Mr. Brown is the author of five books of humor, an illustrator of five others, a frequent contributor of articles to major periodicals, and the co-author and co-artist of the syndicated comic strip, *Boomer*, which appears in 175 newspapers.

The recipient of a Tony nomination and a Drama Desk Award for his book for *The Wiz*, Mr. Brown is soon to be represented on Broadway again with two new productions—a revue, *The Only World in Town*, which will co-star Cab Calloway and dancer Judith Jamison, and *A Broadway Musical*.

Although *The Wiz* marked Charlie Smalls's Broadway debut as lyricist and composer, his work already had been recognized in other fields. A graduate of the Juilliard School of Music with a classical background, he served the usual musical apprenticeship after a stint with the Air Force Band, by playing in Manhattan clubs and touring with gospel singer Esther Marrow and with Harry Belafonte.

After backing various artists, Mr. Smalls went on to form his own group under contract to A&M Records. Primarily a pianist, but proficient on other instruments as well, he has also appeared publicly as an actor and singer. Most recently, he spread his versatility to films by creating the scores for two major releases.

Charlie Smalls was the recipient of a Tony Award for the season's best score as well as a 1976 Grammy Award for the year's best original cast album—both, of course, for *The Wiz*.

PRODUCTION NOTES

The Wiz was first presented by Ken Harper at the Majestic Theatre, New York, on January 5, 1975. The cast was as follows:

Aunt Em	*Tasha Thomas*
Toto	*Nancy*
Dorothy	*Stephanie Mills*
Uncle Henry	*Ralph Wilcox*
Tornado	*Evelyn Thomas*
Munchkins	*Phylicia Ayers-Allen, Pi Douglass, Joni Palmer, Andy Torres, Carl Weaver*
Addaperle	*Clarice Taylor*
Yellow Brick Road	*Ronald Dunham, Eugene Little, John Parks, Kenneth Scott*
Scarecrow	*Hinton Battle*
Crows	*Wendy Edmead, Frances Morgan, Ralph Wilcox*
Tinman	*Tiger Haynes*
Lion	*Ted Ross*
Kalidahs	*Phillip Bond, Pi Douglass, Rodney Green, Evelyn Thomas, Andy Torres*
Poppies	*Lettie Battle, Leslie Butler, Eleanor McCoy, Frances Morgan, Joni Palmer*
Field Mice	*Phylicia Ayers-Allen, Pi Douglass, Ralph Wilcox, Carl Weaver*
Gatekeeper	*Danny Beard*
Emerald City Citizens	*Lettie Battle, Leslie Butler, Wendy Edmead, Eleanor McCoy, Frances Morgan, Joni Palmer, Evelyn Thomas, Philip Bond, Ronald Dunham, Rodney Green, Eugene Little, John Parks, Kenneth Scott, Andy Torres*
The Wiz	*Andre De Shields*
Evillene	*Mabel King*
Lord High Underling	*Ralph Wilcox*
Soldier Messenger	*Carl Weaver*
Winged Monkey	*Andy Torres*
Glinda	*Dee Dee Bridgewater*
Pit Singers:	*Frank Floyd, Sam Harkness, Jozella Reed, Tasha Thomas*

Directed by *Geoffrey Holder*
Choreography and Musical Numbers Staged by *George Faison*
Setting Designed by *Tom H. John*
Costumes Designed by *Geoffrey Holder*
Lighting Designed by *Tharon Musser*
Orchestrations by *Harold Wheeler*
Vocal Arrangements by *Charles H. Coleman*
Dance Arrangements by *Timothy Graphenreed*
Musical Direction by *Tom Pierson*

SCENES AND MUSICAL NUMBERS

Scene 7: Emerald City
          Emerald City Ballet (Pssst)   Friends, Company
                                                          Music by Timothy Graphenreed and George Faison

Scene 8: Throne Room
          So You Wanted to Meet the Wizard   The Wiz
          If I Could Feel   Tinman

ACT TWO

Scene 1: West Witch Castle
          No Bad News   Evillene

Scene 2: Forest
          Funky Monkeys   Monkeys

Scene 3: Courtyard
          Brand New Day   Friends, Winkies
                                                  Music and Lyrics by Luther Vandross

Scene 4: Emerald City Gate

Scene 5: Throne Room
          Who Do You Think You Are?   Friends
          Believe in Yourself   The Wiz

Scene 6: Fairgrounds
          Y'all Got It!   The Wiz

Scene 7: Outskirts
          Quadling Country
          A Rested Body is a Rested Mind   Glinda
          Believe in Yourself (Reprise)   Glinda
          Home   Dorothy

Prologue

Overture.

We see a small, rather ramshackle little farm house in Kansas. Upstage there is a clothesline, and AUNT EM *is unpinning various items of clothing. She keeps an eye on the dark and brooding sky as she drops the clothes in a basket. Both* AUNT EM *and* UNCLE HENRY *are in their late thirties, perhaps, but life has not been easy for them so far, and promises little else.*

A small mongrel dog, TOTO, *runs across the stage, barking playfully.* AUNT EM *gives the dog a glance and shakes her head. Closely behind the dog comes a girl of thirteen or fourteen, wearing her best Sunday dress. Her name is* DOROTHY, *and she's as bright and alive as can be. Somehow, it would seem she's built a life of her own on this dreary farm, and would probably rather remain a child as long as possible instead of accepting the responsibilities of adulthood.*

DOROTHY (*Running on*): Toto! Toto, you come back here!

AUNT EM (*About to ask for help with the wash*): Dorothy . . .

DOROTHY: Toto! You hear me?

AUNT EM (*A little more sharply*): Dorothy, I been needin' help all afternoon!

DOROTHY: Soon as I get Toto, Aunt Em. (*She spies him offstage*) Toto! (*She runs off*).

   (AUNT EM *rolls her eyes as* UNCLE HENRY *enters*)

UNCLE HENRY: You an' Dorothy at it again, Emily?

AUNT EM: Lord, I don't *believe* that child!

   (*He exits as* DOROTHY *returns with* TOTO)

UNCLE HENRY: You'd better hurry up, a big storm is heading this way.

DOROTHY (*To* AUNT EM): Now what was it you wanted me to do?

AUNT EM (*Picks up basket of laundry*): I did it m'self!

DOROTHY: Oh.

AUNT EM (*Testy; crossing to storm cellar*): I *wanted* a hand with these here clothes before the storm blew 'em all away!

DOROTHY: I'm sorry, Aunt Em. I didn't . . .

AUNT EM (*Stops*): ... *think*. No, you never do, child. Now we're fixin' for a twister, an' you're playin' games with that dog! And in your Sunday dress, too! (*Putting basket right of storm cellar doors*) Serve you right if you *both* blew away!

DOROTHY (*Sitting on ground*): I imagine it would.

AUNT EM (*Turning to her*): What was that?

DOROTHY: Aw, I'm not much help around here for you and Uncle Henry. Always daydreamin' an' stuff. I bet it'd be a big load off your back if I *did* blow away, wouldn't it?
Music in: "The Feeling We Once Had"
(AUNT EM, *in mock seriousness, ponders this for a moment, then putting* DOROTHY *on:*)

AUNT EM: I imagine it would.

DOROTHY (*Hurt*): It *would*?

AUNT EM: Dorothy ... you know how much your Uncle Henry and I love you, don't you? (*Sings*)

Put your arms around me, child
Like when you bumped your shin
Then you'll know I love you now
As I loved you then

Though you may be trying sometimes
And I'll need you and you're not there
I may get mad and turn you away
But I still care

(*She takes* DOROTHY'S *hand; kneels*)

But you shouldn't ask for more
Than can come from me
I am different than you are
And one day you'll see

If I lose my patience with you
And I suddenly start to scream
It's only because I want you to be
What I see in my dreams.

And I'd like to know it's there
The feeling we once had

Knowing that you can come to me
If ever times are bad, bad

(Both rise)

Though you are growing older now
And I'm watching you grow
And if I make you sad sometimes
I see your feelings show

And one day I'll look around
And you will be grown
You'll be out in the world, such a pretty girl
But you'll be on your own

And I'd like to know it's there
The feeling we once had
Knowing that you can come to me
Whenever you're feeling sad

Don't lose the feeling
Don't lose the feeling
Don't lose the feeling
The feeling we once had!

(DOROTHY *hugs* AUNT EM. *The storm grows worse.* UNCLE HENRY *runs in, picking up milk can, on his way to them)*
UNCLE HENRY: Em! Dorothy! Hurry! This here's a big one!
(*He throws milk can in house, left of cellar doors*)
Music in: "Tornado Ballet"
(UNCLE HENRY *pulls* AUNT EM *and* DOROTHY *against the wind toward the doors of the storm cellar. They fight against the wind toward the cellar doors losing ground the first two tries. On the third try* UNCLE HENRY *succeeds in opening the doors.* AUNT EM *manages to enter the doors first.* UNCLE HENRY *enters next.* DOROTHY *hands laundry basket to* UNCLE HENRY. *A gust of wind catches* DOROTHY *and sweeps her away. The wind slams the cellar doors shut, and as* UNCLE HENRY *battles, from the inside, to get them open again, the wind rips the porch off the house, and the house moves offstage right.*
Now DANCERS *appear, symbolizing the storm itself, sweeping up* DOROTHY *and the porch in their path.* DOROTHY *makes it*

back to the porch and collapses on it, as the EYE OF THE TORNADO *appears, and the tornado whirls* DOROTHY *and the porch round and round; spinning it on its journey through time and space. When the tornado blows itself out,* DOROTHY *is far, far from Kansas)*

Blackout

Act One

The land of the MUNCHKINS. *Some time later.*
The porch has come to rest in a strange land, full of strange
shapes, with a strange sun in the sky. As lights come up slowly,
we see three MUNCHKINS *approaching the wreckage cautiously.*

DOROTHY (*On porch*): Aunt Em! Aunt Em! Where are you?
   Aunt Em! Aunt Em!
FIRST MUNCHKIN: Aunt Em?
SECOND MUNCHKIN: Aunt Em?
THIRD MUNCHKIN: Aunt Em?
   (*Now* DOROTHY *sees the strange little people, and draws back*
from them in fear)
DOROTHY: *You're* not Aunt Em!
THIRD MUNCHKIN: Who's Aunt Em?
DOROTHY: Where am I?
FIRST MUNCHKIN: In the land of Oz, where the Munchkins live!
   (*Now the* THIRD MUNCHKIN *discovers a pair of familiar feet*
sticking out from under the porch)
THIRD MUNCHKIN: Look! She done set that house down on
   Evvamene!
FIRST MUNCHKIN: Is she dead?
SECOND MUNCHKIN: Yeah, and I don't think she's gonna like it!
   (DOROTHY, *off porch, sees legs and backs away from them*)
FIRST MUNCHKIN (*Crossing to* DOROTHY): Congratulations!
SECOND MUNCHKIN (*Following*): You just killed the Wicked
   Witch of the East!
DOROTHY: Oh, no!
THIRD MUNCHKIN: Oh, yeah!
FIRST MUNCHKIN: Girl, I'm gonna wear *white* to the funeral!
   (DOROTHY *runs from them, scared, toward a strange shape at*
stage left)
DOROTHY: I didn't mean to kill nobody!
   (*The shape opens, and in a puff of smoke,* ADDAPERLE, *the*
GOOD WITCH OF THE NORTH, *appears*)

14 |

ADDAPERLE: What's goin' on around here?

MUNCHKINS: Addaperle!

(They swarm around her)

FIRST MUNCHKIN: Let me have your autograph, girl!

(She favors the MUNCHKINS *with a finger-kiss autograph, through:)*

DOROTHY *(Wide-eyed)*: Who are *you?*

ADDAPERLE: The Good Witch of the North.

DOROTHY: The Good Witch of the *North?*

ADDAPERLE: Maybe you know me better by my stage name . . . Addaperle the Feelgood Girl!

DOROTHY: Your *stage* name?

ADDAPERLE: Yes, I have a magic act! *(She whips a small bouquet of flowers out of her bag)* I do tricks!

THIRD MUNCHKIN: Does she ever!

ADDAPERLE: You better cool it, or I'll turn you into somethin'.

THIRD MUNCHKIN: Addaperle, this child here, she done gone and set her house down on your sister Evvamene!

FIRST MUNCHKIN: That *is* old Evvamene, ain't it?

ADDAPERLE *(Crossing up to porch, examining the feet)*: Oh, I'd know that tacky pantyhose of hers anywhere! *(She thinks)* That means there's only three witches left in Oz! *(Then, to* DOROTHY*)* Me, the Good Witch of the North . . . my sister Glinda, the Good Witch of the South . . . Oh, you oughta see *her* act, honey! And then there's Evillene. . .

ALL *(As they bless themselves)*:—Evillene!

ADDAPERLE: . . . the Wicked Witch of the West. *(She crosses to* DOROTHY*)* Better watch out for her. She's a real downer! Now let's get down to business, honey. What's your name, child?

DOROTHY: Well, my name is . . .

ADDAPERLE: Wait! Don't tell me! I'll ask my magic slate! *(*ADDAPERLE *puts down her magic bag and digs into it for slate)*

DOROTHY: Your *what?*

ADDAPERLE *(Pulling it out of her bag)*: My magic slate. *(She hands slate to* MUNCHKIN*)* Now, I ain't gonna touch this slate, but on it the name of this child shall be written! And that name is . . . Shirley!

DOROTHY: No . . .

ADDAPERLE: Denise?

DOROTHY: No.

ADDAPERLE: Starletta?

DOROTHY: No.

ADDAPERLE: Urylee?

DOROTHY: No.

ADDAPERLE: Mary Bethune?

DOROTHY: No.

ADDAPERLE: Mitzi?

DOROTHY: No . . .

ADDAPERLE (*Grabbing slate and handing it to* DOROTHY): Then *write* your name on this magic slate! *(Then, to the* MUNCHKINS *as* DOROTHY *writes)*: Well, you can't win 'em all.

(DOROTHY *hands her the slate.* ADDAPERLE *pretends magic)* Ibiddy, dibiddy, an' more of the same . . . Now I'm beginnin' to see the name . . . *Dorothy!*

DOROTHY: You call that *magic?*

ADDAPERLE (*Crossing to bag, putting her slate away*): Listen, I'm doing the best I can.

(two other MUNCHKINS *appear on the scene, curious to see what's going on)*

DOROTHY (*Crossing to* ADDAPERLE): Then could you help me get home to Kansas?

ADDAPERLE: Kansas? Oh, I don't think so. That comes under the headin' of transportin' a minor across state lines. Maybe you better go see the Wiz!

(ADDAPERLE puts bag down)

Music In: "He's The Wiz"

FIRST MUNCHKIN: Yeah! She'll have to go see the Wiz!

SECOND MUNCHKIN: I bet he could do it!

THIRD MUNCHKIN: Dorothy'll have to go see the Wiz!

DOROTHY: *Who?*

ADDAPERLE AND THE MUNCHKINS:

Sweet thing, let me tell you 'bout
The world and the way things are
You've come from a different place
And I know you've traveled far
Now that you've told me what it is
I'd better point you toward the Wiz

He's the Wiz,
He's the man, he's the only one
Who can give your wish right to ya—he's the Wizard
He can send you back through time

By runnin' magic through ya
All of the super power's his
Listen and I'll tell you where he is
He's the Wiz and he lives in Oz
He's the Wizard

There's the way to the Emerald City
Now that's not too far, is it? He's the Wizard
Just take your dilemma, child
And lay it on the Wizard
He'll fix you a drink that'll bubble and foam
And in a flash you will be home

He's the Wiz
He's the Wiz of Oz
He's got magic up his sleeve—He's the Wizard
And you know without his help
'Twould be impossible to leave
Fantastic powers at his command
And I'm sure that he will understand

He's the Wiz
And he lives in Oz
He's the Wizard!—He's the Wizard

DOROTHY: *He's the Wizard!*

ADDAPERLE: But before you go, maybe you ought to take Evvamene's silver slippers!
DOROTHY: Silver slippers?
(*The* THIRD MUNCHKIN *takes them off* EVVAMENE's *feet and hands them to* ADDAPERLE, *who puts them on* DOROTHY's *feet through:*)
ADDAPERLE (*Kneeling*): She always wanted me to have 'em. Here. I hope you don't mind secondhand shoes.
DOROTHY: I never had a pair this beautiful.
ADDAPERLE: But you gotta *promise* not to take 'em off till you get home!
DOROTHY: All right I promise—but why?
ADDAPERLE: 'Cause they really got some secret powers!
(MUNCHKINS *gather around to hear secret*)
DOROTHY: To do what?

ADDAPERLE: I don't know. That's the secret.

(MUNCHKINS *break away, disgusted*)

DOROTHY (*Helping* ADDAPERLE): Well, they're just my size, anyway.

ADDAPERLE (*As she kisses* DOROTHY): And this kiss will protect you wherever you go! Except in the poppy field.

DOROTHY: What's wrong with poppies?

ADDAPERLE (*As she picks up* DOROTHY's *shoes and crosses to put them in bag*): Oh, this kind'll put you to sleep for a hundred years! It's terrible, wakin' up and your clothes are all outta style ... (*Picks up bag. Pause. As she brings a wanga out of her bag*) And now, with a wave of my wanga ... I'm gonna disappear on you! I just wave this thing three or four times ... in ever-increasing ... (*The wanga turns into two handkerchiefs*) What the hell's goin' on around here? Trouble is, honey, I ain't been disappearin' much lately. I been takin' the bus.

(*She inadvertently waves one of the handkerchiefs, and in a cloud of smoke she disappears. The* MUNCHKINS *laugh and applaud her kooky "act"*)

THIRD MUNCHKIN: Addaperle's done it again, y'all!

DOROTHY: But she didn't tell me how to get to the Emerald City.

FIFTH MUNCHKIN: Oh, darling!

FIRST MUNCHKIN: You can't miss it.

DOROTHY: I can't?

MUNCHKINS: No.

SECOND MUNCHKIN: See that road of yellow bricks?

(FOUR DANCERS *appear dressed as the* YELLOW BRICK ROAD, *carrying staffs with which they will point the way to* DOROTHY. *She looks at them in bewilderment*)

DOROTHY: Right ...

FIRST MUNCHKIN: Just follow that for two days ... now ...

DOROTHY: Right!

(*She moves to* YELLOW BRICK ROAD)

FOURTH MUNCHKIN: But watch out for a lot of spooky things!

DOROTHY (*Stops. Apprehensive*): Like what?

FIFTH MUNCHKIN: Beware of them awful Kalidah people!

(*As* DOROTHY *continues toward* YELLOW BRICK ROAD)

THIRD MUNCHKIN: Watch out for them terrible flyin' monkeys!

FIRST MUNCHKIN: Most of all, watch out for that evil old Wicked Witch of the West! That girl is everywhere!

THIRD MUNCHKIN: Outside of that, have a nice trip!
(DOROTHY *is now in center of* YELLOW BRICK ROAD *as:*)
Music in: "Soon As I Get Home"
(*The* MUNCHKINS *exit, waving good-bye to* DOROTHY, *and she to them, as she joins the* YELLOW BRICK ROAD *and begins her journey, just a little scared of it all*)
DOROTHY:

There's a feeling here inside
That I cannot hide
And I know I've tried
But it's turning me around

I'm not sure that I'm aware
If I'm up or down
If I'm here or there
I need both feet on the ground

Why do I feel like I'm drowning
When there is plenty of air?
Why do I feel like frowning?
I think the feeling is fear.

Oh, here I am in a different place
In a different time
In this time and space
But I don't want to be here

I was told I must see the Wiz
But I don't know what a wizard is
I just hope the Wiz is there

Maybe I'm just going crazy
Letting myself get uptight
I'm acting just like a baby
But I'm gonna be all right
Soon as I get home
Soon as I get home

Music: Segue into "Home"

In a different place
In a different time

Different people around me
I would like to know of their different world
And how different they find me
And just what's a wiz? Is it big? Will it scare me?
If I ask to leave will the Wiz even hear me?
And how will I know then if I'll ever get home again?

Here I am alone, though it feels the same
I don't know where I'm going
I'm here on my own and it's not a game
And a strange wind is blowing
I am so amazed by the things that I see here
Don't want to be afraid, I just don't want to be here
In my mind this is so clear, what am I doing here?

I wish I was home.

(DOROTHY *is stretched out on the ground, crying.*)

SCENE 2

A cornfield. The next instant.
    Three CROWS *enter, fluttering around* DOROTHY. *Frightened, she runs to stage left. She shoos them away, and they proceed to feast on ears of corn as a* SCARECROW *appears, perched high on a pole, upstage of bridge.* DOROTHY *has not yet seen him.*

SCARECROW (*Calling to* DOROTHY): Say, honey, you got any spare change?
DOROTHY (*Startled*): What?
SCARECROW: I said, you got any spare change? Some loose bread? *Anything,* till I get my head together?
DOROTHY: Now what would a scarecrow do with money?
SCARECROW: Well, I been savin' up to buy me some brains.
DOROTHY (*Sitting on ground*): That's silly! You can't buy brains.
SCARECROW: You can't?
DOROTHY: No
SCARECROW: Well, how about that?
DOROTHY: What do you want brains for? Isn't it any fun bein' a scarecrow?
SCARECROW: Well, I *thought* it would be. But after fifteen minutes on this pole, I knew I wasn't goin' anyplace.

DOROTHY (*Getting up*): Scarecrow, how would you like to get *down* off that pole?

SCARECROW (*Beaming*): I thought you'd never ask! (*As* DOROTHY *crosses to the pole under bridge*) Just pull on that string down there. (DOROTHY *does so, and the* SCARECROW *is released, tumbling down off the pole, unable, for the moment to stand on his feet. Finally, with a supreme effort, he pulls himself together and stands up*) Man, it sure feels good to stand on my own two feet again!

DOROTHY: I guess you haven't had it easy, have you?

Music in: "I Was Born on the Day Before Yesterday"

SCARECROW: Honey, you *know* it . . .

(*As he sings, the* CROWS *form a dancing and singing chorus*)

Woo woo woo
Woo woo woo

I was born on the day before yesterday
I had holes in my shoes, I was cryin' the blues
And I didn't have no place to stay

But I know
I know I'm gonna make it this time
'Cause I know
I know I'm gonna make it this time

I was born over on a hill not so far away
Out of three rubber bands, with old gloves for hands,
And a suit that had been thrown away

They took the jacket and pants
Found a brown paper bag, and they filled it
With straw, and to top off the drag
They gave me penciled-in eyes, and a penciled-in nose
Then they stuck me up there and said
Strike me a pose

And I don't know just how I'm gonna make it this time
But I know I know I'm gonna make it this time
Now listen to me
Woo woo woo
Gonna sing one

Woo woo woo
So you all can hear it
Woo woo woo
Gonna lift my head up
Woo woo woo
Can you feel my spirit?
Can you feel my spirit?

And now that I know
That I wasn't born yesterday
And that I'm fully grown
I can stand on my own
And nothing's gonna get in my way

Because I'm gonna get mine
Gonna turn things around
Gonna get myself together
Gonna get on down

And when I feel that rain comin'!
Through the bottoms of my shoes
I'm gonna leave them by the roadside
And quit cryin' the blues

'Cause I know
I know I'm gonna make it this time
Yes, I know
I know I'm gonna make it this time

Woo woo woo
Gonna sing one so you all can hear it
Woo woo woo
Gonna lift my head up
Woo woo woo
Can you feel my spirit?
Can you feel my spirit?
Can you feel my spirit?
Woo woo woo

(DOROTHY *starts to leave. The* SCARECROW *calls after her*)
SCARECROW: Say, girl, what's your name?

DOROTHY (*Stops*): Dorothy.

SCARECROW (*Moves on knees to Stage Center*): Where you headed for?

DOROTHY (*Crossing to him*): To Emerald City. You see, there's this great big powerful Wiz, and they say he can do miracles. So he's gonna get me back to Kansas. (*He struggles to get up. She helps him. An idea hits her*) Hey, you know what? (*He is on his feet*)

SCARECROW (*Moving right*): Of course not. I don't know anything.

DOROTHY (*Following*): Maybe he could get you some brains!

SCARECROW (*Freezes*): Brains? You mean that?

DOROTHY: Yeah!

SCARECROW (*Laughs*): I'm gonna get my brains! I hope my hat can handle it.

SCENE 3

Music in: "Ease on Down the Road"
DOROTHY *and the* SCARECROW *join the* YELLOW BRICK ROAD *and go on their way with them.*

ROAD, DOROTHY, SCARECROW:
Come on ease on down, ease on down the road
Come on ease on down, ease on down the road
Don't you carry nothin'
That might be a load
Come on ease on down, ease on down the road

DOROTHY:
Ease on down, ease on down the road
Ease on down, ease on down the road
Don't you carry nothin'
That might be a load
Ease on down, ease on down the road

SCARECROW:
'Cause there may be times
When you think you've lost your mind

And the steps you're takin'
Leave you three, four steps behind

DOROTHY:
Just you keep on keepin'
On the road that you choose
Don't you give up walkin'
'Cause you gave up shoes

DOROTHY & SCARECROW:
Ease on down, ease on down the road
Ease on down, ease on down the road
Don't you carry nothin'
That might be a load
Come on
Ease on down, ease on down
Ease on down, ease on down
Ease on down, down the road!

(From the vicinity of a tree, upstage right, we hear a groan)
DOROTHY: What was that?
  (The groan comes again)
SCARECROW *(Pointing)*: It's comin' from over there!
DOROTHY: What should we do?
SCARECROW *(Pointing in the opposite direction)*: Go over there.
DOROTHY *(As she pulls him upstage right)*: No! Somebody needs
  help!
  (DOROTHY and the SCARECROW cross to the root of a big tree,
where they find the TINMAN, almost rusted solid. With an effort,
they push him away from the root of the tree straight
downstage, where they examine him)
DOROTHY: What is it?
SCARECROW: Don't look like an "is" to me. Looks more like a
  "was."
TINMAN: Oil! Oil! I need oil!
DOROTHY: He needs oil!
TINMAN: Oh, please, miss . . . there's some in that little shack
  over there. *(Indicating off left)*
DOROTHY: I'll get it! *(She runs off)*
SCARECROW *(Starting to follow)*: No, Dorothy, wait.
  (The SCARECROW, left alone with the TINMAN, gives him a long
once-over and then crosses to his left. Another long once-over.

TINMAN *turns head to look at him.* SCARECROW *sneaks to his right.* TINMAN *with effort squeaks head to right. Their eyes meet)*

SCARECROW: Man, I have seen me some spaced-out garbage cans in my day . . .

(DOROTHY *returns with an oil can)*

DOROTHY: I found it, Tinman! But now what?

Music in: "Slide Some Oil to Me"

TINMAN: Now what? . . .

(*During the song,* DOROTHY *follows his instructions as to where to oil him. As she does so, he becomes looser and looser, and does a second chorus of the song in dance)*

Slide some oil to me
Let it slip down my spine
If you don't have STP
Crisco will be just fine

Slide some oil to me
Hit my shoulder blade
All y'all that don't have to lubricate
Sure have got it made

Slide some oil to me
Slip some to my side
Standing here in one position
Sure can make one tired

Slip some to my elbows
And my fingers, if you would
Come, slide some oil to me, girl,
Oooh, does that feel good!

Slide some oil to my feet
Look, I have toes again!
Come on and slide some oil to my knees
And let me see if I can bend

Slide some oil to me
I'm beginning to feel fine
Come on and slide some oil down my throat
And let me lubricate my mind

And let me lubricate my mind
And let me lubricate my mind.

SCARECROW *(Pulling* DOROTHY *toward exit)*: Come on, Dorothy,
we gotta be going.
(But she stops to talk to TINMAN*)*
DOROTHY: How did you ever *get* that way?
TINMAN: Well, I wasn't always made outta tin, you know. No, I
used to be a real flesh-and-blood woodchopper, till one day a
wicked witch put a spell on my ax!
DOROTHY: A spell!
TINMAN: Yeah! And she did a number . . . *(Crossing below them
to get ax from* YELLOW BRICK ROAD*)* let me tell you. I mean
one day when I was choppin' down a tree, that ax slipped and
cut off my left leg.
SCARECROW: Mmmmm! Ain't that somethin'?
TINMAN: I thought so. So I went to this here tinsmith I knew,
and I say, "Hey, man . . . you think you could fix me up with
a tin leg?" Well, he did, an' the next day I'm back choppin'
again, doin' my thing, an' damn if that ax don't slip an'
WHAP! cut off my right leg! So I go back to the tinsmith and
get me another leg.
SCARECROW: Now at no time did it dawn on you to get yourself a
new ax?
TINMAN *(Ignoring him, to* DOROTHY*)*: Well, before I knew what
was happening, bit by bit, I was all tin. An' that's the way it
all come about.
DOROTHY: You poor man! *(She crosses to get oil can)*
TINMAN: Well, you can't have everything?
*(*DOROTHY *oils his back during the ensuing exchange)*
SCARECROW: An' that's the truth?
TINMAN: God's honest truth.
SCARECROW: Cross your heart?
(The TINMAN *starts to, then stops)*
TINMAN: No . . . I can't do that.
SCARECROW *(Grabbing* DOROTHY'S *hand to leave)*: I knew it. You
was jivin' us all along! C'mon, Dorothy . . .
TINMAN: No, wait! Wait, wait! *(They stop)* I can't cross my
heart 'cause I don't have no heart.
DOROTHY: You don't have a *heart?*
TINMAN: Well, it didn't come with the suit. You know

nowadays, honey, it isn't enough just bein' good-lookin'.
(TINMAN *strikes a pose*)
DOROTHY (*A moment's conference with the* SCARECROW. *Then*):
Then come with us to the Emerald City and see the Wiz!
They say he can do most anything for anybody!
Music in: "Ease on Down the Road" (Reprise)
TINMAN: Yeah? (*Laugh*) Just show me the way!

DOROTHY, SCARECROW, ROAD:
Pick your left foot up
When your right one's down
Come on, legs keep movin'
Don't you lose no ground
'Cause the road you're walkin'
Might be long sometime
But just keep on steppin'
And you'll be just fine . . .

Come on . . .

DOROTHY, SCARECROW, TINMAN:
Ease on down, ease on down the road
Ease on down, ease on down the road
Don't you carry nothin'
That might be a load
Come on
Ease on down, ease on down the road
Etc.

SCENE 4

Down the road apiece. The next instant.
An offstage roar interrupts the journey of DOROTHY, *the*
SCARECROW, *the* TINMAN, *and the* ROAD. *They scatter in fear to*
downstage right.
Music in: "Mean Ole Lion"
(*To a beat, the* COWARDLY LION *appears, strutting his false*
courage, and trying to intimidate everyone)

LION:
Say what you wanna

But I'm here to stay
'Cause I'm a mean ole lion

You can go where you wanna
But don't get in my way
I'm a mean ole lion

You'll be standing in a draft
If you don't hear me laugh
And if you have to come around
Better hope that I don't frown
'Cause I just might knock you down
I'm a mean ole lion

(Roars)

You know I'm ready to fight
I'll turn your day into night
'Cause I'm a mean ole lion

And if you're half bright
You'll detour to the right
From a mean ole lion

All you strangers better beware
This is the King of the Jungle here
And if I happen to let you slide
Don't just stand there, run and hide
You just caught my better side
I'm a mean ole lion
Mean ole lion!

(While the others cower downstage right, the LION *is very aware of the applause, and reacts to it, milking it, like a ham actor, for all he's worth. During this, the* SCARECROW *and the* TINMAN *re-assess their initial reaction to the* LION *and decide it wasn't called for . . . a quick attitude in mime. Then:)*
SCARECROW: He don't scare me. Do he scare you?
TINMAN: No way, man. No way!
(The LION, *noticing their disrespectful attitude, crosses and swats the* SCARECROW, *knocking him over to stage left. He takes a poke at the* TINMAN, *too, hurting his paw in the process, but*

knocking the TINMAN *away to extreme down right. To protect her friends,* DOROTHY *takes a roundhouse swing at the* LION *and decks him. He cowers*)

LION (*At center, where he has landed*): Don't hit me no more!

TINMAN: Will you dig that?

LION (*To* DOROTHY): Don't you know you could hurt a person that way!

SCARECROW (*Breaking up*): You call yourself the King of the Jungle?

LION (*Rises*): You don't see no other cat beggin' for the gig, do you?

TINMAN: Why, you've got a yellow streak a mile wide!

LION: No, it's my mane. I just had it touched up!

DOROTHY: You coward! Goin' around roarin' at people . . . you oughta be ashamed . . . (*Spanks him*) of yourself!

LION: Oh, I am. But it's not my fault. You see, I was an only cub. My Daddy left home when I was born, and Momma, Momma was such a strong lady . . . you know what I mean? "Do this . . . don't do that . . . you call them paws *clean?* Lick behind your ears, child, or you don't get no dessert!" I tell you I got me such a bunch of schizophobic phrenias . . .

SCARECROW: Oh, wow! Where'd you get all them big words from?

LION: My owl.

(*Perplexed,* SCARECROW *crosses back to* TINMAN)

TINMAN: *What* owl?

LION (*Turns to them*): I've been seeing a high-priced owl for three years now.

DOROTHY: An *owl?*

LION: Yes, my owl. Three times a week. An hour each time. I hate to tell you what kinda bread that runs into.

SCARECROW: And this here . . . uh . . . owl. What does he say is the answer to your disgraceful self?

LION: Owls don't give answers. They just ask questions. Hoo-hoo. So at heart . . . I'll never be anything but a big old scaredy-cat.

(*He starts to cry.* DOROTHY *comforts him*)

TINMAN: Could be worse. At least you *got* a heart.

SCARECROW: And at least you got a brain. Even if it *is* makin' him a pretty mixed-up cat.

LION: What good is a heart? What good is a brain if you ain't got no courage?

DOROTHY: You know, maybe, just maybe, if you came with us and saw the Great Wiz, he could give you some courage . . . just like that!

LION: In only one session? (*They nod yes. He thinks about this, then makes up his mind*) Gentlemen . . . (*Crosses between* TINMAN *and* SCARECROW) little Momma, of course . . . may I fill out your foursome?

Music in: "Ease on Down the Road" (Reprise)

DOROTHY, TINMAN, SCARECROW:

Oh there may be times
When you wish you wasn't born
And you wake one morning
Just to find your courage gone

But just know that feelin'
Only lasts a little while
You just stick with us
And we'll show you how to smile

Come on . . .

DOROTHY, SCARECROW, TINMAN, LION, ROAD:
Ease on down, ease on down the road
Come on, ease on down, ease on down the road
Don't you carry nothin'
That might be a load
Come on
Ease on down, ease on down the road.
                              Etc.

(*As they go further into the forest*)

SCENE 5

In a funky part of the forest. A little later.
During the final phrases of "Ease on Down the Road," the YELLOW BRICK ROAD *takes a turn and exits.* DOROTHY *and her* FRIENDS *fail to see this and plow straight ahead. The music fades out . . .*

LION: Wait a minute, y'all! Where are we?

SCARECROW: I think we're lost.

LION: What makes you say that?

SCARECROW: 'Cause you don't know where we are!

DOROTHY: Then let's go . . . *this way* . . .

(She points downstage. They mime a walk, in place, and hear strange jungle sounds . . . insects and birds and the like. The eyes of the WICKED WITCH OF THE WEST *appear to be watching them. Strange* BEINGS *enter and cross in front of them)*

DOROTHY *(As* FIRST STRANGER *crosses)*: Look!

TINMAN *(As* TWO STRANGERS *cross)*: This one has rhythm. There's a little ugly one.

LION *(As* LAST STRANGER *crosses)*: Oh, Momma!

TINMAN: It can't be Halloween.

LION: I'm sorry, Momma. I didn't mean it.

(Then the light dims. They stop walking)

DOROTHY: Why is it gettin' so dark?

SCARECROW: Beats me.

TINMAN: It's nowhere near sundown yet.

LION *(They run to him)*: I know! This is the part of the forest where the Kalidahs live!

DOROTHY: What's a Kalidah!

LION: I was afraid you was gonna ask me that.

Music in: "Kalidah Battle"

(Now we hear the disembodied laugh of the WICKED WITCH OF THE WEST, *as the* KALIDAHS *leap onstage. The* KALIDAHS *are weird, frightening creatures, intent upon destroying* DOROTHY *and her friends. The* LION *makes an attempt to save* DOROTHY, *but a* KALIDAH *threatens him. The* TINMAN *chases most of the* KALIDAHS *away, swinging his ax at them, but one of them sneaks back to attack* DOROTHY. *However, the* SCARECROW *saves her.* DOROTHY *and the others drag the* LION *from this spot to a safer place.*

Music out as the LAST KALIDAH *exits, chased by* SCARECROW *doing karate kicks. The attack over, they all run to the* LION, *who has fainted. The* LION *yelps on being touched and scoots on all fours to stage right, where he collapses.* DOROTHY *collapses left of the* LION. TINMAN *and* SCARECROW *follow, ending up a little upstage of them)*

SCENE 6

A poppy field. A few moments later.

DOROTHY, SCARECROW, TINMAN, *and* LION *enter, panting. They more or less collapse on the apron.*

LION (*Wiping brow with hankie*): That was too close for comfort!

DOROTHY: Tinman.

TINMAN: Yes, honey.

DOROTHY: You sure saved us all!

TINMAN: Aw, it wasn't no big thing.

DOROTHY: And, Scarecrow, you sure kept your cool, too!

SCARECROW: What can I say?

LION: That's right. The offense always gets the headlines. Nobody ever talks about the defense anymore!

SCARECROW (*Laughing with* TINMAN): What kind of defense were you doing, O Mighty King of the Jungle?

LION: The kind of defense only kings can do!

TINMAN: And what's that?

LION: King Fu!

SCARECROW: King . . .

TINMAN: Fu?

(*They burst into hysterical laughter. In gestures, the* SCARECROW *and the* TINMAN *put him down, but* DOROTHY *defends him*)

DOROTHY (*As she rises*): No, wait a minute! I know the lion was more scared than anybody, (*She helps* LION *up on his knees*) but he saved me three or four times!

LION: Yeah! There you go, Jack, I sure did. An' I would've done more too, but right in the middle of it there, I got this fur ball!

DOROTHY: Yeah, he got a fur ball.

SCARECROW: A *fur ball?*

DOROTHY: He got a fur ball.

TINMAN: A fur ball?

DOROTHY: He got a fur ball.

SCARECROW: Man, you are somethin' *else!*

TINMAN: You ain't nothin' but a big *pussycat!* (*Pokes* LION *with ax*) Meow! Meow!

(*He growls and makes a show of attacking them. They retreat, laughing*)

LION (*Ashamed*): Yes. You're right. A big pussycat, (*Growl*) I guess that's about all I am. That's all I'll *ever* be . . .

(*He seems on the verge of tears as* DOROTHY *comforts him*)

DOROTHY: No, you won't.

Music in: "Be a lion"

LION (*Hopefully*): I won't?

DOROTHY:

There is a place we'll go
Where there is mostly quiet
Flowers and butterflies
A rainbow lives beside it

(LION sits)

And from a velvet sky
A summer storm
I can feel the coolness in the air
But I'm still warm

And then a mighty roar
Will start the sky to cryin'
But not even lightning
Will be frightening my lion

And with no fear inside
No need to run, no need to hide
You're standing strong and tall
You're the bravest of them all
If on courage you must call
Then just keep on tryin' and tryin' and tryin'
You're a lion
In your own way, be a lion!

Come on, be a lion!

DOROTHY & LION:

I'm standing strong and tall
I'm the bravest of them all
If on courage you must call
Then just keep on trying and trying and trying
I'm a lion
In my own way, I'm a lion!

(The TINMAN crosses downstage center and looks out over the
back of the audience. He points excitedly)
TINMAN: Hey! Isn't that the Emerald City out there?
(The others join him to look. Meanwhile, in the background,

five POPPIES *enter; beautiful, dangerous, sinuous; like street-walkers)*

DOROTHY: Look, how beautiful it is!

SCARECROW: Look at all that glitter!

LION: I wonder if I can get a touch-up before we see the Wiz.

(*Now the* TINMAN *and the others begin to notice the* POPPIES *surrounding them)*

Music in: "Lion's Dream"

TINMAN: Hey! What's all this?

SCARECROW: Just looks like a bunch of flowers to me.

LION (*Fascinated by the* POPPIES): Yeah, and I suddenly have the urge to do a little cross-pollinatin'!

(*Suddenly* DOROTHY *remembers* ADDAPERLE'S *warning about the poppy field)*

DOROTHY (*As she runs toward exit left*): No! This is the Poppy Field! We gotta get out of here!

(*The* POPPIES *scatter. They follow and would all exit but the way is blocked by an impassable* FIELD OF POPPIES. *They turn and run right)*

SCARECROW: Hold your nose!

TINMAN: Don't sniff the stuff!

(*They start to fight through the* POPPIES *to exit, with the* LION *bringing up the rear. All of them make it offstage, except the* LION. *A* POPPY *blows dust in his face, and he is hooked)*

LION: Y'all go on ahead. I'll bring up the rear! (*The* POPPIES *surround the* LION, *and he moves among them, trying to touch first this one, then another, getting higher and higher, and having himself a ball, in dance)* All together, ladies—

(*Suddenly we hear a siren)*

Music out

(*They know that whistle—they've been busted before. They exit, leaving the* LION *alone on his poppy-dust high, still tripping, as four* FIELD MICE *enter with a fanciful paddy-wagon. One of the* MICE *makes sure the* POPPIES *have left. The* FIRST MOUSE, *with his police badge, approaches the* LION *who has collapsed)*

FIRST MOUSE: Okay, break it up, we're with the Mice Squad. *He prods the* LION *with his foot)* I said, we're with the Mice Squad, buddy. Get up from there.

LION (*Still high*): The Mice Squad?

FIRST MOUSE: Yeah, the Mice Squad.

(*The* LION *rises slowly, giggling to himself. The* THIRD MOUSE *opens wagon*)

LION: Now look here, Mousifer, how come you can't never find a mouse when you need one?

FIRST MOUSE: Okay, buddy, now where'd you get them poppies from—huh?!

LION: Actually, I'm from out of town . . .

(*The* SECOND MOUSE *grabs one arm*)

SECOND MOUSE: That's what they all say!

FIRST MOUSE (*Grabbing his other arm*): You're under arrest! Get in there!

(*They cross with him to wagon.* FOURTH MOUSE *climbs up on driver's seat. They shove him into the wagon, through:*)

LION: I didn't do nothin'! Hey, wait a minute. You ain't payin' for my clothes! I demand to see my owl! I said I demand . . . (*Then, as they wheel him offstage*) Momma? Momma? Momma! MOMMA!

(*They exit*)

SCENE 7

Outside the gates of Emerald City. A little while later.
DOROTHY, *the* TINMAN, *and the* SCARECROW *enter.*

TINMAN (*Crossing to Emerald City gate*): Dorothy! We're here! I don't believe Emerald City!

SCARECROW (*Following*): Man, we *finally* made it through!

DOROTHY (*At gate*): Now all we got to do is find the Wiz.

(*The* LION *enters, sullenly, prodded by the* FIRST MOUSE)

FIRST MOUSE: C'mon, move it along there, buddy!

LION: Wait till my owl hears about this. I don't believe it. Me— the Kitty of the Kingdom—bein' busted by a *mouse*!

FIRST MOUSE (*To the others*): Look, I wanna tell ya, your cat there was really flying.

TINMAN: We're sorry, officer—very sorry—

FIRST MOUSE: Well, just make sure he never goes in that poppy field again, y' hear?

TINMAN: We'll do our best, sir. Thank you.

(*The* FIRST MOUSE *exits*)

TINMAN: What did you get into?

LION: Myself. (*To* DOROTHY) Little Momma . . . I almost found that rainbow!

(*The* ROYAL GATEKEEPER *enters from the gates. A haughty and arrogant person, he comes between* LION *and* TINMAN)

GATEKEEPER: Excuse me! Will you please carry on in front of another city?

SCARECROW: Who are you?

GATEKEEPER: I am the Royal Gatekeeper! (*Then, examining the* TINMAN) And we don't allow any trash here in the Big Green Apple.

DOROTHY (*Crossing to* KEEPER): But we gotta see the Wiz!

GATEKEEPER: You must be mad! The Wiz never sees anyone. Anywhere. At any time. (*Pause*) But on the other hand, if you care to make it worth my while . . .

TINMAN (*Threatening him with his ax, taking swipes as he speaks*): Oh, sure. Is it worth your while to keep your kneebone connected to your shinbone?

GATEKEEPER (*Who has been backed away*): Now don't get no attitude!

TINMAN (*Crossing back to gate and threatening the scrim with his ax*): You better let us in, or I'm gonna chop down this curtain!

GATEKEEPER: Oh, very well. But first you have to put on these green glasses.

(*He hands them out*)

SCARECROW: Why? (*Taking glasses*)

GATEKEEPER: Why? Because that's the rule, that's why—! Now begone!

TINMAN (*Who has lagged behind. As he exits*): I oughta chop down the old curtain, anyway.

(*They enter Emerald City*)

GATEKEEPER: I said begone! Well, there goes the neighborhood! (*He exits*)

Music in: "Emerald City Ballet"

(*The scrim rises and we see Emerald City in all its glory. The* CITIZENS *of Emerald City are exquisitely and exotically dressed. They are the Beautiful People. Aware of it, proud, and haughty. Their ballet says just this*)

Music out

(DOROTHY *and her friends enter*)

DOROTHY (*Crosses to* CITIZEN): Which way to the Wiz?

(*Everybody laughs at this question*)

LION: All right! What's so funny?

FIRST CITIZEN: Nobody sees the Wiz!

SCARECROW: Why not?

SECOND CITIZEN: They say he's too terrible to behold!

TINMAN: What's he look like?

THIRD CITIZEN (*Mocking*): A giant vulture!

(*They laugh*)

FOURTH CITIZEN: A man-eating elephant!

(*They laugh*)

FIFTH CITIZEN: A nine-foot dragon!

(*They laugh. But the* FIRST CITIZEN *laughs longest and loudest as she approaches* DOROTHY)

FIRST CITIZEN: And you! You want to see the Wiz?

(*She notices* DOROTHY's *silver slippers, and her mood changes. All the other* CITIZENS *notice the slippers, too, and are afraid*)

ALL CITIZENS: The Silver Slippers . . . of the Wicked Witch . . . of the East!

FIRST CITIZEN: If you wanna see the Wiz, honey, you go right ahead!

(*All the Emerald City* CITIZENS *scurry offstage in all directions*)

SCENE 8

The WIZ's *throneroom. The next instant.*

Alone, DOROTHY *and her friends screw up their courage to challenge the* WIZ.

TINMAN: I guess we can go in.

scarecrow: I guess so.

DOROTHY: Well . . . here goes!

(*They start and as they reach the steps, a* SPIDER *jumps out and, startled, they retreat*)

DOROTHY (*Calls*): Mr. Wiz!

Music in: "So You Wanted to Meet the Wizard"

(*Before the terrified eyes of* DOROTHY *and the others, two giant doors slide apart, revealing a mask. The mask flies, revealing yet another aperture. Curtains part and smoke flows out, and through it, riding in on what seems to be a giant tongue, comes the figure of the* WIZ *himself. When the tongue has reached its final position, the* WIZ *strikes a pose, and he is indeed an awesome figure to behold. As he sings, lights flash, fire jumps from hidden pots, and magical effects abound, thoroughly scaring* DOROTHY *and the others)*

WIZ *(Moves down steps)*:
So you wanted to meet the Wizard
Let me tell you that you've come to the right place
Should I make you a frog or a lizard?
You should see the strained expression on your face

If the way I come on is frightening
That's the way I felt like coming on today
Have you ever been kissed by lightning?
Let me tell you that will make you go away.

I fly, and the magic of my power takes me higher
To a level where the clouds turn into fire
In the warmness of the fire I feel fine

Just keep your eyes open and the magic you will see
It will whistle on the wind as it emanates from me
It's a strong and true vibration, you can feel it on your skin
Now come and take my hand and we will dance upon the
wind

So you wanted to meet the Wizard!

(On top step of platform)
All right! Well? Who are you?
DOROTHY: Please, Mr. Wiz. My name is Dorothy *(Indicating each in turn)*, and this is the Scarecrow, an' the Tinman, an' the Lion.
WIZ: And what do you all want?
(They all advance on the WIZ. *In answering the question they all speak at once, so we hear nothing but a garble of:)*
DOROTHY: You see, I want to get back to Kansas . . .
LION: Courage, that's what I came after, courage . . .
SCARECROW: You have a set of used brains lyin' around?
TINMAN: Please, your Wizness, give me a heart . . .
WIZ *(Cutting them off)*: Quiet! *(They all scurry away. You can hear a pin drop now)* That's better. Now, I will listen to your problems one at a time, beginning with . . . *(He singles out*

DOROTHY) ... you! Come here! *(She approaches him tentatively.* LION *follows—but at a safe distance)* Well?

DOROTHY: Oh, please, Mr. Wiz, you just gotta help me get back home to Kansas.

WIZ: I don't *gotta* do anything. The Great Wiz does as he pleases, and no more!

DOROTHY: Oh, no, sir, you don't gotta do nothing at all. But would you?

(For the first time, the WIZ *notices her silver slippers)*

WIZ: Where did you get such a marvelous pair of silver pumps?

DOROTHY: From the Good Witch of the North.

WIZ: Ah, Addaperle, huh? How would you like to trade them for ... *(He shows her a ring on his hand)* ... a beautiful emerald Wizard ring?

DOROTHY: Oh, I can't. I gotta keep 'em on till I get home. I made a *promise.*

WIZ: Break it!

DOROTHY: But I was taught *never* to break a promise!

WIZ *(Annoyed)*: You know, I can understand a child like you wanting to go to Brazil ... Mozambique ... Harlem ... *(Turns to her)* But Kansas? Did I hear you correctly? Get back to *Kansas?*

DOROTHY: Yes, sir.

WIZ *(Advancing on her)*: And what's wrong with it here?

DOROTHY: Nothin'.

WIZ: Does my fantastic Emerald City displease you?

DOROTHY: Oh, no, sir! I think it's the most beautiful place I've ever seen! But there's Aunt Em, and Uncle Henry, an' Toto, and I can't forget about them, can I?

WIZ: You may do whatever you want. Besides, what is home but a place we all leave anyway ... full of faded memories and shattered dreams ... why not forget it? *(He suddenly whirls on the* LION, *who pretends to play a violin)* Lion! What do *you* want?

LION *(Standing)*: I want to get the hell out of here! Help!

WIZ: Is that your *only* request?

LION: No, sir, not really ... and I agree—what's a home but broken furniture—shattered dreams—faded memories—cold oatmeal and—oh, if you only knew my Momma.
(Falls on his knees)

WIZ: But what *is* it you want?

LION (*Ashamed*): Courage!

WIZ: Courage? You mean the mighty king of the jungle is a coward?

LION: Only when I'm scared.

WIZ (*Mocking him*): Weakness! That's your only strength. (*He dismisses the* LION *and turns to confront the* SCARECROW. *He mounts stairs to top of platform.* LION, DOROTHY, *and* TINMAN *scurry to left of steps and watch.* To SCARECROW) Are you a coward, too?

SCARECROW: Oh, no, sir. I haven't got the brains to be afraid of anything.

WIZ: Oh, no?

(*He causes fire to leap from flashpot and the* SCARECROW *tumbles over in fright, as he says:*)

SCARECROW: Except fire! I know that much!

WIZ: Not afraid of anything, you thought? (*Crossing down to him*) How little we know ourselves. Which is the more deceptive . . . the foolish wise man . . . or the wise fool?

SCARECROW: Don't ask me. I never was any good at multiple-choice.

WIZ (*Annoyed, picking him up and throwing him across the room*): Why you dumb sack of straw! Tinman! (*He motions for the* TINMAN *to approach him, which he does, then motions him to kneel which he does*) Do you know anything or not?

TINMAN (*Humbly*): Only that I want a heart, your Wizness.

(*The* WIZ *laughs at his naïveté.* TINMAN *rises and follows him*)

WIZ: What on earth for? Without one, you'll never know pain (*Hits him*) or hurt (*Hits him*) or sorrow.

(*He stares him to his knees*)

TINMAN (*On one knee*): But there's more to feeling things than just that, isn't there?

WIZ: Possibly. But are you sure it's worth the suffering?

Music in: "If I Could Feel"

TINMAN: Oh, I'll take my chances, your Wizness. I'll take my chances . . .

What would I do if I could suddenly feel
And know once again, what I feel is real
I could cry, I could smile

I might lay back for a while
Oh tell me what, what would I do, if I could feel?

(WIZ *goes up and sits on tongue,* TINMAN *rises*)

What would I do, if I could reach inside of me
And know how it feels to say I like what I see
Then I'd be more than glad to share
All that I have inside of here
And the songs that my heart might bring
You'd be more than glad to sing

And if a tear came to my eye
Think of all the wounds they'd mend
And just think of the time I could spend
Being vulnerable again
Oh tell me what, what would I do
What, what would I do
What, what would I do

(*Crosses to platform*)

If I could feel?
If I could feel.

(*Kneeling on step*)
Will you help me get a heart, your Wizness?
WIZ: Oh, lay off that Wizness business! (*As he comes downstage,*
   the SCARECROW *moves out of his way*) Come now! I have
   made my decision! (*To the* TINMAN) I will give you a heart ...
   (TINMAN *ad-libs joy. To the* SCARECROW) ... and you, some
   brains ... (SCARECROW *ad-libs joy. To the* LION) ... and you,
   courage ... (LION *ad-libs joy. To* DOROTHY) ... and I will get
   you back to Kansas ...
DOROTHY: Oh, thank you ...
WIZ: ... *If!*
DOROTHY (*Apprehensively*): If what?
WIZ (*To* DOROTHY): If you kill the most evil, the most wicked,
   the most powerful of all the witches in Oz ... the *Wicked*
   Witch of the West!
DOROTHY: But I couldn't do somethin' like that!

WIZ: Why not? You've already killed one wicked witch.

DOROTHY: But that was an accident!

WIZ: I do not care how it happened. You're the best wicked-witch killer in this country!

SCARECROW: Mr. Wiz, what do I have to do to get my brains?

WIZ: Kill the Wicked Witch of the West, of course! *(He flings him away)*

SCARECROW: But you just told Dorothy *she* had to do that!

WIZ: It does not matter *who* does it! This is a package deal. As long as the Wicked Witch of the West still lives, none of you get anything! *(He starts to exit up the stairs)*

DOROTHY: But I don't want to go around killin' nobody!

WIZ *(Turns to DOROTHY)*: Dorothy, if you want to get back to Kansas bad enough, you're just going to have to pay for it!

DOROTHY: But . . .

WIZ: No! I have spoken!

Music in: "So You Wanted to Meet the Wizard"

(Smoke pours out of the tongue again as the WIZ mounts it. The tongue disappears into the aperture. DOROTHY collapses in tears)

Curtain

Act Two

SCENE 1

The castle of the WICKED WITCH OF THE WEST *(*EVILLENE*). A few days later.*
Music in: "Winkie Chant"
(In the dreadful palace of the WICKED WITCH OF THE WEST, *slavelike* WINKIES *pull and tug on a long rope, at the end of which is something we don't yet see. The* LORD HIGH UNDERLING, *a weak coward of a man, and a bully, and a toady for* EVILLENE, *beats and whips the* WINKIES *as they cross. Through this he shouts:)*

LORD HIGH UNDERLING: Make way! Make way! Make way for the Wicked Witch of the West! Make way for . . . *Evillene!*

(The WINKIES *pull and tug and moan and cry, and now we see they are pulling* EVILLENE'S *massive rolling throne on stage. It's cold and ugly and hung with carcasses.* EVILLENE *herself is lowdown evil. One just knows there isn't a kind bone in her imposing body or a good thought in her rotten mind. She tolerates the moaning and crying of the* WINKIES *for just so long, but not before the throne has settled at downstage center, and then:)*

EVILLENE: Shut up!
(Music and chant out)
'Cause I'm evil with everyone today!

Music in: "No Bad News"

Now when I wake up in the afternoon
Which it pleases me to do
Don't nobody bring me no bad news
'Cause I wake up already negative

And I've wired up my fuse
So don't nobody bring me no bad news

(Rises)

If we're goin' to be buddies
Better bone up on the rules
'Cause don't nobody bring me no bad news
You can be my best of friends
As opposed to payin' dues

(Hits WINKIE *with skirt)*

But don't you never bring me no bad news

No bad news, no bad news
Don't nobody bring me no bad news
Because I'll make you an offer, child
That you cannot refuse
'Cause don't nobody bring me no bad news

When you're talkin' to me
Don't be cryin' the blues 'cause
And don't nobody bring me no bad news
You can verbalize and vocalize
But just give me the clues 'cause
Don't nobody bring me no bad news

Bring the message in your head
Or in something you can't lose
But don't you ever bring me no bad news

(Kicks WINKIE*)*

If you're gonna bring me something
Bring me something I can use
But don't nobody bring me no bad news

(She sits on throne. The throne moves about the stage)

No bad news, no bad news
Don't nobody bring me no bad news

No bad news, no bad news
Don't nobody bring me no bad news

Better watch the way you place the words
That you might chance to choose
'Cause don't nobody bring me

Don't nobody bring me
Don't nobody bring me
Don't nobody bring me
Don't nobody bring me
No bad news!

'Cause I ain't goin' for it!

(All but FOUR WINKIES *leave. The* FOUR *who stay hold behind throne and will move it to a second and third position during the scene. At end of scene they will move it offstage)*

Now where's that Lord High Underling?

LORD HIGH UNDERLING: You summoned me, O Beautiful Mistress?

EVILLENE: Well, what's the situation with Dorothy?

LORD HIGH UNDERLING: I should have news from the front any moment now. Good news.

(For the first time, EVILLENE *notices the* LORD HIGH UNDER-LING *is standing as he speaks to her)*

EVILLENE: On your knees when you speak to me! *(He instantly drops to his knees, groveling.* EVILLENE *raises the hem of her skirt and sticks her foot in his face)* Kiss . . . my . . . foot! *(He kisses it once. Is it enough to please her? No)* One more time. A little higher and about an inch to the right. *(He kisses it again)* Oh, it's so good to be a liberated woman! *(And again. And again, sending* EVILLENE *into an ecstasy of her own, which is interrupted only when* TWO WINKIES *drag in a terrified* MESSENGER. *The* LORD HIGH UNDERLING *moves above throne, where he kneels)*

FIRST WINKIE: O most Wicked Majesty . . . the messenger has arrived!

*(*TWO WINKIES *exit, leaving the* MESSENGER *on his knees, shaking)*

MESSENGER: A message, your Evilness.

EVILLENE: Oh, yeah.

MESSENGER: Yeah.

EVILLENE: Well, for your sake, it had better be *good* news.

MESSENGER (*Lying. Trying to save himself*): Oh, yeah! I got a really good piece of good news for you . . . mostly.

EVILLENE: *Mostly?*

MESSENGER: Yeah!

EVILLENE: What do you mean "mostly"?

MESSENGER: Well, firstly, Dorothy and her friends are still on their way up here and they gonna do you in . . .

EVILLENE (*Laughs*): What?

(*She breaks up laughing. The* LORD HIGH UNDERLING *and* WINKIES *laugh with her. She stops them with a glare*)

MESSENGER: Secondly, we couldn't get the silver slippers away from Dorothy . . .

EVILLENE (*More angry*): What?

MESSENGER: And thirdly, I gotta go now! (*He starts to crawl away, but* EVILLENE *rises from her throne*)

EVILLENE: But you've brought me nothing but *bad* news. Where's the *good* news you promised?

MESSENGER: The good news is . . . there ain't no more bad news! (*He starts to sneak away, this time almost making it.* EVILLENE *whirls on the* LORD HIGH UNDERLING)

EVILLENE: Who hired this jive turkey?

LORD HIGH UNDERLING: Well, I did. Why?

EVILLENE: Well, a pox on your house!

LORD HIGH UNDERLING: A pox on *my* house?

EVILLENE (*With a sweeping gesture taking in the* MESSENGER): A pox on *both* your houses!

LORD HIGH UNDERLING (*In tears*): My summer place, too?

EVILLENE (*To* LORD HIGH UNDERLING): Oh, shut up! (*He dissolves in tears. She now sees the* MESSENGER *trying to sneak away*) Come here, you! (*Her magic draws him back to her, as if she were some sort of a magnet. When he is at her feet, her mood seems to change. She seems to be kinder*) Now, now, now I know it's not your fault . . .

MESSENGER (*Hopefully*): No, it's not my fault . . .

EVILLENE: . . . so I'm going to be very fair about this . . .

MESSENGER (*More hopefully*): . . . Very fair . . . Good, I can leave.

(*On his knees, he crosses toward exit*)

EVILLENE (*Exploding*): Hang that sucker! (TWO WINKIES *from behind the throne drag the* MESSENGER *off to his doom.* EVILLENE *boils, crosses downstage, and, to the audience:*) All right! I'm through being Mr. Nice Guy. I'm going to summon my winged monkeys!

LORD HIGH UNDERLING: Oh, no!

EVILLENE: Oh, yeah!

LORD HIGH UNDERLING (*As he runs off*): Not the winged monkeys!

(*The lights change.* EVILLENE *is bathed in a weird glow, and we hear her utter strange, unintelligible voodoo sounds until the* LEADER *of the* WINGED MONKEYS *leaps onstage. He is an evil, surly fellow, who is not in awe of* EVILLENE, *or anyone else for that matter. A real "hit" man for the syndicate*)

MONKEY: Okay, baby, I'm here, but it's not because of you—it's because of that dumb chant.

EVILLENE: Don't you start signifying to me, you little ape, or I'll put a spell on your coconuts.

MONKEY: So what are you gonna lay on me an' the gang this time?

EVILLENE (*Crossing back to her throne, sitting*): Something right up your alley—couple of cats who need straightening out.

MONKEY: Gotcha. Who?

EVILLENE: A Scarecrow, a Tinman, a Lion, and a little brat named Dorothy.

MONKEY (*This breaks him up*): "A Scarecrow—a Tinman—a Lion—a little brat named Dorothy—" You don't get along with *nobody*, do you?

EVILLENE: Oh, shut up, and do as I command and bring them here! (*She laughs*) When I get my hands on Dorothy's silver slippers . . . all of Oz will kiss my feet!

(WINKIES *drag her throne off. She exits laughing*)

SCENE 2

In the forest leading to EVILLENE's *palace. A little while later. Music in: "Funky Monkeys"*

(*The* LEADER *of the* WINGED MONKEYS *summons his evil band, and a scrim rises, exposing them on a grid, "flying" as it were. They come down from the grid and join him, and in ballet, do their monkey thing. In the background, we see* EVILLENE *watching them get ready for the capture, laughing to herself as she crosses behind them.*

The ballet continues.

Now the LION *enters, carrying an exhausted* DOROTHY *in his arms. Then the* TINMAN *and the* SCARECROW. *They know they are in danger, but not from what source, until the* MONKEYS *confront them; snatch* DOROTHY *out of the* LION's *arms; beat the*

TINMAN; *tear at the* SCARECROW; *and drive the* LION *off, no matter how brave he might be at this moment to protect* DOROTHY.

The WINGED MONKEYS *have accomplished their mission for* EVILLENE)

Music out

Blackout

SCENE 3

EVILLENE's *palace. About a week later.*

Misery continues as the WINKIES *are whipped and beaten again, doing their menial chores. Only now we see the* LION, *carrying two buckets of water, staggering across the stage and disappearing. Finally, when all the* WINKIES *have disappeared,* DOROTHY *stumbles onstage, dirty and grimy and unhappy. She collapses downstage center. Then the* LION *re-enters, still carrying his two water buckets. He sees* DOROTHY, *puts down the buckets and crosses to her.* DOROTHY *turns and runs to him.*

LION: Dorothy!

DOROTHY: Lion!

(They embrace. Then:)

LION: Are you all right?

DOROTHY: I guess so. What's that old witch got *you* doin'?

LION: Carrying all the water outa this place.

DOROTHY: They got you carryin' water?

LION: Little Momma, she got me feeling like Gunga Din. Child, you know that lady is so afraid of water, she don't even take a *bath?*

DOROTHY: She doesn't?

LION: No. She just sends herself out to be dry-cleaned.

(Offstage, we hear EVILLENE's *wicked laugh, and she enters preceded by* THREE *groveling* WINKIES. *She notices* DOROTHY *and the* LION *taking time out from their chores)*

EVILLENE: Well, well, well . . . I don't remember telling anyone to take five!

(Now she notices the two buckets of water and recoils, upset)

DOROTHY: Oh, please, Mrs. Witch. I haven't seen the Lion since I been here!

EVILLENE: So what? Just get back to work. I want you to scrub the floors, polish the silver, vacuum the rugs ... and you *do* do windows, don't you? (*Then, to the* LION) And you! Get that water out of my sight! (DOROTHY *and the* LION *cross to buckets;* EVILLENE *stops them with:*) Dorothy, wait! (*Crosses to her, then, more sweetly, to* DOROTHY) When are you going to give me those lovely silver slippers?

DOROTHY: I can't.

EVILLENE (*Still sweetly*): I'll give you all my beauty tips!

LION: Oh, Lord!

DOROTHY: I'll never take them off!

EVILLENE (*Exploding*): Give them to me! You little brat!
(DOROTHY *hides behind* LION. *The* LION *screws up his courage for once*)

LION (*To* EVILLENE): Big Momma, you know what my owl would say about you?

EVILLENE: Owl? No. What?

LION: You crazy!

EVILLENE (*After a beat*): Is that a put-down?

LION (*Retreating*): No, your Fatness, it's just a ...

EVILLENE (*Cutting him off*): Your *Fatness?* (*She grabs his arm and starts twisting it*) For that, I'm going to have your hide!

LION (*Being forced to his knees in pain*): No! I'm an endangered species!
(DOROTHY *searches for something to stop* EVILLENE *from hurting the* LION)

EVILLENE: This time next year, I'm gonna be wearing you!

DOROTHY: You leave my lion alone, you ... you ...
(*She spies the bucket of water, grabs it and impulsively throws it at* EVILLENE.
As the water hits her, EVILLENE *panics. She starts to melt.*
WINKIES *enter as she melts*)

EVILLENE: Look what you've done! You've ruined me! Water— the only thing I'm powerless against! The only thing that could ever destroy me!
(*She melts into the floor and disappears, as* DOROTHY, *the* LION, *and the* WINKIES *watch in amazement*)

DOROTHY: Oh, Lord, don't tell me. I've done it again!

WINKIES (*Sing*): *Hallelujah!*

LION: What the hell was that?

ONE WINKIE: Thanks to you child, we're all free! Hallelujah!
Music in: "Brand New Day"

WINKIES and DOROTHY:
Everybody rejoice
'Cause there's a reason to rejoice, you see
Everybody come out
And let's commence to singing joyfully

(Through the following, the WINKIES stop being slaves and
become free people once again)

Everybody look up
And feel the hope that we've been waiting for
Everybody be glad
Because our silent fear and dread is gone
Freedom, you see

(LION and DOROTHY exit)

Has got our hearts singing so joyfully
Just look about
You owe it to yourself to check it out
Can't you feel a brand new day?
Can't you feel a brand new day?
Can't you feel a brand new day?

(Through the following, the SCARECROW and the TINMAN
enter, joining DOROTHY and the LION for:)

Everybody be glad
Because the sun is shining just for us
Everybody wake up
Into the morning, into happiness
Hello, world!
It's like a different way of living now
Thank you, world!
We always knew that we'd be free somehow
In harmony
Let's show the world that we've got liberty
It's such a change
For us to live so independently
Freedom, you see
Has got our hearts singing so joyfully
Just look about

You owe it to yourself to check it out
Can't you feel a brand new day
Can't you feel a brand new day
Can't you feel a brand new day
Brand new day!

(Music ends briefly; then, as DOROTHY *and her friends bid good bye to the* WINKIES, *they exit)*

Music in: "Brand New Day" (Reprise)
(After DOROTHY *and her friends have exited, the* WINKIES *reprise another chorus of the song)*

SCENE 4

In front of the gates to Emerald City. Some time later.
The ROYAL GATEKEEPER *enters through gate, peers offstage, sees something, and becomes concerned.*

GATEKEEPER *(To himself):* That bunch is comin' back from seein' the Wicked Witch of the West. Well, the Wiz gave orders they were never gonna be allowed in the city again, so they can just ... *(Now a thought hits him) Back* from seein' the Wicked Witch of the West? *Alive? (He puts two and two together)* So that means that *she* must be ... and if they did that to *her* ... and I tell them they can't ... Uh-oh! I wish I was back on Unemployment!
(He hurriedly seeks cover inside the gates as DOROTHY *and the* OTHERS *enter. The* TINMAN, *the first to enter, crosses to the gate, and calls in)*
TINMAN: Hello in there!
GATEKEEPER *(From the inside):* Good-bye out there!
SCARECROW: Open up in there!
GATEKEEPER: What for?
LION: 'Cause we want to see the Wiz again, dummy!
GATEKEEPER: Impossible. He moved.
TINMAN: He *moved?* How come?
GATEKEEPER: I don't know. It had something to do with urban renewal.
LION: You better urban this gate.
GATEKEEPER: I can't. You see, the man with the keys went on vacation until the middle of next month.

SCARECROW (*With a plan*): Well, then, I guess we better leave the money and go.

GATEKEEPER (*Interested*): Money? What money?

SCARECROW (*Letting the others in on his plan in mime*): Well, we brought back this big bag of loot for the Wiz. How much do you think is in here, Brother Lion?

LION: Well, between in gold and silver alone, I'd say somewhere in the vicinity of a round figure . . .

TINMAN: I think there's at least *twice* that much!

SCARECROW: So when the man with the keys comes back . . . it'll be right here by the mail chute. C'mon, Dorothy, we gotta go before it gets dark.

(*They make footsteps, pretending to walk away,* SCARECROW *and* LION *stomp right.* DOROTHY *and* TINMAN *stomp to left. Then tiptoe back. When the footsteps die down, the* GATEKEEPER *sneaks out the gate*)

GATEKEEPER: Gold? Silver? Where? Where? Where?

(*The* LION *and* SCARECROW *grab him*)

LION and SCARECROW: Gotcha!

GATEKEEPER: Oh, damn! I fall for this every night!

DOROTHY: We're goin' in to see the Wiz!

GATEKEEPER: Oh, all right! But I don't want to be around when you wake him up!

(*He exits through gate as lights change and gate scrim rises*)

SCENE 5

The throneroom of the WIZ. *The next moment.*

The throneroom appears to be empty as DOROTHY *and her friends happily enter to collect their rewards.*

DOROTHY: Mr. Wiz! We're back!

TINMAN: Yeah, old Evillene has been done in!

LION: Would you say the lady was liquidated?

DOROTHY (*Looking under bridge*): I wonder where he is?

(*The disembodied voice of the* WIZ *now seems to surround us as it echoes and reverberates*)

WIZ (*Voice*): I am everywhere.

(*They jump back in fright*)

TINMAN: Well, we've come back to get what you promised.

WIZ (*Voice*): I'm busy—

(DOROTHY *crosses to steps. Now they begin to search for him through:*)

SCARECROW (*Looking around*): Busy? What kinda stuff is that?
  (DOROTHY *climbs steps to bridge*)
TINMAN: It's a copout.
LION: Hey, you owe us everything now, Mr. Wiz!
  (*He backs into engine room door*)
WIZ (*Voice*): Go away! Away . . . away . . . away . . . away . . .
  (SCARECROW *crosses up to steps. The* LION *opens a panel and discovers some wheels and cranks, through:*)
DOROTHY (*On bridge over engine room*): Oh, listen. Mr. Wiz, you promised.
LION: Hey! I think I found the engine room!
  (TINMAN *crosses to* LION)
WIZ (*Voice*): Go away!
SCARECROW (*Runs to* LION) Turn the crank!
  (*The* LION *does so, and the mask in front of the* WIZ's *door begins to move*)
WIZ (*Voice*): Go away! Away . . . away . . . away . . . away . . .
LION: Tell me if anything happens.
SCARECROW (*Pointing*): The mask is movin'! Turn it some more!
  (*The* LION *does so, and the mask flies, revealing an open door to the* WIZ's *bedroom*)
WIZ (*Voice*): No! No . . . no . . . no . . . no . . .
  (*But it's too late. The* WIZ *stands there, mike in hand, in his pajamas, with curlers in his hair. He hurriedly puts down the mike and tries to weasel out of it, especially when there is a moment of doubt from* DOROTHY)
DOROTHY: Have you seen Mr. Wiz?
WIZ: Uh . . . no. I haven't, as a matter of fact. The Wiz isn't here. Right now.
  (*He tries to leave*)
SCARECROW: Then who are *you*?
WIZ: Oh, well, I am . . . um—
LION (*Recognizing him*): A fake!
  (*Advancing on him*)
SCARECROW: A phony!
TINMAN: A fraud!
DOROTHY: And how!
SCARECROW: And you look just like anybody else in the morning!
  Music in: "Who Do You Think You Are?"

DOROTHY, LION, TINMAN, SCARECROW:
  Who, who do you think you are?
  Tell me how, how could you go so far?

The show is over, the curtain is down
And you've got to come clean
The time is now, you must 'fess up
And say what you mean

Baby, your come-on was much too cool
Tell me who, who did you think you'd fool?
You turned us on, then you turned us off
Baby, you're not for real
We see you now, for what you are
Tell us how does it feel?
How does it feel?

Who, who do you think you are?
Who told you that you're the star?
The game is over, it's time to come thru
We got to get over
What you gonna do?
Who do you think you are? Who do you think you are?
Who do you think you are? Who do you think you are?
Who do you think you are? Who do you think you are?

WIZ (*On the floor where he has been thrown at end of number*):
Who do I think I am? Who is the Great . . . the Terrible . . .
the Omnipotent Wizard of Oz in reality?
(*He stands. Pause*)

TINMAN: Yeah!

WIZ: Just a former nobody from Omaha, Nebraska.

DOROTHY: Nebraska? Why, that's near Kansas!

WIZ: Yeah. It's right next door.

SCARECROW: I don't understand . . .

WIZ: Of course not. *Nobody* knows my secret, just as nobody . . .
until now . . . ever sees the real me. Look, y'all (*He crosses to
them*), all I ever wanted were the simple things in life . . .
power . . . prestige . . . and money. I tried everything back in
Omaha. I sold used cars . . . I was a pitchman in a carnival . . .
I even peddled bleaching creams from door to door, but
nothing ever worked! And then one day, I got the call.

TINMAN: The call?

SCARECROW: The call from who?

WIZ: The call from the Almighty himself. And that voice said,
"Son, what you ought to do is spread the good word." And I

said, "Why?" And the voice said, "For the simple things in life—power . . . prestige . . . and money."

TINMAN: Some Almighty voice actually said that to *you?*

WIZ: Well, I can't swear whether that message was coming to me live or on tape, but I heard it. Clear as a bell.

DOROTHY: Then what happened?

WIZ: Well, the very next day I read where five thousand folks were gonna get together at a county fair.

TINMAN: Yeah?

WIZ: So I rented a hot-air balloon . . .

LION: Why?

WIZ: Check this out. I float down out of the heavens, I lay my maiden message on that multitude, and I whip up the granddaddy of all revival meetings! Now, unfortunately, as my balloon was comin' in low from over the carousel, from out of nowhere, a violent wind storm came up! The next thing I knew, I was drifting over this huge desert someplace. Then, through an opening in the clouds, I floated down right here in Oz, right in the middle of a ladies' social!

LION: Come-come-come, Mr. Wiz, what happened next, my man?

WIZ (*Crossing to* LION): Well, these ladies had never seen a balloon before. They thought a miracle had delivered me to them. And before you could say "wizard," they promoted me all over town and sold tickets for a benefit, at which, they said, I was going to perform *another* miracle. (*Then, Proudly*) Naturally, I did.

LION: Well. Yeah, but what kind of another miracle did you put on them, man. Cats and kittens?

WIZ: Green glasses. (*He snaps his fingers*)

SCARECROW: Say what?

WIZ: The glasses with the green lenses. Like the ones everyone's wearing. Just like the pair *I* was wearing when I landed here. (*He crosses to steps.* SCARECROW *and* TINMAN *follow him*)

LION: Yeah. But, wait a minute, Mr. Wiz, there ain't no big miracle about green shades . . . is there?

(LION *and* DOROTHY *cross to the* WIZ)

Music in: "Believe in Yourself"

WIZ: The miracle, my friend, is what you allow your eyes to see through them . . .

If you believe
Within your heart you'll know

That no one can change
The path that you must go

Believe what you feel
And know you're right because
The time will come around
When you say it's yours

(ALL FOUR *sit on steps*)

Believe there's a reason to be
Believe you can make time stand still
And know from the moment you try
If you believe, I know you will

Believe in yourself
Right from the start
And you will have brains, and you'll have a heart
And you will have courage
To last your whole life through

If you believe in yourself
If you believe in yourself
If you believe in yourself
Maybe you can believe in me, too.

(*Then, he crosses to the* SCARECROW) Now then. You *do* believe you have a brain, don't you?

SCARECROW (*Rising from steps*): Well, I'd feel a whole lot better if I knew I had something upstairs besides a bunch of straw.

WIZ (*After a beat*): All right! (*He crosses up onto top of platform to a magic "box." The* SCARECROW *sits on second step. The others stand and watch*) If I found green glasses for all of them out there, maybe I can find a brain somewhere in here for you!

Music in: Underscoring "Believe in Yourself"

(*He fishes in the box and produces a large box marked "All-Bran"*) Look what we got here! "All-Brain"! Through the miracle of modern science, they have dehydrated, pre-frozen, and packaged a distillation of some of the best brains in the world. We're gonna re-stuff your head with this!

(He pours some of the All-Bran into the SCARECROW's *cap, and immediately we see a change. The* SCARECROW *becomes suave, sophisticated, and self-assured)*

SCARECROW: Well, *finally* I know where my head is at!

(He goes to DOROTHY, *picks her up, whirls her, puts her down)*

WIZ *(To the* TINMAN): A heart, you say?

TINMAN: Yes.

WIZ: Then a heart it shall be. *(Gets heart from magic box. Hides it behind his back as he moves back down to* TINMAN*)* You know, once—

TINMAN: Yes.

WIZ: A beautiful young lady sent her heart to me this way. And now I give it to you.

(The WIZ *produces a big valentine heart)*

TINMAN: Oh, yes. *(He pins the heart on the* TINMAN, *who looks at it lovingly)* Are the batteries included?

WIZ: At no extra charge!

TINMAN *(To audience)*: All you ladies out there, ha, ha! Watch out.

(The SCARECROW *joins him to congratulate him. The* LION *mounts platform, crosses to the* WIZ. *The* TINMAN *hugs himself in sheer joy as the* WIZ *deals with the* LION*)*

WIZ: As for you, Jack . . . I bet a couple of totes of the Emerald City courage potion will do the trick!

(He produces a chalice, sets it down, then an extra large whiskey bottle marked "O&Z" and pours something into the chalice; then he squirts some seltzer into the chalice to make a foaming mixture. As the WIZ *mixes the potion, the* LION *moves off the platform. The* WIZ *finishes mixing and crosses to the* LION, *sets the chalice on the floor in front of him and orders him:)*

Drink!

(The LION *falls to his knees and drinks. As he does so, the* WIZ *twists his tail. The* LION *roars in pain, then turns and roars at the* WIZ, *scaring him away, then, pleased with himself, to the* TINMAN *and the* SCARECROW*)*

LION *(Roars)*: All right! Well, all right! All right! All right!

Music out

(They congratulate him. Now DOROTHY *primes herself for her reward, too)*

DOROTHY: Now it's my turn, Mr. Wiz. Whatcha got in there to believe me all the way back home to Kansas?

(*The* WIZ *picks up the chalice, crosses up to the platform.*
DOROTHY *follows him. He stops, turns to her*)

WIZ: Dorothy . . . I'm sorry. I can do a lot of things for a lot of
people, but I don't know how to get you home to Kansas.
The answer's just not in this box.

SCARECROW (*Grandly*): Of course not. (*Sweeping the audience
and the stage with his hand*) It's out there somewhere.

LION and TINMAN: What is?

SCARECROW (*To the* WIZ): My good fellow, do you still have the
balloon that brought you here?

WIZ (*Walks with the* SCARECROW *off platform*): Yes, I do. The
ladies put it up in the park and made a national shrine out of
it.

SCARECROW: Just as I thought. Now, if that balloon brought you
here from Nebraska . . .

WIZ: Uh-huh . . .

SCARECROW: Why couldn't it take Dorothy back to Kansas?

WIZ: Well, it certainly could. But first of all. You—

DOROTHY (*Running eagerly to the* WIZ). LION, TINMAN *and*
SCARECROW *follow*): Yeah! When do we go?

WIZ: Now hold on! There's no way you're gonna get *me* to leave
all *this!*

DOROTHY: All what?

WIZ: All my power, my prestige, and my money . . .

DOROTHY (*Following him*): Your big ole empty room, where
nobody comes to see you, and you're afraid to go out, 'less
people find out you're foolin' them?

WIZ: I am *not* afraid! I just keep a low profile.

DOROTHY: You know, I bet if you got started all over again
someplace, you could do all this and even have some friends.

WIZ (*Turns to her*): Friends? Do you really think so?

DOROTHY: Aw, you're not so bad . . . once a person gets to know
you.

WIZ (*Mulling it over. Are "friends" enough?*): Friends, huh?

DOROTHY (*Takes his hand*): And when we get back to Kansas,
I'll give you my silver shoes.

WIZ: Well, what are we waitin' for?

(*He exits*)

SCENE 6

The balloon site in Emerald City.
On the WIZ's *exit, they move up the steps to top of platform.*

DOROTHY *right of center.* LION *left of her.* SCARECROW *left of* LION. TINMAN *left of* LION.

PEOPLE OF EMERALD CITY *arrive, bearing farewell small balloons for* DOROTHY. *They troop past in their best costumes.*

In a moment, the WIZ *enters in white goggles, jumpsuit and jeweled cape. He circles the stage to his place upstage on platform.*

ALL FOUR *come off platform, join* CROWD *facing upstage as* WIZ *starts sermon.*

Two choruses of "Home" treatment as the WIZ *strolls about, then climbs stairs to pulpit, and music cut-off.*

WIZ: *My fellow Ozians . . .*
No . . . let me just say . . . my friends.
On this memorable day when friends . . . must part . . .
Remember: To everything there is a season (Hmmm) . . .
And remember, there is a Time to Keep *(Hands up)* . . .
And a Time to Cast Away . . .

ALL: Well . . .

WIZ: Yes, I said a Time to Keep *(Hands up)* . . . and a Time to Cast Away.

ALL: Well . . .

WIZ: And today is both times for us.

ALL: Well, well.

WIZ: A Time to Keep. I said a Time to Keep!
And a Time to Remember. Yes, I said a Time to Remember!
And at this very same moment . . . a Time when we must . . .
Cast Away *("Cast Away").*
A Time when we must stop holding
on to the things that make us feel safe! And embrace
what we fear . . . Ourselves, in all our beautiful hang-ups!
(Applause. At first, hesitant, then growing)
We have got to know in our hearts that the things
we hold up as sacred sometimes are holding us down!
Down! When you know you ought to be up!
Down! Afraid to wade through strange and turbulent waters!
Down! Burning in the heat of our own lies,
when you ought to be reaching up! Up! UP!!!
To touch the frozen fingers of truth!
You have got to peel off all your clothes
to find out who you truly are!
But can you do it? *(Silence)*
Shall I do it?
Ow! I have done it *(Cheers)*

I have stepped outside of myself ("*Step!*")
in order to dig inside my soul ("*Step!*")
In order to see what I ought to have seen
before ("*Step! Step!*")
Now you have got to do it!
It is not enough to know where you're going!
You've also got to know where you're coming from!
Y'all got it!

Music in: "Y'All Got It"

I got to leave, so I've packed my bag
And I'm goin'
I got a date, so don't ask me to stay
'Cause I'm showin

You were always ready for new wizardry
You must think that miracles was easy for me
Take what I gave you and put it up on a shelf
'Cause now it's time for this here Wiz,
To wiz on himself
And I'm wizin'

Gi' me a reason why I should stay and I'll judge it
My mind is made up, so nothin' you say, gonna budge it
Y'all copped a whole lot of magic from me
But this the greatest magic that you'll ever see
If you blink more than one time, the kid will be gone
And you will have to hook up the rest on your own
And do you know what I think about that

Your work's cut out for you, so it's not about
If's, but's or and's
'Cause when I leave here I'm leaving it all in your hands
I packed all my clothes, and I packed up my power
I'm leaving this place in less than one-half an hour
If you look up in the sky, you'll know just who it is
It's not a bird, or a plane, it's just the little ol' Wiz
And guess who it's on after that
Y'all got it

Give me a reason why I should stay
And I'll judge it

My mind is made up, so nothing you say
Gonna budge it
I packed all my clothes and I packed up my power
I'm leaving this place
In less than one-half an hour
If you look up in the sky
You'll know just who it is
Not a bird or a plane
Just a little old Wiz
And guess who it's on after that!

Y'all got it, y'all got it, y'all got it
Talkin' 'bout leavin' here.

Y'all got it, y'all got it, y'all got it
Talkin' 'bout leavin' here.

Y'all got it
Y'all got it
Y'all got it
Y'got it!

(On Button of number—the WIZ crosses up the steps and gets into balloon. Balloon rises. DOROTHY, still caught up in the dance, is dancing with the LION, unaware the balloon is leaving without her. The SCARECROW, at the balloon site, waves frantically to get DOROTHY's attention, succeeding finally. She runs upstage, but too late. The balloon has left)

SCENE 7

Somewhere else in Oz. The next moment.
As the balloon disappears and the set changes, the Emerald City CITIZENS *exit.*
Emerald City has disappeared. So has the WIZ. *So has* DOROTHY's *dream of getting home. Despite the fact she still has the* LION, *the* SCARECROW, *and the* TINMAN *with her, she throws a tantrum in her disappointment.*

DOROTHY: Mr. Wiz! You left me! Now I'll bet I'll never get home! *Never!*
(She throws herself down on the ground. There is a puff of smoke. ADDAPERLE appears, dazed and confused as usual)

ADDAPERLE: Where am I?

DOROTHY: Addaperle! *(Rises, runs to her)*

ADDAPERLE: Dorothy! Dorothy! Baby! *(They hug each other.* ADDAPERLE *sees the others)* How come you joined the circus, child?

DOROTHY: No. They're my friends. They came with me to see the Wiz, too.

ADDAPERLE: Oh, you saw him!

DOROTHY: Yeah.

ADDAPERLE: And you got what you wanted!

DOROTHY: Well, *they* did. But I still haven't gotten home to Kansas yet.

ADDAPERLE: Oh, I thought maybe *this* was Kansas.

DOROTHY: No.

ADDAPERLE: Well, listen! Now, how about Glinda? She ought to be able to think of something?

DOROTHY: Who?

ADDAPERLE: I told you about my sister Glinda. The Good Witch of the South? She's the prettiest of all us witches. Takes after me.

TINMAN: Where can we find her?

ADDAPERLE: Oh, don't worry. I'll bring Glinda here before you can say "Great googamooga sugar booga!" Just a wave of my magic hankie . . .

(She waves it, and to her surprise, magic does happen)

Music in: "A Rested Body Is a Rested Mind"

(A tent materializes and along with it, the QUADLINGS, *who are in* GLINDA's *domain)*

Listen! That's Glinda. That's Glinda's theme song!

(Now ADDAPERLE *notices the* QUADLINGS *flooding the area)* Look at 'em! They're coming outta the woodwork! *(Now, as the stage is set for* GLINDA's *grand entrance)* Go ahead, Glinda, work your show, baby!

*(*DOROTHY *and the* SCARECROW *sit on the ground.* TINMAN, LION, *and* ADDAPERLE *stand above them.*

The tent opens, and GLINDA *appears, indeed the prettiest of all the witches, but, like* ADDAPERLE, *a witch who is wise in show-business ways)*

GLINDA:

Come over here and rest awhile
Look at the trip you've made

I know you must be tired by now
So rest here in the shade

Oh, the journey that you had to make
I've watched you bear the load
But you can always stay at my place
When you come off the road

And if you ever need someone
Count on me anytime
I'll be here to lay you down
Because a rested body is a rested mind

And if you ever need someone
Count on me anytime
I'll be here to lay you down
Because a rested body is a rested mind
Because a rested body is a rested mind
Because a rested body is a rested mind
Because a rested body is a rested mind.

(Now ADDAPERLE *rushes up to greet her long-gone little sister*)
ADDAPERLE: Glinda! Glinda! Glinda! It's me! Addaperle!
GLINDA: Addaperle!
    (*They kiss*)
ADDAPERLE: You sure know how to get down.
GLINDA: Well, it may be so. But it's costing me a fortune to do
    it . . .
    (*They move left together;* DOROTHY *interrupts their reunion*)
DOROTHY (*Crossing to* GLINDA): Miss Glinda! My name's Doro-
    thy, and these are my friends . . .
    (*She takes* GLINDA's *hand and pulls her to center.*
    During this, ADDAPERLE *inspects* GLINDA's *company with*
    emphasis on the men)
GLINDA: I know all about you!
DOROTHY: You do?
GLINDA: Oh, I been watchin' you on my crystal ball, hoppin'
    around from one witch to another . . . hittin' 'em with houses
    . . . washin' 'em down the drain . . .
DOROTHY: Yeah. Nobody knows the trouble I've seen.
GLINDA: Well, relax, child.
DOROTHY: Then *you'll* help me get home again?

GLINDA: Why, honey, you got your silver slippers. They'll take you home in no time. Don't you ever talk to your feet?

DOROTHY: No . . .

GLINDA (*Chidingly, to* ADDAPERLE): Well, Addaperle! *You* could have told her the secret right off!

ADDAPERLE: Well, of course I could have! But look at all the people I'd of put out of work.

DOROTHY: Miss Glinda, please tell me the secret!

Music in: "Believe in Yourself" (Reprise)

GLINDA:

If you believe, within your heart you'll know
That no one can change
The path that you must go

(She moves downstage with DOROTHY*)*

Believe that you can go home
Believe you can float on air
Then click your heels three times
If you believe, then you'll be here

Believe in yourself, right from the start
Believe in the magic that's inside your heart
Believe all these things
Not because I told you to

But believe in yourself
If you believe in yourself
Just believe in yourself
As I believe in you

*(*GLINDA *is lifted by the* QUADLINGS *for an exit, and surprisingly,* ADDAPERLE *is lifted by other* QUADLINGS*)*

GLINDA: C'mon, Addaperle . . . we got a lot of catchin' up to do! *(She is carried off)*

ADDAPERLE (*As she is carried off*): What a way to go! Old Addaperle flyin' first class again! Good-bye, Dorothy!

DOROTHY: 'Bye, Addaperle!

ADDAPERLE: 'Bye, baby!

*(*ADDAPERLE *exits)*

DOROTHY: You mean that's all there ever was to it? Just clickin' my heels three times, and I'm home?

LION: Ain't that something, Little Momma? I guess it's about time for you to go, huh?

(She crosses to him. They hug)

SCARECROW: You coulda gone back before you even met me.

TINMAN: Yeah. Before you even got tied up with any of us. Honey, what a shame.

DOROTHY: No! It wasn't a shame! 'Cause if I'd gone back then . . . *(Crosses to* SCARECROW. *Tenderly, to him)* . . . I'd never have seen you get your brains . . . *(Turns to* TINMAN. *Tenderly, to him)* . . . and I'd never known whether you got your heart . . . *(She goes to the* LION, *but can't hold back the tears any longer. For he has been her dearest friend of all)* And— and you . . . *(She collapses in his arms. They hold each other for a moment)*

LION: Dorothy . . . do you really have to go?

(There is another beat, and then the SCARECROW *brightly solves the problem)*

SCARECROW *(Crossing to* DOROTHY*)*: Well, logically, even if she did go, if you kept the silver slippers, you could come back any time you wanted to!

DOROTHY: And I will, Scarecrow. I promise I'll come back . . .

Music in: "Home"

. . . but right now, don't you all see . . .

When I think of home, I think of a place
Where there's love overflowing

*(*TINMAN *and* SCARECROW *move close to her,* TINMAN *to her right,* SCARECROW *to her left)*

I wish I was home, I wish I was back there
With the things I've been knowing
Wind that makes the tall grass bend into leaning
Suddenly the raindrops that fall have a meaning
Sprinkling the scene, makes it all clean

(She crosses to center to LION *who is now on all fours)*

Maybe there's a chance for me to go back
Now that I have some direction
It sure would be nice to be back home
Where there's love and affection

And just maybe I can convince time to slow up
Giving me enough time in my life to grow up
Time, be my friend, let me start again

(The THREE *start a slow exit.* LION *turns and crawls out left.* TINMAN *backs off out right,* SCARECROW *out another exit right)*

Suddenly my world's gone and changed its face
But I still know where I'm going
I have had my mind spun around in space
And yet I've watched it growing
And if you're listening, God, please don't make it hard
To know if we should believe the things we see
Tell us, should we try to stay, should we turn and run away?
Or would it be better just to let things be?

(By now, the SCARECROW, *the* TINMAN, *and the* LION *have disappeared, leaving* DOROTHY *alone, in one, for:)*

Living here in this brand new world might be a fantasy
But it taught me to love, so it's real, real real to me
And I've learned that we must look inside our hearts to find
A world full of love
Like yours, like mine . . .

(She clicks her heels three times)

Like home!

*(*TOTO *runs onstage and jumps into her arms, and the lights go to black)*

Curtain

TWO GENTLEMEN OF VERONA

(Based on the play by William Shakespeare)

Adapted by John Guare and Mel Shapiro

Lyrics by John Guare

Music by Galt MacDermot

EDITOR'S NOTES

One of the most joyous happenings of the 1971–72 Broadway season was the fusion of Shakespeare and the modern beat in the musical variation of the Bard's romantic comedy *Two Gentlemen of Verona*. Originating as a New York Shakespeare Festival outdoor presentation at the Delacorte Theatre, Central Park, it opened on July 27, 1971, and proved so popular with the alfresco audiences that it moved to Broadway in the fall. Once again (this time within the environs of a proscenium) it was glowingly received by press and public.

Clive Barnes declared in *The New York Times:* "It is a lovely fun show ... It is a graffito written across a classic play, but the graffito has an insolent sense of style, and the classic play can still be clearly glimpsed underneath." Jack Kroll reported in *Newsweek* that "*Two Gentlemen of Verona* is a rousing delight, a rare example of how to manhandle Shakespeare for his own and the public's good."

According to Tom Prideaux of *Life*, the musical "stands out for having achieved a consistently celebrative and playful style. What might seem a forced marriage between Elizabethan poetics and neo-hippie hoopla with a Latin-American beat turns out to be a congenial union."

Other professional first-nighters described it as "a musical that has a kink of its own, a certain mirth of mind," while "Mr. Guare's lyrics have a brusque toughness that is admirable, and his rhymes are occasionally as acerbic and as rugged as his sentiments."

The occasion perhaps was best summarized by Brendan Gill in his coverage for *The New Yorker*: "At the end of the opening-night performance of *Two Gentlemen of Verona*, it seemed likely that nobody would ever consent to leave the theatre—neither the merry band of marvelous young people onstage nor the audience that stood applauding."

The musical, which ran for 627 performances, won both the New York Drama Critics' Circle Award and the Antoinette Perry (Tony) Award for best musical of the season, three Drama

Desk Awards, and three citations in *Variety*'s Poll of New York Drama Critics.

John Guare, lyricist and co-adaptor of the libretto with Mel Shapiro, was born in New York City on February 5, 1938. He was educated at Georgetown University and the Yale School of Drama. A prolific contributor to Off-Off-Broadway, Mr. Guare stepped from there to national attention when his short play, *Muzeeka*, opened at the Provincetown Playhouse, New York, in the spring of 1968. Described in the press as "beautifully poetic and always meaningful . . . written with thought, craftsmanship and beauty," it brought him an Obie Award for distinguished writing.

In 1969 Mr. Guare moved up another rung on the ladder to prominence with his Broadway production of *Cop-Out*, the collective title of two short plays. Although the presentation tarried briefly, at season's end Mr. Guare was cited as the year's "Most Promising Playwright" in the annual New York Drama Critics' Poll conducted by *Variety*. That promise was amply fulfilled in 1971 when the author's first full-length play, *The House of Blue Leaves*, was chosen by the New York Drama Critics' Circle as the best American play of the season.

Mr. Guare's other works for the theatre include *The Loveliest Afternoon of the Year, Something I'll Tell You Tuesday, A Day for Surprises, Rich and Famous, Marco Polo Sings a Solo*, and most recently, *Landscape of the Body*, presented by Joseph Papp at the Public Theatre in 1977.

Co-adaptor and director Mel Shapiro shared a second Tony Award with Mr. Guare for "Best Book of a Musical" and was honored with an Obie Award for his robust direction of *Two Gentlemen of Verona*.

One of the theatre's most versatile and sought-after directors, Mr. Shapiro has worked extensively in leading regional theatres throughout the country. Among these: the Tyrone Guthrie Theatre, Minneapolis; Arena Stage, Washington, D.C.; the Old Globe Theatre, San Diego; and the Stanford Repertory Theatre, Palo Alto. He also has directed many New York productions including Mr. Guare's prize-winning *The House of Blue Leaves*.

Galt MacDermot not only received the Tony and New York Drama Critics' Circle Awards for his score for *Two Gentlemen of Verona*, but he also was named by both the Drama Desk and *Variety* Poll the year's outstanding theatre composer. His first

New York score was for the immensely successful *Hair,* which appears later in this volume. Since then he has contributed the music to at least a dozen other stage and film productions and, in more solemn moments, has written an impressive folio of oratorios and sacred music.

PRODUCTION NOTES

Two Gentlemen of Verona was presented by the New York Shakespeare Festival (Joseph Papp, Producer) at the St. James Theatre, New York, on December 1, 1971. The cast was as follows:

Thurio	Frank O'Brian
Speed	Jose Perez
Valentine	Clifton Davis
Proteus	Raul Julia
Julia	Diane Davila
Lucetta	Alix Elias
Launce	John Bottoms
Antonio	Frederic Warriner
Crab	Phineas
Duke of Milan	Norman Matlock
Silvia	Jonelle Allen
Tavern Host	Frederic Warriner
Eglamour	Alvin Lum

Citizens of Verona and Milan: Loretta Abbott, Christopher Alden, Roger Briant, Douglas Brickhouse, Stockard Channing, Paul De John, Nancy Denning, Richard De Russo, Arthur Erickson, Georgyn Geetlein, Sheila Gibbs, Jeff Goldblum, Edward Henkel, Albert Insinnia, Jane Jaffe, Signa Joy, Kenneth Lowry, Sakinah Mahammud, Otis Sallid, Madeleine Swift

Quartet: Black Passion—Sheila Gibbs, Signa Joy, Kenneth Lowry, Sakinah Mahammud

Directed by Mel Shapiro
Setting Designed by Ming Cho Lee
Costumes Designed by Theoni V. Aldredge
Lighting by Lawrence Metzler
Choreography by Jean Erdman
Musical Supervision by Harold Wheeler
Additional Musical Staging by Dennis Nahat
Sound by Jack Shearing
Associate Producer: Bernard Gersten

MUSICAL NUMBERS

ACT ONE

Love in Bloom	Thurio
Summer, Summer	Ensemble
That's a Very Interesting Question	Proteus and Valentine
Love Has Driven Me Sane	Proteus
Thou Hast Metamorphosed Me	Proteus
I'm Not Interested in Love	Julia and Male Ensemble
What Does a Lover Pack?	Proteus, Julia and Ensemble
Pearls	Launce
Loving	Proteus
Where's North?	The Company
Bring All the Boys Back Home	The Duke and Ensemble
Love's Revenge	Valentine
I'm to Marry Thurio	Silvia
To Whom It May Concern Me	Silvia and Valentine
Night Letter	Silvia and Valentine
Love's Revenge (Reprise)	Valentine, Proteus, Launce, Speed
Calla Lily Lady	Proteus

ACT TWO

We Come From the Land of Betrayal	Lucetta
Thurio's Samba	Thurio, The Duke and Ensemble
Hot Lover	Launce and Speed
What a Nice Idea	Julia, Lucetta and Tavern Host
Who is Silvia?	Proteus and Ensemble
Love Me	Silvia
Eglamour	Silvia and Eglamour
Where is Silvia?	The Duke and Ensemble
You Live in the Mansion	Valentine
What's a Nice Girl Like Her	Proteus
Don't Have the Baby	Julia, Lucetta, Speed, Launce
Thurio's Samba (Reprise)	Thurio and Lucetta
Milkmaid	Launce and Milkmaid
Love Has Driven Me Sane (Finale)	The Company

COMPENDIUM

Two Gentlemen of Verona,
Proteus and Valentine,
Pledge a friendship that will last
The length of their lifeline.
Valentine sails to seek his future
In the Emperor's Court of Milan.
Proteus in Verona stays:
To metamorphose Julia is his plan.
Julia's heart is closed,
But, of course, she's metamorphosed
(As everyone eventually is),
And she gives her heart over to his,
(And he only gives her pearls).
Then Proteus, too, sails to Milan,
Leaving two very lonely girls:
Julia who's now preggers,
Lucetta who's her chum.
But choosers must be beggars,
And Two Gentlemen the girls become
To travel thus is safety
To Milan and the Emperor's Court
To find her choice, dear Proteus.
But Love's memory is sometimes short,
For Proteus now loves Silvia,
The Emperor's daughter she, his choice.
But her father would wed her to Thurio—
A fool with lots of money
And a very funny voice.
But Silvia now loves Valentine.
Her book of love is closed,
And even honor-seeking Valentine
Is by Silvia metamorphosed.
Proteus hires Julia,
Who's still dressed as a boy
(He does not recognize her!),
To deliver gifts to Silvia.

Ah, Silvia, he doth prize her!
Poor Julia, doth he despise her?
And Valentine he betrays?
Yes! his very same best friend,
As if love did on proximity
For livelihood depend.
Valentine is banished.
Proteus thinks his way is clear,
But he did not count on Eglamour,
Silvia's previous dear.
And Eglamour saves her
On her wedding Eve,
And far into the forest
Takes her, far from every peeve.
And they make love until the world
Catches up with them.
Proteus tries to take her.
Valentine doth save her.
Julia reveals herself and for a favor
Confesses that she will make a
Life with Proteus, and Silvia chooses Val.
And Thurio wins Lucetta,
Julia's faithful pal.
Everybody falls in love,
Even milkmaids in the field.
Everyone can be metamorphosed:
That is the secret of life,
And that secret is revealed.

John Guare

Place: Verona, Milan and the forest.

Two Gentlemen of Verona was written for outdoor performance, so when it moved inside the back wall of the theater got
painted a luminous Mediterranean blue, a Botticelli blue,
stolen from the sky behind Venus being born. Photographically
real clouds scud across it. The three-level-high set, all crosswalks
and staircases, is painted pink, yellow, orange, and if it looks like
the fire escapes and construction in the tenements of a modern
city, all the better.

Italian farm cottages float down from the flies; green vibrant
trees fly down, lacing the top and sides of the stage.

There is silence.

Then bird calls begin. Whistles. Caws. Crows. Roosters.
Doves cooing. A cacophony of birds.

The actor who will play Thurio runs out on stage dressed in
white. The bird calls grow in volume. The actor who will play
Thurio is deliriously happy. He is the Spirit of Love. We will
call him Vissi D'Amore. He throws his head back and in a
passion-filled Irish tenor voice sings the theme of the old Jack
Benny radio program.

Act One

THURIO (*In his funny, shrill voice*):
Can it be the trees
That fill the breeze
With rare and magic perfume
Oh, no
It isn't the trees
It's love in bloom

Can it be the breeze
That seems to bring
The stars right into my room
Oh, no
It isn't the trees
It's love in bloom

(THURIO *runs off.* CUPID *enters on the top level. The* ENSEMBLE *wanders on*)

ENSEMBLE:
Summer, summer
I was like the summer
Wondering where to go

Autumn, autumn
I was like the autumn
Dying on the vine

Winter, winter
I was like the winter
My heart was cold as snow

Then spring, spring
Spring, spring, spring
I am like the spring

(LUCETTA *appears at the top level and pours thousands of red tissue-paper hearts down on the* ENSEMBLE *and audience*)

Now that you are mine
Cool as a cucumber
Fresh as sweet May wine
Love reminds me of me
I am like all seasons

(CUPID *goes through the* ENSEMBLE *bow and arrowing* EVERYONE)

Love reminds me of me
You are wonderful
You are great
You remind me of me

I am nervous
I am shaking
Love reminds me of me

We are fantastic
We are terrific
We remind me of us

Spring, spring, spring, spring
Love reminds me of me
Spring, spring, spring, spring
Love reminds me of me

I love my father
I want to tell him

I love my mother
I want to tell her

I love my brother
I want to tell him

I love my sister
I want to tell her

I love my mirror
I want to tell me
I want to love me
I want to love me
You can't love another
Without loving yourself.

(ENSEMBLE *freezes.* PROTEUS *and* VALENTINE *enter. They freeze in a tableau of struggle.* SPEED, *the servant, enters carrying luggage. He points at the two of them and bursts out laughing*)

SPEED:
Two Gentlemen of Verona:
A play by William Shakespeare.
(SPEED *and the* ENSEMBLE *run off*)

VALENTINE *(Breaking the tableau):*
Cease to persuade, loving Proteus:
Home-keeping youth have ever homely wits.
Were't not affection chains thy tender days
To the sweet glances of thy honored love,
I rather would entreat thy company
To see the wonders of Milan,
(Music begins)
Than, living dully and sluggardized here in Verona,
Wear out thy youth with shapeless idleness.
What do you want to do with the rest of your life?

PROTEUS:
That's a very interesting question
No one ever asked me that question
Would you mind repeating that question
Say that question once again

VALENTINE:
What do you want to do with your life

PROTEUS:
What do I want to do with my life

That's a very interesting question
No one ever asked me that question
Let me think about that question
My life. My life

(JULIA, *a beautiful Spanish girl, crosses above them on the*
top level. PROTEUS, *in awe, watches her pass*)
I'd like to be a rose
That hangs on Julia's breast

VALENTINE:
I'd like to be that oak tree
That one that towers above the rest

PROTEUS:
I'd like to be a poem that she reads

VALENTINE:
That she rips and throws away
I'd like to be the emperor
Any boy can be, they say

PROTEUS:
I'd rather rule her heart

VALENTINE:
I'd rather rule the world

PROTEUS:
Oh! for a night with Julia

VALENTINE:
Twenty days of wooing for one night of cooing

PROTEUS:
Verona, imagine always living here

VALENTINE:
Milan, imagine always living there

PROTEUS:
Verona, imagine never leaving this place

VALENTINE:
Milan, if everyone knew my face

PROTEUS:
Verona, Julia's name on ev'ry breeze

VALENTINE:
Milan, known by all the maître d's

There's a million wonderful people in the world
I want to know them all
I want them all to bow down
Here's Valentine
Now up, now down

PROTEUS:
There is only one person in my world
I want to know her

VALENTINE:
You don't even know her

PROTEUS:
I'm planning to know her

VALENTINE:
You haven't even met her

PROTEUS:
Not yet

VALENTINE:
Oh, Proteus, you make me laugh

PROTEUS:
I am sorry we don't agree
We've been best friends since we were three

VALENTINE:
Verona is too small for me
Milan is the place to be
Now, thank God, I'll finally be free

There's a million wonderful people in the world
I want to know them all

PROTEUS & VALENTINE:
  We are brothers

  (Sing their school song)

  We are friends
  Up until the day that eternity ends

  (SPEED *enters*)

SPEED:
  Master, the east wind fills the sails.
  I pray you make haste.

  (SPEED *exits*)

VALENTINE (TO PROTEUS):
  Since thou lovest, love still, and thrive therein,
  Even as I would, when I to love begin.

PROTEUS:
  Sweet Valentine, Adieu!
  Think on thy Proteus when thou, haply seest
  Some rare noteworthy object in thy travel:
  Wish me partaker in thy happiness
  When thou dost meet good hap; and in thy danger,
  If ever danger do environ thee,
  Commend thy grievance to my holy prayers,
  For I will be thy beadsman, Valentine.

  (PROTEUS *turns away from* VALENTINE *and cries*)

VALENTINE:
  We are brothers, we are friends

PROTEUS:
  No, we're not . . .

VALENTINE:
Up until the day that eternity ends

(PROTEUS *embraces* VALENTINE)

Peace, brother.

PROTEUS:
Peace.

(VALENTINE *runs off.* PROTEUS *turns out to the audience*)

PROTEUS:
He after honor hunts, I after love:
He leaves his friends to dignify them more;
I leave myself, my friends, and all, for love.

(*Music. He takes out paper and pen and writes*)

Thou, Julia, hast metamorphosed me—

Made me neglect my studies, lose my time
War with good counsel, set the world at nought
Made wit with musing weak, heart sick with thought
Pro-o-o-o-o-o-o-te-us

(PROTEUS *signs his name with a flourish.* JULIA *and* LUCETTA
*enter, carrying rakes and hoes and burlap bales. They stop when
they see* PROTEUS. PROTEUS *is terrified at their proximity. He tries
to speak. He runs off*)

JULIA (*Watching him go*):
Lucetta, wouldst thou counsel me to fall in love?

LUCETTA:
Ay, Madam, so you stumble not unheedfully.

JULIA:
What think'st thou of the gentle Proteus?

LUCETTA:
Lord, Lord! to see what folly reigns in us!

JULIA:
How now! What means this passion at his name?

LUCETTA:
Then, thus, of many good I think him best.

JULIA:
Your reason?

LUCETTA:
I have no other than a woman's reason. I think him so, because I think him so.

JULIA:
And wouldst thou have me cast my love on him?

LUCETTA:
Ay, if you thought your love not cast away.

JULIA:
Why, he of all the rest hath never moved me.

LUCETTA:
Yet he of all the rest, I think, best loves ye.

JULIA:
His little speaking shows his love but small.

LUCETTA:
Fire that's closest kept burns most of all.

JULIA:
They do not love that do not show their love.

LUCETTA:
Oh, they love least, that let men know their love.

JULIA:
I would I knew his mind.

(Music. PROTEUS *enters right on third level. He sings passionately to* JULIA)

PROTEUS:
I'm planning to write a symphony, do you mind
If I dedicate the symphony to you
I'm planning to write a very great book, do you mind
If the heroine is very much like you
Would you mind if I made you immortal
I nat'rally ask your permission
I wouldn't want to make you immortal
Unless you agree to this condition

(PROTEUS *signals the* ENSEMBLE *to enter. They do.* ENSEMBLE
enters right, carrying lighted candles. A triumph of pomposity)

PROTEUS & ENSEMBLE:
I won't write a symphony for you
I won't carve you in stone
If you will not love me forever
Love me forever
Then I will leave you alone

(*During the song,* PROTEUS *passes a letter down through each
member of the* ENSEMBLE *to* LAUNCE. LAUNCE *gives the letter to*
LUCETTA *who gives it to* JULIA. JULIA *looks at it and tears up the
letter*)

PROTEUS:
Cruel, cruel, cruel.

(PROTEUS *and the* ENSEMBLE *run off*)

LUCETTA:
What, Madam, shall these pieces lie here like tell-tales, all
catching cold?

JULIA:
Go! Get you gone and let the papers lie.

LUCETTA:
To plead for love deserves more fee than hate.

JULIA:
Will ye be gone?

LUCETTA:
  That you may ruminate.

  (LUCETTA *exits*)

JULIA:
  I am not interested in poetry
  Poetry's another word for love
  I am not interested in music
  Music is another word for love
  I'm not really interested in romance
  I'm not really interested in love, love, love
  I find love alarming
  I'm happier farming

  (*The air is filled with bird calls for a few seconds*)

  I am not interested in passion
  Passion's just a masquerade for love
  I do not care that much for caring
  Caring's just a careless word for love
  Frankly I don't even care for people
  I'm not really interested in love, love, love
  I only deal with what I feel with

  (*The actor who will play* THURIO *appears again, still in white, still insanely happy. He sings passionately to a* SOPRANO *who appears as insanely happy as he; they sing to each other*)

THURIO:
  Love is that you
  That fills my ears
  That fills my nose
  That fills my heart

SOPRANO:
  Love is that you
  That fills the air
  That fills the sky

THURIO:
  Love is that you
  Speak up

Speak up
Don't be so shy

(*As* THURIO *sings, he crosses to* SOPRANO, *then throws confetti at her, then she throws confetti on him. She circles up right to left as* THURIO *follows her; he throws confetti on* JULIA)

Love is that you
Call out your name
Love love hello
Is that you
Speak up
Love love love
Hello hello

SOPRANO:
Hello hello

(SOPRANO *throws confetti into* THURIO's *face*)

THURIO:
Love, is that you

(*They chase each other off stage, deliriously happy as cupids on a rape.* JULIA *has been metamorphosed and returns to her torn letter*)

JULIA:
O hateful hands! to tear such loving words:
Injurious wasps, to feed on such sweet honey,
And kill the bees that yield it with your stings!
I'll kiss each several paper for amends.
Aye, mira, here is writ "kind Julia." Unkind Julia!
As in revenge of thy ingratitude,
I throw thy name against the bruising stones,
Trampling contemptuously on thy disdain.
Alli tienes tu para que aprendas un poquito.
And here is writ "Love-wounded Proteus."
Poor wounded name! My bosom, as a bed,
Shall lodge thee, till thy wound be thoroughly healed;
And thus I search it with a sovereign kiss.
Un momentito.
Twice or thrice was "Proteus" written down.

Be calm, good wind, blow not a word away,
Till I have found each letter in the letter,
Except mine own name, that some whirlwind bear
Unto a ragged, fearful-hanging rock,
And throw it thence into the raging sea!
Look! Here in one line is his name twice writ,
"Poor forlorn Proteus . . . Passionate Proteus . . ."
"To sweet Julia": that I'll tear away;
And yet I will not, since so prettily
He couples it to his complaining name.
Thus will I fold them one upon another:
Now kiss, embrace, contend, do what you will.

(Music. She writes PROTEUS a letter)

Thou, Proteus, thou hast metamorphosed me
Made me neglect my farming, lose my mind
War with good suitors, kept my temper short
Made sleep a stranger, heartsick with thought
Your loving Juuuuulliiaaaaaaa

Being your slave, what should I do but tend
Upon the hours and times of your desire?
I have no precious time at all to spend
Nor services to do, till you require.

(PROTEUS & LAUNCE enter left)

So true a fool is love that in your will
Though you do anything, he thinks no ill.

(JULIA gives PROTEUS the letter, then crosses right)
I love you.

(JULIA exits)

PROTEUS:
Then roses bloom.

Sweet love! Sweet lines! Sweet life!
Here is her hand, the agent of her heart;
Here is her oath for love, her honor's pawn.

Oh, that our fathers would applaud our loves,
To seal our happiness with their consents!
O heavenly Julia!

(PROTEUS *kisses the letter, then kisses* LAUNCE *on the forehead
as* PROTEUS's *father* ANTONIO *enters carrying luggage*)

LAUNCE (*To the audience*):
Spring comes to Verona.

ANTONIO:
How now! What letter are you reading there?

PROTEUS:
May't please your Lordship, 'tis a word or two
Of commendations sent from Valentine,
Delivered by a friend that came from him.

(PROTEUS *has been holding a letter behind his back.* LAUNCE
takes it and exits quickly)

ANTONIO:
I am resolved that thou shalt spend some time
With Valentine in the court of Milan.

(ANTONIO *has put the luggage down right center stage*)

PROTEUS:	ANTONIO:
No	Yes
No	Yes
No	Huh
No	Huh
No	What
No	What
No	Boy

(PROTEUS *has crossed down right center steps into the audience*)

ANTONIO:
Boy! Boy! Come back here, boy.

(PROTEUS *returns to down center stage by* ANTONIO)

Tomorrow be in readiness to go:
Excuse it not; for I am peremptory.

PROTEUS:
My lord, I cannot be so soon provided:
Please you, deliberate a day or two.

ANTONIO:
Look, what thou wantst shall be sent after thee:
No more of stay! Tomorrow thou must go.

(ANTONIO *is on the left steps. He blows his son a perfunctory kiss, but then sticks his right fist in his elbow in a gesture of pure contempt. He exits*)

PROTEUS:
Thus have I shunned the fire for fear of burning,
And drenched me in the sea, where I am drowned.
I feared to show my father Julia's letter,
Lest he should take exception to my love;
And, with the vantage of mine own excuse
Hath he excepted most against my love.
Oh, how this spring of love resembleth
The uncertain glory of an April day,
Which now shows all the beauty of the sun,
And by and by a cloud takes all away!

(JULIA *enters stage right; she sees the luggage*)

Lovers are lovers best at parting.
When your heart is breaking,
You're in love.

JULIA:
My heart is breaking

PROTEUS:
Then you're in love

JULIA:
Is your heart breaking

(She sits on suitcase)

PROTEUS:
> Mine doesn't have to
> 'Cause I packed my heart away

(The ENSEMBLE enters with a large straw basket)

> What does a lover pack

ENSEMBLE:
> Pack in the sack that he'll stack upon his back

PROTEUS:
> What does a lover pack

ENSEMBLE:
> Bring in the sling that he'll swing beneath his wing

PROTEUS:
> What does a lover pack

ENSEMBLE:
> Sag 'neath the swag that he'll drag into his bag

PROTEUS:
> In his sack

ENSEMBLE:
> Please don't pain yourself
> I don't want you to strain yourself

PROTEUS:
> What does a lover bring

ENSEMBLE:
> Bonbons and sweet mints and boxes of candy

PROTEUS:
> What does a lover bring

ENSEMBLE:
You'll need a toothbrush with all of that candy

PROTEUS:
What does a lover bring

ENSEMBLE:
Roses and daisies and jack-in-the-pulpits

PROTEUS:
In his sling

ENSEMBLE:
You'll need a handkerchief with all of those flowers

PROTEUS:
I'll have to pack my
One thousand love letters
Did you know I wrote
One thousand love letters
I never mailed the
One thousand love letters
I had no one I could mail them to

ENSEMBLE:
Owwwwwwwwwwwwwwwwwwww
Owwwwwwwwwwwwwwwwwwwww
Owwwwwwwwwwwwwwwwwwwww

JULIA:
I'll take them.

PROTEUS:
When I get to Milan
I'll mail them all to you

Pictures of Julia
Portraits of Julia
Albums of Julia
Cameos of Julia
Statues of Julia

ENSEMBLE:
Why not pack the real thing
What does a lover pack

PROTEUS:
I packed my heart away
Along with the bonbons

ENSEMBLE:
What does a lover pack

PROTEUS:
I packed my heart away
Along with the flowers

ENSEMBLE:
What does a lover pack

PROTEUS:
I packed my heart with the statues
Safe and sound
When I get back to Verona

ALL:
I will see you around

(ENSEMBLE *exits.* PROTEUS *pulls out a huge string of pearls from his shoulder bag and puts them around* JULIA'S *neck. She takes* PROTEUS'S *hand and leads him down left, lies on the floor, fixes the pearls and offers herself to him.* PROTEUS *takes off his glasses and looks to the heavens)*

PROTEUS:
Thank you.

(*They embrace on the floor as music begins, and* LAUNCE *enters up right to get the luggage.* LAUNCE *sees them, does a take, then crosses over to them)*

LAUNCE:
You leaned down to kiss me

And your pearls got in my mouth
Your pearls got in my mouth

So I brushed back the pearls
And I kissed your mouth

I leaned down to love you
And your pearls caught on the sheet
Your pearls caught on the sheet
So I took off the pearls
And put them in the ashtray

Then you said that you loved me
You said that you loved me
And nothing got in the way
You didn't choke
You didn't joke
You just said you loved me
And the pearls came out of your mouth
And pearls came out of your mouth
And made a necklace fit
For the emperor of Milan

(LAUNCE *does a dance and exits with a leap off right. He re-enters*)

Sir Proteus, your father calls for you.
He is in haste; therefore I pray you hurry.

PROTEUS:
Why, this it is: My heart accords there to.
And yet a thousand times it answers: "No."

(JULIA *tearfully hangs on to* PROTEUS)

JULIA:
No.

PROTEUS:
Have patience, gentle Julia.

JULIA:
I must. There is no remedy.

PROTEUS:
I will return as soon as I can . . .
Soon . . . soon . . . soon . . .

(They sing a Spanish folk song)

JULIA & PROTEUS:
Soon soon soon soon soon ba ba eh
Pajaro lindo de la madruga
Pajaro lindo soon soon

JULIA:
Don't say soon so much, and you will return sooner.
Keep this remembrance for thy Julia's sake.

(JULIA gives her ring to PROTEUS. He tries to put it on his finger)

Empuja.

(Pushes it)

PROTEUS:
It's a little too fat, my pinkie.

(It fits)

Why, then, we'll make exchange; here, take you this.

(PROTEUS gives his ring to JULIA)

JULIA:
And seal the bargain with a holy kiss.

(They go to kiss, but the pearls get in the way. JULIA stops)

Wait a minute.

(She throws the pearls out of the way to her back. They kiss)

PROTEUS:
Here is my hand for my true constancy;

(*He shakes her hand vigorously*)

And when that hour o'erslips me the day
Wherein I sigh not, Julia, for thy sake.
The next ensuing hour some foul mischance
Torment me for my love's forgetfulness.

JULIA:
No! No!

PROTEUS:
Yes! Yes!

ANTONIO (*Calls offstage*):
Proteus! Proteus!

PROTEUS:
In my short absence, let thy lips do this:
Give my dead picture one engendering kiss.

(PROTEUS *takes a picture of himself from his pocket, kisses it, and gives it to* JULIA)

Work that to life, and let me ever dwell
In thy remembrance, Julia.

ANTONIO (*Offstage*):
Proteus!

(PROTEUS *exits left platform to answer his father's call.* JULIA *exits down left, weeping.* PROTEUS *re-enters left platform*)

PROTEUS:
What! gone without a word?
Ay, so true love should do: it cannot speak;
For truth hath better deeds than words to grace it.

(PROTEUS *exits.* LAUNCE *enters down right with* CRAB, *his dog*)

LAUNCE:

Master Proteus! Master Proteus!
I think my master Proteus be a kind of a knave.
He sends me to give my very dog Crab as a parting
present to his lady Julia. I present the cur to Julia.
Hang down your head, Crab. Did I not bid thee still, mark
me and do as I do. I give the dog to Julia. When didst
thou ever see me heave up my leg and make water against
a gentle woman's farthingale. Didst thou ever see me do
such a trick? Now I'm leaving Verona and I'm going with
Sir Proteus to the Imperial Court in Milan. I don't
want to leave Verona. I love Verona.

Verona, imagine never seeing you again

Oh, Crab, doesn't it tear your heart? Crab? Crab?
I think Crab be the sourest-natured dog that lives.
When I left home, my mother weeping, my father wailing,
my sister crying, the maid howling, and the cat wringing
his hands, and the whole house is in a great perplexity.
Yet did not this cruel-hearted cur shed but one tear,
Cry . . . Go on. Cry . . . Just one time . . . He is a stone
. . . a very pebble stone, and has no more pity in him than
a dog. Why, my great grandam having no eyes, mind
you, wept herself blind at my parting. And now I'm leaving
Verona and this dog sheds not a tear, nor speaks a word;
but see how I lay the dust with my tears.

(*Women of the* ENSEMBLE *enter right, men enter left;*
ANTONIO *and* PROTEUS *enter platform left, crying at the leaving.*
ALL *embrace and leave* PROTEUS, LAUNCE *and* CRAB *alone on
stage with baggage . . . During the farewell,* PROTEUS *sings*)

PROTEUS:

Don't want to travel
Don't want to travel
Don't want to travel
Don't want to travel
Don't want to travel
Don't want to travel
I don't give a damn
How many miles to Milan

(ANTONIO *ad-libs goodbyes in various languages. They mime sailing.* PROTEUS *sings as* LAUNCE *paddles*)

I love my father
I want to tell him
I love my mother
I want to tell her

I love my brother
I want to tell him
I love my sister
I want to tell her
I love my mirror
I want to tell me
I want to love me
You can't love another
Without loving yourself

(As PROTEUS *and* LAUNCE *hit land, lights change and they mime getting out of the ship and exit up right center. As they exit, music changes.* WORKING WOMEN *enter. Two* SCARECROWS *appear at the top level*)

WOMEN:
  In Verona
  In Verona
  In Verona

(LUCETTA *and* JULIA *very dejectedly*)

LUCETTA & JULIA:
  It's very lonely for two ladies in Verona
  It must be nice to be a man
  And sail off to Milan

JULIA:
  It must be nice to be a man
  And not be pregnant

JULIA:	LUCETTA & WOMEN:
If I were a young man	
I wouldn't be pregnant	*In Verona*

If I were a young man
I wouldn't be pregnant   *In Verona*

LUCETTA:
I think, madam, that you should tell him
Write a letter made of vellum
Tell him tell him tell him write it down

JULIA:
Dear Proteus, I hate to bother
But you know you'll be a father
No, I think I'd rather tell him personally

WOMEN:
Tell him tell him he's a papa
Tell him tell him he's a papa
Tell him tell him that he is going to be a dad

JULIA: LUCETTA & WOMEN:
I'm not a young man
So I never can travel   *From Verona*
I'm not a young man
So I never can travel   *From Verona*

JULIA:
It's not safe for girls to go off
Men can show off. Girls can't go off

LUCETTA:
Throw off all the fears you have
We'll dress like men

JULIA:
Ay sie cuanto cuanto la gusta
This hen's become a rooster

LUCETTA:
And a booster on your pilgrimage to love

(Two WOMEN *undress* LUCETTA *and* JULIA *while two* WOMEN
cross up to third level and pull the clothes off the SCARECROWS)

WOMEN:
Please don't travel dressed like girls
Please don't travel dressed like girls
Please don't travel dressed like girls
Dress like men

LUCETTA:
Okay

JULIA:	WOMEN:
How lucky that scarecrow	
He's dressed like a young man	*From Verona*
How lucky that scarecrow	
He's dressed like a young man	*From Verona*

(The WOMEN *throw the* SCARECROWS' *clothes down.* JULIA *and* LUCETTA *dress in their new "old" clothes)*

JULIA & LUCETTA:
Dame, dame, la comisa
Toma, ponte, la comisa
Donne, donne, pantalones
Toma, ponte pantalones
Donne, donne, el sombero
Donne, donne, la corbata
Donne, donne, calzoncillos
Dame, donne, los zapatos
Donne, donne, la chaketa
Toma, ponte la chaketa

JULIA:
Ay no puedi.
Est arme.
Quieta.

ALL:
Take the clothes right off that scarecrow
And if that scarecrow dare crow
Tell him he is dealing with
Two gentlemen
Two gentlemen of Verona

Two gentlemen
Two gentlemen
Two gentlemen

LUCETTA & JULIA:
We are brothers, we are friends
Up until the day that eternity ends

WOMEN:
Tell him tell him he's a papa
Tell him tell him he's a papa
Tell him tell him he's a papa
Tell him tell him he's a papa

(LUCETTA *and* JULIA *call good-bye to each girl*)

LUCETTA & JULIA:
Adios muchachas

(JULIA *and* LUCETTA *exit center.*
The Travel Section: traveling to Milan. The lighting is
mysterious but a rainbow is evident. The CHORUS *appears in*
black capes and black masks and forces the travelers to weave
in and out of its path)

VALENTINE:
Follow the rainbow
Then turn right at the sun
Which you see going (down)

SPEED:
Down in the valley
Then underneath the waterfall
And mountain (pass)

VALENTINE:
Pass by the pine trees
The mass is always growing
On the northern (side)

SPEED:
Sidesaddle, we'll straddle

    Rattlesnakes and fiddle
    While we paddle (down)

VALENTINE:
    Down through the rapids
    And somersault the waterfall
    And whirling (pool)

    (VALENTINE *and* SPEED *exit as* PROTEUS *appears*)

PROTEUS:
    Pool all of our knowledge
    Keep us safe and sound
    How can we ever be lost

    (LAUNCE *enters left*)

LAUNCE:
    How can we ever be found

    (*They exit as* VALENTINE *and* SPEED *appear on third level*)

SPEED:
    We found the igloo
    Now turn right at the palm tree
    Which is bearing (fruit)

VALENTINE:
    Fruitlessly didn't this territory
    Pass before our eyes to(day)

SPEED:
    Day of all days
    When we need every drop
    We waved in our can(teen)

VALENTINE:
    Teenier and teenier
    Is any chance
    That we had to get to Mi(lan)

VALENTINE & SPEED:
    Land

Is that land
No, it's sea
No, it's you
No, it's me
It's mirage
Snakes

(VALENTINE *and* SPEED *exit.* LUCETTA *and* JULIA *enter*)

LUCETTA:
Rajahs and bloodthirsty sheiks
Cause those shrieks
Girls being forced
We are lost

ALL:
We are lost
We are lost
We are lost
We are lost

LUCETTA:
Indians and wild Mongol hordes
With curved swords
Take all their slaves
Up to their caves

(To JULIA)

This way.

(LUCETTA *and* JULIA *exit.* VALENTINE *and* SPEED *enter*)

SPEED:
Tea leaves once told me I'd travel
But who believes what's in a (cup)

VALENTINE:
Cup your hands up to your eyes
And look and tell me what you are seeing

(*The whole scene changes. It's Milan, and it's the most exciting place in the world. The* ENSEMBLE *dances. One* GIRL *in the* ENSEMBLE *at the beginning speaks to* VALENTINE. *Music begins)*

SIGNA:
  Hey, sugar, come here, I want to talk to ya.

  (Dance)

VALENTINE:
  Milan we finally got here
  Where's fame
  How do I apply
  Where's fortune
  And how do I get it
  The noise
  The size
  I can't believe my eyes

(All dance as the DUKE, SILVIA, *his beautiful daughter, and* THURIO *enter up center and cross down center. The* ENSEMBLE *falls to the floor)*

DUKE:
  The duke
  I am the boss here
  Silvia
  This is my little girl
  This is Thurio
  He's going to wed her

  (To SILVIA)

  Don't miss the boat
  Go dance me up some votes

*(*SILVIA *and* THURIO *begin to waltz because that's the kind of jerk he is. A dancer cuts in, and we have a lively dance with* SILVIA *and male* ENSEMBLE *dancers)*

VALENTINE & ENSEMBLE:
  Here's north
  Forget the compass

It's noon
I know the time
I'm here

Call me fortune's pet
Milan
I'll lick you yet

(SILVIA *ends her dance.* THURIO *crosses to her, but she's no dummy and she snubs him. The* DUKE *appears at the top of the stage.* EVERYONE *cheers him*)

DUKE:
When I got into office
There was too much peace
I said it leads to trouble
All this peace
Since I've been elected
I've put troops from here to Rome
And if I'm re-elected
I'll bring all the boys back home

ENSEMBLE:
Bring 'em home
Bring 'em home
Bring all the boys back home

DUKE:
I've sent the boys to warfare
To save our who—knows—what
To protect our hey—who—dere
And defend our hey—why—not
If I am re-elected
Where e'er our troops may roam
If I'm re-elected
I'll bring all the boys back home

ENSEMBLE:
Bring 'em home
Bring 'em home
Bring all the boys back home

DUKE:
If we didn't have a war
Then where
Would we spend our money
Where
Welfare, clean air, child care

ENSEMBLE:
Clean air only
makes you wheeze

Welfare keeps you
on your knees

DUKE:
I'll raise the tax
We should adore
The fact we can
Afford a war

The boys all get in trouble
The spunky little chaps
I'll teach the little children
Their favorite song is taps

(THURIO *commands the* ENSEMBLE *in close-order drill*)

THURIO:
Company fall in. First squad left. Third squad right.
Face forward march.

ENSEMBLE:
Bring 'em home
Bring 'em home
Bring all the boys back home

DUKE:
You should be proud
And feel all warm
A shroud's
A lovely uniform

Who's that boy
He smoked a joint
Send him off
At rifle point

What's that sign
Says me and graft
Put that guy
Into the draft

I'm patriotic
To a man
For God, for country
And Milan

Bring 'em back
Bring 'em back
I'll bring all the boys back
Bring all the boys back

I sent 'em over and I can bring 'em back. Re-elect me!

THURIO (*The Drill Sergeant*):
Second squad to the rear march
to the rear march
to the rear march
to the left flank march
to the right flank march

First squad right flank march

(*To a* MAN)

give me ten
give me ten push-ups
Second squad left flank march

ENSEMBLE:
Yea!

DUKE:
Re-elect me!

ENSEMBLE:
Yea!

DUKE:
Re-elect me!

DUKE & ENSEMBLE:
And I'll bring all the boys back home

(The ENSEMBLE *marches off.* DUKE *and* THURIO *shake hands and exit.* VALENTINE's *Letter Writing Shoppe appears on stage.* VALENTINE *is trying to work.* SILVIA *appears at the top level and sings)*

SILVIA & VALENTINE:
Who is Silvia
What is she
That all our swains commend her
Holy, fair and wise is she
That heaven such grace did lend her
That she might
Admired be

*(*SPEED *has entered right and seen* SILVIA*)*

SPEED:
Silvia! Silvia!

*(*SILVIA *exits)*

VALENTINE:
Who bade you call her?

SPEED:
She that you love?

VALENTINE:
Why how know you that I am in love?

SPEED:
First, you have learned like Sir Proteus to wreath your arms like a malcontent; to walk alone, like one that had

the pestilence; to sigh like a schoolboy that had lost
his ABC; to weep like a young wench that had buried her
grandam; to fast, like one that takes diet; to watch, like
one that fears robbing. You were wont, when you laughed,
to crow like a cock, when you walked, to walk like one of
the lions; when you fasted, it was presently after dinner;
when you looked sadly, it was for want of money; and now
you are metamorphosed with a mistress that, when I look
on you, I can hardly think you my master.

(A GIRL *enters the writing shop and gives letter and money to*
VALENTINE. SPEED *sings to her and frightens her as she exits*)

I want to feel it
I love to feel it
I love the whole world
I love policemen
I love the lawyers
I love our soldiers
I want to tell them
I want to love them
Telling love is half the fun
You can't lock it in

SPEED:
All right! I have loved her since I first saw her.

SPEED:
If you love her, you cannot see her, for love is blind.

VALENTINE:
Belike boy, then, you are in love, for last morning you could
not see to wipe my boots.

(VALENTINE *gives mailbag to* SPEED)

SPEED:
True sir, I was in love with my bed. I thank you, you
beat me for my love, which makes me the bolder to chide
you for yours.

(VALENTINE *chases* SPEED. SPEED *exits laughing*)

VALENTINE:
No appetite
Love took it away
To show me how starved I was
Love's revenge

Insomnia
Love gave it to me
To show me I didn't dream
Love's revenge

The little I sleep
Is just for a nightmare
The little I eat
Is to taste the dregs
Where is my reason
What is my name
What is this terrible shake in my legs

My future plans
Love took them away
To show me I have no future
Love's revenge

I have no future
I have no past
Without love
Nothing can last

Without love
Nothing can last
That's love
That's love's revenge

(SILVIA *enters left with a scarf over her face; crosses to* VALENTINE *behind counter*)

SILVIA (VALENTINE *is dazed*):
I'd like to send a letter.

I'm to marry Thurio
No

I have a secret lover
That I do adore
But my pappy
Sent him off to war
My darlin's name is
Eglamour
And all my passions do inform his mind

VALENTINE *(Falsetto)*:
   To whom . . .

(He clears his throat)

To whom shall I send this?

SILVIA:
   You write it. I'll take care of the rest. Make it fancy.

(VALENTINE *picks up a large feather quill pen and takes down*
what she says)

To whom it may concern me
And oh, you do
Oh, my darlin'
My arms and legs and fingers and knees
Long to wrap around your chest and neck and back and legs
And my lips and tongue and teeth long to
Bite these words into your arms and back and ankles
And elbow and neck
Do I make myself clear
I want you
I wouldn't know a spiritual relationship
If I tripped over it and broke my nose and
My foot and my heart and my hands
All reach out to you and say
Hi there

Save me, Eglamour.

(SILVIA *lies on counter)*

Save me.

(VALENTINE *takes a deep, nervous breath and repeats her letter, tapping it out on the wireless*)

VALENTINE:
   To whom it may concern me:
   And oh, you do,
   Oh, my darlin.
   My arms and legs and fingers and knees
   Long to wrap around your chest and neck and back and legs
   And my lips and tongue and teeth long to
   Bite these words into your arms and back and ankles
   And elbows and neck.
   Do I make myself clear?
   I want you.

   I wouldn't know a spiritual relationship
   If I tripped

(SILVIA *reacts with all her body*)

   Over it and broke my nose and
   My foot and my heart and my hands
   All reach out to you and say
   Hi there
   Save me, Silvia, save me

(SILVIA *sits up and reacts to his mistake*)

SILVIA:
   Eglamour.

VALENTINE:
   Eglamour.

(*He taps out "Eglamour" in Morse code*)

Eglamour. How shall I send this, my lady?

SILVIA:
   What are the rates?

VALENTINE *(He shows her a chart)*:
We have night rates and day rates. The day rates are more
expensive, however . . .

SILVIA:
Night letter
So divine
Night letter
Come be mine
Nothing better than a
Hot night letter
Night letter
Oh, so cool
Night letter
Hear me drool
Nothing wetter than a
Hot night letter
Did you remember to lick the stamp
Night letter
Did you remember to slap the flap
Night letter
Did you remember you have to say
S–W–A–K
Night letter
Mail it early
Night letter
Avoid the rush
Hope you get a
Night letter

Oh, my father would enforce me to marry a vain and foolish
Suitor of fabulous great wealth to stuff the coffers
Of his government and pay for the vain and foolish
War my father uses for his own ends.
Help me . . .

VALENTINE:
Valentine.

(SILVIA *falls into* VALENTINE's *arms)*

SILVIA:

Help me, Valentine.
The marriage is tomorrow
I have to be saved tonight.

Could you save me
Tonight at nine

VALENTINE:

I could save you
Tomorrow at nine

SILVIA:

That's too late, too late
To escape my fate
Tomorrow noon is my wedding day
Come save me
I want to be very far away
Come save me
When the groom comes
To look for me
I didn't R.S.V.P.

VALENTINE:

I could save you
Tonight at eight

SILVIA:

Tonight at eight
Would be just great

VALENTINE:

I'm your man now
Let me make my plan now

SILVIA:

It's a high tower they keep me prisoner in.

VALENTINE:

A high tower?

SILVIA:
A very, very high tower.

VALENTINE:
Let me think
It's a high tower
And you've got to be saved
By tonight at eight

VALENTINE: SILVIA:
Let me think

                                              Think baby, think think baby
I got to think
Oh yah
                                              Think baby, think think baby
I got to get my thoughts
Together
                                              Think baby, think think baby
I got to get organized
                                              Think baby, think think baby
I think I got it   *(Screams at him)*
I think I got it
                                              Think baby, think think baby
Oh, yes I got it
I know I got it
                                              Think baby, think baby
Talkin' bout a night
ladder

Night ladder
Good and strong

SILVIA *(Joyous)*:
Night ladder
Ten feet long

VALENTINE & SILVIA:
Nothing gladder
Than a long
Night ladder

SILVIA:
I will see ya
Tonight at eight

VALENTINE:
Tonight at eight
Will be just great

VALENTINE & SILVIA:
Nothing sadder than a
Short night ladder

Night ladder
Good and strong

Night ladder
Ten feet long

Nothing gladder
Than a long
Night ladder

O baby

O baby

O baby

(GUARD *enters left and carries* SILVIA *off down left still singing*)

SILVIA:
O baby

O baby

VALENTINE:
O baby—baby—baby—come on back

(SILVIA *re-enters and they embrace.* PROTEUS *enters, unobserved*)

SILVIA:
I came in here to write to my lover Eglamour.
Instead I found a truer love.

(They kiss. The GUARD *enters left and carries* SILVIA *off again)*

Adieu.

VALENTINE *(Whispers joyously)*:
Eight!

*(*LAUNCE *has followed* PROTEUS. SPEED *enters down left from the house and sees* LAUNCE. *They yell greetings to each other, embrace and fall in a pile of bodies, left center)*

LAUNCE:
Speed.

VALENTINE *(To* PROTEUS*)*:
How does your lady? How thrives your love?

LAUNCE:
His tales of love were wont to weary you.

PROTEUS:
I know you joy not in love discourse.

VALENTINE:
Ay, Proteus, but that life is altered now.

SPEED:
He has done penance for condemning love;
Love hath chased sleep from his enthralled eyes
And made them watchers of his own heart's sorrow.

VALENTINE:
My love is as a fever, longing still
For that which longer nurseth the disease,
Feeding on that which doth preserve the ill,
The uncertain sickly appetite to please.
My reason hath left me.

Past cure I am, now reason is past care
And frantic-mad with evermore unrest;
My thoughts and my discourse as madmen's are
Only from the truth expressed:

No appetite—Love took it away

PROTEUS, LAUNCE, SPEED *(In a fifties back-up)*:
Dup-de-do

VALENTINE:
To show me how starved I was

PROTEUS, LAUNCE, SPEED:
Ow-ow

VALENTINE:
Love's revenge

PROTEUS, LAUNCE, SPEED:
Love's revenge

VALENTINE:
Insomnia

PROTEUS, LAUNCE, SPEED:
Dup-de-do

VALENTINE:
Love gave it to me

PROTEUS, LAUNCE, SPEED:
Dup-de-do

VALENTINE:
To show me I didn't dream

PROTEUS, LAUNCE, SPEED:
Ow-ow

VALENTINE:
Love's revenge

PROTEUS, LAUNCE, SPEED:
Love's revenge

VALENTINE: PROTEUS, LAUNCE, SPEED:
The little I sleep   *Ah-ah-ow-ow*
Is just for a nightmare
The little I eat   *Ah-ah-ow-ow*
Is to taste the dregs
Where is my reason   *Ow-ow*
What is my name
What is this terrible shake   *Ah-ah*
In my legs

VALENTINE:
My future plans

PROTEUS, LAUNCE, SPEED:
Dup-de-do

VALENTINE:
Love took them away

PROTEUS, LAUNCE, SPEED:
Dup-de-do

VALENTINE:
To show me I had no future

PROTEUS, LAUNCE, SPEED:
Ow-ow

VALENTINE:
Love's revenge

PROTEUS, LAUNCE, SPEED:
Love's revenge

VALENTINE:
I have no future

PROTEUS, LAUNCE, SPEED:
He has no future

VALENTINE:
I have no past

PROTEUS, LAUNCE, SPEED:
He has no past

VALENTINE:
Without love

PROTEUS, LAUNCE, SPEED:
Without love

VALENTINE:
Nothing can last
Without love nothing can last
That's love's
Ow-ow

It happened so suddenly, my Lady Silvia just
Blew my mind.

And it's love's revenge

SPEED:
Do-do-do-do

VALENTINE:
My foolish rival, that her father likes
Only for his possessions are so huge,
Is gone with her along, and I must after.

(VALENTINE *exits right and reappears with his bike: a golden Renaissance/Baroque version of a Schwinn*)

For love, thou know'st, is full of jealousy.

PROTEUS:
But she loves you?

VALENTINE:
Aye.

SPEED:

Master, you just met her.

VALENTINE (*As he exits on bike down left*):

I must find me a long night ladder.

(PROTEUS *exits behind* VALENTINE)

LAUNCE:

Dup-de-do

SPEED:

What sayest thou that my master is become a notable lover?

LAUNCE:

I never knew him otherwise.

SPEED:

Than how?

LAUNCE:

A notable lubber, as thou reportest him to be.

SPEED:

Why, thou whoreson ass, thou mistakest me.

LAUNCE:

Why, fool, I meant not thee, I meant thy master.

SPEED:

I tell thee, my master has become a hot lover.

LAUNCE:

Why, I tell thee, I care not though he burn himself in Love. If thou wilt go with me to the alehouse.

SPEED:

How did thy master part with Madame Julia?

LAUNCE:
Marry, after they closed in earnest, they parted very
fairly in jest.

SPEED:
Will they marry?

LAUNCE:
No.

SPEED:
How does the matter stand with them?

LAUNCE:
Marry thus: when it stands well with him, it stands well
with her.

(SPEED *gets the joke*)

SPEED:
To the alehouse.

LAUNCE:
To the alehouse.

(*They exit.* PROTEUS *enters up left and leaps down center*)

PROTEUS:
I'm very happy
For my best friend
He found a wonderful girl
She's a calla lily lady
She's a water lily lady
La la la la la la

She must be a very nice person
To fall in love with my friend
She's a calla lily lady
She's a water lily lady
La la la la la la

I assume she knows he's thrifty
What I mean to say is cheap
His I.Q. is fifty
Nevertheless he is deep

So I'm very happy
For my best friend
You're looking at a picture of glee
I want my best friend
To be ha-ha-ha-happy
But not happier than me
Once again now
But not happier than me

She's a calla lily lady
She's a water lily lady
She's a brocco lily lady
I love brocco lily
Carrots and peas
I want to swoon
Between her knees
Yea

So I'm very happy
For my best friend
You're looking at a picture of glee
I want my friend
To be ha-ha-ha-ha-happy
So what if he's happier than me
Once again now
So what if he's happier than me
Up the mountain
So what if he's happier than me
Arroz con pollo
So what if he's happier than me
A little softer
So what if he's happier than me

To leave my Julia, shall I be forsworn;
To love fair Silvia, shall I be forsworn;

To wrong my friend, I shall be much forsworn;
And even that power which gave me first my oath
Provokes me to this three-fold perjury:
Love bade me swear, and love bids me forswear.

O sweet-suggesting love, if thou hast sinned,
Teach me, thy tempted subject, to excuse it!
At first I did adore a twinkling star,
But now I worship a celestial sun.

Julia I lose, and Valentine I lose:
If I keep them, I needs must lose myself;

If I lose them, thus find I by their loss,
For Valentine, myself; for Julia, Silvia.
I to myself am dearer than a friend,
For love is still most precious in itself;
And Silvia, witness heaven that made her fair,
Shows Julia but a swarthy Ethiope.
I will forget that Julia is alive,
Rememb'ring that my love to her is dead;

And Valentine I'll hold an enemy,
Aiming at Silvia as sweeter friend.
I cannot now prove constant to myself
Without some treachery used to Valentine.
This night he meaneth with a corded ladder
To climb celestial Silvia's chamber window;
Myself in counsel, his competitor:
Now presently I'll give her father notice
Of their disguising and pretended flight;
Who, all enraged, will banish Valentine.

(*The orchestra hisses* PROTEUS)

Love, lend me wings to make my purpose swift,
As thou hast lent me wit to plot this drift!

(PROTEUS *crosses left as orchestra plays music to*):

I'm very happy for my best friend
He's found a wonderful girl (boom)!

(*Stage lights go to black.* PROTEUS *exits left*)

Act Two

(Orchestra plays music to):

Thou, Silvia, thou hast metamorphosed me
Made me neglect my studies, lose my mind
War with good counsel, set the world at nought
Made wit with musing weak, heart sick with thought
Proteus

PROTEUS:
Love, lend me wings to make my purpose swift.
As thou hast lent me wit to plot this drift!

(PROTEUS dials a Renaissance telephone. THURIO enters carrying his ringing Baroque telephone. The DUKE follows)

THURIO:
Hello, Silvia! Who is this? Who is this?

(PROTEUS breathes heavily into the phone. To the DUKE)

It's for you.

DUKE:
Hello, who is this? Who is this?

PROTEUS:
My gracious Lord, that which I would discover
The law of friendship bids me to conceal;
But when I call to mind your gracious favors
Done to me, undeserving as I am,
My duty pricks me on to utter that
Which else no worldly good should draw from me.

DUKE:
Hummmmm.

PROTEUS:
Know, worthy prince, Sir Valentine, my friend,
This night intends to steal away your daughter.

DUKE:
Who is this?

THURIO:
Who is this?

DUKE:
Who is this?

THURIO:
Who is this?

PROTEUS:
Myself am one made privy to the plot.
I know you have determined to bestow her
On Thurio, whom your gentle daughter hates.

THURIO:
Who is this?

PROTEUS:
And should she thus be stol'n away from you,
It would be much vexation to your age.
Thus, for my duty's sake, I rather chose
To cross my friend in his intended drift
Than, by concealing it, heap on your head
A pack of sorrows, which would press you down,
Being unprevented, to your timeless grave.

(SILVIA *enters at the top level of the stage looking for*
VALENTINE, *waiting for him to save her*)

THURIO:
My Lord,
We nightly lodge her in an upper tower,
The key whereof myself have ever kept;
And thence she cannot be conveyed away.

(They laugh)

PROTEUS:
Know, noble lord, they have devised a means
How he her chamber window will ascend,
And with a corded ladder fetch her down;
For which the youthful lover now is gone,
And this way comes he with it presently;
Where, if it please you, you may intercept him.
But, good my lord, do it so cunningly
That my discovery be not aimed at;
For love of you, not hate unto my friend,
Hath made me publisher of this pretense.

(SILVIA *exits*)

DUKE:
Who is this?

THURIO:
Who is this?

(PROTEUS *breathes heavily into the phone, then hangs up. The* DUKE *and* THURIO *exit. As* JULIA *and* LUCETTA, *disguised as boys, appear, they react in horror as* PROTEUS *turns to the pictures of* SILVIA *that fill the stage)*

PROTEUS:
Silvia! Silvia! Silvia! Silvia! Silvia!
Even as one heat another heat expels,
Or as one nail by strength drives out another.
So the remembrance of my former love
Is by a newer object quite forgotten,
Silvia, Silvia.

(He sees the "boys")

Who are you?

(LUCETTA *stammers*)

Good, I like thee well, and will employ thee in some service
presently
Regarding my Lady Silvia . . .

Holy fair and wise is she . . .

(JULIA *and* LUCETTA *sneak away.* PROTEUS *sees them running*)

Wait! Wait!
Come Back, Come Back!
I would employ thee.

(PROTEUS *runs down center and catches* JULIA *and* LUCETTA)

PROTEUS:
What are your names?

JULIA:
Sebastian.

LUCETTA:
Caesario.

PROTEUS:
Sebastian and Caesario . . .
You look familiar.
Where do you come from?

LUCETTA:
We come from the land of betrayal
An Indian word meaning hate
But the people smile all the time there
And the cultural advantages are great

PROTEUS:
Follow me.

LUCETTA:
The air that we breathe is polluted
The wars that we fight are the same
But no one is quite sure who leads us
So no one is ever to blame

Our principal export is lying
Truth, youth and beauty we ban
Our principal pastime is loving
The kind they stamp made in Japan

I must say you do look familiar
Could it be that you've ever been there
We live in the heart of the city
Where deceit double-crosses despair

I'm happy to talk of the old town
I see now I am not away
The town changed it's name to everywhere
And I live in it every day

We come from the land of betrayal
An Indian word meaning hate
But the people smile all the time there
And the cultural advantages are great

PROTEUS:
Come, you are now in the service of my Lady, Silvia.

(They exit right. As PROTEUS, JULIA *and* LUCETTA *exit stage right, the* DUKE *enters from up center, looks around then blows his whistle.* THURIO *enters up center followed by three* GUARDS, *whom he positions offstage to wait for* VALENTINE, *as he positions himself on the second level stage, left. The* DUKE *has crossed down right center and steps into the audience, and we see* VALENTINE *enter up left center on his bike wearing a long cloak. He rides down center)*

DUKE:
Sir Valentine.

THURIO:
Ah, Sir Valentine.

DUKE:
Whither away so fast?

VALENTINE:
Please it, your Grace, there is a messenger
That stays to bear my letters to my friends,
And I am going to deliver them.

DUKE:
Be they of much import?

VALENTINE:
The tenor of them doth but signify
My health and happy being at your court.

DUKE:
Nay then, no matter; stay with me awhile.

(The DUKE crosses the stage to down left to lean against a pole as THURIO crosses to VALENTINE)

THURIO:
Aye, stay.

DUKE:
I am to break with thee of some affairs
That touch me near, wherein thou must be secret.
'Tis not unknown to thee that I have sought
To match my friend, Sir Thurio, to my daughter.

VALENTINE:
I know it well, my Lord; and, sure, the match
Were rich and honorable; besides, the gentleman
Is full of virtue, bounty, worth, and qualities
Beseeming such a wife as your fair daughter.

THURIO:
You're very perceptive.

DUKE:
Sir Valentine.

(He motions for VALENTINE to come closer, and THURIO balances the bike as VALENTINE crosses to the DUKE)

THURIO:
My, what a lovely bike!

DUKE:
There is a lady in Milan here,
Whom I affect; but she is nice, and coy,
And nought esteems my aged eloquence:
Now, therefore, would I have thee to my tutor—

THURIO:
And I would have thee for my tutor.

DUKE:
For long ago I have forgot to court;
Besides, the fashion of the time is changed—
How, and which way, I may bestow myself,
To be regarded in her sun-bright eye.
But she I mean is promised by her friends
Unto a youthful gentleman of worth,
And kept severely from resort of men,
That no man hath access by day to her.

VALENTINE (*Nervously*):
Why, then I would resort to her by night.

THURIO:
Ay, but the doors be locked and the keys kept safe.

DUKE:
That no man hath recourse to her by night.

VALENTINE:
What lets but one may enter at her window?

THURIO:
Oh, no. Her chamber is aloft.

DUKE:
And built so shelving that one cannot climb it
Without apparent hazard of his life.

VALENTINE:
  Why, then, a ladder . . .

THURIO:
  A ladder.

DUKE:
  A ladder.

THURIO:
  Oh, a ladder!

VALENTINE:
  A ladder made quaintly with cords,
  With a pair of anchoring hooks to cast up,
  Would serve to scale another Hero's tower,
  So bold Leander would adventure it.

  (All laugh)

DUKE:
  Now, as thou art a gentleman of blood,
  Advise me where I may have such a ladder.

VALENTINE:
  Pray tell, when would you use it?

THURIO:
  This very night.

  (The DUKE *removes his sunglasses)*

DUKE *(A threat)*:
  For love is like a child
  That longs for everything that he can come by.

VALENTINE:
  By seven o'clock . . .

THURIO:
  Seven o'clock . . .

VALENTINE:
I'll get you such a ladder.

DUKE:
Hark thee; I will go to her alone.
How shall I best convey the ladder thither?

VALENTINE:
It will be light, my lord, that you may bear it
Under a cloak.

(*The* DUKE *puts on his sunglasses.* THURIO *goes into a dancing frenzy*)

THURIO:
A cloak, a cloak, a cloak!

VALENTINE:
That is of my length.

DUKE:
A cloak as long as thine will serve the turn?

VALENTINE:
Ay, my good lord.

DUKE:
Then let me see thy cloak.
I'll get me one of such another length.

VALENTINE:
Why, any cloak will serve the turn, my lord.

DUKE:
How shall I fashion me to wear a cloak?
I pray thee, let me feel thy cloak upon me.

(THURIO *has now reached* VALENTINE *and takes the cloak from his back, exposing the rope ladder under the cape. The* DUKE *prepares to blow the whistle to bring on the* GUARDS)

THURIO:
Night ladder, so divine.

(*The* DUKE *blows the whistle and the* GUARDS *appear as* THURIO *does a dance with the cape.* VALENTINE *tries to escape. He is blocked at the right*)

Night ladder, now you're mine.

(VALENTINE *tries to escape to the left. Once again the* DUKE *blows the whistle, and another* GUARD *appears stage right with army clothes, which* THURIO *takes after handing the* GUARD *the cape*)

Oh, nothing is gladder than a long night ladder.

(THURIO *hands the uniform to* VALENTINE)

DUKE:
No need to look so quizzical
You just passed your physical

You have no future and no past
The army is your home at last

I don't know why he looks so sad
Army life it ain't so bad

He's patriotic is this man
To God, to country, and Milan

(DUKE *and* THURIO *exit up center.* DUKE *smiles at* VALENTINE *just before exiting*)

VALENTINE:
And why not death, rather than living torment?
To die is to be banished from myself;
And Silvia is myself: banished from her,
Is self from self; a deadly banishment!
What light is light, if Silvia be not seen?
What joy is joy, if Silvia be not by?

Unless it be to think that she is by,
And feed upon the shadow of perfection.
Except I be by Silvia in the night
There is no music in the nightingale;
Unless I look on Silvia in the day,
There is no day for me to look upon.
She is my essence; and I leave to be,
If I be not by her fair influence
Fostered, illumined, cherished, kept alive.

(PROTEUS *enters*)

PROTEUS:
Cease to lament for that thou canst not help.
And study help for that which thou lament'st.
Time is the nurse and breeder of all good.
Here if thou stay thou canst not see thy love;
Besides, thy staying will abridge thy life.
Hope is a lover's staff; walk hence with that,
And manage it against despairing thoughts.
Thy letters may be here, though thou art hence;
Which, being writ to me, shall be delivered
Even in the dark-ebony bosom of thy love.

(VALENTINE *starts to protest*)

PROTEUS:
The time now serves not to expostulate;
Come, I'll convey thee through the city gate.

(SILVIA *runs on the top level of the stage*)

SILVIA:
Valentine!

PROTEUS:
Don't look back. You'll turn into salt.

(PROTEUS *leads* VALENTINE *off. The* ENSEMBLE *runs on*)

DUKE:
Now, now, daughter.

SILVIA:
Oh, you.
First I loved Eglamour, and you sent him away.
Now I love Valentine, and you sent him away.
Why do you send away everyone I love?

DUKE:
Go back to your tower, dear.

SILVIA:
I don't want to go back to my tower.
No. No. Valentine! Valentine!

(DUKE *carries* SILVIA *off*)

THURIO:
My lord, My lord.

DUKE *(Running back on)*:
Yes.

THURIO:
She takes his going grievously.

DUKE:
No! No!
I just talked to her and she said you were a poet,
And she mentioned how Orpheus' lute was strung with
poet's sinews,
Whose golden touch could soften steel and stones,
Make tigers tame and huge leviathans
Forsake unsounded deeps to dance on sands.

THURIO:
She said all that?

DUKE:
All that and more.

THURIO:
What did she say to my nose
I—I—I

What did she say to my clothes
I—I—I
Please don't fake it
I can take it

DUKE:
She said
Boom chicka chicka chicka
Fuck fucka wucka wucka
Cock cocka wocka wocka
Puss pussa wussa wussa
Fuck fucka wucka wucka wow

THURIO:
Wow!

THURIO & ENSEMBLE:
Boom chicka chicka chicka
Fuck fucka wucka wucka
Cock cocka wocka wocka
Puss pussa wussa wussa
Fuck fucka wucka wucka wow!

THURIO:
Now
What did she say to my cheeks
I—I—I
What did she say to my hands
I—I—I
What did she say to my glands
I—I—I
Please don't slow up

DUKE:
I may throw up
She said
Boom chicka chicka chicka
Fuck fucka wucka wucka
Cock cocka wocka wocka
Puss pussa wussa wussa
Fuck fucka wucka wucka wow

THURIO:
>Love
>I made you lucky
>Love
>You lucky duck
>Love
>When you met up with me
>You met up with lady luck

THURIO:
>Is that what she said
>Did you hear what she said

DUKE:
>*You're going to be wed*

THURIO:
>Bring out the bed
>What did she say to my chest
>I–I–I
>What thinks my fabulous gal
>I–I–I
>Of my alimentary canal
>I–I–I

(*The* DUKE *starts to pin medals on* THURIO *held by four* MALE
MEMBERS *of the* ENSEMBLE *while rest of* ENSEMBLE *is down right
as if at a revival meeting*)

DUKE:
>She said,
>His legs bestride the ocean; his reared arm
>Crested the world. His voice was propertied
>As all the tuned spheres, and that to friends,
>But when he meant to quail and shake the orb
>He was as rattling thunder. For his bounty,
>There was no winter in't. An autumn 'twas
>That grew the more by reaping. His delights
>Were dolphin like: they showed his back above
>The element they liv'd in. In his livery
>Walked crowns and crownets; realms and islands
>Were as coins dripped from his pocket.

THURIO:
> Oh no, she didn't. She said:

ENSEMBLE:
> *Boom chicka chicka chicka*
> *Fuck fucka wucka wucka*
> *Cock cocka wocka wocka*
> *Puss pussa wussa wussa*
> *Boom chicka chicka chicka*
> *Fuck fucka wucka wucka wow wow*
> *Boom chicka chicka chicka*
> *Fuck fucka wucka wucka*
> *Cock cocka wocka wocka*
> *Pussa pussa wussa wussa*
> *Fuck fucka wucka wucka now*

THURIO & ENSEMBLE:
> *Boom chicka chicka chicka*
> *Fuck fucka wucka wucka*
> *Cock cocka wocka wocka*
> *Puss pussa wussa wussa*
> *Fuck fucka wucka wucka wow*

THURIO:
> Gold
> Gold can buy you love
> As long as you have gold
> You always will have love

ENSEMBLE:
> *Boom chicka chicka chicka*
> *Fuck fucka wucka wucka*
> *Cock cocka wocka wocka*
> *Puss pussa wussa wussa*
> *Boom chicka chicka chicka*
> *Fuck fucka wucka wucka wow wow*
>
> *Boom chicka chicka chicka*
> *Fuck fucka wucka wucka*
> *Cock cocka wocka wocka*
> *Puss pussa wussa wussa*
> *Fuck fucka wucka wucka wow*

(Dance with no words)

THURIO:
Love
I made you lucky love
You lucky duck love
When you met up with me
You met up with lady luck

ENSEMBLE:
Boom chicka chicka chicka
Fuck fucka wucka wucka
Cock cocka wocka wocka
Puss pussa wussa wussa
Boom chicka chicka chicka
Fuck fucka wucka wow

Boom chicka chicka chicka
Fuck fucka wucka wucka
Cock cocka wocka wocka
Puss pussa wussa wussa
Fuck fucka wucka wucka wow

THURIO:
All of my fears have been
killed

ENSEMBLE:
Owwwwwwwwwwwwwwwwwwww

ENSEMBLE:
Love love love

THURIO:
Love is a dream I can build

ENSEMBLE:
Owwwwwwwwwwwwwwwwwwww

ENSEMBLE:
Love love love

THURIO:
Now I am tot'ly fulfilled

Love
Love
Love

ENSEMBLE:
Owwwwwwwwwwwwwwwwwwwww

Love love
Boom chick chicka chicka
Boom chick chicka chicka boom

(*As* THURIO, DUKE *and* ENSEMBLE *exit,* LAUNCE *and* SPEED *enter up center. They are in the tavern and are glowingly drunk*)

LAUNCE & SPEED:
Young folks spend their time lovin'
Rich folks can afford lovin'
I've been
Dog catcher, bartender, log roller, truck driver
But not lover
I want to be a hot lover
A hoooooooot lover
Like the kids in the play

SPEED:
Take it, Launcy.

LAUNCE:
Oh, I've had lovin'
Oh, God—the pain
To be rejected by a poodle
Then by a Great Dane—oh—oh—oh

LAUNCE & SPEED:
Oh—
Old folks take their time lovin'
Poor folks can't afford lovin'
I've been
Hair cutter, house painter, meat chopper, road runner

But not lover
I want to be a hot lover
A hot, hot lover
Like the kids in the play   *Elect!*

(LAUNCE *and* SPEED *exit as* INNKEEPER *enters left and* PROTEUS, JULIA *and* LUCETTA *enter from up center)*

INNKEEPER:
Bravo! You all come back here.

PROTEUS:
Who is Silvia

INNKEEPER:
What is she

PROTEUS:
That all our swains commend her

INNKEEPER:
Holy fair and wise is she

PROTEUS:
The heaven such grace did lend her

INNKEEPER:
That she might

PROTEUS & INNKEEPER:
Admired be

PROTEUS:
Sebastian, I have entertained thee,
Partly that I have need of such a youth,
That can with some discretion do my business.
Take this ring with thee;
Deliver it to Madam Silvia.
She loved me well, delivered it to me.

INNKEEPER:
It's a good thing this isn't Venice.

(INNKEEPER *exits ramp down right*)

JULIA:
It seems you loved not her, to leave her token.
She is dead, belike?

PROTEUS:
Not so; I think she lives.

LUCETTA:
Alas!

PROTEUS:
Why dost thou cry, Alas?

LUCETTA:
I cannot choose
But pity her.

PROTEUS:
Wherefore shouldst thou pity her?

JULIA:
Because, methinks, that she loved you as well
As you do love your Lady Silvia.
She dreams on him that has forgot her love;
You dote on her that cares not for your love.
'Tis pity love should be so contrary;
And thinking on it makes us cry, Alas!

LUCETTA:
Right.

PROTEUS:
Do as thou art told!

(PROTEUS *exits*)

JULIA:
Because he loves her
He despises me

Because I love him
I pity him

If I could be her
Just for a moment
When he was holding her
I would insult him
Then he'd be unhappy
And not know where to run

I could turn back into me
And I would comfort him
What a nice idea
What a sweet idea
But easier said than done

Wait!

If I could be him
Just for a moment
I'd hold her so close
And yell insults at her
She'd never speak to him again

I could turn back into me
And I would comfort him
It ends up the same
Either way

All I want to do
Is have someone scold him
Then I'd come on the scene
And gladly hold him
That's my idea of fun

Que bonita idea
Que idea mas linda
Que idea mas dulce
Que idea mas rica
What a nice idea
What a sweet idea

But easier said than done
But easier said than done

(PROTEUS *enters from right and whistles for the* ENSEMBLE, *which enters,* ALL *vocalizing and bearing presents for* SILVIA. INNKEEPER *follows* PROTEUS)

PROTEUS:
Cut! Cut!

INNKEEPER:
What a terrible noise.

(PROTEUS *blows pitch pipe, then conducts* ENSEMBLE)

ENSEMBLE:
Who is Silvia? What is she
That all our swains commend her
Holy, fair, and wise is she
That heaven such grace did lend her
That she might admired be

(SILVIA *enters with* GUARD)

PROTEUS:
Silvia.

(SILVIA *crosses down to stage level and crosses down right as* ENSEMBLE *goes wild applauding her*)

BLACK PASSION GIRLS:
Silvia
Silvia
Silvia

PROTEUS:
Is she kind as she is fair
For beauty lives with kindness
Love doth to her eyes repair
To help him of his blindness
And being helped inhabit there

ENSEMBLE:
> *Ahh Ahh Ahh*
> *Ahh Ahh Ahh*
> *Aaaaaaahhhhhhhhahhhh*

ENSEMBLE:
> *Then to Silvia let us sing*
> *That Silvia is excelling*
> *She excels each mortal thing*
> *Upon the dull earth dwelling*
> *To her let garlands bring*

(During the ENSEMBLE *singing,* PROTEUS *tries to get the ring from* JULIA. *She will not give it to him.* PROTEUS *exits ramp right and immediately re-enters with* LAUNCE *carrying* CRAB *as a gift to* SILVIA. ALL *converge on* SILVIA *down center with gifts. She breaks up center as* ALL *fall down or stand stunned)*

SILVIA:
> Stop it.
> Stop it. Who the hell is Silvia?

> *Love me*
> *Not your idea of me*
> *Release me*
> *From your fantasy*
> *Love me*
> *Forget your fear of me*

SILVIA:
> *Let me go*
> *Let me go*
> *Let me go*
> *Let me go*
> *Set me free*
> *Love me*
> *I am not solid gold*
> *Touch me*
> *I am flesh blood and bone*
> *Love me*
> *Don't want karate holds*

Let me go
Let me go
Let me go
Let me go
Set me free
Let me go
Let me go
Let me go
Let me go
Set me free
Don't tell me to keep my chin up
Stick a baby in my womb
I won't be nobody's pin up
In nobody's locker room
Why don't you love me
Not your idea of me
Release me from your fantasy
Love me
Forget your fear of me
Let me go
Let me go
Let me go
Let me go
Set me free
Let me go
Let me go
Let me go
Let me go
Set me free
Let me go
Let me go
Let me go
Let me go
Set me free

(SILVIA *runs up to third level*)

BLACK PASSION:
Don't keep her
A prisoner
Of your imagination

Don't keep her
A prisoner
Of your imagination

Don't keep her
A prisoner
Of your imagination

(A dove has flown to SILVIA *over the heads of the audience.*
She puts a note on the dove)

SILVIA:
This magic dove
Will find my love
In his jungle destination

(The DOVE *flies back into the theater)*

BLACK PASSION:	SILVIA:	ENSEMBLE:
Let it go		
	Higher	
Let it go		
	Higher	
Let it go		
	Why don't you let it	
Let it go	*Go a little bit higher*	*Don't keep her*
		A prisoner
Let it go	*It's got to get there*	*Of your*
		Imagination
Let it go	*It's got to get there*	*Don't keep her*
		A prisoner
Let it go	*I think I spot him*	*Of your*
		Imagination
Let it go	*What if it's not him*	*Don't keep her*
		A prisoner
Let it go	*I don't know*	*Of your*
		Imagination
Let it go	*Well yes I can tell*	
Let it go	*Yeah yeah yeah yeah*	
Let it go	*Yeah yeah yeah yeah*	

Let it go	*Yeah yeah yeah yeah*
Let it go	*Yeah yeah yeah yeah*
Let it go	*Yeah yeah yeah yeah*

SILVIA:
Eglamour!

(*From the rear balcony of the theater,* EGLAMOUR *is heard: a thrilling baritone voice*)

EGLAMOUR:
Did I hear someone call my name
It's been so long and rare
Since someone called my name
Call my name

(EGLAMOUR *climbs down a ladder from the balcony to the orchestra. He wears an army uniform. He carries the magic dove on his shoulder. He is Chinese*)

SILVIA:
Eglamour, Eglamour

EGLAMOUR:
Call me Eglamour
It's been so long since someone did
It sounds so sweet and fair
To hear me called my name once again

SILVIA:
Eglamour, Eglamour

(As EGLAMOUR *reaches the stage, a* GUARD *moves to stop* EGLAMOUR. EGLAMOUR *taps the* GUARD, *who collapses in slow motion.* ELGAMOUR *travels to the top level*)

EGLAMOUR:
I was always there
You only had to call my name
I'd gladly lose my soul

To save your life
Lucky you
I was there
Lucky me
Now I'm here

(EGLAMOUR *has now reached* SILVIA. PROTEUS *runs on the top level.* EGLAMOUR *gives him one of his magic taps and* PROTEUS *collapses in slow motion*)

SILVIA:
Now you're here

EGLAMOUR:
Now I'm here
Your father sent me off to war
I think your father thought
That I'd be killed
No luck
Here I am
Lucky you

EGLAMOUR & SILVIA:
Lucky me
Lucky me

LUCETTA:
Go get 'em, Eglamour.

EGLAMOUR & SILVIA:
Lucky me

(ENSEMBLE *comes back to the stage from the house as* EGLAMOUR *and* SILVIA *exit third level.* DUKE *enters left third level.* THURIO *enters left platform.* DUKE *blows his whistle*)

DUKE:
Silvia! Silvia! Silvia!

GUARD:
She's gone, my lord.

THURIO (*To the* GUARD):
  She has my jewels upon her and my ducats.

(THURIO *chases* GUARD *up left and throws apple at him*)

DUKE:
  Where is she?

PROTEUS (PROTEUS *has recovered from* EGLAMOUR'S *supernatural power. He also is on the third level*):
  She's gone with that Eggg Eggg Eggg—whatever his name is.

JULIA (*From down left center*):
  Where is Silvia
  Where is she

ENSEMBLE:
  That some one came and kidnapped

DUKE:
  Kidnapped
  My daughter has been kidnapped
  My precious little girl
  Bring my baby home to me

(ENSEMBLE *crosses to* THURIO)

ENSEMBLE:
  Your fiancée is missing
  And the wedding is today
  Capture them before they go

PROTEUS:
  The lovers have been sighted
  And they're headed right this way
  Follow me into the fray

ENSEMBLE:
  What did you say

PROTEUS:
  Follow me into the fray

ENSEMBLE:
Into which fray

PROTEUS:
Pick up your bows and arrows
And follow me into the fray

ENSEMBLE:
Into the fray
Into the fray
Into the fray
Into the fray

(ALL *exit. We are now in the forest. Trees appear. A full moon rises. A tent appears stage center.* SILVIA *and* EGLAMOUR *enter*)

EGLAMOUR:	SILVIA:
Now I'm here	*Now you're here*
Your father sent me off to war	*My father sent you off*
I think your father	*to war*
Thought that I'd be killed	
No luck	
Here I am	
Lucky you	
Lucky me	*Lucky me*
Lucky me	*Lucky me*
Lucky me	*Lucky me*

(As SILVIA *and* EGLAMOUR *enter the tent,* VALENTINE *enters third level left in his army uniform. He is on guard duty*)

VALENTINE:
How use doth breed habit in a man!
This shadowy desert, unfrequented woods,
I better brook than flourishing peopled towns:
Here I can stand alone, unseen of any,
And to the nightingale's complaining notes
Tune my distress and record my woes.
Silvia, Silvia . . .

You live in the mansion
I call my heart
I keep beneath my doublet
You live there on a permanent lease
Nothing like a sublet

You've got to move in
You never can let
The property gets run down
The thought of you
Moved in this morning
I want you here by sundown

You've rent my heart
Now you control it
If this is rent control
Then I extol it

You live in the mansion
I call my heart
I keep beneath my doublet
You live there on a permanent lease
Nothing like a sublet

Everybody needs a home
Here is your vacancy
You already are my love
Come live with me
Silvia, Silvia

You live in the mansion
I call my heart
I keep beneath my doublet
You live there on a permanent lease
Nothing like a sublet
Nothing like a sublet
Nothing like a sublet

SILVIA (*From inside the tent*):
  Eglamour

VALENTINE:
  I know I've heard that name before.

(VALENTINE *exits.* PROTEUS *enters, singing the triumphal march from* Aida)

PROTEUS *(Furious):*
  Pa pa paaa paa pa pah

EGLAMOUR: SILVIA:
  Here I am
  Lucky you
  Lucky me   *Lucky me*
  Lucky me   *Lucky me*
  Lucky me   *Lucky me*

(*As* EGLAMOUR *and* SILVIA *sing in the tent,* PROTEUS *reacts. He lifts the flap, looks into the tent, throws flap shut*)

PROTEUS:
  What's a nice girl like her
  Doing in this place
  Why are nice lips like hers
  Kissing his
  What's a nice heart like hers
  Doing on her sleeve
  What's a nice heart like mine
  Doing in my mouth
  I should have stayed down south
  I want to kiss her mouth

  Still
  It makes me ill
  I've had my fill
  Of that silly billy
  Playing Jack to her Jill
  It makes me ill
  I need a pill
  I'll sing a trill

  Now I'm angry
  La la la
  La la la
  What's a nice girl like her
  Doing in this place
  Lighting Christmas tree ornaments

Up in my face
I'm glad I didn't stay south
I'm going to kiss her mouth

(PROTEUS *jumps into the tent.* SILVIA *jumps out of the tent followed by* EGLAMOUR *followed by* PROTEUS. EGLAMOUR *exits.* SILVIA *watches escaping* EGLAMOUR, *then turns on* PROTEUS)

SILVIA:
  Oh, miserable unhappy that I am.

PROTEUS:
  What I would not undergo for one calm look!
  Oh, 'tis the curse of love, and still approved,
  When women cannot love where they're beloved!
  If the gentle spirit of moving words
  Can no way change you to a milder form,
  I'll woo you like a soldier, at arm's length,
  And love you 'gainst the nature of love—force you.

(PROTEUS *forces* SILVIA *to the ground*)

SILVIA:
  O Heaven!

PROTEUS:
  I'll force thee. Yield to my desire.

(*And he plops himself on top of her. Starts to kiss her. He removes his glasses.* VALENTINE *enters left platform. Crosses down left of* PROTEUS *and* SILVIA. SILVIA *giggles in delight. They become aware of* VALENTINE. PROTEUS *puts on his glasses*)

  Valentine!

(PROTEUS *and* SILVIA *untangle, and* SILVIA *falls into the tent*)

VALENTINE:
  Proteus, I must never trust thee more,
  But count the world a stranger for thy sake.
  O time must accurst,
  'Mongst all foes that a friend should be the worst!

PROTEUS (*On his knees*):

My shame and guilt confound me.

(EGLAMOUR *enters right platform*)

EGLAMOUR:
Charge.

(A CHINESE DRAGON *enters down right with lighted eyes and fire and smoke coming from its mouth.* EGLAMOUR *crosses down center and leads the assault. The* DRAGON *circles the tent as* PROTEUS *and* VALENTINE *defend themselves with swords. Then the* DRAGON *turns on* EGLAMOUR *and chases him off*)

PROTEUS:
Forgive me, Valentine: if hearty sorrow
Be sufficient ransom for offense,
I tender't here; I do as truly suffer
As e'er I did commit.

VALENTINE:
Then I am paid;
And once again I do receive thee honest.
Who by repentance is not satisfied
Is nor of Heaven nor earth; for these are pleased.

(JULIA, *still in disguise, enters*)

By penitence the Eternal's wrath's appeased:
And, that my love may appear plain and free,
All that was mine in Silvia I give thee.

PROTEUS:
Oh, thank you.

(PROTEUS *crosses to tent.* JULIA *swoons*)

JULIA:
O me unhappy!

VALENTINE:
  Look to the boy.

(LAUNCE, LUCETTA *and* SPEED *enter down left.* SILVIA *comes out of the tent*)

PROTEUS (*Crosses to* JULIA):
  Why, boy! Why, wag! What's the matter?

(PROTEUS *sees the ring he has given to* JULIA)

  Why, this is the ring I gave to Julia.
  But how cam'st thou by this ring? At my depart
  I gave this unto Julia.

JULIA:
  Julia herself did give it me;
  And Julia herself hath brought it hither.

(JULIA *pulls off her cap. Her hair tumbles down*)

PROTEUS:
  JULIA! And pregnant, too.

(*He sees she is pregnant. He feigns innocence*)

LUCETTA:
  Don't have the baby
  Don't have the baby
  We have too many babies
  It's time to start the ban

SPEED:
  You must have the baby
  You must have the baby
  But tell the baby his father
  Was a terrible man

LAUNCE:
  No, have the baby
  But lie to the baby

Tell the baby his father
Was Emperor of Milan

JULIA:
I'll have the baby
I'll have the baby
I won't lie to the baby
I'll just tell the baby
I loved his father
And when we made him
Oh, how his father loved me

O Proteus, let this habit make thee blush!
Be thou ashamed.
It is the lesser blot, modesty finds,
Women to change their shapes than men their minds.

PROTEUS:
Than men their minds! 'tis true, O heaven, were man
But constant, he were perfect! That one error
Fills him with faults; makes him run through all the sins:
What is in Silvia's face but I may spy
More fresh in Julia's with a constant eye?

JULIA:
Sinverguenza!
A buena hora se te occurre que.

PROTEUS:
Si.

JULIA:
Me quieres.

PROTEUS:
Okay.

JULIA:
Porque no pensaste antes.

PROTEUS:
Si.

JULIA:
De meterte con la otra.

PROTEUS:
Okay.

JULIA:
En realidad es un problema.

PROTEUS:
Si.

JULIA:
Porque no se si perdonarte oh no.

PROTEUS:
Si. Si. Si. Si!

(PROTEUS *and* JULIA *exit.* DUKE *and* THURIO *enter right third level*)

DUKE:
Yonder is Silvia.

THURIO:
Yonder is Silvia, and Silvia's mine.

(THURIO *crosses down stairs as* SPEED *and* LUCETTA *and* LAUNCE *exit.* VALENTINE *confronts* THURIO, *who is on right platform*)

VALENTINE:
Thurio, give back, or else embrace thy death!

(VALENTINE *has drawn his sword.* THURIO *realizes he is unarmed*)

THURIO:
I'm unarmed.

(VALENTINE *drops his sword and chases* THURIO *across the second level.* THURIO *cries*)

THURIO:

Sir Valentine, I care not for her, I.
I hold him but a fool that will endanger
His body for a girl that loves him not:
I claim her not, and therefore she is thine.

DUKE:

The more degenerate and base art thou,
To make such means for her as thou hast done,
And leave her on such slight conditions.

THURIO:

Give me back my ducats.

(THURIO *cries*)

DUKE:

Now, by the honor of my ancestry.
I do applaud thy spirit, Valentine,
And think thee worthy of an empress' love:
Know, then, I here forget all former griefs,
Cancel all grudge, repeal thee home again.
Plead a new state in thy unrivaled merit,
To which I thus subscribe, Sir Valentine,
Thou art a gentleman and well derived;
Take thou thy Silvia, for thou hast deserved her.

(THURIO *cries*. VALENTINE *comes to* SILVIA)

VALENTINE:

I thank your Grace; the gift hath made me happy.

(VALENTINE *picks up* SILVIA)

Come on, baby.

(*They exit left.* DUKE *crosses up center.* LUCETTA *enters right platform as* THURIO *crosses down to left platform.* THURIO *sees* LUCETTA. *It's love at first sight*)

THURIO:
Love is that you
That fills my ears
That fills my nose
That fills my heart

(LUCETTA *throws off cap followed by jacket and crosses down right*)

LUCETTA:
Love is that you
That fills the air
That fills the sky
Owwwwwwwwwwww

THURIO:
Love is that you? Speak up
Speak up, don't be so shy

(THURIO *and* LUCETTA *cross to each other down right*)

LUCETTA & THURIO:
Boom chicka chicka chicka
Boom chicka chicka chicka
Boooomm

(THURIO *douses her with confetti. They embrace as* MILKMAID *and* LAUNCE *enter down left*)

MILKMAID:
What happened to everybody else here tonight
Finally happened to me

LAUNCE:
I met this little milkmaid an hour ago
And it finally happened to me

MILKMAID:
I know you're kinda busy tyin' up the plot
But I thought I'd tell you just to add one more knot

LAUNCE & MILKMAID:
So what happened to everybody else here tonight
Finally happened to
Finally happened to
Finally happened to me

(THURIO *and* LUCETTA *exit right;* MILKMAID *and* LAUNCE *exit left.* DUKE *crosses down center and blows his whistle. The tent is cleared*)

DUKE:
Our day of marriage shall be yours;
One feast, one house, one mutual happiness.

(*He bows to the audience.* SILVIA *enters up center*)

SILVIA:
I love my father
I want to tell him
I love my mother
I want to tell her
I love my brother
I want to tell him
I love my sister
I want to tell her
I love my mirror

I want to tell me
I want to love me
I want to love me
You can't love another
Without loving yourself

(SILVIA *exits. Three* ENSEMBLE MALES *and* LAUNCE *enter up center playing basketball*)

ENSEMBLE:
My pace was frantic
My mood was tortured
Now love has driven me sane

LAUNCE:
My life resembled
"The Cherry Orchard"

ALL:
Now love has driven me sane

Am I healthy? Am I happy? Yes
Gone is all the angst and crappiness
The big shock is the shock of happiness
Love love love love love love love love love

(*The* MEN, *led by* PROTEUS, *enter with yo-yos, doing elaborate tricks with yo-yos, with Frisbees. All the* GIRLS *appear on top level and blow soap bubbles into the audience. Paper hearts fly down on the stage.* VALENTINE *sails on stage on a gold Baroque scooter*)

ALL:
I was into all perversions
Now love has driven me straight
Homo! necro! just diversions
Now love has driven me straight

Trade my straitjacket
For a wedding veil
Throw away my needle and spoon

Sado-mas
And all that jazz
Lobotomized
Right out of my brain

(*Everybody does healthy exercises*)

ALL:
Life's a prison
And love's the pardon
Love's the gardener

And I'm the garden
Love's the doctor
And I give in
I was sick
But love has driven
Me sannnnnnnnne
Love has driven me sannnnnnnnnnne

(ALL *do Tai Chi*)

I love my father
I want to tell him
I love my mother
I want to tell her
I love my brother
I want to tell him
I love my sister
I want to tell her
I love my mirror
I want to tell me
I want to love me
I want to love me
You can't love another
Without loving yourself

(SPEED *does karate and* ALL *fall down*)

I lived in terror
I lived in panic
Now love has driven me calm
At least depressive's
A break from manic
Now love has given me balm

(THURIO *enters and leads* COMPANY *in ballet*)

LAUNCE:
Panic put me in paralysis
Terror kept me in analysis
Wonderland is not where Alice is

THURIO:
Fifth
Passe
Attitude
Tendu
Battu
Arabesque

ALL:
Love love love love love love love love love

(LUCETTA *enters on a pogo stick*)

LUCETTA:
Each delusion
Made me merrier
Reality is so damned flat
Penis envy
And hysteria
I was into all that

(JULIA *and* SILVIA *come on from opposite sides of the stage and lead everybody in a dance. Everybody is juggling, doing handstands, cartwheels, baton-twirling, swinging from the rafters*)

ALL:
Life is passion
And fear is treason
There's no ration
On my reason
Love's the mansion
That I live in
Love's the chauffeur
Who has driven me sane
Love has driven me
Sane
Sane
Sane
Love has driven me sane

(The CHORUS *members are standing on their heads)*

*You can't love another
Without loving yourself*

Curtain

GREASE

A New 50's Rock 'N' Roll Musical

Music, Book and Lyrics by Jim Jacobs and Warren Casey

EDITOR'S NOTES

Although it never won any major awards, *Grease* continues to be a phenomenon of the American musical theatre. Now in its sixth consecutive year on Broadway and, as of this writing, well past its 2,500th performance, it ranks as the fourth-longest-running musical in our theatrical history, and there is every indication that it might topple these records before its final curtain has fallen. *Grease*'s enormous popularity with audiences is not confined to the New York metropolitan area: since it opened in 1972, five road companies have been playing regularly throughout the country and a sixth *Grease* contingent is permanently based in Las Vegas.

Originating at the Kingston Mines Theatre, Chicago, in 1971, it came to New York during the following year in a new guise. While the Eden Theatre, which initially housed the presentation, was technically an Off-Broadway operation, the production played under a standard Actors' Equity Broadway contract, thereby facilitating a move uptown if audience response warranted it. Once the reviews were perused and box-office lines continually grew, the enterprising producers decided that the time for a move indeed was at hand. On June 7, 1972, *Grease* and its merry band of mummers settled in at the Broadhurst Theatre for what was to become one of the most successful and longest engagements in Broadway annals.

The first-night reviewers embraced the show with an outpouring of their most felicitous adjectives. The representative from the New York *Daily News* exclaimed: "*Grease* is a winner! A rollicking, lively and funny musical. It brings back the look and sound of the 1950s with glee." The chronicler for *The New York Times* found it "brash, charming, unsentimental, lighthearted, spunky and high-spirited. Thanks to *Grease*, all those words are applicable. The musical comedy is both musical and comic once more."

Fellow journalists were in accord, hailing it as "a fascinating song-and-dance show" that "isolates and frames on a stage the early rock 'n' roll era in full furor" and, resultantly, is "great fun and one of the niftiest musicals around!"

A collaborative effort of two gifted theatre craftsmen, Jim Jacobs and Warren Casey, *Grease* may be as all-American as the memories it evokes of the fifties, but its appeal seems to be universal for it also has been successfully performed in many foreign countries and in many languages.

Jim Jacobs was born and raised in Chicago. During the "golden era" of rock 'n roll (1956–1960) he was a "greaser" at Taft High School, where he played guitar and sang with several small groups. Around 1963, he became involved with a local theatre company and there met his future collaborator, Warren Casey.

During the next five years, Mr. Jacobs worked with Paul Sills and appeared in over fifty community theatre productions in and around Chicago while employed as a writer during the day. Professionally, he has worked both as an actor and writer for theatre, films, recordings, and commercials.

Warren Casey grew up in Yonkers, New York, and attended Syracuse University. During the "grease" period of the late 1950s, he learned a good deal about teenagers of the time while working as a teacher in upstate New York. He also fulfilled a desire to act by appearing with local little theatre groups.

In the early 1960s he moved to Chicago and worked as a record salesman and assistant manager of a chain of apparel shops. Meanwhile, he continued acting and appeared in about thirty shows in Chicago community theatres. He also taught himself how to play the guitar and began writing songs for the amusement of himself and his friends—a pursuit that soon was to come to full fruition when he and Mr. Jacobs began to work on *Grease*.

A motion-picture version of the musical was released in 1978, with John Travolta and Olivia Newton-John as the two youthful protagonists and such seasoned players as Eve Arden, Sid Caesar, Joan Blondell, Frankie Avalon, Dody Goodman, and Alice Ghostley in special "adult" cameo roles.

PRODUCTION NOTES

Grease was first presented by Kenneth Waissman and Maxine Fox, in association with Anthony D'Amato, at the Eden Theatre, New York on February 14, 1972. On June 7, 1972, the production transferred to the Broadhurst Theatre, New York. The cast was as follows:

Miss Lynch	*Dorothy Leon*
Patty Simcox	*Ilene Kristen*
Eugene Florczyk	*Tom Harris*
Jan	*Garn Stephens*
Marty	*Katie Hanley*
Betty Rizzo	*Adrienne Barbeau*
Doody	*James Canning*
Roger	*Walter Bobbie*
Kenickie	*Timothy Meyers*
Sonny	*Jim Borrelli*
Frenchy	*Marya Small*
Sandy Dumbrowski	*Carole Demas*
Danny Zuko	*Barry Bostwick*
Vince Fontaine	*Don Billett*
Johnny Casino	*Alan Paul*
Cha-Cha Di Gregorio	*Kathi Moss*
Teen Angel	*Alan Paul*

Directed by *Tom Moore*
Musical Numbers and Dances staged by *Patricia Birch*
Scenery by *Douglas W. Schmidt*
Costumes by *Carrie F. Robbins*
Lighting by *Karl Eigsti*
Orchestrations by *Michael Leonard*
Musical Direction and Vocal Arrangements by *Louis St. Louis*

SCENES

MUSICAL NUMBERS

ACT ONE

Alma Mater	Miss Lynch, Patty and Eugene
Alma Mater Parody	Pink Ladies, Burger Palace Boys
Summer Nights	Sandy and Danny, Pink Ladies, Burger Palace Boys
Those Magic Changes	Doody, Burger Palace Boys and Pink Ladies
Freddy, My Love	Marty, Jan, Frenchy and Rizzo
Greased Lightnin'	Kenickie and Burger Palace Boys
Mooning	Roger and Jan
Look at Me, I'm Sandra Dee	Rizzo
We Go Together	Pink Ladies and Burger Palace Boys

ACT TWO

Shakin' at the High School Hop	Entire Company
It's Raining on Prom Night	Sandy and Radio Voice
Shakin' at the High School Hop (Reprise)	Entire Company
Born to Hand-Jive	Johnny Casino and Company
Beauty School Dropout	Teen Angel, Frenchy and Choir
Alone at a Drive-In Movie	Danny and Burger Palace Boys
Rock 'n' Roll Party Queen	Doody and Roger
There Are Worse Things I Could Do	Rizzo
Look at Me, I'm Sandra Dee (Reprise)	Sandy
All Choked Up	Sandy, Danny and Company
We Go Together (Reprise)	Entire Company

CHARACTERS:

DANNY: *The leader of the Burger Palace Boys. Well-built, nice-looking, with an air of cool, easygoing charm. Strong and confident.*

SANDY: *Danny's love interest. Sweet, wholesome, naïve, cute, like Sandra Dee of the "Gidget" movies.*

THE PINK LADIES: *the club-jacketed, gum-chewing, hip-swinging girls' gang that hangs around with the Burger Palace Boys—*

RIZZO: *Leader of the Pink Ladies. She is tough, sarcastic and outspoken, but vulnerable. Thin, Italian, with unconventional good looks.*

FRENCHY: *A dreamer. Good-natured and dumb. Heavily made-up, fussy about her appearance—particularly her hair. She can't wait to finish high school so she can be a beautician.*

MARTY: *The "beauty" of the Pink Ladies. Pretty, looks older than the other girls, but betrays her real age when she opens her mouth. Tries to act sophisticated.*

JAN: *Chubby, compulsive eater. Loud and pushy with the girls, but shy with boys.*

THE BURGER PALACE BOYS, *A super-cool, d.a.-haired, hard-looking group of high school wheeler-dealers . . . or so they think—*

KENICKIE: *Second in command of the Burger Palace Boys. Tough-looking, tattooed, surly, avoids any show of softness. Has an offbeat sense of humor.*

DOODY: *Youngest of the guys. Small, boyish, open, with a disarming smile and a hero-worshiping attitude toward the others. Plays the guitar.*

ROGER: *The "anything-for-a-laugh" stocky type. Full of mischief, half-baked schemes and ideas. A clown who enjoys putting other people on.*

SONNY: *Italian-looking, with shiny black hair and dark oily skin. A braggart and wheeler-dealer who thinks he's a real lady-killer.*

PATTY: *A typical cheerleader at a middle-class American public high school. Attractive and athletic. Aggressive, sure of herself, given to bursts of disconcerting enthusiasm. Catty, but in an All-American-Girl sort of way. She can twirl a baton.*

CHA-CHA: *A blind date. Slovenly, loudmouthed and homely. Takes pride in being "the best dancer at St. Bernadette's."*

EUGENE: *The class valedictorian. Physically awkward, with weak eyes and a high-pitched voice. An apple-polisher, smug and pompous but gullible.*

VINCE FONTAINE: *A typical "teen audience" radio disc jockey. Slick, egotistical, fast-talking. A veteran "greaser."*

JOHNNY CASINO: *A "greaser" student at Rydell who leads a rock 'n' roll band and likes to think of himself as a real rock 'n' roll idol.*

TEEN ANGEL: *A good-looking, falsetto-voiced, Fabian look-alike. A singer who would have caused girls to scream and riot back in 1958.*

Act One

SCENE 1

*Lights come up on the singing of the Rydell Alma Mater.
Enter three people:* MISS LYNCH, *an old maid English teacher
who leads the singing;* PATTY, *former high school cheerleader
and honor student, now a professional married career woman;
and* EUGENE FLORCZYK, *former class valedictorian and honor
student, now vice-president of an advertising agency. Behind
them is a large sign trimmed in green and brown that reads:
"Welcome Back: Rydell High, Class of '59."*

ALL:

> *As I go trav'ling down life's highway*
> *Whatever course my fortunes may foretell*
> *I shall not go alone on my way*
> *For thou shalt always be with me, Rydell.*
>
> *When I seek rest from worldly matters*
> *In palace or in hovel I may dwell*
> *And though my bed be silk or tatters*
> *My dreams shall always be of thee, Rydell.*

(EUGENE, PATTY *and* MISS LYNCH *enter*)

> *Through all the years, Rydell,*
> *And tears, Rydell,*
> *We give three cheers, Rydell, for thee.*
> *Through ev'rything, Rydell,*
> *We cling, Rydell,*
> *And sing, Rydell, to thee.*

(*As the song ends,* MISS LYNCH *introduces* EUGENE *and then
takes her seat*)
MISS LYNCH: Thank you. It is my pleasure at this time to

introduce Mrs. Patricia Simcox Honeywell, your class yearbook editor, and Mr. Eugene Florczyk, class valedictorian
and today vice-president of "Straight-Shooters Unlimited,"
Research and Marketing.

EUGENE: Miss Lynch, fellow graduates, honored guests, and
others. Looking over these familiar faces really takes me back
to those wonderful bygone days. Days of working and playing
together, days of cheering together for our athletic teams—
Yay, Ringtails!—and days of worrying together when examina-
tion time rolled around. Perhaps some of those familiar faces
of yesteryear are absent this evening because they thought
our beloved Miss Lynch might have one of her famous
English finals awaiting us. (*To* MISS LYNCH) I was only joking.
(*To audience*) However, the small portion of alumni I notice
missing tonight are certainly not missing from our fond
memories of them . . . and I'm sure they'd want us to know
that they're fully present and accounted for in spirit, just the
way we always remember them.

(*School bell rings—Chuck Berry-style guitar run is heard. The*
GREASERS *are revealed in positions of laziness, defiance, boredom
and amusement. They sing a parody of the Alma Mater as they
take over the stage*)

GREASERS:

*I saw a dead skunk on the highway
And I was goin' crazy from the smell
'Cause when the wind was blowin' my way
It smelled just like the halls of old Rydell.
And if ya gotta use the toilet
And later on you start to scratch like hell,
Take off your underwear and boil it
'Cause you got memories of old Rydell.*

*I can't explain, Rydell, this pain, Rydell.
Is it ptomaine Rydell gave me?
Is it v.d., Rydell? Could be, Rydell.
You oughta see the faculty.
If Mr. Clean, Rydell, had seen Rydell
He'd just turn green and disappear.
I'm outta luck, Rydell, dead duck, Rydell.
I'm stuck, Rydell, right here!*

SCENE 2

The GREASERS *stalk off as the scene shifts to the high school cafeteria.* JAN *and* MARTY *enter, wearing their Pink Ladies jackets and carrying trays,* JAN's *loaded with food. As each female character enters, she joins the others at one large table.*

JAN: Jeez, I wish it was still summer. Christ, it's only a quarter after twelve and I feel like I been here a whole year already.

MARTY: Yeah, what a drag. Hey, you wanna sit here?

JAN: Yeah. Rizzo's comin', and Frenchy's bringin' that new chick. Hey, Marty, who'd ya get for Economics? Old Man Drucker?

MARTY: Yeah, what a pain in the ass. He keeps makin' passes.

JAN: For real? He never tried nothin' with me!

MARTY: Huh. You want my coleslaw?

JAN: I'll see if I have room for it. *(She takes coleslaw)*

MARTY: Hey, Rizzo, over here!

RIZZO *(Enters, carrying tray)*: Hey, hey, hey! Hey, where's all the guys?

JAN: Those slobs? You think they'd spend a dime on their lunch? They're baggin' it.

RIZZO: Pretty cheap.

(Lights fade on the cafeteria, come up on ROGER AND DOODY *sitting on the school steps)*

DOODY: Hey, Rump, I'll trade ya a sardine for a liver sausage.

ROGER: I ain't eatin' one of those things. You had 'em in your icebox since last Easter.

DOODY: Nah, this was a fresh can. My ma just opened it this morning.

ROGER: You mean your old lady dragged her ass out of bed for ya?

DOODY: Sure. She does it every year on the first day of school.

KENICKIE *(Enters)*: Hey, where ya at?

ROGER: Hey, Kenickie. What's happening?

DOODY: Hey, Kenickie, whatcha got in the bag? I'll trade ya half a sardine.

KENICKIE: Get outta here with that dog food. I ain't messin' up my stomach with none of that crap. *(He pulls a pack of Hostess Sno-Balls out of the bag and starts unwrapping it)*

ROGER: Hey, Kenicks, where were ya all summer?

KENICKIE: What are you, the F.B.I.?

ROGER: I was just askin'.

KENICKIE: I was workin'. Which is more than either of you two skids can say.

ROGER: Workin'! Yeah? Where?

KENICKIE: Luggin' boxes at Bargain City.

ROGER: Nice job!

KENICKIE: Hey, eat me! I'm savin' up to get me some wheels. That's the only reason I took the job.

ROGER: You gettin' a car, Kenick?

DOODY: Hey, cool! What kind?

KENICKIE: I don't know what kind yet, moron. But I got a name all picked out. "Greased Lightning"!

ROGER (*Putting him on*): Oh, nifty!

DOODY: Yeah. Maybe you oughtta get a hamster instead.

(DOODY *and* ROGER *laugh*)

KENICKIE: Go ahead, laugh it up. When I show up in that baby, you suckers'll be laughin' out your ass.

ROGER: Will we ever!

(SONNY *enters wearing wraparound sunglasses. As he enters, he pulls a class schedule out of his pocket*)

KENICKIE: Hey, whattaya say, Sonny?

SONNY: Son of a bitch. I got old lady Lynch for English again. She hates my guts. (*Lights a cigarette*)

ROGER: Nah, she's got the hots for ya, Sonny. That's why she keeps puttin' ya back in her class.

KENICKIE: Yeah, she's just waitin' for ya to grow up.

SONNY: Yeah, well, this year she's gonna wish she never seen me.

KENICKIE: Yeah? What are ya gonna do to her?

SONNY: I'm just not gonna take any of her crap, that's all. I don't take no crap from nobody.

MISS LYNCH (*Enters*): What's all the racket out here?

DOODY: Hi, Miss Lynch, did you have a nice summer?

SONNY (*He hides his cigarette by cupping it in his hand and shoving his hand in his pocket*): Hello, Miss Lynch, we was . . . uh . . .

MISS LYNCH: Dominic, aren't you supposed to be in class right now?

SONNY: I . . . I . . .

MISS LYNCH: You're just dawdling, aren't you? That's a fine way to start the new semester, Mr. LaTierri. Well? Are you going to stand there all day?

SONNY: No, ma'am.

DOODY: No, ma'am.

MISS LYNCH: Then move! (*Exits*)

SONNY: Yes, ma'am. (*He takes his hand out of his pocket and inhales on the still-burning cigarette*)

ROGER: I'm sure glad she didn't give you no crap. Son. You would have really told her off, right?

SONNY: Shaddup.

(*Lights fade on steps, come up again on GIRLS in the cafeteria*)

MARTY (*Squinting and putting her glasses on*): Hey, Jan, who's that chick with Frenchy? Is she the one you were tellin' me about?

JAN: Yeah, her name's Sandy. She seems pretty cool. Maybe we could let her in the Pink Ladies.

RIZZO: Just what we need. Another broad around.

(*FRENCHY and SANDY enter, carrying trays*)

FRENCHY: Hi, you guys, this is my new next-door neighbor, Sandy Dumbrowski. This here's Rizzo, and that's Marty, and you remember Jan.

JAN: Sure. Hi.

SANDY: Hi. Pleased to meet you.

FRENCHY (*To* SANDY): Come on, sit down. Hey, Marty, those new glasses?

MARTY: Yeah, I just got 'em for school. Do they make me look smarter?

RIZZO: Nah. We can still see your face.

MARTY: How'dja like rice pudding down your bra?

JAN: *I'll* take it! (*She reaches over and grabs the pudding*)

RIZZO: How long you been livin' around here?

SANDY: Since July. My father just got transferred here.

MARTY: Hey, French, what'dja do to your hair? It really looks tough.

FRENCHY: Ah, I just touched it up a little

JAN: You gonna eat your coleslaw, Sandy?

SANDY: It smells kinda funny.

FRENCHY (*To divert* SANDY's *attention while* JAN *grabs her coleslaw*): Wait'll you have the chipped beef. Better known as "Shit on a Shingle."

MARTY: Don't mind her, Sandy. Some of us like to show off and use dirty words.

RIZZO: Some of us? Check out Miss Toilet-Mouth over here.

MARTY (*Giving her "the finger"*): Fuck you, Rizzle!

JAN (*Trying to change the subject*): How do ya like the school so far, Sandy?

SANDY: Oh, it seems real nice. I was going to go to Immaculata, but my father had a fight with the Mother Superior over my patent-leather shoes.

JAN: What do ya mean?

SANDY: She said boys could see up my dress in the reflection.

MARTY: Swear to God?

JAN: Hey, where do ya get shoes like that?

PATTY (*Offstage*): Hi, kids!

RIZZO: Hey, look who's comin'. Patty Simcox, the Little Lulu of Edgebrook Heights.

MARTY: Yeah. Wonder what she's doin' back here with us slobs?

RIZZO: Maybe she's havin' her period and wants to be alone.

PATTY (*Enters*): Well, don't say hello.

RIZZO: We won't.

PATTY: Is there room at your table?

MARTY (*Surprised*): Oh, yeah, move over, French.

PATTY: Oh, I just love the first day of school, don't you?

RIZZO: It's the biggest thrill of my life.

  (FRENCHY *starts doing* RIZZO's *hair*)

PATTY: You'll never guess what happened this morning.

RIZZO: Prob'ly not.

PATTY: Well, they announced this year's nominees for the Student Council, and guess who's up for vice-president?

MARTY (*Knowing what's coming*): Who?

PATTY: Me! Isn't that wild?

RIZZO: Wild.

PATTY: I just hope I don't make *too* poor a showing.

RIZZO: Well, we sure wish ya all the luck in the world.

PATTY: Oh, uh, thanks. Oh, you must think I'm a terrible clod! I never even bothered to introduce myself to your new friend.

SANDY: Oh, I'm Sandy Dumbrowski.

PATTY: It's a real pleasure, Sandy. We certainly are glad to have you here at Rydell.

SANDY: Thank you.

PATTY: I'll bet you're going to be at the cheerleader tryouts next week, aren't you?

SANDY: Oh, no. I'd be too embarrassed.

PATTY: Don't be silly. I could give you a few pointers if you like.

MARTY: Aaaaahhh, son of a bitch!

PATTY: Goodness gracious!

RIZZO: Nice language. What was that all about?

MARTY (*Examining her glasses*): One of my diamonds fell in the macaroni.

(*Lights fade on* GIRLS, *come up on* GUYS *on the steps*)

DOODY: Hey, ain't that Danny over there?

SONNY: Where?

KENICKIE: Yeah. What's he doin' hangin' around the girls' gym entrance?

ROGER: Maybe he's hot for some chick!

SONNY: One of those skanks we've seen around since kindergarten? Not quite.

DOODY (*Yells*): Hey, Danny! Whatcha doin'?

ROGER: That's good, Dood. Play it real cool.

KENICKIE: Aw, leave him alone. Maybe he ain't gettin' any.

DANNY (*Enters, carrying books and lunch*): Hey, you guys, how they hangin'? (*Fakes* SONNY *out with a quick goose*)

SONNY: Whattaya say, Zuko—'dja see any good-lookin' meat over there?

DANNY: Nah, just the same old chicks everybody's made it with!

DOODY: Where ya been all summer, Danny?

DANNY: Well, I spent a lot of time down at the beach.

KENICKIE: Hey, 'dja meet any new broads?

DANNY: Nah. Just met this one who was sorta cool, ya know?

SONNY: Ya mean she "puts out"?

DANNY: Is that all you ever think about, Sonny?

SONNY (*Looking around at the other* GUYS): Fuckin' A!

ROGER: Aahh, come off it, Zuko. Ya got in her drawers, right?

DANNY: Look, man. That's none of you guys' business.

KENICKIE: Okay, if that's the way you're gonna be.

DANNY: You don't want to hear all the horny details, anyway.

SONNY (*Starts tickling* DANNY): Sure we do! Let's hear a little!

ROGER (*Joining in*): C'mon, Zuko, koochee koochee!

(*All* GUYS *join in playfully mauling* DANNY *as the lights fade on them and come back up on the* GIRLS *at the cafeteria table*)

SANDY: I spent most of the summer at the beach.

JAN: What for? We got a brand-new pool right in the neighborhood. It's real nice.

RIZZO: Yeah, if ya like swimmin' in Clorox.

SANDY: Well—actually, I met a boy there.

MARTY: You hauled your ass all the way to the beach for some guy?

SANDY: This was sort of a special boy.

RIZZO: Are you kiddin'? There ain't no such thing.

(*Lights stay on* GIRLS, *come up on* GUYS)

DANNY: Okay, you guys, ya wanna know what happened?

GUYS: Yeah! Let's hear it! (*Etc. ad lib*)

SANDY: No he was really nice. It was all very romantic.

(DANNY *rises and sings* "Summer Nights" *to the* GUYS. SANDY *sings her version to the* GIRLS)

DANNY:
Summer lovin'! Had me a blast.

SANDY:
Summer lovin'! Happened so fast.

DANNY:
Met a girl crazy for me.

SANDY:
Met a boy cute as can be.

BOTH:
Summer day, drifting away, to
Uh-oh, those summer nights.

GUYS:
Tell me more, tell me more,
Didja get very far?

GIRLS:
Tell me more, tell me more,

MARTY:
Like does he have a car?

DANNY:
She swam by me, she got a cramp.

SANDY:
He ran by me, got my suit damp.

DANNY:
Saved her life, she nearly drowned.

SANDY:
He showed off, splashing around.

BOTH:
Summer sun, something begun, then
Uh-oh, those summer nights.

GIRLS:
Tell me more, tell me more.

FRENCH:
Was it love at first sight?

(Lights stay up on both groups after song)
PATTY: Gee, he sounds wonderful, Sandy.
DOODY: She really sounds cool, Danny.
RIZZO: A guy doesn't touch ya and it's true love. Maybe he was a
   fairy.
   (SANDY gives RIZZO a puzzled look)
ROGER: Big knockers, huh?
FRENCHY: Hey, nice talk, Rizzo!
KENICKIE: She Catholic?
JAN: What if we said that about Danny Zuko?
SONNY: Hot box, huh, Zuker?
SANDY: Did you say Danny Zuko?
DANNY: I didn't say that, Sonny!
RIZZO: Hey, was he the guy?
DOODY: Boy, you get all the neats!
SANDY: Doesn't he go to Lake Forest Academy?
   (PINK LADIES laugh)
KENICKIE: She doesn't go to Rydell, does she?
   (DANNY shakes his head "no")
MARTY: That's a laugh!
SONNY: Too bad. I'd bet she'd go for me.
PATTY *(Confidentially)*: Listen, Sandy, forget Danny Zuko. I
   know some really sharp boys.
RIZZO: So do I. Right, you guys? C'mon, let's go.
   (PINK LADIES get up from the table, SANDY following them.
   The GUYS all laugh together)
FRENCHY: See ya 'round, Patty!
RIZZO: Yeah, maybe we'll drop in on the next Student Council
   meeting.

(RIZZO *nudges* MARTY *in the ribs. Lights go down on the lunchroom.* GIRLS *cross toward* GUYS *on steps)*

MARTY: Well, speaking of the devil!

SONNY *(To* GUYS*):* What'd I tell ya, they're always chasin' me.

MARTY *(Pushing* SONNY *away):* Not you, greaseball! Danny!

RIZZO: Yeah. We got a surprise for ya.

(PINK LADIES *shove* SANDY *toward* DANNY*)*

SANDY *(Surprised and nervous):* Hello, Danny.

DANNY *(Uptight):* Oh, hi. How are ya?

SANDY: Fine.

DANNY: Oh yeah ... I ... uh ... thought you were goin' to Immaculata.

SANDY: I changed my plans.

DANNY: Yeah! Well, that's cool. I'll see ya around. Let's go, you guys. *(Pushes* GUYS *out)*

DOODY: Where do you know her from, Danny?

DANNY: Huh? Oh, just an old friend of my family's.

SONNY *(To* DANNY*):* She's pretty sharp. I think she's got eyes for me, didja notice?

(DANNY *gives* SONNY *"a look," pulls him off.* GUYS *exit)*

JAN *(Picking up* DANNY*'s lunch):* Gee, he was so glad to see ya, he dropped his lunch.

SANDY: I don't get it. He was so nice this summer.

FRENCHY: Don't worry about it, Sandy.

MARTY: Hey listen, how'd you like to come over to my house tonight? It'll be just us girls.

JAN: Yeah, those guys are all a bunch of creeps.

(DANNY *returns for his lunch)*

RIZZO: Yeah, Zuko's the biggest creep of all.

(RIZZO, *seeing* DANNY, *exits. Other* GIRLS *follow)*

SCENE 3

School bell rings and class change begins. GREASERS, PATTY *and* EUGENE *enter, go to lockers, get books, etc.* DANNY *sees* DOODY *with guitar.*

DANNY: Hey, Doody, where'dja get the guitar?

DOODY: I just started takin' lessons this summer.

DANNY: Can you play anything on it?

DOODY: Sure. *(He fumbles with the frets and strikes a sour chord)* That's a C. *(He sits and waits for approval)*

MARTY *(Baffled):* Hey, that's pretty good.

DOODY (*Hitting each chord*): Then I know an A minor, and an F, and I've been workin' on a G.

FRENCHY: Hey! Can you play "Tell Laura I Love Her"?

DOODY: I don't know. Has it got a C in it?

DANNY: Hey, come on; let's hear a little, Elvis.

DOODY (*Pulling out instruction book*): *Magic Changes*, by Ronnie Dell . . . (*Sings off key while strumming sour chords*)

C-C-C-C-C-C
A-A-A-A *minor*
F-F-F-F-F-F
G-G-G-G *seventh*

DANNY: That's terrific.

DOODY: Thanks—want to hear it again?

ALL: Sure! Yeah! (*Etc. ad lib*)

(DOODY *starts to sing "Those Magic Changes," and other* KIDS *transform into rock 'n' roll, "doo-wop" group backing him as he suddenly becomes a teen idol rock 'n' roll star*)

DOODY and GROUP:

C-C-C-C-C-C
A-A-A-A *minor*
F-F-F-F-F-F
G-G-G-G *seventh*

What's that playing on the radio?
Why do I start swaying to and fro?
I have never heard that song before
But if I don't hear it any more
It's still familiar to me,
Sends a thrill right through me,
'Cause those chords remind me of
The night that I first fell in love to
Those magic changes.

My heart arranges
A melody
That's never the same.
A melody
That's calling your name
And begs you, please, come back to me,

Please return to me,
Don't go away again.
Oh, make them play again
The music I long to hear
As once again you whisper in my ear.
Ohhhh, my darling.

I'll be waiting by the radio.
You'll come back to me someday, I know.
Been so lonesome since your last goodbye
But I'm singing as I cry-y-y.
While the bass is sounding,
While the drums are pounding,
Beating of my broken heart
Will climb to first place on the chart.
Ohhh, my heart arranges
Ohhh, those magic changes.

C-C-C-C-C-C
A-A-A-A-A minor
G-G-G-G seventh
Shoop-doo-wah bom!

(At the end of the song, MISS LYNCH *enters to break up the group. All exit except* GUYS *and* SONNY*)*
MISS LYNCH *(To* SONNY*)*: Mr. LaTierri, aren't you due in Detention Hall right now?
*(*GUYS *all make fun of* SONNY *and lead him off to Detention Hall)*

SCENE 4

A pajama party in MARTY'S *bedroom.* MARTY, FRENCHY, JAN *and* RIZZO *are in pastel baby-doll pajamas,* SANDY *in a quilted robe buttoned all the way up to the neck. The WAXX jingle for the Vince Fontaine Show is playing on the radio.*
VINCE'S VOICE: Hey, hey, this is the Main Brain, Vince Fontaine, at Big Fifteen! Spinnin' the stacks of wax, here at the House of Wax—W-A-X-X. *(Ooo-ga horn sound)* Cruisin' time, 10:46. *(Sound of ricocheting bullet)* Sharpshooter pick hit of the week. A brand-new one shootin' up the charts like a rocket by The Vel-Doo Rays—goin' out to Ronnie and Sheila, the kids

down at Mom's School Store, and especially to Little Joe and the LaDons—listen in while I give it a spin! (*Radio fades*)

FRENCHY (*Looking at a fan magazine that has a big picture of Fabian on the cover*): Hey, it says here that Fabian is in love with some Swedish movie star and might be gettin' married.

JAN: Oh, no!

MARTY: Who cares, as long as they don't get their hooks into Kookie.

RIZZO: Hey, Frenchy, throw me a ciggie-butt, will ya?

(FRENCHY *throws* RIZZO *a cigarette*)

MARTY: Me too, while ya got the pack out.

FRENCHY: Ya want one, Sandy?

SANDY: Oh, no, thanks. I don't smoke.

FRENCHY: Ya don't? Didja ever try it?

SANDY: Well, no, but . . .

RIZZO: Go. on, try it. It ain't gonna kill ya. Give her a Hit Parade!

(FRENCHY *throws* SANDY *a Hit Parade*)

Now, when she holds up the match, suck in on it.

(FRENCHY *lights the cigarette,* SANDY *inhales and starts coughing violently*)

Oh, I shoulda told ya, don't inhale if you're not used to it.

MARTY: That's okay. You'll get better at it.

FRENCHY: Yeah, then I'll show ya how to French inhale. That's really cool. Watch. (*She demonstrates French inhaling*)

JAN: Phtyyaaagghh! That's the ugliest thing I ever saw!

FRENCHY: Nah, the guys really go for it. That's how I got my nickname, Frenchy.

RIZZO: Sure it is. Jesus Christ, you guys, I almost forgot! (*She removes a half-gallon of wine from her overnight bag*) A little Sneaky Pete to get the party goin'.

JAN: Italian Swiss Colony. Wow, it's imported.

(RIZZO *passes bottle to* MARTY)

FRENCHY: Hey, we need some glasses.

RIZZO: Just drink it out of the bottle, we ain't got cooties.

MARTY: It's kind of sweet. I think I like Thunderbird better.

RIZZO: Okay, Princess Grace. (*Takes bottle away from* MARTY)

MARTY (*Grabbing bottle back*): I didn't say I didn't want any, it just don't taste very strong, that's all.

(MARTY *passes bottle to* SANDY, *who quickly passes it to* JAN)

JAN: Hey, I brought some Twinkies, anybody want one?

MARTY: Twinkies and wine? That's real class, Jan.

JAN (*Pointing to label on bottle*): It says right here it's a dessert wine! (*Passes wine to* FRENCHY)

RIZZO: Hey, Sandy didn't get any wine. (*Hands bottle to* SANDY)

SANDY: Oh, that's okay. I don't mind.

RIZZO: Hey, I'll bet you never had a drink before either.

SANDY: Sure I did. I had some champagne at my cousin's wedding once.

RIZZO: Oh, ring-a-ding-ding. (*Hands her wine*)

(SANDY *sips wine cautiously*)

RIZZO: Hey, no! Ya gotta chug it. Like this! (RIZZO *takes a big slug from the bottle*) Otherwise you swallow air bubbles, and that's what makes you throw up.

JAN: I never knew that.

MARTY: Sure, Rudy from the Capri Lounge told me the same thing.

(SANDY *takes a slug from the bottle and holds it in her mouth, trying to swallow it*)

JAN: Hey, Sandy, you ever wear earrings? I think they'd keep your face from lookin' so skinny.

MARTY: Hey! Yeah! I got some big round ones made out of real mink. They'd look great on you.

FRENCHY: Wouldja like me to pierce your ears for ya, Sandy? I'm gonna be a beautician, y'know.

JAN: Yeah, she's real good. She did mine for me.

SANDY: Oh no, my father'd probably kill me.

MARTY: You still worry about what your old man thinks?

SANDY: Well . . . no. But isn't it awfully dangerous?

RIZZO (*Leans down to* SANDY): You ain't afraid, are ya?

SANDY: Of course not!

FRENCHY: Good. Hey, Marty, you got a needle around? (*She rummages in dresser for needle*)

MARTY: Hey, how about my virgin pin! (*She reaches for her Pink Ladies jacket and takes off "circle pin," handing it to* FRENCHY)

JAN: Nice to know it's good for somethin'.

MARTY: What's that crack supposed to mean?

JAN: Forget it, Marty, I was just teasing ya.

MARTY: Yeah, well, tease somebody else. It's my house.

(FRENCHY *begins to pierce* SANDY'S *ears.* SANDY *yelps*)

FRENCHY: Hey, would ya hold still!

MARTY: *(To the rescue)* Hey, French . . . why don't you take Sandy in the john? My old lady'd kill me if we got blood all over the rug.

SANDY: Huh?

FRENCHY: It only bleeds for a second. Come on.

JAN: Aaaww! We miss all the fun!

(JAN opens a second package of Twinkies as FRENCHY begins to lead SANDY off)

FRENCHY: Hey, Marty, I need some ice to numb her earlobes.

MARTY *(Exasperated)*: Ahh . . . look, why don'tcha just let the cold water run for a little while, then stick her ear under the faucet?

SANDY: Listen, I'm sorry, but I'm not feeling too well, and I . . .

RIZZO: Look, Sandy, if you think you're gonna be hangin' around with the Pink Ladies—you gotta get with it! Otherwise, forget it . . . and go back to your hot cocoa and Girl Scout cookies!

GUYS:
Tell me more, tell me more.

KENICKIE:
Did she put up a fight?

DANNY:
Took her bowling, in the arcade.

SANDY:
We went strolling, drank lemonade.

DANNY:
We made out, under the dock.

SANDY:
We stayed out till ten o'clock.

BOTH:
*Summer fling, don't mean a thing, but
Uh-oh, those summer nights.*

GUYS:

Tell me more, tell me more,
But ya don't have to brag.

GIRLS:

Tell me more, tell me more.

RIZZO:

'Cause he sounds like a drag.

SANDY:

He got friendly, holding my hand.

DANNY:

She got friendly, down on the sand.

SANDY:

He was sweet, just turned eighteen.

DANNY:

She was good, ya know what I mean?

BOTH:

Summer heat, boy and girl meet, then
Uh-oh, those summer nights!

GIRLS:

Tell me more, tell me more,

JAN:

How much dough did he spend?

GUYS:

Tell me more, tell me more,

SONNY:

Could she get me a friend?

SANDY:

It turned colder, that's where it ends.

DANNY:

So I told her we'd still be friends.

SANDY:

Then we made our true love vow.

DANNY:

Wonder what she's doin' now.

BOTH:

Summer dreams, ripped at the seams, but
Uh-ohh! Those summer nights!

SANDY: Okay, come on . . . Frenchy.

JAN: Hey, Sandy, don't sweat it. If she screws up, she can always fix your hair so your ears won't show.

FRENCHY: Smart ass.

RIZZO: That chick's gettin' to be a real pain in the ass.

JAN: Ah, lay off, Rizzo.

MARTY: Yeah, she can't help it if she ain't been around.

RIZZO: Yeah, well, how long are we supposed to play baby-sitter for her? *(Suddenly a loud "urp" sound is heard offstage)* What the hell was that? *(The GIRLS all look at each other, bewildered, for a couple of seconds, then FRENCHY runs back into the room)*

FRENCHY: Hey, Marty, Sandy's sick. She's heavin' all over the place!

JAN: Dja do her ears already?

FRENCHY: Nah. I only did one. As soon as she saw the blood she went *bleugh!*

RIZZO: God! What a party poop!

MARTY: Jeez, it's gettin' kinda chilly. I think I'll put my robe on. *(She pulls out a gaudy kimono and makes a big show of putting it on)*

JAN: Hey, Marty, where'dja get that thing?

MARTY: Oh, you like it? It's from Japan.

RIZZO: Yeah, everything's made in Japan these days.

MARTY: No, this guy I know sent it to me.

FRENCHY: No kiddin'!

JAN: You goin' with a Jap?

MARTY: He ain't a Jap, stupid. He's a Marine. And a real doll, too.

FRENCHY: Oh, wow! Hey, Marty, can he get me one of those things?

JAN: You never told us you knew any Marines.

RIZZO: How long you known this guy?

MARTY: Oh . . . just a couple of months. I met him on a blind date at the roller rink . . . and the next thing I know, he joins up. Anyway, right off the bat he starts sendin' me things—and then today I got this kimono. *(Trying to be cool)* Oh yeah, look what else! *(She takes a ring out of her cleavage)*

FRENCHY: Oh, neat!

MARTY: It's just a tiny bit too big. So I gotta get some Angora for it.

FRENCHY: Jeez! Engaged to a Marine!

RIZZO: *(Sarcastically)* Endsville.

JAN: What's this guy look like, Marty?

FRENCHY: You got a picture?

MARTY: Yeah, but it's not too good. He ain't in uniform. *(She takes her wallet out of the dresser. It's one of those fat bulging ones with rubber bands around it. She swings wallet and accordion picture folder drops to floor)* Oh, here it is . . . next to Paul Anka.

JAN: How come it's ripped in half?

MARTY: Oh, his old girlfriend was in the picture.

JAN: What's this guys's name, anyway?

MARTY: Oh! It's Freddy. Freddy Strulka.

JAN: He a Polack?

MARTY: Naah, I think he's Irish.

FRENCHY: Do you write him a lot, Marty?

MARTY: Pretty much. Every time I get a present.

JAN: Whattaya say to a guy in a letter, anyway?

(MARTY *and* GIRLS *suddenly become a rock 'n' roll quartet and sing "Freddy, My Love")*

MARTY:

Freddy, my love, I miss you more than words can say.
Freddy, my love, please keep in touch while you're away.
Hearing from you can make the day so much better,
Getting a souvenir or maybe a letter.
I really flipped over the gray cashmere sweater.
Freddy, my love
(Freddy, my love, Freddy, my love, Freddy, my lo-oove.)

Freddy, you know, your absence makes me feel so blue.
That's okay, though, your presents make me think of you.
My ma will have a heart attack when she catches
Those pedal pushers with the black leather patches.
Oh, how I wish I had a jacket that matches.
Freddy, my love
(Freddy, my love, Freddy, my love, Freddy, my lo-oove)

Don't keep your letters from me,
I thrill to every line.
Your spelling's kinda crummy
But honey, so is mine.
I treasure every giftie,
The ring is really nifty.
You say it cost you fifty
So you're thrifty,
I don't mind!
(Woe-ohh-ohh-oh)

Freddy, you'll see, you'll hold me in your arms someday
And I will be wearing your lacy lonjeray.
Thinking about it, my heart's pounding already
Knowing when you come home we're bound to go steady
And throw your service pay around like confetti
Freddy, my love
(Freddy, my love, Freddy, my love, Freddy, my lo-oove)

(On the last few bars of song the GIRLS *fall asleep one by one, until* RIZZO *is the only one left awake. She pulls pants on over her pajamas and climbs out the window. Just at that moment,* SANDY *comes back into the room, unnoticed by* RIZZO, *and stands looking after her)*

SCENE 5

GUYS *come running on, out of breath and carrying quarts of beer and four hubcaps.* DANNY *has a tire iron.*

DANNY: I don't know why I brought this tire iron! I coulda yanked these babies off with my bare hands!
SONNY: Sure ya could, Zuko! I just broke six fingernails!

ROGER: Hey, you guys, these hubcaps ain't got a scratch on 'em. They must be worth two beans apiece easy.

DOODY: No kiddin'? Hey, how much can we get for these dice? *(Pulls out foam rubber dice)*

ROGER: Hey, who the hell would put brand new chromers on a secondhand dodgem car!

DANNY: Probably some real tool!

SONNY: Hey, c'mon, let's go push these things off on somebody!

DANNY: Eleven o'clock at night? Sure, maybe we could go sell 'em at a police station!

DOODY: A police station, what a laugh! They don't use these kinda hubcaps on cop cars.

(A car horn is heard)

SONNY: Hey, here comes that car we just hit! Let's tear ass! Ditch the evidence!

(GUYS run, dropping hubcaps. SONNY tries to scoop them up as KENICKIE drives on in "Greased Lightning")

DANNY: Hey, wait a minute—it's Kenickie!

KENICKIE: All right, put those things back on the car, dipshit!

SONNY: Jeez, whatta grouch! We was only holdin' 'em for ya so nobody'd swipe 'em.

DOODY *(Handing back dice)*: Hey, where'dja get these cool dice?

DANNY: Kenickie, whattaya doin' with this hunka junk, anyway?

KENICKIE: Whattaya mean? This is "Greased Lightning!"

("Whats" and puzzled looks go up from the GUYS)

SONNY: What? You really expect to cop some snatch in this sardine can?

KENICKIE: Hey, get bent, LaTierri!

ROGER: Nice color, what is it? Candy-Apple Primer?

KENICKIE: That's all right—wait till I give it a paint job and soup up the engine—she'll work like a champ!

DANNY *(Looking at car and picking up mike)*: The one and only Greased Lightning!

(Hard-driving guitar begins playing "Greased Lightnin' ")

KENICKIE:
I'll have me overhead lifters and four-barrel quads, oh, yeah.
A fuel-injection cutoff and chrome-plated rods, oh, yeah.
With a four-speed on the floor, they'll be waitin' at the door.
Ya know that ain't no shit, I'll be gettin' lotsa tit
In Greased Lightnin'.

KENICKIE AND GUYS:

Go, Greased Lightnin', you're burnin' up the quarter mile.
(Greased Lightnin', go, Greased Lightnin')
Yeah, Greased Lightnin', you're coastin' through the heat-lap
trials.
(Greased Lightnin', yeah, Greased Lightnin')
You are supreme
The chicks'll cream
For Greased Lightnin'!

KENICKIE:

I'll have me purple frenched tail-lights and thirty-inch fins,
oh, yeah.
A palomino dashboard and dual-muffler twins, oh, yeah.
With new pistons, plugs, and shocks, I can get off my rocks.
Ya know that I ain't braggin', she's a real pussy-wagon.
Greased Lightnin'!

KENICKIE AND GUYS:

Go, Greased Lightnin', you're burnin' up the quarter mile.
(Greased Lighnin', go, Greased Lightnin')
Yeah, Greased Lightnin', you're coastin' through the heat-lap
trials.
(Greased Lightnin', yeah, Greased Lightnin')
You are supreme
The chicks'll cream
For Greased Lightnin'!

(As song ends, RIZZO enters)

RIZZO: What the hell is that thing?

KENICKIE: Hey, what took you so long?

RIZZO: Never mind what took me so long. Is that your new custom convert?

KENICKIE: This is it! Ain't it cool?

RIZZO: Yeah, it's about as cool as a Good Humor truck.

KENICKIE: Okay, Rizzo, if that's how you feel, why don'tcha go back to the pajama party? Plenty of chicks would give their right tit to ride around in this little number.

RIZZO: Sure they would! Out! What do ya think this is, a gangbang? *(She opens the passenger door, shoving GUYS out)* Hey, Danny! I just left your girl friend at Marty's house, flashin' all over the place.

DANNY: Whattaya talkin' about?

RIZZO: Sandy Dumbrowski! Y'know . . . Sandra Dee.

KENICKIE: Be cool, you guys.

(RIZZO *immediately starts crawling all over him*)

DANNY: Hey, you better tell that to Rizzo!

(*Siren sounds*)

KENICKIE: The fuzz! Hey, you guys better get ridda those hubcaps.

DANNY: Whattaya mean, man? They're yours!

KENICKIE: Oh, no they're not! I stole 'em. (*He starts to drive off*)

(*Siren sounds again.* GUYS *leap on car and drive off, singing,* "Greased Lightnin' " *as the lights change*)

SCENE 6

SANDY *runs on with pom-poms, dressed in a green baggy gymsuit. She does a Rydell cheer.*

SANDY:

Do a split, give a yell,

Throw a fit for old Rydell.

Way to go, green and brown,

Turn the foe upside-down.

(SANDY *does awkward split.* DANNY *enters*)

DANNY: Hiya, Sandy. (SANDY *gives him a look and turns her head so that* DANNY *sees the Band-Aid on her ear*) Hey, what happened to your ear?

SANDY: Huh? (*She covers her ear with her hand, answers coldly*) Oh, nothing. Just an accident.

DANNY: Hey, look, uh, I hope you're not bugged about that first day at school. I mean, couldn't ya tell I was glad to see ya?

SANDY: Well, you could've been a little nicer to me in front of your friends.

DANNY: Are you kidding? Hey, you don't know those guys. They just see ya talkin' to a chick and right away they think she puts . . . well, you know what I mean.

SANDY: I'm not sure. It looked to me like maybe you had a new girl friend or something.

DANNY: Are you kiddin'! Listen, if it was up to me, I'd never even look at any other chick but you. (SANDY *blushes*) Hey, tell ya what. We're throwin' a party in the park tonight for Frenchy. She's gonna quit school before she flunks again and go to Beauty School. Howdja like to make it on down there with me?

SANDY: I'd really like to, but I'm not so sure those girls want me around anymore.

DANNY: Listen, Sandy. Nobody's gonna start gettin' salty with ya when I'm around. Uh-uhh!

SANDY: All right, Danny, as long as you're with me. Let's not let anyone come between us again, okay?

PATTY *(Rushing onstage with two batons and wearing cheerleader outfit)*: Hiiiiiiii, Danny! Oh, don't let me interrupt. *(Gives* SANDY *baton)* Here, why don't you twirl this for a while. *(Taking* DANNY *aside)* I've been dying to tell you something. You know what I found out after you left my house the other night? My mother thinks you're cute. *(To* SANDY*)* He's such a lady-killer.

SANDY: Isn't he, though! *(Out of corner of mouth, to* DANNY*)* What were you doing at her house?

DANNY: Ah, I was just copying down some homework.

PATTY: Come on, Sandy, let's practice.

SANDY: Yeah, let's! I'm just dying to make a good impression on all those cute lettermen.

DANNY: Oh, that's why you're wearing that thing—gettin' ready to show off your skivvies to a bunch of horny jocks?

SANDY: Don't tell me you're jealous, Danny.

DANNY: What? Of that buncha meatheads! Don't make me laugh. Ha! Ha!

SANDY: Just because they can do something you can't do?

DANNY: Yeah, sure, right.

SANDY: Okay, what have *you* ever done?

DANNY *(To* PATTY, *twirling baton)*: Stop that! *(Thinking a moment)* I won a Hully Gully contest at the "Teen Talent" record hop.

SANDY: Aaahh, you don't even know what I'm talking about.

DANNY: Whattaya mean, look, I could run circles around those jerks.

SANDY: But you'd rather spend your time copying other people's homework.

DANNY: Listen, the next time they have tryouts for any of those teams I'll show you what I can do.

PATTY: Oh, what a lucky coincidence! The track team's having tryouts tomorrow.

DANNY *(Panic)*: Huh? Okay, I'll be there.

SANDY: Big talk.

DANNY: You think so, huh? Hey, Patty, when'dja say those tryouts were?

PATTY: Tomorrow, tenth period, on the football field.

DANNY: Good, I'll be there. You're gonna come watch me, aren't you?

PATTY: Oooohh, I can't wait!

DANNY: Solid. I'll see ya there, sexy. *(Exits)*

PATTY: Toodles! *(Elated, turns to* SANDY*)* Ooohh, I'm so excited, aren't you?

SANDY: Come on, let's practice.

SANDY AND PATTY *(Sing Rydell fight song, twirling batons,* SANDY *just missing* PATTY'S *head with each swing)*:

Hit 'em again, Rydell Ringtails
Tear 'em apart, green and brown.
Bash their brains out, stomp 'em on the floor
For the glory of Rydell evermore.

Fight, team, fight; fight, team, fight.
Chew 'em up—spit 'em out.
Fight, team, fight.

*(*SANDY *and* PATTY *exit doing majorette march step)*

SCENE 7

A deserted section of the park. JAN *and* ROGER *on picnic table.* RIZZO *and* KENICKIE *making out on bench.* MARTY *sitting on other bench.* FRENCHY *and* SONNY *on blanket reading fan magazines.* DANNY *pacing.* DOODY *sitting on a trash can. They're all eating food or drinking beer. A portable radio is playing The Vince Fontaine Show.*

VINCE'S RADIO VOICE: Hey, gettin' back on the rebound here for our second half. *(Cuckoo sound)* Dancin' Word Bird Contest comin' up in a half hour, when maybe I'll call you. Hey, I think you'll like this little ditty from the city, a new group discovered by Alan Freed. Turn up the sound and stomp on the ground. Ohhh, yeah!!! *(Radio fades)*

DANNY: Hey, Frenchy, when do ya start beauty school?

FRENCHY: Next week. I can hardly wait. No more dumb books and stupid teachers.

MARTY (*Holding out a package of Vogues*): Hey, anybody want a Vogue?

FRENCHY: Yeah, you got any pink ones left?

SONNY: Yeah, give me one. (*Puts it in his mouth*) How about one for later?

MARTY (*Throwing him another cigarette*): God, what a mooch!

DOODY: Hey, Rump, you shouldn't be eatin' that cheeseburger. It's still Friday, y'know!

ROGER: Son-of-a-bitch! What'dja remind me for? Now I gotta go to confession. (*He takes another bite of the cheeseburger*)

JAN: Well, I can eat anything. That's the nice thing about bein' a Lutheran.

ROGER: Yeah, that's the nice thing about bein' Petunia Pig.

JAN (*Giving ROGER "the finger"*): Hey, right here, lard-ass!

FRENCHY: Hey, Sonny, don't maul that magazine. There's a picture of Ricky Nelson in there I really wanna save.

SONNY: I was just lookin' at Shelley Farberay's jugs.

FRENCHY (*Leaning over to look at picture and primping*): Y'know, lotsa people think I look just like Shelley Farberries.

SONNY: Not a chance. You ain't got a set like hers.

FRENCHY: I happen to know she wears falsies.

SONNY: You oughtta know, foam-domes.

JAN: You want another cheeseburger?

ROGER: Nah, I think I'll have a Coke.

JAN: You shouldn't drink so much Coke. It rots your teeth.

ROGER: No shit, Bucky Beaver.

JAN: I ain't kiddin'. Somebody told me about this scientist once who knocked out one of his teeth and dropped it in this glass of Coke, and after a week, the tooth rotted away until there was nothing left.

ROGER: For Christ's sake, I ain't gonna carry a mouthful of Coke around for a week. Besides, what do you care what I do with my teeth? It ain't your problem.

JAN: No, I guess not.

MARTY: (*Wearing extra-large college letterman sweater and modeling for DANNY*): Hey, Danny, how would I look as a college girl?

DANNY (*Pinching boobs*): Boola-boola . . .

MARTY: Hey, watch it! It belongs to this big jock at Holy Contrition.

DANNY (*Indicating* MARTY's *sweater*): Wait'll ya see me wearin' one of those things. I'm gonna try out for the track team tomorrow.

(*Several heads turn and look at* DANNY. *Ad libs of "What?" "Zuko, no!," etc.*)

MARTY: Are you serious? With those bird legs?

(KIDS *all laugh.* ROGER *does funny imitation of* DANNY *as a gung-ho track star*)

DANNY: Hey, better hobby than yours, Rump.

(*Other* GUYS *laugh at remark, all giving* ROGER *calls of "Rump-Rump"*)

JAN (*After a pause*): How come you never get mad at those guys?

ROGER: Why should I?

JAN: Well, that name they call you. Rump!

ROGER: That's just my nickname. It's sorta like a title.

JAN: Whattaya mean?

ROGER: I'm king of the mooners.

JAN: The what?

ROGER: I'm the mooning champ of Rydell High.

JAN: You mean showin' off your bare behind to people? That's pretty raunchy.

ROGER: Nah, it's neat! I even mooned old lady Lynch once. I hung one on her right out the car window. And she never even knew who it was.

JAN: Too much! I wish I'd been there. (*Quickly*) I mean ... y'know what I mean.

ROGER: Yeah. I wish you'd been there, too.

JAN (*Seriously*): You do?

ROGER (*Answers her by singing "Mooning"*):
I spend my days just mooning,
So sad and blue.
I spend my nights just mooning
All over you.

JAN:
All over who?

ROGER:

> *Oh, I'm so full of love,*
> *As any fool can see,*
> *'Cause angels up above*
> *Have hung a moon on me.*

JAN:

> *Why must you go?*

ROGER:

> *Why must I go on mooning*
> *So all alone.*
> *There would be no more mooning*
> *If you would*

JAN:

> *Call me up on the phone.*

ROGER:

> *Oh, lying by myself in bed I*
> *Cry and give myself the red eye*
> *Mooning over you.*
> *I'll stand behind you mooning*
> *Forevermore.*

JAN:

> *Forevermore.*

ROGER:

> *Someday you'll find me mooning*
> *At your front door.*

JAN:

> *At my front door!*

ROGER:

> *Oh, every day at school I watch ya*
> *Always will until I gotcha*
> *Mooning, too.*
> *(There's a moon out tonight!)*

DOODY *(Loudly)*: Hey, Danny, there's that chick ya know.

(SANDY *and* EUGENE *enter,* EUGENE *wearing Bermuda shorts and argyle socks.* BOTH *have bags of leaves.* RIZZO *and* KENICKIE *sit up to look.* DANNY *moves to* EUGENE *and stares)*

EUGENE: Well, Sandy, I think I have all the leaves I want. Uh . . . why don't I wait for you with Dad in the station wagon.

(DANNY, *looking at* EUGENE, *outlines a square with head movement.* EUGENE *exits. As* DANNY *walks away,* SONNY *crosses to* SANDY)

SONNY: Hi ya, Sandy. What's shakin'? How 'bout a beer?

SANDY *(Giving* DANNY *a look)*: No, thanks, I can't stay.

DANNY: Oh, yeah! Then whattaya doin' hangin' around? *(He casually puts his hand on* MARTY's *shoulder and* MARTY *looks at him, bewildered)*

SANDY: I just came out to collect some leaves for Biology.

SONNY: Oh, yeah? There's some really neat yellow ones over by the drainage canal. C'mon, I'll show ya'! *(He grabs* SANDY *and starts off)*

KENICKIE: *(Shouting)* Those ain't leaves. They're used rubbers.

(SONNY *gives* KENICKIE *a look as he drags* SANDY *offstage)*

DOODY: Hey, Danny . . . aren't you gonna fellow 'em?

DANNY: Why should I? She don't mean nothin' to me.

RIZZO *(To* DANNY)*: Sure, Zuko, every day now! Ya mean you ain't told 'em?

KENICKIE: Told us what?

RIZZO: Oh, nothin'. Right, Zuko?

KENICKIE: Come off it, Rizzo. Whattaya tryin' to do, make us think she's like you?

RIZZO: What's that crack supposed to mean? I ain't heard you complainin'.

KENICKIE: That's 'cause ya been sittin' on my face all night.

DANNY: Hey, cool it, huh?

RIZZO: Yeah, Kenickie, if you don't shut up it's gonna be your ass.

KENICKIE: Ohh, I'm really worried, scab!

RIZZO: Okay, you bastard! *(She pushes him off bench and they fight on ground)*

ROGER AND DOODY: Fight! Fight! Yaayy! *(Etc.)*

DANNY *(Separating them)*: Come on, cut it out! (RIZZO *and* KENICKIE *stop fighting and glare at each other)* Jesus, what a couple of fruitcakes!

RIZZO: Well, he started it.

KENICKIE: God, what a yo-yo! Make one little joke and she goes apeshit. *(He sulks over to garbage can)*

DOODY: Jeez, nice couple.

(There is an uncomfortable pause onstage as the KIDS *hear* VINCE FONTAINE *on radio)*

VINCE'S VOICE: . . . 'cause tomorrow night yours truly, the Main Brain, Vince Fontaine, will be M.C.ing the big dance bash out at Rydell High School—in the boys' gym, and along with me will be Mr. T.N.T. himself, Johnny Casino and the Gamblers. So, make it a point to stop by the joint, Rydell High, 7:30 tomorrow night.

RIZZO: Hey, Danny, you goin' to the dance tomorrow night?

DANNY: I don't think so.

RIZZO: Awww, you're all broke up over little Gidget!

DANNY: Who?

RIZZO: Ahh, c'mon, Zuko, why don'tcha take me to the dance—I can pull that Sandra Dee crap, too. Right, you guys?

*(*ROGER *and* DOODY *do* MGM *lion, and* RIZZO *sings, "Look at Me, I'm Sandra Dee")*

RIZZO:

Look at me, I'm Sandra Dee
Lousy with virginity.
Won't go to bed till I'm legally wed.
I can't, I'm Sandra Dee.

Watch it, hey, I'm Doris Day.
I was not brought up that way.
Won't come across, even Rock Hudson lost
His heart to Doris Day.

I don't drink or swear,
I don't rat my hair.
I get ill from one cigarette.
Keep your filthy paws off my silky drawers.
Would you pull that stuff with Annette?

*(*SANDY *enters, hearing the last part of the song.* SONNY *is behind her)*

As for you, Troy Donahue,
I know what you wanna do.
You got your crust, I'm no object of lust.
I'm just plain Sandra Dee.
No, no, no, Sal Mineo,
I would never stoop so low.
Please keep your cool, now you're starting to drool, fongool!
I'm Sandra Dee!

(SANDY *crosses to* RIZZO)

SONNY: Hey, Sandy, wait a minute . . . hey . . .

SANDY (*to* RIZZO): Listen, just who do you think you are? I saw you making fun of me. (SANDY *leaps on* RIZZO *and the two girls start fighting.* DANNY *pulls* SANDY *off*) Let go of me! You dirty liar! Don't touch me!

(SONNY *and* ROGER *hold* RIZZO)

RIZZO: Aaahh, let me go. I ain't gonna do nothin' to her. That chick's flipped her lid!

SANDY (*To* DANNY): You tell them right now . . . that all those things you've been saying about me were lies. Go on, tell 'em!

DANNY: Whattaya talkin' about? I never said anything about you.

SANDY: You creep! You think you're such a big man, don't ya? Trying to make me look like just another tramp. (RIZZO *charges at her. The* GUYS *hold* RIZZO *back*) I don't know *why* I ever liked you, Danny Zuko.

(SANDY *runs off in tears, stepping on* FRENCHY's *fan magazine.* DANNY *starts after her, gives up.* FRENCHY *sadly picks up torn Ricky Nelson picture*)

DANNY (*Turning to the others*): Weird chick! (*Pause*) Hey, Rizzo. You wanna go to the dance with me?

RIZZO: Huh? Yeah, sure. Why not?

ROGER: Hey, Jan. You got a date for the dance tomorrow night?

JAN: Tomorrow? Let me check. (*She takes out a little notebook and thumbs through it*) No, I don't. Why?

ROGER: You wanna go with me?

JAN: You kiddin' me? (*As* ROGER *shakes his head "no"*) Yeah, sure, Roge!

DOODY (*Moving to* FRENCHY): Hey, Frenchy, can you still go to the dance, now that you quit school?

FRENCHY: Yeah. I guess so. Why?

DOODY: Oh. Ahh, nothin' . . . I'll see ya there.

SONNY: Hey, Kenickie, how 'bout givin' me a ride tomorrow, and I'll pick us up a couple a broads at the dance.

KENICKIE: Nah, I got a blind date from 'cross town. I hear she's a real bombshell.

MARTY: Gee, I don't even know if I'll go. All those silly kids.

DANNY: Okay, you can be the chaperone.

DOODY (*Laughs*): Hey, Neat-o!

(DANNY *pinches* MARTY'S ASS. MARTY *starts to chase* DANNY. *All sing "We Go Together"*)

ALL:

We go together, like
Rama-lama-lama, ka-dinga da ding-dong,
Remembered forever, as
Shoo-bop sha-wadda-wadda
Yippity boom-de-boom
Chang chang changitty-chang shoo-bop.
That's the way it should be (Whaa-oohh! yeah!)

We're one of a kind, like
Dip-da-dip-da-dip
Doo-wop da-dooby-doo.
Our names are signed
Boogedy, boogedy, boogedy, boogedy
Shooby-doo-wop-she-bop
Chang chang-a changitty-chang shoo-bop.
We'll always be like one (Whaa-wha-wha-whaaaaaah)

When we go out at night
And stars are shining bright
Up in the skies above,
Or at the high school dance
Where you can find romance
Maybe it might be la-a-a-ah-ove

We're for each other, like
A-wop-baba-lu-mop and wop-bam-boom!
Just like my brother, is
Sha-na-na-na-na-na yippity-dip-de-doom

Chang chang-a changitty-chang shoo-bop
We'll always be together!

(At the end of the song, the lights fade on the KIDS *as they go off, laughing and horsing around, improvising various falsetto riffs)*

Act Two

SCENE 1

The GREASERS *run on and sing "Shakin' at the High School Hop." They are preparing for the high school dance—the BOYS combing hair, polishing shoes, etc., the GIRLS spraying hair, putting on crinolines, stuffing Kleenex into bras, etc.*

ALL:
   Well, honky-tonk baby, get on the floor.
   All the cats are shoutin', they're yellin' for more.
   My baby likes to rock, my baby likes to roll,
   My baby does the chicken and she does the stroll.
   Well, they shake it
   Ohh, shake it
   Yeah, shake it
   Everybody shakin'
   Shakin' at the high school hop.

DANNY:
   Well, sock-hop baby,

GIRLS:
   Roll up her crazy jeans.

GUYS:
   Gonna rock to the music,

ALL:
   Gonna dig the scene.

GIRLS:
   Shimmy to the left,

GUYS:
   Cha-cha to the right

ALL:

We gonna do the walk
Till broad daylight

(Repeat Chorus)

GIRLS:

Well, we're gonna Alley-oop
  On blueberry hill.

GUYS:

Hully gully with Lucille,
  Won't be standin' still.

GIRLS:

Hand-jive baby,

ALL:

Do the stomp with me.
I calypso, do the slop,
Gonna bop with Mr. Lee.

Well, they shake it
Ohh, shake it
Yeah, shake it
Everybody's shakin'
Shakin' at the high school hop.

(Instrumental chorus and dance while the GREASERS *move into the high school gym and are joined by* PATTY, EUGENE AND MISS LYNCH, *all dancing wildly)*

Shake, rock and roll
Rock, roll and shake
Shake, rock and roll
Rock, roll and shake
Shake, rock and roll
Long live rock and roll.

(Lights fade on dance and SANDY *is revealed in her bedroom. She turns up the volume on radio)*

ANNOUNCER: . . . continuing lovely dreamtime music on WLDL with a popular success from last summer: "It's Raining on Prom Night" . . .

(Song comes on radio. SANDY *sings lead vocal with the radio voice in harmony)*

RADIO VOICE:
> *I was deprived of a young girl's dream*
> *By the cruel force of nature from the blue.*

SANDY AND RADIO VOICE:
> *Instead of a night full of romance supreme*
> *All I got was a runny nose and Asiatic flu.*
>
> *It's raining on prom night,*
> *My hair is a mess.*
> *It's running all over*
> *My taffeta dress.*
> *It's wilting the quilting in my Maidenform*
> *And mascara flows right down my nose because of the storm.*
> *I don't even have my corsage, oh gee*
> *It fell down a sewer with my sister's I.D.*

*(*SANDY *talks verse while* RADIO VOICE *continues to sing)*

> *Yes, it's raining on prom night.*
> *Oh, my darling, what can I do? I miss you.*
> *It's raining rain from the skies*
> *It's raining real tears from my eyes*
> *Over you.*

> *Dear God, let him feel the same way I do right now. Make him want to see me again!* (SANDY *resumes singing the lead)*

> *Oh, what can I do?*
> *It's raining rain from the skies,*
> *It's raining tears from my eyes*
> *Over you-ooo-ooo-ooo—rain-ing.*

(After song, instrumental version of "Shakin' at the High School Hop" continues. Lights fade out on SANDY, *come up on*

the high school dance. The couples are DANNY *and* RIZZO, JAN *and* ROGER, FRENCHY *and* DOODY, PATTY *and* EUGENE. MISS LYNCH *is overseeing the punchbowl.* MARTY *is alone and* SONNY *is drinking from a half-pint in the corner. At the end of "Shakin'," the* KIDS *cheer and yell.* JOHNNY CASINO, *with guitar on bandstand, introduces* VINCE FONTAINE, *announcer for radio station* WAXX)

JOHNNY CASINO: Hang loose, everybody. Here he is, the Main Brain—Vince Fontaine.

VINCE (*Dashes on and grabs mike*): I've had a lot of requests for a slow one. How 'bout it, Johnny Casino?

JOHNNY CASINO (*Grabbing mike*): Okay, Vince, here's a little number I wrote called "Enchanted Guitar."

VINCE (*Grabbing mike back*): And don't forget, only ten more minutes till the big Hand-Jive Contest. (*Cheers and excited murmurs from the* CROWD) So, if you've got a steady, get her ready.

(JOHNNY CASINO *and the* BAND *do slow two-step instrumental as* VINCE *leaves bandstand and mills among* KIDS)

RIZZO: Hey, Danny, you gonna be my partner for the dance contest?

DANNY: Maybe, if nothing better comes along.

RIZZO: Drop dead!

JAN (*Stumbling on* ROGER's *feet*): Sorry.

ROGER: Why don'tcha let *me* lead, for a change?

JAN: I can't help it. I'm used to leading.

FRENCHY (*Dancing with* DOODY, *who is rocking back and forth in one spot*): Hey, Doody, can't you at least turn me around or somethin'?

DOODY: Don't talk, I'm tryin' to count.

(PATTY *dances near* DANNY *with* EUGENE, *who is pumping her arm vigorously*)

PATTY: Danny, Danny!

DANNY: Yeah, that's my name, don't wear it out.

PATTY: How did the track tryouts go?

DANNY (*Nonchalantly*): I made the team.

PATTY: Oh, wonderful! (*She starts signaling in pantomime for* DANNY *to cut in*)

RIZZO: Hey, Zuko, I think she's tryin' to tell ya somethin'! (PATTY's *pantomime becomes more desperate as* EUGENE *pumps harder*) Go on, dance with her. You ain't doin' me no good.

DANNY *(Going up to* EUGENE): Hey, Euuu-gene, Betty Rizzo thinks you look like Pat Boone.

EUGENE: Oh? *(He walks over and stands near* RIZZO, *staring. He polishes his white bucks on the back of his pants legs)*

(DANNY dances with PATTY)

RIZZO: Whataya say, fruit-boots?

EUGENE: I understand you were asking about me?

RIZZO: Yeah! I was wondering where you parked your hearse.

(EUGENE sits next to RIZZO as RIZZO offers him SONNY's half-pint. SONNY grabs it back. PATTY and DANNY are in a close dance clinch, not moving)

PATTY: I never knew you were such a fabulous dancer, Danny. So sensuous and feline.

DANNY: Huh? Yeah?

(Music tempo changes to cha-cha. KENICKIE and CHA-CHA DI GREGORIO enter)

CHA-CHA: God, nice time to get here. Look, the joint's half-empty already.

KENICKIE: Ahh, knock it off! Can I help it if my car wouldn't start?

CHA-CHA: Jeez, what crummy decorations!

KENICKIE: Where'd ya think you were goin', American Bandstand?

CHA-CHA: We had a sock hop at St. Bernadette's once. The Sisters got real pumpkins and everything.

KENICKIE: Neat. They probably didn't have a bingo game that night. *(He walks away and CHA-CHA trails behind him)*

VINCE *(Coming up to MARTY)*: Pardon, me, weren't you a contestant in the Miss Rock 'n' Roll Universe Pageant?

MARTY: Yeah, but I got disqualified 'cause I had a hickey on my neck.

(The song ends and KIDS cheer. JOHNNY CASINO looks for VINCE FONTAINE on the dance floor)

JOHNNY CASINO: Hey, Vince . . . any more requests?

VINCE *(Irritated, still looking at MARTY. Motions JOHNNY away with his hand)*: Yeah, play anything!

JOHNNY CASINO: Okay, here's a little tune called "Anything."

(Band plays instrumental stroll. MARTY, JAN and FRENCHY, VINCE, ROGER AND DOODY form facing lines as DANNY and PATTY come through center)

PATTY: I can't imagine you ever having danced with Sandy like this.

DANNY: Whattaya mean?

PATTY: I mean her being so clumsy and all. She can't even twirl a baton right. In fact, I've been thinking of having a little talk with the coach about her.

DANNY: Why? Whatta you care?

PATTY: Well, I mean . . . even you have to admit she's a bit of a drip. I mean . . . isn't that why you broke up with her?

DANNY: Hey, listen . . . y'know she used to be a halfway decent chick before she got mixed up with you and your brown-nose friends.

(DANNY *walks away from her.* PATTY, *stunned, runs to punch table.* KENICKIE *walks up to* RIZZO)

RIZZO: Hey, Kenickie, where ya been, the submarine races?

KENICKIE: Nah. I had to go to Egypt to pick up a date.

RIZZO: You feel like dancin'?

KENICKIE: Crazy. (*He starts to dance off with* RIZZO)

EUGENE: It's been very nice talking to you, Betty.

RIZZO: Yeah, see ya around the bookmobile.

(CHA-CHA *moves to* EUGENE, *hoping* EUGENE *might ask her to dance, as band continues.* SONNY *gets up and crosses dance floor*)

DOODY (*Dropping out of the stroll line*): Hey, Rump, let's go have a weed.

ROGER: Yeah, okay.

JAN: Oh, Roger, would ya get me some punch?

ROGER: Whatsa matter? You crippled?

(JAN *sticks her tongue out at* ROGER *as he and* DOODY *start off. They bump into* SONNY. *The band plays a cha-cha*)

VINCE (*To* MARTY): I'm Vince Fontaine. Do your folks know I come into your room every night? Over WAXX, that is! I'm gonna judge the dance contest. Are you gonna be in it?

MARTY: I guess not. I ain't got a date.

VINCE: What? A knockout like you? Things sure have changed since I went to school . . . last year. Ha-Ha!

(MARTY *stares at him dumbly for a few seconds, then starts laughing.* DOODY, SONNY, ROGER *and* DANNY *are drinking and smoking in corner.* CHA-CHA *is dancing around* EUGENE *at bench*)

DOODY (*Pointing to* CHA-CHA): Hey, ain't that the chick Kenickie walked in with?

SONNY: Where?

DOODY: The one pickin' her nose over there.

SONNY: That's the baby.

ROGER: Jesus, is she a gorilla!

SONNY: I thought she was one of the steam-table ladies.

(*The* GUYS *crack up*)

CHA-CHA (*To* EUGENE): Hey, did you come here to dance or didn't ya?

EUGENE: Of course, but I never learned how to do this dance.

CHA-CHA: Ahh, there's nothing to it. I'm gonna teach ballroom at the CYO. (*She grabs* EUGENE *in dance position*) Now, one-two-cha-cha-cha! Three-four-cha-cha-cha ... very-good-cha-cha-cha ... keep-it-up-cha-cha-cha ...

EUGENE: You certainly dance well.

CHA-CHA: Thanks, ya can hold me a little tighter. I won't bite cha. (*She grabs* EUGENE *in a bear hug*)

(*Music ends, and* KIDS *applaud*)

JOHNNY CASINO: Thank you. This is Johnny Casino telling you when you hear the tone it will be exactly one minute to Hand-Jive Time!

(*Excited murmurs and scrambling for partners takes place on the dance floor as the band's guitarist makes a "twang" sound on his E string*)

EUGENE (*To* CHA-CHA): Excuse me, it was nice meeting you.

CHA-CHA: Hey, wait a minute ... don'tcha want my phone number or somethin'?

EUGENE (*To* PATTY): Patty, you promised to be my partner for the dance contest, remember?

PATTY: That's right. I almost forgot. (*She looks longingly toward* DANNY *as* EUGENE *pulls her away*)

DANNY (*Walking over to* RIZZO *and* KENICKIE): Hey, Rizzo. I'm ready to dance with you now.

RIZZO: Don't strain yourself ... I'm dancin' with Kenickie.

KENICKIE: That's all right, Zuko, you can dance with my date. (*He yells*) Hey, Charlene! C'mere.

CHA-CHA (*Walking over to* KENICKIE): Yeah, whattaya want?

KENICKIE: How'dja like to dance this one with Danny Zuko?

CHA-CHA: The big rod of the Burger Palace Boys? I didn't even know he saw me here.

DANNY (*Giving* CHA-CHA *a dismayed look*): I didn't.

(CHA-CHA *looks around in ecstasy*)

JOHNNY: Okay, alligators, here it is. The big one ... (*Drum roll*) The Hand-Jive Dance Contest. (*The* KIDS *cheer*) Let's get things under way by bringing up our own Miss Lynch.

(*The* KIDS *react.* GUITAR PLAYER *in band plays a few chords of* "Rydell Fight Song" *as* MISS LYNCH *comes up to the mike*)

MISS LYNCH (*To* JOHNNY CASINO): Thank you, Clarence. (*All the* KIDS *break up.* JOHNNY CASINO *mouths, "Fuck you, man" and gives* KIDS *"the finger"*) Whenever you're finished. (*Noise subsides a little*) Before we begin, I'd like to welcome you all to "Moonlight in the Tropics." And I think we all owe a big round of applause to Patty Simcox and her committee for the wonderful decorations.

(*Mixed reaction from* CROWD)

CHA-CHA: They shoulda got real coconuts!

MISS LYNCH: Now, I'm sure you'll be glad to know that I'm not judging this dance contest. (*A few* KIDS *cheer*) All right. All right. I'd like to present Mr. Vince Fontaine. (KIDS *cheer, as she looks around*) Mr. Fontaine?

VINCE (*Still with* MARTY, *yells*): Comin' right up! (*Aside to* MARTY *as he starts for the bandstand*) Stick around, cupcake. I'll be right back.

MISS LYNCH: As most of you know, Mr. Fontaine is an announcer for radio station WAXX. (VINCE, *on the bandstand, whispers in her ear*) Uh ... (*Uncomfortably*) "Dig the scene on Big Fifteen." (*Cheer goes up*) Now for the rules! One: All couples must be boy-girl. Two: Anyone using tasteless or vulgar movements will be disqualified. Three: If Mr. Fontaine taps you on the shoulder, you must clear the dance floor immediately ...

VINCE (*Grabbing the mike from* MISS LYNCH): I just wanna say, truly in all sincerity, Miss Lynch, that you're doing a really, really terrific job here, terrific. And I'll sure bet these kids are lucky to have you for a teacher, 'cause I'll bet in all sincerity that you're really terrific. *Is she terrific, kids?* (*The* KIDS *cheer*) Only thing I wanna say, in all sincerity, is enjoy yourselves, have a ball, 'cause like we always say at Big Fifteen where the jocks hang out—"If you're having fun, you're number one!" And some lucky guy and gal is gonna go boppin' home with a stack of terrific prizes. But don't feel bad if I bump yez out, 'cause it don't matter if you win or lose, it's what ya do with those dancing shoes. So, okay, cats, throw your mittens around your kittens ... and *away we go!* (VINCE *does Jackie Gleason pose*)

(JOHNNY CASINO *sings "Born to Hand-Jive." During the dance,* COUPLES *are eliminated one by one as* VINCE FONTAINE *mills through the crowd, tapping each* COUPLE *and occasionally letting one of his hands slither down to rub one of the girls across the ass, or nonchalantly trying to "cop a feel."*

JOHNNY CASINO:

> *Before I was born, late one night,*
> *My papa said, "Everything's all right."*
> *The doctor laughed, when ma laid down*
> *With her stomach bouncin' all around*
> *'Cause a be-bop stork was 'bout to arrive*
> *And mama gave birth to the hand-jive!*
>
> *I could barely walk when I milked a cow*
> *And when I was three I pushed a plow.*
> *While choppin' wood I'd move my legs*
> *And started dancin' while I gathered eggs.*
> *The townfolk clapped, I was only five,*
> *He'll outdance 'em all, he's a born hand-jive!*

(*Short guitar solo. Dance chorus*)

> *Born to hand-jive, babeeeeeee!!*
> *Born to hand-jive, baby!!*

(*Dance chorus*)

> *So I grew up dancin' on the stage,*
> *Doin' the hand-jive became the rage.*
> *But a jealous stud pulled a gun*
> *And said "Let's see how fast you run."*
> *Yeah, natural rhythm kept me alive*
> *Out-dodgin' bullets with the ol' hand-jive!*
> *Now, can you hand-jive, babeeeeeee??*
> *Oh, can you hand-jive, baby?*
> *Oh, yeah, oh, yeah, oh, yeah. Born to hand-jive!*

(*Eventually, all the* COUPLES *are eliminated except* DANNY *and* CHA-CHA. *On the final chorus, the* KIDS *stand around in a circle and clap in time.* VINCE FONTAINE *pulls* MISS LYNCH *onto the dance floor and tries to hog the spotlight from* DANNY *and* CHA-CHA. *At the end of the dance,* MISS LYNCH, *out of breath, returns to the bandstand,* VINCE FONTAINE *right behind her*)

MISS LYNCH: My goodness! Well, we have our winners. Will you step up here for your prizes? Daniel Zuko and ... and ...

(DANNY *and* CHA-CHA, *swamped by the other* KIDS, *battle their way to the bandstand*)

CHA-CHA: Cha-Cha Di Gregorio.

MISS LYNCH: *(Taken aback at having to repeat the first name)* Uh . . . Cha-Cha Di Gregorio.

CHA-CHA *(Grabbing mike)*: They call me Cha-Cha 'cause I'm the best dancer at St. Bernadette's.

(Mixed reaction and ad libs from CROWD*)*

MISS LYNCH: Oh . . . that's very nice. Congratulations to both of you, and here are your prizes: Two record albums, "Hits from the House of WAXX," autographed by Mr. Vince Fontaine. *(She holds up album with large letters WAXX.* KIDS *cheer)* Two free passes to the Twi-Light Drive-In Theater . . . good on any week night. *(*KIDS *cheer)* A coupon worth ten dollars off at Robert Hall. *(*KIDS *boo)* And last but not least, your trophies, prepared by Mrs. Schneider's art class. *(Cheers and applause.* MISS LYNCH *presents* DANNY *and* CHA-CHA *with two hideous ceramic nebbishes in dance positions, mounted on blocks of wood)*

VINCE *(Grabbing the mike from* MISS LYNCH*)*: Weren't they terrific? C'mon let's hear it for these kids! *(*KIDS *cheer)* Only thing I wanna say before we wrap things up is that you kids at Rydell are the greatest!

KENICKIE: Fuckin' A!

VINCE: Last dance, ladies' choice.

(Band plays slow instrumental. DANNY *takes record album from* CHA-CHA, *giving her his trophy in exchange and exits.* COUPLES *leave dance, one by one, until* CHA-CHA *is left alone.* PATTY, EUGENE *and* MISS LYNCH *clean up after dance. Each exits as the lights change to new scene)*

SCENE 2

It is evening a few days later in front of the Burger Palace. FRENCHY *is pacing around, magazine in hand, looking at sign on Burger Palace window: "Counter Girl Wanted." After a few moments* SONNY, KENICKIE *and* DOODY *enter with weapons:* DOODY *with a baseball bat,* SONNY *with a zip gun,* KENICKIE *with a lead pipe and chain. They wear leather jackets and engineer boots.*

KENICKIE: Hey, Sonny, what Cracker Jack box ja' get that zip gun out of, anyway?

SONNY: What do ya mean, I made it in shop. *(Seeing* FRENCHY*)* Hey, what's shakin', French? You get out of beauty school already?

FRENCHY: Oh . . . I cut tonight. Those beauty teachers they got working there don't know nothin'. Hey, what's with the arsenal?

DOODY: We gotta rumble with the Flaming Dukes.

FRENCHY: No lie! How come?

KENICKIE: Remember that scurvy broad I took to the dance? (FRENCHY *looks blank*)

DOODY (*Helpfully*): Godzilla!

DOODY AND KENICKIE (*They do imitation of* CHA-CHA *and* EUGENE *dancing*): "One-two-cha-cha-cha!"

FRENCHY: Oh! Y'mean Cha-Cha Dee Garage-io . . . the one Danny won the dance contest with?

SONNY: Well, it turns out she goes steady with the leader of the Flaming Dukes. And she told this guy Danny got in her silks.

KENICKIE: If he did, he musta been makin' a bug collection for Biology.

(*All* GUYS *laugh.* KENICKIE *joins in, laughing at his own joke.* DANNY *enters jogging, wearing a white track suit with a brown and green number four on his back. The trunks are white with a thin green and brown stripe running vertically on each side. He has a relay-race baton*)

FRENCHY (*Seeing* DANNY): Hey look . . . ain't that Danny?

DOODY: Hey, Danny!

FRENCHY: What's he doing in his underwear?

DOODY: That's a track suit! Hiya, Danny.

(DANNY *stops. He's panting.* GUYS *gather around him*)

KENICKIE: Jesus, Zuko, where do you keep your Wheaties?

DANNY (*Reaching in front of jock strap and pulling out a crumpled pack of Luckies*): Ha-ha. Big joke. (*He lights a cigarette*)

SONNY: Hey, it's a good thing you're here. We're supposed to rumble the Dukes tonight!

DANNY (*Alarmed*): What time?

KENICKIE: Nine o'clock.

DANNY (*Annoyed*): Nice play! I got field training till nine-thirty.

KENICKIE: Can't ya sneak away, man?

DANNY: Not a chance! The coach'd kick my ass.

SONNY: The coach!

DANNY: Besides, what am I supposed to do, stomp on somebody's face with my gym shoes? (*He puts cigarettes back in jock*)

KENICKIE: Ahh, c'mon, Zuko, whattaya tryin' to prove with this track-team crap!?

DANNY: Why? Whatta you care? Look, I gotta cut. I'm in the middle of a race right now. See ya later.

SONNY: You got the hots for that cheerleader or somethin'?

DANNY: How'd you like a fat lip, Sonny? Nine o'clock, huh? I'll be back if I can get away. Later! *(Silence.* DANNY *stands glaring at the* GUYS *for a moment and then he runs off, cigarette in his mouth)*

SONNY: Neat guy, causes a ruckus and then he cuts out on us!

KENICKIE: Jeez, next thing ya know he'll be gettin' a crew cut!

DOODY: He'd look neater with a flat top.

KENICKIE: C'mon, let's go eat. *(He and* SONNY *start toward Burger Palace)*

SONNY: Hey, Kenicks, you wanna split a superburger?

KENICKIE: Yeah. All right.

SONNY: Good. Lend me a half a buck.

*(*SONNY AND KENICKIE *exit into Burger Palace, stashing their weapons in a painted oil drum used for garbage)*

DOODY: Hey, Frenchy, maybe I'll come down to your beauty school some night this week ... we can have a Coke or somethin'.

FRENCHY *(Uncertain)*: Yeah ... yeah, sure.

*(*DOODY *smiles and, depositing his baseball bat in the same oil drum, exits into the Burger Palace)*

FRENCHY *(To her movie magazine)*: Jeez! What am I gonna do? I mean, I can't just tell everybody I dropped out of beauty school. I can't go in the Palace for a job ... with all the guys sittin' around. Boy, I wish I had one of those Guardian Angel things like in that Debbie Reynolds movie. Would that be neat ... somebody always there to tell ya what's the best thing to do.

(Spooky angelic guitar chords. FRENCHY's *Guardian* TEEN ANGEL *appears. He is a Fabian-like rock singer. White Fabian sweater with the collar turned up, white chinos, white boots, a large white comb sticking out of his pocket. He sings "Beauty School Dropout." After the first verse, a chorus of* ANGELS *appears: a group of* GIRLS *in white plastic sheets with their hair in white plastic rollers, arranged in a halo effect. They provide background doo-wahs)*

TEEN ANGEL:

> *Your story's sad to tell:*
> *A teenage ne'er-do-well,*

Most mixed-up nondelinquent on the block,
Your future's so unclear now.
What's left of your career now?
Can't even get a trade-in on your smock.

(ANGEL CHORUS *enters*)

Beauty school dropout,
No graduation day for you.
Beauty school dropout,
Missed your midterms and flunked shampoo.
Well, at least you could have taken time
To wash and clean your clothes up
After spending all that dough to have
The doctor fix your nose up.
Baby, get movin',
Why keep your feeble hopes alive?
What are you provin'?
You got the dream but not the drive.
If you go for your diploma you could join a steno pool
Turn in your teasing comb and go back to high school.

Beauty school dropout,
Hangin' around the corner store.
Beauty school dropout,
It's about time you knew the score.
Well, they couldn't teach you anything,
You think you're such a looker,
But no customer would go to you
Unless she was a hooker.
Baby, don't sweat it,
You're not cut out to hold a job.
Better forget it,
Who wants their hair done by a slob?
Now your bangs are curled, your lashes twirled,
But still the world is cruel.
Wipe off that angel face and go back to high school.

(*At the end of the stanza the* TEEN ANGEL *hands* FRENCHY *a high school diploma, which she uncurls, looks at, crumples up and throws away. The* TEEN ANGEL *and* CHOIR *look on.* FRENCHY *walks away*)

Baby, ya blew it.
You put our good advice to shame.
How could you do it?
Betcha Dear Abby'd say the same.
Guess there's no way to get through to you,
No matter who may try.
Might as well go back to that malt shop in the sky.

(*The* TEEN ANGEL *and* CHOIR *exit.* DOODY, KENICKIE *and* SONNY *come out of Burger Palace as the place is closing. The* GUYS *retrieve their weapons from the trash can*)

SONNY: Looks like they ain't gonna show. They said they'd be here at nine.

DOODY: What time is it?

SONNY (*Looking at his watch*): Hey man, it's almost five after. C'mon, let's haul ass.

KENICKIE: Give 'em another ten minutes. Hey, what the hell happened to Rump?

SONNY: Who cares about lard-ass. Who'da ever thought Zuko'd punk out on us.

KENICKIE: Nice rumble! A herd of Flaming Dukes against you, me and Howdy Doody.

DOODY: Hey, I heard about this one time when the Dukes pulled a sneak attack by drivin' up in a stolen laundry truck. That really musta been cool.

SONNY (*Suddenly*): Hey, you guys, watch out for a fuckin' laundry truck.

(SONNY *and* KENICKIE *tense up, looking around.* DOODY *stares blankly.* ROGER *comes charging on in a frenzy with a car antenna in his hand*)

ROGER (*Shouting*): Okay, where the fuck are they? (*Looking around*) Hey, where's Zuko?

SONNY: Well, look who's here. Where you been, chub-nuts?

ROGER: Hey, bite the weenie, moron. My old man made me help him paint the goddamned basement. I couldn't even find my bullwhip. I had to bust off an aerial.

SONNY: Ha, whattaya expect to do with that thing?

KENICKIE (*Grabbing* ROGER'S *antenna and imitating a newscaster*): This is Dennis James bringing you the play-by-play of Championship Gangfighting!

ROGER (*Grabbing antenna back*): Hey, listen, I'll take this over any of *those* Tinker Toys!

KENICKIE: Oh, yeah? Okay, Rump, how 'bout if I hit ya over the head with that thing and then I hit ya over the head with my lead pipe and ya can tell me which one hurts more—okay?

ROGER: Okay. C'mon and get it! C'mon, Kenickie! (*He holds out the antenna. As* KENICKIE *reaches for it he lashes the air above* KENICKIE*'s head and almost hits* SONNY *behind him*)

SONNY: Hey, watch it with that thing, pimple-puss!

ROGER: Hey, whatsamatter, LaTierri, afraid ya might get hurt a little?

SONNY: Listen, chickenshit, you're gonna look real funny cruisin' around the neighborhood in a wheelchair.

ROGER: Well, why don'tcha use that thing, then? You got enough rubber bands there to start three paper routes.

KENICKIE (*Grabbing* DOODY*'s baseball bat*): Hey, Rump! C'mon, let's see ya try that again.

ROGER: What'sa matter, Kenicks? What happened to your big bad pipe?

(SONNY, DOODY, KENICKIE AND ROGER *begin circling.* KENICKIE *knocks antenna out of* ROGER*'s hand with bat.* KENICKIE *and* SONNY *close in on* ROGER, *now defenseless*)

KENICKIE: Okay, Rump, how's about mooning the Flaming Dukes? Pants 'em!

(SONNY *and* KENICKIE *leap on* ROGER *and get his pants off.* DOODY *helps with the shoes.* SONNY *and* KENICKIE *run off with* ROGER*'s pants as* DOODY *gathers up weapons*)

DOODY: Hey, you guys, wait up! (*He starts to run off, goes back to hand* ROGER *his antenna, then exits*)

ROGER: Oh, shit! (*He stands a moment, bewildered, holding antenna, then exits, disgusted*)

SCENE 3

Lights come up on Greased Lightning at the Twi-Light Drive-In Theater. SANDY *and* DANNY *are sitting alone at opposite ends of the front seat staring straight ahead in awkward silence. Movie music is coming out of a portable speaker.* DANNY *is sipping a quart of beer. Dialogue from the movie begins to come out of the speaker.*

GIRL'S VOICE: It was . . . like an animal . . . with awful clawing hands and . . . and . . . hideous fangs. Oh, it was like a nightmare!

HERO'S VOICE: There, there, you're safe now, Sheila.

SCIENTIST's VOICE: Poor Todd. The radiation has caused him to mutate. He's become half-man, half-monster ... like a werewolf.

SHEILA's VOICE: But, doctor ... he ... he's my *brother*. And his big stock-car race is tomorrow!

(A werewolf cry is heard)

HERO's VOICE: Great Scott! It's a full moon!

(Silence. DANNY stretches, puts arm across SANDY's shoulder. He tries to get arm around her. She moves away)

DANNY: Why don'tcha move over a little closer? *(Removes his arm from the back of the seat)*

SANDY: This is all right.

DANNY: Well, can't ya at least smile or somethin'? Look, Sandy, I practically had to bust Kenickie's arm to get his car for tonight. The guys are really p.o.'d at me. I mean, I thought we were gonna forget all about that scene in the park with Sonny and Rizzo and everything. I told ya on the phone I was sorry.

SANDY: I know you did.

DANNY: Well, you believe me, don't ya?

SANDY: I guess so. It's just that everything was so much easier when there was just the two of us.

DANNY: Yeah, I know ... but ... *(Suddenly)* Hey, you ain't goin' with another guy, are ya?

SANDY: No. Why?

DANNY *(Trying to take off his high school ring)*: Err ... oh, ah ... nothin'. Well, yeah ... uh ... ahhh, shit! I was gonna ask ya to take my ring. *(He finally holds out the ring)*

SANDY: Oh, Danny. I don't know what to say.

DANNY: Well, don'tcha want it?

SANDY *(Smiles shyly)*: Uh-huh.

(DANNY puts ring on SANDY's finger. She kisses him lightly)

DANNY: I shoulda gave it to ya a long time ago. *(They kiss)* I really like you, Sandy.

(They kiss again, DANNY getting more aggressive and passionate as the kiss goes on)

SANDY: Danny, take it easy! What are you trying to do? *(She squirms away from him)*

DANNY: Whatsa' matter?

SANDY: Well, I mean ... I thought we were just gonna—you know—be steadies.

DANNY: Well, whattaya' think goin' steady is, anyway? *(He grabs her again)* C'mon, Sandy!

SANDY: Stop it! I've never seen you like this.

DANNY: Relax, willya, nobody's watchin us!

SANDY: Danny, please, you're hurting me.

(DANNY lets go and SANDY breaks away)

DANNY: Whattaya' gettin' so shook up about? I thought I meant somethin' to ya.

SANDY: You do. But I'm still the same girl I was last summer. Just because you give me your ring doesn't mean we're gonna go all the way. *(She opens the car door and gets out)*

DANNY: Hey, Sandy, wait a minute.

(SANDY slams car door on DANNY's hand. He howls in pain)

SANDY: I'm sorry, Danny. Maybe we better just forget about it. *(She gives DANNY his ring back. When he refuses, she leaves it on the car hood and exits)*

DANNY: Hey, Sandy, where you goin'? You can't just walk out of a drive-in!

(Movie voices are heard again)

HERO'S VOICE: Look, Sheila! The full moon is sinking behind "Dead Man's Curve."

(DANNY gets out of car to get the ring)

SHEILA'S VOICE: Yes, Lance . . . and with it . . . all our dreams.

*(Werewolf howl. DANNY sings "Alone at a Drive-In Movie,"
with werewolf howls coming from movie and the BURGER PALACE
BOYS singing background "doo-wops" in DANNY's mind)*

DANNY:

*I'm all alone
At the drive-in movie.
It's a feelin' that ain't too groovy,
Watchin' werewolves without you.*

(Offstage wolf howl)

*Gee, it's no fun
Drinkin' beer in the back seat.
All alone just ain't too neat
At the passion pit, wanting you.*

*And when the intermission elf
Moves the clock's hands
While he's eating everything
Sold at the stand.*

(DANNY *gets into car*)

When there's one minute to go
Till the lights go down low,
I'll be holding the speaker knobs
Missing you so.

I can't believe it,
Unsteamed windows I can see through.
Might as well be in an igloo
'Cause the heater doesn't work . . .
As good as you.

(Lights fade on DANNY *as he drives off in car*)

SCENE 4

A party in JAN's *basement*. ROGER and DOODY *are sitting on barstools singing* "Rock 'n' Roll Party Queen" *accompanied by* DOODY's *guitar*. KENICKIE and RIZZO *are dancing*. SONNY and MARTY *are on couch tapping feet and drinking beer*. FRENCHY *is sitting on floor next to record player keeping time to the music*. JAN *is swaying to the music*. SANDY *sits alone on stairs trying to fit in and enjoy herself*. DANNY *is not present*.

DOODY AND ROGER:
Little girl—y'know who I mean—
Pretty soon she'll be seventeen.
They tell me her name's Betty Jean,
The-ha-ha rock 'n' roll party queen.

Friday night and she's got a date.
Goin' places—just a-stayin' out late,
Droppin' dimes in the record machine.
Ah-ho-ho, rock 'n' roll party queen.

Pa-pa-pa-pa-pa oh no,
Can I have the car tonight?
Bay-ba, bay-bee, can I be the one
To love you with all my might (I-yi-yi-yi-)

She's the girl that all the kids know,
Talk about her wherever she goes.

I could write a fan magazine
About that rock 'n' roll party queen.

Bomp-ba bomp-ba-bomp, you should see her
Shake to the latest dance.
Bay-ba bay-bee, no, don't call it puppy love,
Don'tcha wanna true romance? (I-yi-yi-yi)

Oh rockin' and-a rollin' little party queen.
We gonna do the stroll, hey, party queen.
Know I love you so, my party queen,
You're my rockin' and my rollin'
Party quee-een!

SANDY: Don't put too many records on, Frenchy. I'm going to leave in a couple of minutes.

KENICKIE: Aahh, come on! You ain't takin' your record player already! The party's just gettin' started.

RIZZO (*Moving to* SANDY *at steps*): Yeah, she's cuttin' out 'cause Zuko ain't here.

SANDY: No, I'm not! I didn't come here to see him.

RIZZO: No? What'dja come for, then?

SANDY: Uh . . . because I was invited.

RIZZO: We only invited ya 'cause we needed a record player.

JAN (*Trying to avoid trouble, motions* FRENCHY *to come out to the kitchen*): Hey, French!

FRENCHY (*Putting her hand on* SANDY's *arm*): Don't mind her, Sandy. C'mon, let's go help Jan fix the food.

(*The* GUYS *all gather together at the couch looking at a Viewmaster*)

MARTY (*Moving to* RIZZO, *who is sitting alone on steps*): Jesus, you're really a barrel of laughs tonight, Rizzo. You havin' your friend?

RIZZO: Huh?

MARTY: Your friend. Your period.

RIZZO: Don't I wish! I'm about five days late.

MARTY: You think maybe you're p.g.?

RIZZO: I don't know—big deal.

MARTY: How'd you let a thing like that happen anyway?

RIZZO: It wasn't my fault. The guy was usin' a thing, but it broke.

MARTY: Holy cow!

RIZZO: Yeah. He got it in a machine at a gas station. Y'know, one of those four-for-a-quarter jobs.

MARTY: Jeez, what a cheapskate! (KENICKIE *walks past them to get a can of beer*) Hey, it's not Kenickie, is it?

RIZZO: Nah! You don't know the guy.

MARTY: Aahh, they're all the same! Ya remember that disc jockey I met at the dance? I caught him puttin' aspirin in my Coke.

RIZZO: Hey, promise you won't tell anybody, huh?

MARTY: Sure, I won't say nothin'.

RIZZO (*Moves to* GUYS *at couch*): Hey, what happened to the music? Why don't you guys sing another song?

ROGER: Okay. Hey, Dude, let's do that new one by the Tinkletones?

(JAN, FRENCHY *and* SANDY *enter to hear song*)

DOODY AND ROGER:
Each night I cry myself to sleep,
The girl I love is gone for keeps.
Ooo-wa ooo-ooo-wa . . .

(*During the song,* MARTY *whispers to* KENICKIE, *who angrily goes over to* RIZZO)

KENICKIE: Hey, Rizzo, I hear you're knocked up.

(*Song stops*)

RIZZO (*Glaring at* MARTY): You do, huh? Boy, good news really travels fast!

KENICKIE: Hey, listen, why didn't you tell me?

RIZZO: Don't worry about it, Kenickie. You don't even know who the guy is.

KENICKIE: Huh? Thanks a lot, kid.

(*He walks away, hurt, leaves the party. The* GROUP *urges him to stay.* RIZZO, *upset, sits looking after him*)

SONNY (*Coming over to* RIZZO): Hey, Rizz, how's tricks? Look, if you ever need somebody to talk to . . .

RIZZO: You think you can get a little without usin' a safety, right? Get lost, Sonny.

DOODY: Tough luck, Rizzo.

ROGER: Listen, Rizz, I'll help you out with some money if you need it.

RIZZO: Forget it, I don't want any handouts.

FRENCHY: It ain't so bad, Rizz—you get to stay home from school.

JAN: Hey, you want to stay over tonight, Rizz?

RIZZO: Hey, why don't you guys just flake off and leave me alone?

(There is an awkward silence)

JAN: It's getting late, anyway—I guess it might be better if everybody went home. C'mon, let's go!

(JAN gives SONNY a push. DOODY and FRENCHY exit)

MARTY: Hey, French . . . wait up!

(MARTY gets her purse, which is near RIZZO; she avoids eye contact. RIZZO glares viciously at her)

ROGER: See ya. Rizz. *(Looks at RIZZO a moment and exits)*

SONNY *(To JAN)*: Tell her I didn't mean anything, will ya? *(Exits)*

(RIZZO begins to clean up)

JAN: Just leave that stuff, Rizzo. I'll get it.

RIZZO: Look, it's no bother. I don't mind.

(JAN exits)

SANDY *(Collecting her record player and purse)*: I'm sorry to hear you're in trouble, Rizzo.

RIZZO: Bullshit! What are you gonna do—give me a whole sermon about it?

SANDY: No. But doesn't it bother you that you're pregnant?

RIZZO: Look, that's my business. It's nobody else's problem.

SANDY: Do you really believe that? Didn't you see Kenickie's face when he left here?(RIZZO *turns away*) It's Kenickie, isn't it? *(Awkward pause)* Well, I guess I've said too much already. Good luck, Rizzo. *(She starts to leave)*

RIZZO *(Turns and glares at her)*: Just a minute, Miss Tight-Ass! Who do you think you are? Handing me all this sympathy crap! Since you know all the answers, how come I didn't see Zuko here tonight? You just listen to me, Miss Sandra Dee. *(Sings "There Are Worse Things I Could Do")*

There are worse things I could do
Than go with a boy or two,
Even though the neighborhood
Thinks I'm trashy and no good.
I suppose it could be true
But there's worse things I could do.

I could flirt with all the guys,
Smile at them and bat my eyes,

Press against them when we dance
Make them think they stand a chance,
Then refuse to see it through.
That's a thing I'd never do.

I could stay home every night,
Wait around for Mister Right,
Take cold showers every day,
And throw my life away
For a dream that won't come true.

I could hurt someone like me
Out of spite or jealousy.
I don't steal and I don't lie,
But I can feel and I can cry,
A fact I'll bet you never knew,
But to cry in front of—
That's the worst thing I could do.

(Lights fade out on RIZZO *as* SANDY *exits in tears carrying her record player. She goes into her bedroom and sits down on her bed, dejectedly. She sings a reprise of "Look at Me, I'm Sandra Dee.")*

SANDY:
Look at me, there has to be
Something more than what they see.
Wholesome and pure, also scared and unsure,
A poor man's Sandra Dee.
When they criticize and make fun of me,
Can't they see the tears in my smile?
Don't they realize there's just one of me
And it has to last me a while?

(She picks up the phone and dials) Hello, Frenchy? Can you come over for a while? And bring your makeup case. *(She hangs up)*

Sandy, you must start anew.
Don't you know what you must do?
Hold your head high,
Take a deep breath and cry

Good-bye
To Sandra Dee.

(On last line of song she reaches for Kleenex and stuffs tissues into her bra. Lights fade)

SCENE 5

Lights come up on the inside of the Burger Palace. ROGER, DOODY, KENICKIE *and* SONNY *are sitting at counter.*

ROGER: Hey, you guys wanta come over to my house to watch the Mickey Mouse Club? (PATTY *enters in cheerleader costume, dragging pom-poms dispiritedly*) Hey, whattaya say, Mary Hartline?
(PATTY *ignores them*)
SONNY *(Loudly)*: She ain't talkin'.
DOODY: Maybe she had a fight with Danny.
KENICKIE: Hey, jugs! Why don't ya make me a track star, too?
SONNY: Nah, get me out on that field. I'm a better broad-jumper than Zuko.
(The GUYS *laugh*)
PATTY *(Turning on them)*: You're disgusting, all of you! You can have your Danny Zuko, you worthless bums.
ROGER: Nice talk!
DOODY: Whatsa matter? Don't you like Danny anymore?
PATTY: As if you didn't know. He quit the track team!
GUYS: Huh?
PATTY: I just found out. The other day the coach asked Danny, perfectly nicely, to try to get to practice on time. Danny made a shamefully crass gesture and walked off the field.
SONNY: He gave him the finger!
(GUYS *crack up*)
ROGER: What a neat!
PATTY: Not only that, before he left the locker room, he . . . he . . . smeared Ben-Gay in the team captain's athletic supporter.
(*The* GUYS *double up.* DANNY *enters. The* GUYS *immediately crowd around him*)
DANNY: Hey, you guys!
KENICKIE: Hey, Zuko!
SONNY: Whattaya say, Zuke? Where ya been?
DOODY: Hi, Danny.

(DANNY *stands open-mouthed, bewildered by all the sudden attention.* PATTY *looks on disapprovingly*)

DANNY: I guess you got the word, huh?

ROGER: Hey, come on, we were just goin' over to my house to watch the Mickey Mouse Club.

DANNY (*Enthusiastically*): Yeah?

PATTY: Danny! I want to talk to you.

(DANNY *motions to* GUYS *to be cool for a second as he crosses to* PATTY)

DANNY: Ease off, Patty!

PATTY (*Dagger eyes*): It's very important, Danny!

(GUYS *all crowd around* DANNY *again*)

SONNY: Aaahh, come on, Zuko! It'll be neat. Annette's startin' to get big knockers!

DANNY (*Smiles*): Solid! Later, Patty.

(GUYS *start to leave.* MARTY, FRENCHY, RIZZO *and* JAN *in Pink Ladies jackets enter silently, gesturing the* GUYS *to be cool as they take up defiant positions.* SANDY *enters, now a Greaser's dream girl. A wild new hair style, black leather motorcycle jacket, skin-tight slacks, gold hoop earrings. Yet she actually looks prettier and more alive than she ever has. She is chewing gum and smoking a cigarette. She slouches casually and French inhales*)

RIZZO (*Aside to* SANDY): Remember, play it cool.

DANNY (*Turns and sees* SANDY): Hey Sandy! Wow, what a total! Wick-ed!

SANDY (*Tough and cool*): What's it to ya, Zuko?

DANNY: Hey, we was just goin' to check out The Mouseketeers. How would you like to come along?

PATTY: Danny, what's gotten into you? You couldn't possibly be interested in that . . . that floozy.

(SANDY *looks to* RIZZO *for her next move. Then she strolls over to* PATTY, *studies her calmly, and punches her in the eye.* PATTY *falls*)

GIRLS: *Yaa-aay!*

PATTY: Oh, my God, I'm going to have a black eye! (*She bawls*)

FRENCHY (*Opening purse*): Don't sweat it. I'll fix it up. I just got a job demonstrating this new miracle makeup at Woolworth's.

DANNY: Hey, Sandy, you're somethin' else!

SANDY: Oh, so ya noticed, huh? (*She looks him calmly in the eye and walks coolly over to microphone, picks it up, walks back to* DANNY. *She makes a classic gesture: Right hand strikes left inner elbow; left forearm swings up, mike in hand. Better known as an "up yours" gesture)* Tell me about it, stud!

DANNY *(Sings "All Choked Up."* BURGER PALACE BOYS *join in, doing background)*:

Well, I feel so strange, well, upon my word.
Now my brain is reeling and my eyesight's blurred,
I tremble a lot,
I'm nervous and hot,
Uh-huh! I'm all choked up.

There's a fire alarm wailin' in my head,
And my circulation says "Condition Red."
I'm in a cold sweat,
My T-shirt's all wet,
Uh-huh! I'm all choked up.

Oh, baby, baby, baby,
Take my heart before it breaks.
My knees are weak, my backbone quakes,
My hands are colder than ice,
My throat's locked in a vise.
Come on and change my pain to paradise.

There's a fever runnin' through my skin.
Can'tcha hear me knockin', won'tcha let me in?
You know I'm your fool,
Now don'tcha be cruel.
Uh-huh! I'm all choked up.

GIRLS:
Now, listen here:

SANDY:
So you're spinnin' round in a dizzy spell,
It's a situation I know pretty well.
Yeah, I've been there too
So I feel for you
Uh-huh! I'm all choked up

GIRLS:
And furthermore:

SANDY:

> So you're down and out, you're against a wall,
> And you're sayin' I'm the one that did it all.
> I'm sure you're sincere,
> It gets me right here.
> Uh-huh! I'm all choked up!
>
> Oh, baby, take it slow and don't complain.
> My poor heart just can't stand the strain.
> Hey, I can cure your disease.
> Let's hear you say "Pretty please,"
> And take your medicine down on your knees!

DANNY AND GUYS:

> Got a fever, a hundred four Fahrenheit.
> Need your lovin', can I come over tonight?
> Feelin' low-down, my equilibrium's shot,
> Gimme, gimme, that tranquilizer you got.

DANNY:

> Oh, baby, take my ring
>   'Cause you're my match.

SANDY:

> Well, I still think
>   There's strings attached.

DANNY:

> You're writin' my epitaph.

SANDY:

> Well, that's just tough and a half.

DANNY:

> You're gonna make me die!

SANDY:

> Don't make me laugh!

DANNY AND SANDY:

> Well, I might forgive what you put me through,
> 'Cause I do believe you really love me too.
> I look in your eyes,

The suffering dies.
Uh-huh! I'm all choked up.

ALL:
　Hey, hey, hey, hey,
　I'm all choked up.
　Hey, hey, hey, hey.

DANNY AND SANDY (*To a "Hum shoo-bee doo-wop" background*
　by the OTHERS):
　　I'm all choked up
　　Uh-huh!
　　Uh-huh!

ALL:
　Ow!
DANNY: Hey, I still got my ring! I guess you're still kinda mad at
　me, huh? (*He holds out his ring*)
SANDY: Nah. Fuck it
　(*They kiss and hug quickly*)
ROGER: Hey, we just gonna stand around here all day? Let's get
　outta here!
DOODY: Yeah, we're missin' "Anything-Can-Happen" Day! (*He
　pairs off with* FRENCHY)
DANNY: Yeah, let's cut! You comin', Big D?
SANDY: Solid! Hey, Patty, you wanna come?
PATTY: Oh. Well, thanks, but I wouldn't want to be in the way.
SANDY: Nah. It don't matter. Right?
DANNY: Hell, no. C'mon, Patty!
　(PATTY *crosses up to door near* DANNY)
SONNY (*Goes over to* MARTY): Hey, Marty, did I tell ya I'm
　gettin' a new Impala?
MARTY: Ohh, would you paint my name on it?
　(SONNY *nods "sure" and puts arm around her. They head for*
　door area)
RIZZO (*Crossing to* KENICKIE): Hey, Kenickie, can we stop at the
　drugstore? I think I'm getting my friend.
　(KENICKIE *puts arm around her as all* KIDS *smile and cheer for*
　RIZZO)
FRENCHY: Gee, the whole crowd's together again. I could cry.

JAN: Gee, me too!

SANDY: Yeah, I'm all choked up.

(The KIDS *all have their arms around each other as they sing a one-verse reprise of "We Go Together" and go off dancing and singing)*

Curtain

JESUS CHRIST SUPERSTAR

A Rock Opera

Lyrics by Tim Rice

Music by Andrew Lloyd Webber

EDITOR'S NOTES

Hailed by *Variety* as "the biggest all-media parlay in show business history," *Jesus Christ Superstar* started its phenomenal career as a record album with sales soaring into the millions, a subsequent concert attraction, a full-scale stage spectacle, a motion picture, then television presentation, and a theatre piece destined for perennial revivals.

With its exciting score composed by Andrew Lloyd Webber and dramatically persuasive lyrics by Tim Rice, the success of the rock opera has been international and has been performed in countless languages throughout the world.

Its initial theatrical performance took place at the Mark Hellinger Theatre in New York City on October 12, 1971, and, admittedly, was greeted with loud controversy, both from professional critics and laymen. Denounced by some religious groups and fervently defended by others, the work engendered more newspaper reportage, both pro and con, and more feverish excitement than any stage production within recent memory.

Charges of irreverence aside, some of the criticism (or, if you will, approbation) was prompted by the overlavish, often flamboyant and overwhelming production conceived and staged by Tom O'Horgan. Nonetheless, the presentation ran for 711 performances in New York and has populated stages across the land in one form or another ever since.

Douglas Watt of the New York *Daily News* led the parade of journalistic enthusiasts:

Jesus Christ Superstar is so stunningly effective a theatrical experience that I am still finding it difficult to compose my thoughts about it. It is, in short, a triumph.

As I'm sure you know, *Jesus Christ Superstar,* which tells its story entirely through song, considers the last seven days of Christ in contemporary pop terms and, it must be added, with complete reverence. Andrew Lloyd Webber's score is vibrant, richly varied and always dramatically right and much the same things can be said for Tim Rice's lyrics.

The songs are, indeed, marvelous and although they rock a

good deal of the time there are other interesting influences in it and some lovely string and choral writing. The story itself is, of course, almost unbearably moving, but the great accomplishment of Webber and Rice has been to make it so strikingly immediate.

In covering the London production (where it opened on August 9, 1972) *Variety*'s correspondent observed that though it was "toned down somewhat from the flamboyance of Tom O'Horgan's Broadway conception," it remained "an exciting show. Whatever else may be said, it's certainly reverential, and it effectively purveys a seminal message of Christ's gospel stripped of the doctrinology piled on over the centuries." The West End presentation is now in its sixth year and has become the longest-running musical in London theatre history.

Lyricist Tim Rice was born at Amersham, Buckinghamshire, on November 10, 1944. He went to two "very religious" schools—one of them in Japan, where his father worked for a year. At Lancing College in Sussex, he was more interested in singing with a pop group than academic pursuits and after leaving there, briefly attended a French university. He next— and quite unsuccessfully—studied law for two years.

Mr. Rice met Andrew Lloyd Webber in 1965 and started his collaboration with the composer in the following year. In 1966 Mr. Rice joined EMI Records as assistant to the recording manager and two years later moved over to the Norrie Paramor Organization as a record producer. In 1969 he left that post to form a new recording company with his collaborator.

In addition to his work with Mr. Webber, Mr. Rice has fashioned the lyrics for songs for the films *Gumshoe* and *The Odessa File*, and has appeared frequently on British television, including two of his own series, "Musical Triangles" and "Disco."

Composer Andrew Lloyd Webber was born in London on March 22, 1948, into a distinguished musical family. His father is a well-known composer and organist as well as director of the London College of Music.

Mr. Webber's first composition was published when he was nine years old, providing an auspicious start for the youthful creator. Later, he won a Queen's Scholarship to the Westminster School and a History Exhibition to Magdalen College, Oxford. After one term, he left Oxford to study music and ultimately joined the Royal College of Music.

Although Mr. Webber started his collaboration with Mr. Rice in 1966, it wasn't until 1968 that the team earned its first real recognition with the recording of their pop oratorio, *Joseph and the Amazing Technicolor Dream Coat*. After the enormous success of *Jesus Christ Superstar*, it, too, was presented on the London stage, opening at the Albery Theatre in 1973. It also has been performed in the New York area, notably as an annual Christmas presentation at the Brooklyn Academy of Music.

The team's newest musical, *Evita*—based on the life and times of Eva Peron, wife of the late Argentine dictator—is scheduled to open in London in mid-1978.

The Norman Jewison–Robert Stigwood motion picture version of *Jesus Christ Superstar*, filmed in the Holy Land, was released in 1973.

PRODUCTION NOTES

Jesus Christ Superstar was produced by Robert Stigwood, in association with MCA, Inc. and by arrangement with David Land, at the Mark Hellinger Theatre, New York, on October 12, 1971. The cast was as follows:

Judas Iscariot	*Ben Vereen*
Jesus of Nazareth	*Jeff Fenholt*
Mary Magdalene	*Yvonne Elliman*
First Priest	*Alan Braunstein*
Second Priest	*Michael Meadows*
Caiaphas	*Bob Bingham*
Annas	*Phil Jethro*
Third Priest	*Steven Bell*
Simon Zelotes/Merchant/Leper	*Dennis Buckley*
Pontius Pilate	*Barry Dennen*
Peter/Merchant/Leper	*Michael Jason*
Maid by the Fire/Leper	*Linda Rios*
Soldier/Judas's Tormentor	*Tom Stovall*
Old Man/Apostle/Leper	*Peter Schlosser*
Soldier/Judas's Tormentor	*Paul Sylvan*
King Herod/Merchant/Leper	*Paul Ainsley*
Cured Leper/Temple Lady	*Robin Grean*
Cured Leper/Apostle/Merchant/Tormentor (Judas's Death)	*James Sbano*
Cured Leper/Temple Lady	*Laura Michaels*
Cured Leper/Apostle/Merchant/Tormentor (Judas' Death)	*Clifford Lipson*
Cured Leper/Temple Lady/Reporter	*Bonnie Schlon*
Cured Leper/Apostle/Reporter	*Pi Douglass*
Cured Leper/Apostle Woman/Temple Lady	*Celia Brin*
Cured Leper/Apostle/Tormentor (Judas's Death)	*Dennis Cooley*
Reporter/Apostle Woman/Temple Lady/Leper	*Anita Morris*
Reporter/Leper	*Ted Neeley*
Reporter/Apostle Woman/Temple Lady/Leper	*Kay Cole*
Reporter/Leper	*Kurt Yaghjian*

Reporter/Leper	*Margaret Warncke*
Reporter/Apostle/Leper	*Willie Windsor*
Reporter/Apostle Woman/Temple Lady/Leper	*Ferne Bork*
Reporter/Apostle/Leper	*Samuel E. Wright*
Apostle Woman/Temple Lady/Leper	*Denise Delapenha*
Apostle/Merchant/Leper/Reporter	*Robalee Barnes*
Apostle/Leper/Reporter/Tormentor (Judas's Death)	*Doug Lucas*
Soul Girl/Leper	*Charlotte Crossley*
Soul Girl/Leper	*Cecelia Norfleet*
Soul Girl/Leper	*Janet Powell*
Judas's Tormentor/Soldier	*Edward Barton*
Judas's Tormentor/Soldier	*Tony Gardner*

And various Palm Sunday Attendants, Alabaster Monsters, The Mob, and Members of the Crowd

Conceived for the Stage and Directed by *Tom O'Horgan*
Scenic Design by *Robin Wagner*
Lighting Designed by *Jules Fisher*
Costumes Designed by *Randy Barcelo*
Sound Designed by *Abe Jacob*
Musical Direction by *Marc Pressel*
Orchestrations by *Andrew Lloyd Webber*
Production Supervisor: *Charles Gray*
Associate Producers: *Gatchell and Neufeld*

THE LAST SEVEN DAYS IN THE LIFE OF JESUS OF NAZARETH

Synopsis of Scenes and Musical Numbers

ACT ONE

Overture   The Company
Heaven on Their Minds   Judas
What's the Buzz—Bethany, Friday Night
         Jesus, Mary, The Apostles and their Women
Strange Thing Mystifying
         Judas, Jesus, The Apostles and their Women
Then We Are Decided   Caiaphas and Annas
Everything's Alright
         Mary, Judas, Jesus, The Apostles and their Women
This Jesus Must Die—Jerusalem, Sunday
         Caiaphas, Annas, The Priests and The Company
Hosanna   Caiaphas, Jesus and The Company
Simon Zealotes   Simon and The Company
Poor Jerusalem   Jesus
Pilate's Dream—Pontius Pilate's House, Monday   Pilate
The Temple   Jesus and The Company
I Don't Know How to Love Him   Mary and Jesus
Damned for All Time—Tuesday
         Judas, Annas, Caiaphas and Priests

ACT TWO

The Last Supper—Thursday Night
Jesus, Judas and The Apostles

Gethsemane—The Garden Jesus

The Arrest
Peter, Jesus, Apostles, Reporters, Caiaphas, Annas

Peter's Denial Maid, Peter, Soldier, Old Man, Mary

Pilate and Christ—Pilate's Palace, Friday
Pilate, Soldier, Jesus and The Company

King Herod's Song—House of Herod Herod

Judas's Death Judas, Annas, Caiaphas

Trial Before Pilate—Pilate's Palace
Pilate, Caiaphas, Jesus and The Mob

Superstar Voice of Judas and The Company

The Crucifixion—Golgotha Jesus and The Company

John 19:41 The Orchestra

OVERTURE

Heaven on Their Minds

JUDAS:
My mind is clearer now—at last all too well
  I can see where we all soon will be
If you strip away the myth from the man
  you will see where we all soon will be
Jesus! You've started to believe
The things they say of you
You really do believe
This talk of God is true
And all the good you've done
Will soon get swept away
You've begun to matter more
Than the things you say

Listen, Jesus, I don't like what I see
All I ask is that you listen to me
And remember—I've been your right-hand man all along
You have set them all on fire
They think they've found the new Messiah
And they'll hurt you when they find they're wrong

I remember when this whole thing began
No talk of God then—we called you a man
And believe me—my admiration for you hasn't died
But every word you say today
Gets twisted 'round some other way
And they'll hurt you if they think you've lied

Nazareth, your famous son should have stayed
  a great unknown
Like his father carving wood—he'd have made good
Tables, chairs and oaken chests would have suited Jesus best
He'd have caused nobody harm—no one alarm

Listen, Jesus, do you care for your race?
Don't you see we must keep in our place?
We are occupied—have you forgotten how put down we are?
I am frightened by the crowd
For we are getting much too loud
And they'll crush us if we go too far

Listen, Jesus, to the warning I give
Please remember that I want us to live
But it's sad to see our chances weakening with every hour
All your followers are blind
Too much heaven on their minds
It was beautiful, but now it's sour
Yes, it's all gone sour

BETHANY, FRIDAY NIGHT

What's the Buzz

APOSTLES:
What's the buzz? Tell me what's happening . . .

JESUS:
Why should you want to know?
Don't you mind about the future, don't you try to think ahead
Save tomorrow for tomorrow, think about today instead

APOSTLES:
What's the buzz? Tell me what's happening . . .

JESUS:
I could give you facts and figures—even give you plans and forecasts
Even tell you where I'm going—

APOSTLES:
When do we ride into Jerusalem? . . .

JESUS:
Why should you want to know?
Why are you obsessed with fighting times and fates you can't defy?
If you knew the path we're riding, you'd understand it less than I

APOSTLES:
What's the buzz? Tell me what's happening . . .

MARY MAGDALENE:
Let me try to cool down your face a bit . . .

250 |

JESUS:

> Mary—mm—that is good
> While you prattle through your supper—where and when and
> who and how
> She alone has tried to give me what I need right here and
> now

APOSTLES:

> What's the buzz? Tell me what's happening? . . .

Strange Thing Mystifying

JUDAS:

> It seems to me a strange thing, mystifying
> That a man like you can waste his time on women of her
> kind
> Yes I can understand that she amuses
> But to let her kiss you, stroke your hair, that's hardly in your
> line
>
> It's not that I object to her profession
> But she doesn't fit in well with what you teach and say
> It doesn't help us if you're inconsistent
> They only need a small excuse to put us all away

JESUS:

> Who are you to criticize her? Who are you to despise her?
> Leave her, leave her, let her be now
> Leave her, leave her, she's with me now
> If your slate is clean—then you can throw stones
> If your slate is not then leave her alone
>
> I'm amazed that men like you can be so shallow thick and
> slow
> There is not a man among you who knows or cares if I come
> or go

ALL (Save JUDAS):

No you're wrong! You're very wrong! ... How can you say
that? ...

JESUS:
    Not one—not one of you!

Then We Are Decided

CAIAPHAS:
    We've been sitting on the fence for far too long

ANNAS:
    Why let him upset us?
    Caiaphas—let him be
    All those imbeciles will see
    He really doesn't matter

CAIAPHAS:
    Jesus is important
    We've let him go his way before
    And while he starts a major war
    We theorize and chatter

ANNAS:
    He's just another scripture-thumping hack
      from Galilee

CAIAPHAS:
    The difference is they call him King—the
      difference frightens me
    What about the Romans
    When they see King Jesus crowned?
    Do you think they'll stand around
    Cheering and applauding?

    What about our people
    If they see we've lost our nerve?
    Don't you think that they deserve
    Something more rewarding?

ANNAS:

> They've got what they want—they think so
>   anyway
> If he's what they want why take their toy away?
> He's a craze

CAIAPHAS:

> Put yourself in my place
> I can hardly step aside
> Cannot let my hands be tied
> I am law and order
>
> What about our priesthood?
> Don't you see that we could fall?
> If we are to last at all
> We cannot be divided

ANNAS:

> Then say so to the council
> But don't rely on subtlety
> Frighten them or they won't see

CAIAPHAS:

> Then we are decided?

ANNAS:

> Then we are decided.

Everything's Alright

MARY MAGDALENE:

> Try not to get worried, try not to turn on to
> Problems that upset you, oh, don't you know
> Everything's alright, yes, everything's fine
> And we want you to sleep well tonight
> Let the world turn without you tonight
> If we try, we'll get by, so forget all about us tonight

APOSTLES' WOMEN:
  Everything's alright, yes, everything's alright, yes

MARY MAGDALENE:
  Sleep and I shall soothe you, calm you and anoint you
  Myrrh for your hot forehead, oh, then you'll feel
  Everything's alright, yes, everything's fine
  And it's cool and the ointment's sweet
  For the fire in your head and feet
  Close your eyes close your eyes
  And relax think of nothing tonight

APOSTLES' WOMEN:
  Everything's alright, yes, everything's alright, yes

JUDAS:
  Woman your fine ointment—brand new and expensive
  Could have been saved for the poor
  Why has it been wasted? We could have raised maybe
  Three hundred silver pieces or more
  People who are hungry, people who are starving
  Matter more than your feet and hair

MARY MAGDALENE:
  Try not to get worried, try not to, turn on to
  Problems that upset you, oh, don't you know
  Everything's alright, yes, everything's fine
  And we want you to sleep well tonight
  Let the world turn without you tonight
  If we try, we'll get by, so forget all about us tonight

APOSTLES' WOMEN:
  Everything's alright, yes, everything's alright, yes

JESUS:
  Surely you're not saying we have the resources
  To save the poor from their lot?
  There will be poor always, pathetically struggling—
  Look at the good things you've got!
  Think! while you still have me
  Move! while you still see me
  You'll be lost and you'll be so sorry when I'm gone

MARY MAGDALENE:

Sleep and I shall soothe you, calm you and anoint you
Myrrh for your hot forehead, oh, then you'll feel
Everything's alright, yes, everything's fine
And it's cool and the ointment's sweet
For the fire in your head and feet
Close your eyes close your eyes
And relax think of nothing tonight
Close your eyes close your eyes and relax

ALL:

Everything's alright, yes, everything's alright, yes

JERUSALEM, SUNDAY

This Jesus Must Die

PRIEST 1:
  Good Caiaphas, the council waits for you
  The Pharisees and priests are here for you

CAIAPHAS:
  Ah, gentlemen—you know why we are here
  We've not much time and quite a problem here

CROWD *(Outside):*

  Hosanna! Superstar! . . .

ANNAS:
  Listen to that howling mob of blockheads in the street!
  A trick or two with lepers and the whole town's on its feet

ALL:
  He is dangerous

CROWD: *(Outside):*
  Jesus Christ Superstar—tell us that you're who they say you
    are

ALL:
  He is dangerous

PRIEST 2:
  That man is in town right now to whip up some support

PRIEST 3:
  A rabble-rousing mission that I think we must abort

ALL:
  He is dangerous!

CROWD *(Outside)*:
Jesus Christ Superstar!

ALL:
He is dangerous!

PRIEST 4:
Look, Caiaphas—they're right outside our yard

PRIEST 5:
Quick, Caiaphas—go call the Roman guard

CAIAPHAS:
*No wait—we need a more permanent solution to our
    problem . . .*

ANNAS:
*What then to do about Jesus of Nazareth
Miracle wonderman—hero of fools?*

PRIEST 6:
No riots, no army, no fighting, no slogans

CAIAPHAS:
One thing I'll say for him—Jesus is cool

ANNAS:
*We dare not leave him to his own devices
His half-witted fans will get out of control*

PRIEST 1:
How can we stop him?

PRIEST 2:
His glamour increases

PRIEST 3:
By leaps every minute

PRIEST 4:
He's top of the poll

CAIAPHAS:
> *I see bad things arising—the crowd crown him king*
> *Which the Romans would ban*
> *I see blood and destruction, our elimination because of one*
> * man*
> *Blood and destruction because of one man*

ALL:
> *Because, because, because of one man*

CAIAPHAS:
> *Our elimination because of one man*

ALL:
> *Because, because, because of one, 'cause of one, 'cause of one*
> * man*

PRIEST 6:
> *What then to do about this Jesusmania?*

ANNAS:
> *How do we deal with the carpenter king?*

PRIEST 1:
> *Where do we start with a man who is bigger*

PRIEST 3:
> *Than John was when John did his Baptism thing?*

CAIAPHAS:
> *Fools! You have no perception!*
> *The stakes we are gambling are frighteningly high!*
> *We must crush him completely—*
> *So like John before him, this Jesus must die*
> *For the sake of the nation this Jesus must die*

ALL:
> *Must die, must die, this Jesus must die*

CAIAPHAS:
> *So like John before him, this Jesus must die*

ALL:

> *Must die, must die, this Jesus must, Jesus must, Jesus must die!*

Hosanna

CROWD:

> *Hosanna Heysanna Sanna Sanna Ho*
> *Sanna Hey Sanna Ho Sanna*
> *Hey JC, JC won't you smile at me?*
> *Sanna Ho Sanna Hey Superstar*

CAIAPHAS:

> *Tell the rabble to be quiet, we anticipate a riot*
> *This common crowd is much too loud*
>
> *Tell the mob who sing your song that they are fools and they are wrong*
> *They are a curse, they should disperse*

CROWD:

> *Hosanna Heysanna Sanna Sanna Ho*
> *Sanna Hey Sanna Ho Sanna*
> *Hey JC, JC you're alright by me*
> *Sanna Ho Sanna Hey Superstar*

JESUS:

> *Why waste your breath moaning at the crowd?*
> *Nothing can be done to stop the shouting*
> *If every tongue was still the noise would still continue*
> *The rocks and stones themselves would start to sing:*

CROWD (With JESUS):

> *Hosanna Heysanna Sanna Sanna Ho*
> *Sanna Hey Sanna Ho Sanna*
> *Hey JC, JC won't you fight for me?*
> *Sanna Ho Sanna Hey Superstar*

Simon Zealotes

CROWD:

>Christ, you know I love you
>Did you see I waved?
>I believe in you and God
>So tell me that I'm saved
>Christ, you know I love you
>Did you see I waved?
>I believe in you and God
>So tell me that I'm saved
>Jesus, I am with you
>Touch me, touch me, Jesus
>Jesus, I am on your side
>Kiss me, kiss me, Jesus

SIMON ZEALOTES:

>Christ, what more do you need to convince you
>That you've made it and you're easily as strong
>As the filth from Rome who rape our country
>And who've terrorized our people for so long?

CROWD (With SIMON):

>Jesus, I am with you
>Touch me, touch me, Jesus
>Jesus, I am on your side
>Kiss me, kiss me, Jesus
>Christ, you know I love you
>Did you see I waved?
>I believe in you and God
>So tell me that I'm saved
>Christ, you know I love you
>Did you see I waved?
>I believe in you and God
>So tell me that I'm saved

>Christ, you know I love you
>Did you see I waved?
>I believe in you and God
>So tell me that I'm saved

Christ, you know I love you
Did you see I waved?
I believe in you and God
So tell me that I'm saved
Jesus, I am with you
Touch me, touch me, Jesus
Jesus, I am on your side
Kiss me, kiss me, Jesus

SIMON ZEALOTES:
There must be over fifty thousand

GIRLS:
Fifty thousand!

SIMON ZEALOTES:
Screaming love and more for you

GIRLS:
Love! Love! Love!

SIMON ZEALOTES:
And every one of fifty thousand
Would do whatever you asked them to

GIRLS:
Tell us, Simon!

SIMON ZEALOTES:
Keep them yelling their devotion
But add a touch of hate at Rome
You will rise to a greater power
We will win ourselves a home
You'll get the power and the glory
For ever and ever and ever . . .

GIRLS:
You'll get the glory
Ever and ever . . .

ALL:
Amen!

Poor Jerusalem

JESUS:

Neither you Simon, nor the fifty thousand
Nor the Romans, nor the Jews, nor Judas nor the Twelve,
Nor the Priests, nor the Scribes
Nor doomed Jerusalem itself,
Understand what power is
Understand what glory is
Understand at all . . . understand at all

If you knew all that I knew, my poor Jerusalem
You'd see the truth, but you close your eyes
But you close your eyes
While you live your troubles are many, poor Jerusalem
To conquer death, you only have to die
You only have to die

PONTIUS PILATE'S HOUSE, MONDAY

Pilate's Dream

PILATE:
> I dreamed I met a Galilean
> A most amazing man
> He had that look you very rarely find
> The haunting hunted kind
>
> I asked him to say what had happened
> How it all began
> I asked again—he never said a word
> As if he hadn't heard
>
> And next the room was full of wild and angry men
> They seemed to hate this man—they fell on him and then
> They disappeared again
>
> Then I saw thousands of millions
> Crying for this man
> And then I heard them mentioning my name
> And leaving me the blame

The Temple

CROWD:
> Roll on up, Jerusalem
> Come on in, Jerusalem
> Sunday here we go again
> Live in me, Jerusalem
> Here you live, Jerusalem
> Here you breathe, Jerusalem

While your temple still survives
You at least are still alive

MEN:

I got things you won't believe
Name your pleasure I will sell
I can fix your wildest needs
I got heaven I got hell

CROWD:

Roll on up—for my price is down
Come on in—for the best in town
Take your pick of the finest wine
Lay your bets on this bird of mine

WOMEN:

What you see is what you get
No one's been disappointed yet
Don't be scared give me a try
There is nothing you can't buy

CROWD:

Name your price, I got everything
Hurry, it's all going fast
Borrow cash on the finest terms
Hurry now while stocks still last.

Roll on up, Jerusalem
Come on in, Jerusalem
Sunday here we go again
Live in me, Jerusalem
Here you live, Jerusalem
Here you breathe, Jerusalem
While your temple still survives
You at least are still alive
I got things you won't believe
Name your pleasure—I will sell—

JESUS:

My temple should be a house of prayer
But you have made it a den of thieves
Get out! Get out!

My time is almost through
Little left to do
After all I've tried for three years, seems like thirty
Seems like thirty

LEPERS:

See my eyes, I can hardly see
See me stand, I can hardly walk
I believe you can make me whole
See my tongue, I can hardly talk
See my skin, I'm a mass of blood
See my legs, I can hardly stand
I believe you can make me well
See my purse, I'm a poor, poor man

Will you touch, will you mend me, Christ?
Won't you touch, will you heal me, Christ?
Will you kiss, you can cure me, Christ?
Won't you kiss, won't you pay me, Christ?

See my eyes, I can hardly see
See me stand, I can hardly walk
I believe you can make me whole
See my tongue, I can hardly talk
See my skin, I'm a mass of blood
See my legs, I can hardly stand
I believe you can make me well
See my purse, I'm a poor, poor man

Will you touch, will you mend me, Christ?
Won't you touch, will you heal me, Christ?
Will you kiss, you can cure me, Christ?
Won't you kiss, won't you pay me, Christ?

See my eyes I can hardly see
See me stand, I can hardly walk
I believe you can make me whole
See my tongue, I can hardly talk
See my skin, I'm a mass of blood
See my legs, I can hardly stand
I believe you can make me well
See my purse, I'm a poor, poor man

Will you touch, will you mend me, Christ?
Won't you touch, will you heal me, Christ?
Will you kiss, you can cure me, Christ?
Won't you kiss, won't you pay me, Christ?

See my eyes, I can hardly see
See me stand, I can hardly walk
I believe you can make me whole
See my tongue, I can hardly talk
See my skin, I'm a mass of blood . . .

JESUS:
There's too many of you—don't push me
There's too little of me—don't crowd me
Leave me alone!

Everything's Alright

MARY MAGDALENE:
Try not to get worried, try not to turn on to
Problems that upset you, oh, don't you know
Everything's all right, yes, everything's fine

JESUS:
And I think I shall sleep well tonight
Let the world turn without me tonight

MARY MAGDALENE:
Close your eyes, close your eyes
And forget all about us tonight

I Don't Know How to Love Him

MARY MAGDALENE:
I don't know how to love him
What to do how to move him

I've been changed, yes, really changed
In these past few days when I've seen myself
I seem like someone else

I don't know how to take this
I don't see why he moves me
He's a man, he's just a man
And I've had so many men before

In very many ways
He's just one more

Should I bring him down, should I scream and shout
Should I speak of love, let my feelings out
I never thought I'd come to this—what's it all about

Don't you think it's rather funny
I should be in this position
I'm the one who's always been
So calm so cool, no lover's fool
Running every show
He scares me so

I never thought I'd come to this—what's it all about
Yet if he said he loved me
I'd be lost, I'd be frightened
I couldn't cope, just couldn't cope
I'd turn my head, I'd back away
I wouldn't want to know
He scares me so
I want him so
I love him so

TUESDAY

Damned for All Time

JUDAS:
> Now, if I help you, it matters that you see
> These sordid kind of things are coming hard to me
> It's taken me some time to work out what to do
> I weighed the whole thing up before I came to you
> I have no thought at all about my own reward
> I really didn't come here of my own accord
> Just don't say I'm
> Damned for all time

> I came because I had to—I'm the one who saw
> Jesus can't control it like he did before
> And furthermore I know that Jesus thinks so, too
> Jesus wouldn't mind that I was here with you
> I have no thought at all about my own reward
> I really didn't come here of my own accord
> Just don't say I'm
> Damned for all time

> Annas, you're a friend, a worldly man and wise
> Caiaphas, my friend, I know you sympathize
> Why are we the prophets? Why are we the ones?
> Who see the sad solution—know what must be done
> I have no thought at all about my own reward
> I really didn't come here of my own accord
> Just don't say I'm
> Damned for all time

ANNAS:
> Cut the protesting, forget the excuses
> We want information—get up off the floor

CAIAPHAS:
We have the papers we need to arrest him
You know his movements—we know the law

ANNAS:
Your help in this matter won't go unrewarded

CAIAPHAS:
We'll pay you in silver—cash on the nail
We just need to know where the soldiers can find him

ANNAS:
With no crowd 'round him

CAIAPHAS:
Then we can't fail

Blood Money

JUDAS:
I don't want your blood money!

CAIAPHAS:
Oh, that doesn't matter—our expenses are good

JUDAS:
I don't need your blood money!

ANNAS:
But you might as well take it—we think that you should

CAIAPHAS:
Think of the things you can do with that money
Choose any charity—give to the poor
We've noted your motives—we've noted your feelings
This isn't blood money—it's a

ANNAS:
A fee!

CAIAPHAS:
A fee—nothing more.

JUDAS:
On Thursday night you'll find him where you want him
Far from the crowds in the Garden of Gethsemane

CHOIR:
Well done, Judas
Good old Judas

THURSDAY NIGHT, THE LAST SUPPER

The Last Supper

APOSTLES:

Look at all my trials and tribulations
Sinking in a gentle pool of wine
Don't disturb me now—I can see the answers
Till this evening is this morning life is fine
Always hoped that I'd be an apostle
Knew that I would make it if I tried
Then when we retire we can write the gospels
So they'll still talk about us when we've died

JESUS:

The end ...
Is just a little harder when brought about by friends
For all you care, this wine could be my blood
For all you care, this bread could be my body
The end!
This is my blood you drink
This is my body you eat
If you would remember me when you eat and drink ...

I must be mad thinking I'll be remembered—yes
I must be out of my head!
Look at your blank faces! My name will mean nothing
Ten minutes after I'm dead!
One of you denies me
One of you betrays me—

APOSTLES:

How can he say that?
Betray you?—Who?—Not me! ...

JESUS:
  Peter will deny me

PETER:
  No, not me!

JESUS:
  In just a few hours
  Three times will deny me—and that's not all I see
  One of you here dining, one of my twelve chosen
  Will leave to betray me—

JUDAS:
  Cut out the dramatics! You know very well who—

JESUS:
  Why don't you go do it?

JUDAS:
  You want me to do it!

JESUS:
  Hurry—they are waiting

JUDAS:
  If you knew why I do it . . .

JESUS:
  I don't care why you do it!

JUDAS:
  To think I admired you
  Well, now I despise you

JESUS:
  You liar—you Judas

JUDAS:
  You want me to do it!
  What if I just stayed here
  And ruined your ambition?
  Christ, you deserve it!

JESUS:

Hurry, you fool, hurry and go,
Save me your speeches, I don't want to know—Go! Go!

APOSTLES:

Look at all my trials and tribulations
Sinking in a gentle pool of wine
What's that in the bread—it's gone to my head
Till this morning is this evening life is fine
Always hoped that I'd be an apostle
Knew that I would make it if I tried
Then when we retire we can write the gospels
So they'll all talk about us when we've died

JUDAS:

You sad, pathetic man—see where you've brought us to
Our ideals die around us all because of you
And now the saddest cut of all—
Someone has to turn you in
Like a common criminal, like a wounded animal
A jaded mandarin
A jaded mandarin
A jaded, faded mandarin

JESUS:

Get out! They're waiting! They're waiting for you!

JUDAS:

Every time I look at you I don't understand
Why you let the things you did get so out of hand
You'd have managed better if you'd had it planned—

APOSTLES:

Look at all my trials and tribulations
Sinking in a gentle pool of wine
Don't disturb me now—I can see the answers
Till this evening is this morning life is fine
Always hoped that I'd be an apostle
Knew that I would make it if I tried
Then when we retire we can write the gospels
So they'll still talk about us when we've died

JESUS:
> *Will no one stay awake with me?*
> *Peter? John? James?*
> *Will none of you wait with me?*
> *Peter? John? James?*

IN THE GARDEN OF GETHSEMANE

Gethsemane (I only want to say)

JESUS:
I only want to say
If there is a way
Take this cup away from me for I don't want to taste its
  poison
Feel it burn me, I have changed. I'm not as sure
As when we started
Then I was inspired
Now I'm sad and tired
Listen, surely I've exceeded expectations
Tried for three years, seems like thirty
Could you ask as much from any other man?
But if I die
See the saga through and do the things you ask of me
Let them hate me, hit me, hurt me, nail me to their tree
I'd wanna know, I'd wanna know my God
I'd wanna see, I'd wanna see my God
Why I should die?
Would I be more noticed than I was ever before?
Would the things I've said and done matter any more?
I'd have to know, I'd have to know my Lord
I'd have to see, I'd have to see my Lord
If I die, what will be my reward?
I'd have to know, I'd have to know my Lord
Why should I die?
Can you show me now that I would not be killed in vain?
Show me just a little of your omnipresent brain
Show me there's a reason for your wanting me to die
You're far too keen on where and how and not so hot on why
Alright, I'll die!
Just watch me die!

See how I die!
Then I was inspired
Now I'm sad and tired
After all, I've tried for three years, seems like ninety
Why then am I scared to finish what I started?
What you started—I didn't start it
God, thy will is hard
But you hold every card
I will drink your cup of poison, nail me to the cross and break
* me*
Bleed me, beat me, kill me, take me now—before I change
* my mind*

The Arrest

JESUS:
Judas—must you betray me with a kiss?

PETER:
What's the buzz? Tell me what's happening
What's the buzz? Tell me what's happening
What's happening

PETER AND APOSTLES:
What's the buzz? Tell me what's happening . . .
Hang on, Lord—we're gonna fight for you . . .

PETER:
Hang on, Lord—we're gonna fight for you

JESUS:
Put away your sword
Don't you know that it's all over?
It was nice but now it's gone
Why are you obsessed with fighting?
Stick to fishing from now on

CROWD:

> *Tell me, Christ, how you feel tonight*
> *Do you plan to put up a fight?*
> *Do you feel that you've had the breaks?*
> *What would you say were your big mistakes?*
> *Do you think that you may retire?*
> *Did you think you would get much higher?*
> *How do you view your coming trial?*
> *Have your men proved it's all worthwhile?*

> *Come with us to see Caiaphas*
> *You'll just love the High Priest's house*
> *You'll just love seeing Caiaphas*
> *You'll just die in the High Priest's house*

> *Come on, God, this is not like you*
> *Let us know what you're gonna do*
> *You know what your supporters feel*
> *You'll escape in the final reel*
> *Tell me, Christ, how you feel tonight*
> *Do you plan to put up a fight?*
> *Do you feel that you've had the breaks?*
> *What would you say were your big mistakes?*

> *Come with us to see Caiaphas*
> *You'll just love the High Priest's house*
> *You'll just love seeing Caiaphas*
> *You'll just die in the High Priest's house*

> *Now we have him! Now we have got him! . . .*

CAIAPHAS:

> *Jesus, you must realize the serious charges facing you*
> *You say you're the Son of God in all your handouts—well, is*
>   *it true?*

JESUS:

> *That's what you say—you say that I am*

ANNAS:

> *There you have it, gentlemen—what more evidence do we*
>   *need?*

Judas, thank you for the victim—stay a while and you'll see it
bleed!

CROWD:
Now we have him! Now we have got him! . . .
Take him to Pilate! . . .

Peter's Denial

WOMAN:
I think I've seen you somewhere—I remember
You were with that man they took away
I recognize your face

PETER:
You've got the wrong man, lady, I don't know him
And I wasn't where he was tonight—never near the place

SOLDIER:
That's strange, for I am sure I saw you with him
You were right by his side and yet you denied—

PETER:
I tell you I was never ever with him

OLD MAN:
But I saw you too—he looked just like you

PETER:
I don't know him!

MARY MAGDALENE:
Peter—don't you know what you have said?
You've gone and cut him dead

PETER:

I had to do it—don't you see?
Or else they'd go for me

MARY MAGDALENE:

It's what he told us you would do—
I wonder how he knew . . .

FRIDAY

Pilate and Christ

PILATE:

Who is this broken man cluttering up my hallway?
Who is this unfortunate?

SOLDIER:

Someone Christ—King of the Jews

PILATE:

Oh, so this is Jesus Christ—I am really quite surprised
You look so small—not a king at all
We all know that you are news—but are you king?
King of the Jews?

JESUS:

Your words—not mine

PILATE:

What do you mean by that?
That is not an answer
You're deep in trouble, friend—
Someone Christ—King of the Jews
How can someone in your state be so cool about his fate?
An amazing thing—this silent king
Since you come from Galilee, then you need not come to me
You're Herod's race! You're Herod's case!

CROWD:

Hey Hosanna Hey Sanna Sanna Sanna Ho
Sanna Hey Sanna Ho and how
Hey JC, JC please explain to me
You had everything—where is it now?

King Herod's Song

HEROD:

Jesus, I am overjoyed to meet you face to face
You've been getting quite a name all around the place
Healing cripples, raising from the dead
And now I understand you're God—at least that's what
  you've said

So you are the Christ, you're the great Jesus Christ
Prove to me that you're divine—change my water into wine
That's all you need do and I'll know it's all true
C'mon, King of the Jews

Jesus, you just won't believe the hit you've made round here
You are all we talk about, the wonder of the year
Oh, what a pity if it's all a lie
Still I'm sure that you can rock the cynics if you try
So you are the Christ, you're the great Jesus Christ
Prove to me that you're no fool—walk across my swimming
  pool
If you do that for me then I'll let you go free
C'mon, King of the Jews

I only ask things I'd ask any superstar
What is it that you have got that puts you where you are?
I am waiting, yes, I'm a captive fan
I am dying to be shown that you are not just any man

So if you are the Christ, yes, the great Jesus Christ
Feed my household with this bread—you can do it on your
  head
Or has something gone wrong? Why do you take so long?
C'mon, King of the Jews

Hey! Aren't you scared of me, Christ? Mr. Wonderful Christ!
You're a joke, you're not the Lord—you are nothing but a
  fraud

Take him away—he's got nothing to say!
Get out, you King of the Jews! Get out of my life!

Judas' Death

JUDAS:

My God! I saw him—he looked three-quarters dead!
And he was so bad I had to turn my head
You beat him so hard that he was bent and lame
And I know who everybody's gonna blame
I don't believe he knows I acted for our good
I'd save him all this suffering if I could
Don't believe . . . our good . . . and I'd save him . . . if I could

ANNAS:

Cut the confessions, forget the excuses
I don't understand why you're filled with remorse
All that you've said has come true with a vengeance
The mob turned against him—you backed the right horse

CAIAPHAS:

What you have done will be the saving of everyone
You'll be remembered forever for this
And not only that you've been paid for your efforts
Pretty good wages for one little kiss

JUDAS:

Christ! I know you can't hear me
But I only did what you wanted me to
Christ! I'd sell out the nation
For I have been saddled with the murder of you
I have been spattered with innocent blood
I shall be dragged through the slime and the mud
I have been spattered with innocent blood
I shall be dragged through the slime
And the slime and the slime and the mud!

I don't know how to love him.
I don't know why he moves me

He's a man—he's just a man
He is not a king—he's just the same
As anyone I know
He scares me so
When he's cold and dead will he let me be?
Will he love—does he love me too?
Does he care for me?
My mind is—it's in darkness now—God
God, I'm sick, I've been used
And you knew all the time, God
God! I'll never know why you chose me for your crime
For your foul bloody crime
You have murdered me! Murdered me! . . .

CHOIR:
   Poor old Judas
   So long, Judas . . .

Trial Before Pilate
(Including the Thirty-Nine Lashes)

PILATE:
   And so the king is once again my guest
   And why is this? Was Herod unimpressed?

CAIAPHAS:
   We turn to Rome to sentence Nazareth
   We have no law to put a man to death
   We need him crucified—it's all you have to do
   We need him crucified—it's all you have to do

PILATE:
   Talk to me, Jesus Christ
   You have been brought here—manacled, beaten
   By your own people—do you have the first idea why you
      deserve it?
   Listen, King of the Jews

Where is your kingdom?
Look at me—am I a Jew?

JESUS:

I have no kingdom in this world—I'm through

CROWD:

Talk to me, Jesus Christ

JESUS:

There may be a kingdom for me somewhere—if I only knew

PILATE:

Then you are a king?

JESUS:

It's you that say I am
I look for truth and find that I get damned

PILATE:

But what is truth? Is truth unchanging law?
We both have truths—are mine the same as yours?

CROWD:

Crucify him! Crucify him!

PILATE:

What do you mean? You'd crucify your king?

CROWD:

We have no king but Caesar!

PILATE:

He's done no wrong—no, not the slightest thing

CROWD:

We have no king but Caesar! Crucify him!

PILATE:

Well this is new—respect for Caesar
Till now this has been noticeably lacking

Who is this Jesus? Why is he different?
You Jews produce Messiahs by the sackful

CROWD:

We need him crucified
It's all you have to do
We need him crucified
It's all you have to do

PILATE:

Talk to me, Jesus Christ
Look at your Jesus Christ
I'll agree he's mad
Ought to be locked up
But that is not a reason to destroy him
He's a sad little man
Not a king or God
Not a thief—I need a crime

CROWD:

Crucify Him! Crucify him!

PILATE:

Behold a man—behold your shattered king

CROWD:

We have no king but Caesar

PILATE:

You hypocrites—you hate us more than him

CROWD:

We have no king but Caesar! Crucify him!

PILATE:

I see no reason—I find no evil
This man is harmless, so why does he upset you?
He's just misguided—thinks he's important
But to keep you vultures happy I shall flog him!

CROWD:

> Crucify him! Crucify him!
> Crucify! Crucify! Crucify! Crucify! . . .

(Thirty-nine lashes)

PILATE:

> Where are you from, Jesus? What do you want, Jesus? Tell
> me
> You've got to be careful—you could be dead soon—could well
> be
> Why do you not speak when I hold your life in my hands?
> How can you stay quiet! I don't believe you understand

JESUS:

> You have nothing in your hands
> Any power you have comes to you from far beyond
> Everything is fixed and you can't change it

PILATE:

> You're a fool, Jesus Christ—how can I help you?

CROWD:

> Pilate! Crucify him! Crucify!
> Remember Caesar—you have a duty
> To keep the peace, so crucify him!
> Remember Caesar—you'll be demoted, you'll be deported
> Crucify him!
>
> Remember Caesar—you have a duty
> To keep the peace, so crucify him!
> Remember Caesar—you'll be demoted, you'll be deported
> Crucify him!
>
> Remember Caesar—you have a duty
> To keep the peace, so crucify him!
> Remember Caesar—you'll be demoted, you'll be deported
> Crucify him!

PILATE:

> Don't let me stop your great self-destruction
> Die if you want to, you misguided martyr

I wash my hands of your demolition
Die if you want to, you innocent puppet!

Superstar

VOICE OF JUDAS:

Every time I look at you, I don't understand
Why you let the things you did get so out of hand
You'd have managed better if you'd had it planned
Why'd you choose such a backward time and such a strange
  land?
If you'd come today, you would have reached a whole nation
Israel in 4 BC had no mass communication
Don't you get me wrong—I only want to know

CHOIR:

Jesus Christ, Jesus Christ
Who are you? What have you sacrificed?
Jesus Christ Superstar
Do you think you're what they say you are?

VOICE OF JUDAS:

Tell me what you think about your friends at the top
Who d'you think besides yourself's the pick of the crop?
Buddha—was he where it's at? Is he where you are?
Could Mahomet move a mountain or was that just PR?
Did you mean to die like that? Was that a mistake or
Did you know your messy death would be a record-breaker?
Don't you get me wrong—I only want to know

CHOIR:

Jesus Christ, Jesus Christ
Who are you? What have you sacrificed?
Jesus Christ Superstar
Do you think you're what they say you are?

THE CRUCIFIXION

The Crucifixion

JESUS:
God forgive them—they don't know what they're doing
Who is my mother? Where is my mother?
My God, My God, why have you forgotten me?
I am thirsty
It is finished
Father into your hands I commend my spirit

John 19:41

THE WIZ: Dorothy (Stephanie Mills), Adaperle (Clarice Taylor) and the Munchkins.
Photo: Martha Swope

THE WIZ: Dorothy (Stephanie Mills) and her three companions, Tinman (Tiger Haynes), Scarecrow (Hinton Battle) and Lion (Ted Ross). *Photo: Martha Swope*

TWO GENTLEMEN OF VERONA: Silvia (Jonelle Allen) and Valentine (Clifton Davis) after dictating a "Night Letter." *Photo: Joseph Abeles Studio*

TWO GENTLEMEN OF VERONA: Proteus (Raul Julia) and Company in "Love Has Driven Me Sane." *Photo: Joseph Abeles Studio*

GREASE: The Burger Palace Boys and their Pink Ladies. *Photo: Joseph Abeles Studio*

GREASE: Members of the Company "Shakin' at the High School Hop." *Photo: Joseph Abeles Studio*

JESUS CHRIST SUPERSTAR: Mary Magdalene (Yvonne Elliman) comforts Jesus of Nazareth (Jeff Fenholt) as she sings "I Don't Know How to Love Him." *Photo: Joseph Abeles Studio*

JESUS CHRIST SUPERSTAR: Jesus of Nazareth (Jeff Fenholt) surrounded by his disciples. *Photo: Joseph Abeles Studio*

YOUR OWN THING: Olivia (Marcia Rodd) and Sebastian (Rusty Thacker). *Photo: Bert Andrews*

YOUR OWN THING: Viola (Leland Palmer) cavorts with members of the Apocalypse rock 'n roll group. *Photo: Bert Andrews*

HAIR: "Black Boys" and "White Boys" as interpreted by two singing trios.
Photo: Bert Andrews

HAIR: Members of The Tribe in a persuasive moment. *Photo: Bert Andrews*

TOMMY: Above, "Sparks," Roger Daltrey (left) and Pete Townshend (right). Below, The Who performing *Tommy*. Although "Tommy" was performed at the New York Metropolitan Opera House, it did not appear on Broadway. These two photos were taken during performances in California. *Photos: Sansara-Nirvana*

PROMENADE: 105 (Ty McConnell), Servant (Madeline Kahn) and 106 (Gilbert Price).
Photo: Joseph Abeles Studio

PROMENADE: In the foreground, left to right, Carrie Wilson, Michael Davis, Gilbert Price, Shannon Bolin, Ty McConnell, Madeline Kahn and George S. Irving. *Photo: Joseph Abeles Studio*

YOUR OWN THING

By Hal Hester and Danny Apolinar

Book by Donald Driver

Music and Lyrics by Hal Hester and Danny Apolinar

(Suggested by William Shakespeare's *Twelfth Night*)

(*Produced for the New York Stage by* Zev Bufman and
Dorothy Love)

EDITOR'S NOTES

"*Your Own Thing*," which arrived at the Orpheum Theatre on Saturday night is cheerful, joyful and blissfully irreverent to Shakespeare and everything else," wrote Clive Barnes in *The New York Times*. "The work is as modern as today; its vitality and charm are terrific!"

The rock transformation of *Twelfth Night*, with its good-humored irreverencies, its freshness and engaging score, had the entire press corps rocking with superlatives. "A delightful inspiration that is brilliant, brisk and funny. It's a groovy non-stop caprice that is bound to become the 'in' thing."

Soon after its opening numerous road companies were dispatched across the land while offers for foreign productions poured in from more than a dozen countries. *Your Own Thing* did indeed become the "in" thing of the late 1960s, and it was the second American rock musical—the first was *Hair*—to attain national and international success.

The original production ran for 933 performances and went on to break a precedent by becoming the very first Off-Broadway show to win the coveted New York Drama Critics' Circle Award for the season's best musical.

The genesis of *Your Own Thing* came about in a somewhat circuitous manner. As co-composer and co-lyricist Hal Hester recounted in his foreword to the publication of the musical:

> In the spring of 1966, my collaborator, Danny Apolinar, and I suffered a bad experience in preparing a musical score for a property by a well-known author, for which we had no legal authority for the musical rights. We presented the score to the author's agent, and were told that we had no talent and should return to Puerto Rico (where we both lived). We did go back to Puerto Rico, not because we thought we had no talent, but to look for an idea for a musical based on a property in the public domain so as not to repeat our mistake.
>
> One evening, Paulette Girard, an actress friend of mine, was reading aloud to me all the synopses of Shakespeare's plots. When she came to *Twelfth Night*, the parallel of the

look-alike situation of the sexes seemed to me to be a natural, inasmuch as the dress and hair affectations of the younger generation are one of the main topics of thought with today's youth. The youth of today did not have to use the Establishment's standards of masculinity and femininity. I discussed the idea with Danny, and he liked it very much, so the two of us sat down to write a twenty-five-page outline using the Shakespeare plot and its parallel to the revolution that was occuring among young people all over the world.

When we finished our outline and score, we auditioned it for another actress friend of ours, Dorothy Love, who owns the Orpheum Theatre in New York.... When it became obvious that we would not interest an established producer, Dorothy offered to produce it at her theatre, and we started having backers' auditions. We raised half of the money needed; but we still didn't have a writer for the book. While inquiring among our theatrical friends in New York, Donald Driver's name kept cropping up as a writer and director with imagination and we auditioned the show for him. Besides Dorothy, Donald was the only other professional person to see the show's potential. He and I worked together for about three weeks and he took over the completion of the book. Danny and I got busy rewriting the score for the many new songs which were born of the many new ideas Donald was bringing to the book.

We had felt all along that we had something new and different to contribute to the theatre, both musically and visually, and the critics proved that we were right.... The many productions of *Your Own Thing* throughout the U.S.A. and many other countries have made "doing your thing" a household phrase. One critic, although liking the show, thought our title had a dirty meaning, which just goes to prove that when you do your thing, in our case *Your Own Thing*, your thing may not necessarily be his thing, but we hope it is your thing.

Donald Driver, director and author of the book, was born in Portland, Oregon. He graduated from Pomona College in Southern California and served in the Navy in World War II. He started in the theatre as a performer, first as a dancer then as an actor. His initial Broadway engagement was in 1952 when he appeared in the musical *Buttrio Square*. A series of other appearances, in plays and musicals, followed until he branched out as a writer and director with *From Paris with Love* which toured the United States and Canada in 1962. From then on, he staged many productions in theatres across the country, including a fresh concept of *The Taming of the Shrew* presented in 1965 at the American Shakespeare Festival in Stratford, Connecticut. In 1967 he came to Broadway as director of the American production of *Marat/Sade*, for which he was cited in the annual Tony nominations.

Following his success with *Your Own Thing*, Mr. Driver staged *Mike Downstairs; Jimmy Shine* (with Dustin Hoffman); a revival of *Our Town* with Henry Fonda; and his own comedy, *Status Quo Vadis*.

Hal Hester, co-composer and co-lyricist with Danny Apolinar, was born in Paducah, Kentucky. He studied at the Cincinnati Conservatory of Music, where he majored in piano and composition. After his graduation, he began writing songs and soon became an ASCAP writer with more than thirty published and recording credits. He also managed to conduct two other successful careers: as part of a singing trio that appeared in popular New York nightclubs, and the owner-operator of *The Sand and Sea Club* (named for his first million-record song, which he wrote for Nat King Cole) in San Juan, Puerto Rico.

Danny Apolinar was born in Brooklyn, New York, and educated at the High School of Industrial Arts and Pratt Institute. While working as a free-lance commercial artist he also managed to pursue a career in show business—he first became stagestruck when he did a show at a resort hotel in the Catskills.

His first professional contact with the entertainment milieu was as a singer with his collaborator, Hal Hester, for Atlantic Records in an act called *The Madhattans*. But their subsequent piano-and-songs act on which the pair had pinned high hopes was short-lived; Apolinar received his army induction notice just as the club tour was launched.

Later, with his own Danny Apolinar Trio, he toured the Playboy Club circuit and was featured as solo pianist in a series of Manhattan bistros.

Your Own Thing was Mr. Apolinar's initial experience in the theatre, both as an author and performer.

PRODUCTION NOTES

Your Own Thing was first presented by Zev Bufman and Dorothy Love at the Orpheum Theatre, New York, on January 13, 1968. The cast was as follows:

Apocalypse Singing Group:

Danny	*Danny Apolinar*
John	*John Kuhner*
Michael	*Michael Valenti*
Orson	*Tom Ligon*
Olivia	*Marian Mercer*
Viola	*Leland Palmer*
Sebastian	*Rusty Thacker*
Purser; Stage Manager	*Igors Gavon*
Nurse	*Imogene Bliss*

Directed by *Donald Driver*
Musical Direction and Dance Arrangements by *Charles Schneider*
Scenery by *Robert Guerra*
Costumes by *Albert Wolsky*
Lighting by *Tom Skelton*
Orchestrations by *Hayward Morris*
Technical Direction by *Richard Thayer*
Associate Producer: *Walter Gidaly*
Slide Sequences Designed by *Michael W. Lunstead*
Slide Photography by *Frank Derbas*
Motion Picture Sequences by *Michael Morse*

MUSICAL NUMBERS

No One's Perfect, Dear   Sebastian, Viola
The Flowers   Viola
I'm Me! (I'm Not Afraid)   Apocalypse
Baby! Baby!   Apocalypse, Viola
Come Away, Death   Sebastian
I'm on My Way to the Top   Sebastian
Let It Be   Olivia
She Never Told Her Love   Viola
Be Gentle   Viola, Orson
What Do I Know?   Viola
Baby! Baby! (Reprise)   Apocalypse, Sebastian, Viola
The Now Generation   Apocalypse, Viola
The Middle Years   Sebastian
The Middle Years (Reprise)   Olivia
When You're Young and in Love   Orson
Hunca Munca   Apocalypse, Company
Don't Leave Me   Olivia, Sebastian, Orson
Do Your Own Thing   Company

CHARACTERS

OLIVIA: *A very charming, witty and deliciously droll woman of thirty who owns and operates a discotheque. She loves to be surrounded by the young and is dressed in very chic versions of the latest fashion fad.*

ORSON: *A graduate of the beat generation who has become a theatrical agent and whose biggest client is the Apocalypse rock-and-roll group. His love affair with Olivia has been long and literary; his attempts to emulate the Now generation are heartfelt and hopeless. He is a square.*

VIOLA AND SEBASTIAN: *Brother and sister, members of the Now generation who, previous to their separation in the shipwreck, had been a rock duo. They are completely uninhibited and adventuresome. Their identical dress and hairstyle cause them to be mistaken for one another.*

APOCALYPSE: DANNY, JOHN, and MICHAEL. *Members of a four-man rock-and-roll group. They wear far-out clothes, long hair, and say and do anything that pleases them.*

NURSE: *A nurse.*

PURSER: *A sailor who befriends Viola after the shipwreck.*

STAGE MANAGER: *Runs Olivia's discotheque for her and is constantly frustrated by the behavior and language of the Now generation.*

PREFACE

When reading the following script, one must keep in mind the fact that film and slide projections, taped and live sound effects accompany the written word to form a mixed-media collage which is the final effect of the script.

Nine actors portray the ten characters: Viola, Sebastian, Olivia, Orson, The Apocalypse (Danny, John, and Michael), the Nurse, the Purser, and the Stage Manager. The following characters are projected on slides and their voices are recorded on tape: Everett Dirksen, Mayor Lindsay, Queen Elizabeth, Buddha, the Sistine God, W. C. Fields, John Wayne. Shirley Temple, Shakespeare, the Pope, Jesus Christ, and Louis XIV. Other slide projections are either scenic environments, comic-strip balloon writing (projected over the head of the actor thinking those thoughts), or projections which are extensions of what an actor is thinking; for example, slides of Viola appear when Orson is singing of his love for her. And further, when Orson is fantasizing his fears of homosexuality, the characters he imagines are projected around him.

Motion picture is used in conjunction with slide effects to provide a more total environment such as a shipwreck, or to depict the size of New York City, or to produce a psychedelic effect—as in the "Hunca Munca" dance.

Setting

The all-white setting suggests a Shakespearian stage. Upstage there are two platform-ramps, one higher than the other, running from one wing to the other. Behind them is a cyclorama or rear-projection screen. There are five entrances from the wings on either side: right 1 and left 1 are sliding doors and on both sides of each door there is a bench; right 2 and left 2 are wing entrances; right 3 and left 3 are the first platform-ramp; right 4 and left 4 are the second platform-ramp; right 5 *and left 5 are upstage of the platform-ramps and have a set of stairs leading up to the top platform-ramp. There is no act curtain used.*

Lighting

Normal stage lighting is used except when there are projections. When projections are used, backlighting is used on the set, and the actors are lit by follow spots.

Music

The orchestra consists of an electric organ, an electric guitar, an electric fender bass, and percussion.

TIME: *The present.*
PLACE: *Manhattan Island, Illyria.*

Overture: "Baby"
Music cut off.
DIRKSEN:

If music be the food of love, play on! I can't remember if that's Marlowe or Bacon.

(The shipwreck: The film begins with an explosion aboard ship and continues throughout the scene showing a shipwreck at sea and the ship finally sinking. Accompanying slide projections are stills taken from that movie and projected on the set surrounding the surface upstage on which the film is projected to complete the environmental picture)

VOICE OVER:

Passengers, please don't be alarmed. Please don't panic. The lifeboats are being lowered. We'll take on women and children as soon as the ship's Xerox and IBM machines are loaded.

(During the shipwreck scene the entire company appear as passengers running about, trying to put on life preservers, jump overboard, and generally escape the disaster. VIOLA and SEBAS-TIAN are finally the last passengers left on board)

SEBASTIAN:

Viola, where are you going?

VIOLA:

I'm going back to the cabin.

SEBASTIAN:

Vi, you can't go back to the cabin!

VIOLA:

I've got to save our orchestrations.

SEBASTIAN:
Stupid sister, we're sinking.

VIOLA:
Then you get them.

SEBASTIAN:
The hell you say. What do they matter if I drown getting them?

VIOLA:
Okay, Phi Bete, how'll we get work?

SEBASTIAN:
We get new orchestrations.

VIOLA:
Wonderful! They cost a fortune!

SEBASTIAN:
Then God dammit, I'll hum.

VIOLA (*Laughing*):
You're always off pitch.

SEBASTIAN:
All right, you go get them!

VIOLA (*Sudden anger*):
You'd let me, wouldn't you?

SEBASTIAN:
Why can't you ever be nice?
Why can't you ever be nice?
Why can't you ever be nice,
Be nice once or twice?

VIOLA:
Look who's talkin',
Look who's squawkin',
Look who's callin' the pot black.

SEBASTIAN:
> *Look who's talkin'*
> *Look who's squawkin',*

VIOLA:
> *Get off my back.*

BOTH:
> *No one's perfect dear.*

SEBASTIAN:
> *Why can't you be kind to me?*

VIOLA *(Laughing)*:
> See, you're off pitch!

SEBASTIAN:
> Vi-o-la, listen to me . . .

VIOLA:
> Some brother you are. You don't give a damn if we end up back in Akron, Ohio.

SEBASTIAN:
> You want a singing job in the bottom of the ocean?

VIOLA:
> It's no farther under than Akron!

SEBASTIAN:
> Why do you always have to argue? God damn you, Vi, we're sinking!

VIOLA:
> *Why can't you ever be nice?*
> *Why can't you ever be nice?*
> *Why can't you be nice to me,*
> *Nice and brotherly?*

SEBASTIAN:
> *Look who's talkin',*
> *Look who's squawkin',*

Look who's callin' the pot black.
Look who's talkin',
Look who's squawkin',

VIOLA:
Get off my back.
No one's perfect.

SEBASTIAN:
No one's perfect.

VIOLA:
No one's perfect.

SEBASTIAN:
No one's perfect.

BOTH:
No one is perfect, dear.

SEBASTIAN:
One of these days, Vi . . .

VIOLA:
Oh, I hate you so much!

PURSER (*enters, addressing* VIOLA):

For christ sakes! Don't just stand there, fella, get your sister to the lifeboat! (*Exits*)

(SEBASTIAN, *in anger, starts to follow* PURSER *off*)

VIOLA:
Oh, no! You're not going anywhere without those orchestrations!

SEBASTIAN:
All right then! I'll get them! (*Exits*)

VIOLA (VIOLA *starts to follow, bending over at orchestra pit*):
I should think you would!

SEBASTIAN *(Mimic)*:
I should think you would.

PURSER *(Enters)*:
Come on! Move your ass, mister, we're going fast! *(Slaps*
VIOLA's *ass)* Move your ass, lady, we're going fast.

(Blackout. PURSER *and* VIOLA *exit. Film out. Slides out.
Projections: Slides of waterfront buildings in semiabstract.
Lights. Enter* PURSER *and* VIOLA*)*

VIOLA:
What country, friend, is this?

PURSER:
This is Illyria, lady.

VIOLA:
And what should I do in Illyria?
My brother, he is in Elysium.
Perchance he is not drowned;
What think you, sailor?

PURSER:
It is perchance that you yourself were saved.

VIOLA:
And so perchance may he be.

PURSER:
True, madam; and, to comfort you with chance,
Assure yourself, after our ship did split,
When you, and those poor number saved with you
Hung on our driving boat, I saw your brother
Most provident in peril, bind himself
(Courage and hope both teaching him the practice)
To a strong mast that lived upon the sea:
Where, like Orion on the dolphin's back,
I saw him hold acquaintance with the waves.
So long as I could see.

VIOLA:
Know'st thou this country?

PURSER:
Ay, madam, well, for I was bred and born
Not three hours' travel from this place.

(Exits)

VIOLA (Calling after PURSER):

Who governs here?

(Lights down)

MAYOR LINDSAY:
Illyria is a fun city. Cough, cough.

VIOLA:
And what should I do in Illyria?

(During this song the motion-picture film shows varying shots
of New York City skyline and skyscrapers. The film is at the
same time beautiful and impersonal; and in a nutshell, cap-
sulizes the exterior shapes of twentieth-century urban life. The
slide projections which accompany this film are stills of steel
and glass structures and change constantly during the song)

VIOLA:
So much glass, so much steel,
What's there to care? What's there to feel?
All that glass, all that chrome,
Can I ever call this place home?

Here the air is gray and smoggy.
My eyes burn and my head seems groggy.
How do the flowers grow
In their sweet little box
In their neat little row?

Here come the men to plant new flowers.
The beautiful people must see beautiful flowers
From their beautiful ivory towers.

So much glass, so much steel,
What's there to care? What's there to feel?
All that glass, all that chrome,
Can I ever call this place home?

Time to change another season.
If I watch I may find the reason
Why flowers never die
In their glass-covered box
'Neath their gas-covered sky.

Here come the men to plant new flowers.
The beautiful people must see beautiful flowers
From their beautiful ivory towers.

So much glass, so much steel,
What's there to care? What's there to feel?
All that glass, all that chrome,
Can I ever call this place home?
Can I ever call this place home?

BALLOON (*Over* VIOLA's *head*):
   "Oh dear God. I fear Sebastian lost in the shipwreck."

SISTINE GOD:
   She's talking to me. Shipwrecks, you know, are my specialty.

BALLOON (*Over* VIOLA's *head*):
   "I've never been without him. How will I ever get a singing job?"

BUDDHA:
   Disaster may be your speciality; but next to harmony, mine is rock.

(BUDDHA *bell rings and* BUDDHA *hand appears with card*)

VIOLA (*Reading* BUDDHA *card*):
   "Boy wanted."
(VIOLA *inspects herself; collapses her chest*)
Why not?

(VIOLA *does choreographed dance, exits*)

(Projection: Telephone environment. ORSON *enters;* OLIVIA *enters separately. Both close doors; lights up. This scene is played like a normal scene without pantomiming use of telephones)*

ORSON *(Speaking front):*
Hello, Olivia.

OLIVIA *(Speaking front):*
Orson, old charmer, that's got to be you.

ORSON:
It is, Olivia, I love you.

OLIVIA:
Orson, is this a business call?

ORSON:
Olivia, I love you.

OLIVIA *(Turning to* ORSON*):*
No, you're just stimulated by rejection.

ORSON *(Turning to* OLIVIA*):*
I am not.

OLIVIA:
All right, then you're too old for me.

ORSON:
I am not; we're the same age.

OLIVIA:
That proves it; I like younger men. Orson is this a business call? Are you calling me about your rock group?

ORSON:
Will you have dinner with me?

OLIVIA:
Soon, Orson, soon.

ORSON:
Olivia—

OLIVIA:
Orson, did you call me up for another emotional setback?

ORSON:
No! It *is* about my singing group, The Four Apocalypse.

OLIVIA:
Well, finally! What about them? Don't tell me the boys dropped you for a new agent?

ORSON:
Ha! Ha! Only one.

OLIVIA:
What?

ORSON:
I lost one of the Apocalypse.

OLIVIA:
Oh no! You didn't lose Death? Or Famine?

ORSON:
No, Disease. He's been drafted.

OLIVIA (*Going center to* ORSON):
Oh! That's terrible. I've advertised all four.

ORSON (*Going center to* OLIVIA):
Now look, Olivia—

OLIVIA:
How would you like to go to a discotheque to hear a quartet and get a trio? Business is business, Orson. I want all four or none.

ORSON:
Surely you wouldn't cancel out?

OLIVIA:

Orson, what good are Death, War, and Famine without Disease?

ORSON:

With all those postpubic, long-haired, beriberi types hanging around, can't you recommend one?

OLIVIA:

They're all matched sets. I wouldn't want to break up any.

ORSON:

Olivia . . .

OLIVIA:

There goes that tone again.

ORSON:

But I do love you.

OLIVIA:

Orson, believe me, what you have is just an unresolved umbilical sense memory. *(Opens door)*

ORSON:

Oh, Olivia.

OLIVIA:

I want all four or none. *(Exits, closing door)*

ORSON:

I'll get a new Disease . . . Olivia, are you listening to me? She's mean.

(Projection: Interior, ORSON's office. Lights build. APOCALYPSE enter)

DANNY:

What did Olivia say this time, Orson, baby?

MICHAEL:

How's the romance going?

JOHN:
Going to be a June wedding?

(*All grab* ORSON *and hum various wedding marches*)

ORSON:
She says she'll cancel if we don't come up with a fourth Apocalypse for her discotheque.

JOHN:
Four? We're only three.

MICHAEL:
Yeh. Three was always bad news.

DANNY (*Stirring caldron*):

Like the three witches in *Macbeth*.

MICHAEL (*Stabbing himself*):
The Triumvirate!

JOHN:
Don't forget the waltz!

(DANNY *grabs* ORSON *and begins waltzing*)

ORSON:
God damn you guys. I need help!

MICHAEL:
God damn you guys. He needs help!

JOHN:
I think you can safely say that.

DANNY (*Overlapping above line*):
There's a sense of desperation there.

ORSON:
We'll discuss finding a replacement for your drafted leader if you clowns all will come down a minute.

MICHAEL:
Down everybody.

ORSON:
We've got thirty-two ... (APOCALYPSE *fall to their knees imitating the three monkeys, "Hear no evil, see no evil, speak no evil." John blows high toot on kazoo for "Speak no evil"*) We've got thirty-two weeks of bookings. The contract reads a rock group of four. We've now got three. As I see it, we need one more.

(APOCALYPSE *follow* ORSON *on their knees*)

DANNY:
Now we're getting somewhere.

JOHN:
Orson, I have a split personality. Will that help?

MICHAEL:
I know his other half. He can't do anything.

JOHN:
He can, too. He can lie, cheat, and steal.

DANNY:
I'll verify that.

ORSON:
Miserable children!

JOHN, MICHAEL, DANNY:
Orson!

ORSON:
Can't you creeps ever be serious?

MICHAEL:
Okay, creeps, get serious. Let's give it a little Corelli fugue here.

(APOCALYPSE *play a perfect three-part Corelli fugue on kazoos, and dance a minuet*)

ORSON:

They should have drafted all four of you!

DANNY:

Hey, look. There's sadness in the room.

MICHAEL:

Don't cry, boys, it's bad for your nasal passages.

ORSON:

Go on. Keep it up. Keep it up. When you're all starving, let's see you come up with the funnies.

MICHAEL:

He needs help. Okay, brain pool, give it the Auguste Rodin.

(APOCALYPSE *imitate pose of Rodin's* The Thinker)

JOHN:

I've got it. Nobody would know if there were only three of us, if we just kept shifting position all night. (APOCALYPSE *get in close line, all facing same direction,* JOHN *in the middle*) We could call ourselves the Lucky Pierres.

MICHAEL *(Falsetto)*:

I love it.

DANNY:

It's an "In" joke.

ORSON:

Get out! . . . Get out!

APOCALYPSE *(Barbershop harmony)*:

The roses are blooming in Picardy . . .

(As APOCALYPSE *exit, lights down*)

QUEEN ELIZABETH:

Why do they need a fourth musician? In my day troubadors sang alone.

BOGART:

We call that folk singing. The government frowns on it.

SISTINE GOD:

The old queen's right. Four's not a Biblical number.

QUEEN ELIZABETH:

Did I hear that Vatican Manifestation on the ceiling refer to me as the "old queen"?

JOHN WAYNE:

It don't matter who they put in the group. I can't tell the boys from the girls anyway.

BOGART:

You do have a problem. (*Lights up*)

ORSON:

I can't get through to these guys. God knows I've tried. There's no generation gap with me. I read *Ramparts* and *The East Village Other*. I've been to the Electric Circus. I've studied their language. I read that article in *McCalls* by Lynda Bird. I've studied their music, and everything teen, their every scene. I try every way I can to get through to them with God knows what-not. Even pot. Blahh. It makes you hungry. I gained four pounds on the candy bars alone. To them I'm Orson Uptight. Big Square. Nowhere. But I'm not! I'm the personification of all the accumulated knowledge of the beat generation and I try to be it. Why can't they see it. What do I have to do to show, I know . . . how to be one of them? (*Exits*)

(APOCALYPSE *enter during end of* ORSON'S *speech*)

DANNY:

I don't have to show anyone
I want to be one of them;
'Cause deep inside is the feeling of pride,
The me from which the mighty oaks stem.

MICHAEL:

This is a man, look at his hair,
Not your idea of a he-man.

DANNY:

Think what you will, what do I care?
I just want to be a free man,
To be me, man.

JOHN:

This is a man, look at his clothes,
Not your idea of a tough man.

DANNY:

Think what you will, this is no pose.
Don't have to pretend I'm a rough man,
I'm enough, man.

MICHAEL:

This is a man, look at his eyes,
They're expressive.

DANNY:

I can feel.

JOHN:

This is a man, look at his heart,
It's impressive.

DANNY:

I am real.

ALL:

Why does everybody have to be afraid to be a human being?
Why does everybody have to be afraid of other people
seeing?

DANNY:

Everybody has emotion buried deep inside.
When they feel one truthful emotion,
They feel that's what they've got to hide.

JOHN:

Me—I'm not afraid to cry,
Me—I'm not afraid to die,
I'm not afraid to weep when I'm sad,

I'm not afraid to laugh when I'm glad,
I'm not afraid to know when I'm bad,
I'm not afraid to love.

MICHAEL:

Me—I'm not afraid to live,
Me—I'm not afraid to give,
I'm not afraid when the nights are too long,
I'm not afraid to admit when I'm wrong,
I'm not afraid to sing a new song,
I'm not afraid to love.

DANNY:

Me—I'm not afraid to be,
Me—I'm not afraid to see,
I'm not afraid to give all my love,
I'm not afraid of heaven above,
I am the new man, a true man, more human and free,
But most of all, I'm not afraid of me.

ALL:

Our generation can't live in the past.
I know that tomorrow won't last.
That's the reason our hearts beat much faster.

DANNY:

I'm not the starry-eyed boy next door,
I'm not the life of the party,
I've got to be what I've got to be.
I'm me!
I'm not the prince in a fairy tale,
I'm not as strong as an oak tree,
I like the feeling of feeling free.
I'm me!

My generation can't live in the past.
I know that tomorrow won't last.
That's the reason my heart beats much faster.

ALL:

I can do anything I want to do.
I can make every dream I dream come true.

There may be things that I'll never
Completely see.
But look at me! Look! You can see that I'm real!
I'm alive! I'm me.

(Blackout. APOCALYPSE *exit)*

SHIRLEY TEMPLE:
Death, War, Disease and Famine. That's not very nice.

BUDDHA:
Best you go with it. It makes your stocks rise.

JOHN WAYNE:
Why don't they call themselves "The He-Men" or something?

LOUIS IV:
What were those magical items on the boys' costumes, that run up and down?

BOGART:
They're called zippers, Louis.

(Lights up. Projection: Interior, ORSON's *office.* VIOLA *enters, with short dance. Stops)*

VIOLA *(Reading* BUDDHA *card)*:
Buddha says: "Boy Wanted." Out of sight. [VIOLA *continues dance cross to door.* ORSON *enters through door.* APOCALYPSE *enter during the end of* VIOLA's *dance*]

ORSON *(Taking* BUDDHA *card from* VIOLA)*:
Buddha. That your agent? [APOCALYPSE *cross down to* VIOLA *and* ORSON. *Music vamp starts and continues under dialogue to song*] What's your instrument?

VIOLA:
I'm a boy. *(Realizing . . .) Oops! (Takes tambourine from* MICHAEL*) Yes! (Plays tambourine)*

ORSON:
Can you sing?

VIOLA (*In high soprano voice*):
"AAHHH!" . . . I'm a tenor.

ORSON:
Name?

VIOLA:
Uh . . Charlie! Uh . . . Charlie . . . uh . . .

ORSON:
Disease! Let's see your work.

(*While* APOCALYPSE *sing "Baby, Baby,"* VIOLA, *making mistakes, tries to sing along with them, play the tambourine, dance and give a good audition. The impression is more frantic than anything as she tries to copy each of their styles. She wins them over as they end up copying hers*)

VIOLA & APOCALYPSE:
Somethin's happenin' makes me want to fly,
Baby! Baby! Baby! Baby!
Somethin's happenin', some new kind of high,
Baby! Baby! Baby! Baby!
Over and over and over and over and over
And over and over and over
Over and over and over and over and over
And over and Oh!

Somethin's happenin' makes me want to pop,
Baby! Baby! Baby! Baby!
Somethin's happenin' goin' to the top,
Baby! Baby! Baby! Baby!
Over and over and over and over and over
And over and over and over
Over and over and over and over and over
And over and Oh!

Somethin's happenin' makin' me feel good,
Baby! Baby! Baby! Baby!
Somethin's happenin', gonna knock on wood,
Baby! Baby! Baby! Baby!
Over and over and over and over and over

And over and over and over,
Baby! Baby!
Over and over and over and over and over
And over and
Rockabye, bye-bye, baby!

(*All ad-lib*)

ORSON:
You're real groovy. You're . . . you know . . . ah . . .

DANNY:
Solid?

ORSON:
Yeh, solid.

JOHN:
Jackson!

ORSON:
Jack . . . Bug out!

JOHN:
You'll learn to cope with the parochial entrenchment of the Victorians.

ORSON:
Get out!

APOCALYPSE (*Barbershop harmony as they exit, backing out*):

Daddy, dear old daddy,
You've been more like a mother to me.

VIOLA:
They're very unusual. Thanks, thanks for the audition!

ORSON:
I'm Orson. Your new agent.

VIOLA:
Really! Then I can join the group?

ORSON (*Starting to kneel*):
Want me to get down on my knees and beg you?

VIOLA (*Stopping him*):
No! You don't have to do that!

ORSON:
I was about to grow long hair and plug myself in. (VIOLA *laughs but switches to "bad joke" take*) But I don't sing that well. I have trouble staying on pitch. You know, Charlie, that never struck me before. Could a little thing like that make me square?

VIOLA:
Oh, not. Just the right square can be awfully groovy.

ORSON:
I wish someone would tell that to Olivia.

VIOLA:
Olivia?

ORSON:
She's the woman I love.

VIOLA:
Oh. And she thinks you're square?

ORSON:
Like Bert Parks! Look! Olivia listens to young kids like you. If I give you a letter, you could deliver it to her in person, and then maybe you could put in a good word for me . . . like what you just said.

VIOLA:
What'd I just say?

ORSON:
That I'm not square.

VIOLA:
You're not? Oh, no. You're not!

ORSON:
She will attend it better in thy youth
Than in a nuncio's of more grave aspect.

VIOLA:
Hmm?

ORSON:
Dear lad, believe it;
For they shall yet belie thy happy years
That say thou art a man. Diana's lip
Is not more smooth and rubious;

(VIOLA *sneaks a look at her upper lip*)
thy small pipe
Is as the maiden's organ, shrill of sound,

(VIOLA *feels her throat*)
And all is semblative a woman's part.

(VIOLA *covers her breasts;* ORSON *opens door*)
I know thy constellation is right apt
For this affair.

(ORSON *pulls* VIOLA *off*)

VIOLA:
This scene's getting freaky!

(*Blackout. As* ORSON *pulls* VIOLA *off, closing door, music*)

SHAKESPEARE:
Why do they always quote my commercial crappe!

(*Music. Projection: Exterior environment of trees and foliage.* SEBASTIAN *enters, in wheelchair, and hospital robe, covered with blanket*)

SEBASTIAN:
My stars shine darkly over me; my sister

Vi, though it was said she much resembled me,
Was yet of many accounted beautiful;
She bore a mind that envy could not but call fair.
Drowned in salt water. I'll drown her remembrance
In more stinging brine of despair.

Come away, come away, death,
And in sad cypress let me be laid.
Fly away, fly away, breath:
I am slain by a lost lovely maid.

My shroud of white, stuck all with yew,
O, prepare it!
My part of death, no one so true
Did share it.

Not a flower, not a flower sweet
On my black coffin let there be strown.
Not a friend, not a friend greet
My poor corpse, where my bones shall be thrown.

A thousand, thousand sighs to save.
Lay me, O, where
Sad brother never find my grave
To weep there!

Come away, come away, death
And in sad cypress let me be laid.
Fly away, fly away, breath:
I am slain by a lost lovely,
Lost lovely maid.

(*Lights up; slide environment out.* NURSE *enters with basin,
thermometer, and washcloth, closes door*)

NURSE (*Seeing only the back of* SEBASTIAN *in wheelchair*):

Good morning, Miss, I'm the relief nurse; all right, Miss . . .
(*She shakes down thermometer*)

SEBASTIAN:
    Now, look . . .

NURSE (*Putting thermometer in* SEBASTIAN's *mouth*):
Keep this under your tongue, Miss, while I give you your sponge bath.

SEBASTIAN:
Ub-blub . . .

NURSE:
You do want me to bathe you, don't you?

SEBASTIAN (*High voice*):

Uh-huh!

NURSE (*Puts chair in bed position*):
Well, then, just relax, honey. Relax! Take your arm out of your sleeve. Well, you got quite a little crack on the head there, didn't you? What happened?

SEBASTIAN (*Still sitting up; takes arm out of its sleeve*):
Uhh . . .

NURSE (*Going to basin*):
Ah, ah, ah, that's a rhetorical question, girl. (SEBASTIAN *lies down. Crossing back to* SEBASTIAN, NURSE *lifting his left arm up to wash it*) Give me your arm. (*Pause*) Do we always wear our armpits Italian style?

SEBASTIAN (*Falsetto*):
Uh . . . mn . . .

NURSE (*Continuing to wash arm*):
Chacun à son goo, as the French say. Like I say, I'm just here until Thursday. I'm relieving the regular nurse so she can have her varicose veins removed. (*Puts arm down, having finished washing it*) Boy, if the cement floors don't break them down, the patients snapping your girdle will. (*Slaps* SEBASTIAN *with washcloth*) I just passed my Army nurse's exam. I'm on my way to Vietnam next Thursday. (NURSE *slaps* SEBASTIAN *with cloth again, crosses to basin, wrings out cloth*) I figure it's a lot safer to face a spread of Vietcong mortars, than one convalescent with a well-aimed finger. (*Crossing back to* SEBASTIAN, *continu-*

ing to bathe him, this time starting with the back): We girls must stick together, right?

SEBASTIAN *(High voice)*
    Right!

NURSE *(Washing him and getting progressively lower on his body):*
You know, being a nurse is no Florence Nightingale movie. The patients couldn't care less how much work you put in. They're just interested in ... *(She reaches* SEBASTIAN's *crotch. She does a take front, looks under robe, screams! and throws down rag)* You ought to be ashamed of yourself!

SEBASTIAN *(He takes out thermometer as he sits up):*
    Oh, dear. I'm sorry to hear that. You really think so? *(Opens robe, ducks his head inside to inspect himself)*

NURSE *(Taking thermometer and reading it):*
    We'll have to take this over.

SEBASTIAN *(Lighting up):*
    The bath, too?

NURSE:
    You should be in the army with a haircut.

SEBASTIAN:
    I don't quite see the connection.

NURSE:
    It would straighten you out.

SEBASTIAN:
    Well, you've already done that. Zabadabadoo! *(He falls back down)*

NURSE *(Putting chair into upright position again):*
    You see! That's what I mean. Okay, that's enough. In the army with a haircut!

SEBASTIAN:
    I'll probably get there soon enough without you wishing it on

me. Who said, "A coward, a most devout coward, religious in it"?

NURSE *(Starting to push wheelchair off. Lights start down)*:
  You're not afraid of going to war, are you?

SEBASTIAN:
  Oh, no, just of being shot.

(SEBASTIAN *and* NURSE *exit*)

DIRKSEN:
  That sort of thing gives aid and comfort to the enemy.

JOHN WAYNE:
  My country right or wrong!

BOGART:
  I think Hitler said the same thing.

POPE:
  But God is on our side.

BUDDHA:
  Which one?

(Projection: Return to slides of trees and foliage used in previous scene. SEBASTIAN *and* NURSE *enter.* SEBASTIAN *on foot, dressed. Lights restore)*

NURSE:
  I won't be seeing you again. Will you write to me and let me know whither you are bound?

SEBASTIAN *(He kisses* NURSE *on the cheek)*:
  My determinate voyage is mere extravagancy. Fare you well at once.

NURSE:
  The gentleness of all the gods go with thee. *(Exits)*

SEBASTIAN:
   And what should I do in Illyria?

(Music introduction into song: "I'm on My Way to the Top." During the introduction, the environment changes from trees to city skyscrapers and skyline. The slides are of the same type used in the song "The Flowers." The last slide to appear is the BUDDHA. BUDDHA *bell rings and* BUDDHA *hand appears with card)*

SEBASTIAN *(Reading* BUDDHA *card)*:
   "Boy Wanted." Groovy.

*(*BUDDHA *hand exits)*
(First verse of song is sung to BUDDHA*)*

I'm a guy going places, and I'm leaving today.
I've got plenty to do and I'd do it with you,
But I've no time to stop.

*(*BUDDHA *hand appears. During next line of song,* SEBASTIAN *and* BUDDHA *shake hands)*

I'm on my way to the top.

*(*BUDDHA *hand exits.* BUDDHA *slide goes out and is replaced with a skyscraper slide to go with the rest of the environment)*

I've got all of the aces, hear me holler hooray!
Don't you wait up for me, I've got places to see
That would make your eyes pop.
I'm on my way to the top.

*(*SEBASTIAN *crosses to* ORSON's *door, knocks on door.* ORSON *enters)*

ORSON *(Taking* BUDDHA *card from* SEBASTIAN*)*:
   This Buddha must be a poor loser. I'm your new agent.

SEBASTIAN:
   You are?

ORSON:
Look, Charlie, the first thing you've got to learn to do is trust me.

SEBASTIAN:
Right, right, I will.

ORSON:
I've been thinking about that letter to Olivia.

SEBASTIAN:
What letter?

ORSON:
You got the letter?

SEBASTIAN:
No, sir.

ORSON:
Charlie, didn't my secretary give you a letter?

SEBASTIAN:
No, sir.

ORSON:
Well, it doens't matter. I wrote a stronger one. One I know will really get through to her. Here.

SEBASTIAN:
What do I do with it?

ORSON (*Pushing* SEBASTIAN *on his way*):
Good youth, address they gait unto her;
Be not denied access; stand at her doors
And tell them there thy fixed foot shall grow
Till thou have audience!

(ORSON *exits, closing door*)

SEBASTIAN:
He's freaked out!

This is the life I was made for!
I'm giving all that I've got!
This is the time that I've prayed for!
Here I come ready or not!

I don't care if time races, I'm determined to stay.
Don't say anything more, hang a sign on my door,
'Cause I'm closing up shop!
I'm on my way to the top!
I'm on my way to the top!
I'm on my way to the top!

(Lights out. SEBASTIAN *exits. Projection: Interior.* OLIVIA'S *wallpaper. Bright-colored flowers.* APOCALYPSE *and* VIOLA *enter.* MICHAEL *first. He enters in a follow spot, then lights up. Door is closed by last person)*

MICHAEL *(High, Southern accent):*
Fifth floor, ladies lingerie, everybody out.

*(*OLIVIA *enters, closing door behind her. To* OLIVIA*)*
Olivia, Charlie.

OLIVIA *(To* VIOLA*):*
Hi! Well, I'm certainly glad Orson got a fourth.

MICHAEL *(To* VIOLA*):*
Charlie, Olivia.

VIOLA:
I'm the new Disease.

OLIVIA *(To* VIOLA*):*
You're kinda young, aren't you? *(To* MICHAEL*)* He doesn't even have a beard.

JOHN:
The fault is not in his stars, dear Olivia, but in his genes.
(Lights down)

BALLOON *(Slide, over* VIOLA'S *head):*
"My God! Do you think they've guessed?"
(Lights restore)

OLIVIA:
How did you meet up with the Dead End Kids?

MICHAEL:
Dead End Kids?

DANNY:
Miss Olivia's frame of reference is late thirties.

JOHN:
It makes for mischieviously medieval witticisms.

MICHAEL:
It's like joking in a foreign language.

VIOLA:
Come on, you guys, you'll embarrass her.

OLIVIA:
Naw! If I can turn 'em on, I can turn 'em off.

DANNY (*Whacking tambourine on his knee*):
Score one!

VIOLA:
Are you guys always such a bunch of fools?

(*The following section takes on the quality of Shakespeare low comedy. The* APOCALYPSE *become the clowns,* OLIVIA *and* VIOLA *the straight men. The staging is Elizabethan burlesque, with the lines accented with a series of "freezes" (or poses). Additional accent comes from the drums. Projection: A line drawing of Shakespeare's Globe Theatre, in black and white*)

JOHN:
Good, sir, I'll bet I can prove you're a fool.

VIOLA:
You can?

JOHN (*Sitting on floor in front of* VIOLA):
Dexteriously, good sir.

VIOLA:
Good fool, make your proof.

MICHAEL:
Good sir, why mourn'st thou?

VIOLA:
Good fool, for my brother's death.

DANNY (*Rolling over* MICHAEL's *back*):
I think his soul is in hell, sir, and black.

VIOLA:
I know his soul is in heaven, fool, and white.

JOHN:
The more fool, sir, to mourn for your brother's soul, being in heaven and *white*. Think if he were on earth and *black*.

(APOCALYPSE *with music accompaniment, do back roll up stage to first step of platform. They sit and remain motionless. Lights down to pin spots on* OLIVIA *and* VIOLA. VIOLA *stands center stage in a "freeze," tambourine hanging on one arm*)

OLIVIA:
No beard! That really does it.
How now?
Methinks I feel this youth's perfections
With an invisible and subtle stealth
To creep in at mine eyes.
Even so quickly may one catch the plague?
Well, let it be.

(*During the following song, the stage continues to remain motionless, except for* OLIVIA, *who uses the tambourine during song*)

You can catch cold very fast, well, let it be.
It can take hold very fast, well, let it be.
If this happens to me, well, let it be.
Well, let it be.

If I've found love very fast, well, let it be.
And if this love doesn't last, well, let it be.
If this happens, at least it happens to me,
So let it be.

Have I really found my groove? Well, let it be.
Or is this a stupid move? Well, let it be.
Whatever happens, I'll have to wait and see,
Just let it be.

You can call it what you will, but let it be.
If this happens, I'll take what's coming to me.
Just let it be, well, let it be.
Well, let it be.

(OLIVIA *flips tambourine back on* VIOLA's *arm. Lights change.*
APOCALYPSE *and* VIOLA *come out of their freezes*)
Now Jove in his next commodity of hair
Send thee a beard.

VIOLA:
By my troth, I'll tell thee, I am sick for one, 'though I would
not have it grow on my chin.

(Led *by* VIOLA, *who does not actually leave the stage,*
APOCALYPSE *exit in single file, still playing the clowns. Their exit
is with music.* OLIVIA *pantomimes paying them, as they pass by
her. Projection: On music cut off, environment restores to*
OLIVIA's *wallpaper*)

Orson wanted me to wait until the guys weren't around.
He asked me to deliver this letter. He wanted it delivered in
person.

(Hands OLIVIA *the letter*)

OLIVIA:
Oh! Here, you read it.

VIOLA:
Oh, I couldn't do that.

OLIVIA (*Nonchalantly tossing letter on the floor*):
Then let's just forget it; and in the meantime, why don't you sit down and we can get acquainted?

VIOLA (*Picking up letter*):
... I'll read it! Orson's really very nice, you know.

"You couldn't really mean it.
You're only kidding.
You couldn't really mean it."

OLIVIA:
Here we go.

VIOLA:
"Anyone can see, you prefer me
To those kids you've been hanging around."

OLIVIA:
Stop. That line again.

VIOLA:
"To those kids you've been hanging around."

OLIVIA:
The line before that.

VIOLA:
"Anyone can see you prefer me."

OLIVIA (*Seductively*):
You read very well.

VIOLA (*Giving* OLIVIA *the letter*):
Orson's really not as square as you'd think. Anyway, he's really very nice, and he loves you.

OLIVIA (*Smiling*):
Yes, well, tell him it's hopeless ... but, have him send another letter by ...

VIOLA:
By tomorrow?

OLIVIA:

No, by boy. (OLIVIA *exits, closing door*)

VIOLA:

Fortune forbid my outside have not charmed her,
Poor lady, she were better love a dream. (VIOLA *does dance
cross to* ORSON'S *door*)

ORSON (*Enters*):
Did she get it? Did she send an answer?

VIOLA:

Hopeless. But she said send another letter.

ORSON:

I knew it! She's hooked!

(ORSON *exits left 1, closing door.* VIOLA *takes letter and does
dance exit right 4, with letter in her teeth.* SEBASTIAN *enters right
3, with letter in his teeth and does dance cross to* OLIVIA'S *door
right 1*)

OLIVIA (*Enters right 1 door.* SEBASTIAN *gives her the letter.* OLIVIA
   gives it back to him):
You read it.

SEBASTIAN (*Reading*):
"You can't deny you love me.
You're only faking.
You can't deny you love me."

OLIVIA:

No, I can't.

SEBASTIAN (*Reading*):

"Anyone can see how happy you'd be
With me always hanging around."

OLIVIA:

Repeat the last line.

SEBASTIAN (*Reading*):
  "With me always hanging around."

OLIVIA:
  I like it!

SEBASTIAN (*Folding up the letter and giving it to* OLIVIA):
  Right, shall I take an answer?

OLIVIA:
  No, but bring another letter. (*Exits right 1, closing door*)

SEBASTIAN:
  She made good view of me; indeed, so much
  That methought her eyes had lost her tongue.

(SEBASTIAN *does dance cross to* ORSON'S *door left 1.* ORSON *enters left 1 before* SEBASTIAN *gets there and* SEBASTIAN *knocks on* ORSON'S *forehead*)

Another letter ought to land her.

ORSON (*Staggering from the clubbing* SEBASTIAN *has accidentally given him, takes out a letter and gives it to* SEBASTIAN *and exits left 1, closing door*):
  Right!

(SEBASTIAN *does dance cross and exits right 4, with letter in his teeth.* VIOLA *enters right 3, with letter in her teeth, and does dance cross to* OLIVIA'S *door right 1.* OLIVIA *enters right 1;* VIOLA *gives her the letter.* OLIVIA *gives the letter back and sits, waiting to be read to*)

VIOLA (*Reading*):
  "I can't believe you mean it. I think you're kidding.
  I know I really love you."

OLIVIA:
  Hold it! That line again.

VIOLA (*Catching* OLIVIA; *reading*):
  "I think you're kidding."

OLIVIA *(Laughing)*:
Wrong! The last one.

VIOLA *(Reading)*:
"I know I really love you."

OLIVIA:
Well, you said it. (OLIVIA *ogles* VIOLA. VIOLA gives the letter to OLIVIA)

VIOLA:
These are Orson's words. They're not very persuasive, are they?

OLIVIA:
Doggerel.

VIOLA:
If I did love you with dear Orson's flame . . .

OLIVIA *(Anxious)*:
What would you do?

VIOLA:
Make me a willow cabin at your gate
And call upon my soul within the house,
Write loyal cantons of contemned love
And sing them loud, even in the dead of night.

OLIVIA *(Rising)*:
I'll bring my Ovaltine and meet you about two. (OLIVIA *unzips* VIOLA's *zipper*)

VIOLA:
Whoa! (VIOLA *turns quickly upstage and zips her zipper up*)
I meant if I were Orson.

OLIVIA:
Oh, yes. Well, tell him the answer's the same, it's nowhere.
But . . . uh . . . uh . . . let's sleet and snow it with another letter. Shall we? (*Exits right 1, closing door.* VIOLA *does dance cross to* ORSON's *door left 1*)

VIOLA:
Soft, now follows prose.

(ORSON *enters*)

ORSON:
She flipped.

VIOLA:
Nowhere.

ORSON:
Is the Post Road still open?

VIOLA:
Right.

(ORSON *puts letter in* VIOLA's *open hand and exits left 1, closing door on his own arm.* VIOLA *does dance cross center; she attaches letter to string and exits right 4, dragging letter behind her.* SEBASTIAN *struts on right 3 with letter on a twig; crosses to bench up of right 1 door, stands on it with branch hidden behind his back and knocks.* OLIVIA *enters right door.* SEBASTIAN *offers her the twig with the letter and* OLIVIA *takes it*)

OLIVIA:
How thoughtful. (OLIVIA *takes the letter off the twig and gives it to* SEBASTIAN. *She then turns with the twig, giving it a confused look*)

SEBASTIAN (*Reading*):
"Let's make a date for dinner.
Let's go this evening.
Let's make a date for dinner."

OLIVIA:
What time?

SEBASTIAN:
It says eight o'clock. Shall I tell him? (SEBASTIAN *folds letter and gives it to* OLIVIA)

OLIVIA:
Why? And spoil his dinner. (OLIVIA *exits right 1, closing door*)

SEBASTIAN:
Right.

(SEBASTIAN *starts dance cross to* ORSON's *door right 1 but gives up, finishes it walking, and opens Right 1 door*)

ORSON *(Revealed Left 1 in doorway)*:
How's the Post Road?

SEBASTIAN:
Fast, man, fast.

ORSON:
Dinner?

SEBASTIAN:
I think you could safely say that. But she wants another letter around eight.

ORSON *(Giving* SEBASTIAN *another letter)*:
Charlie, you're a real friend to take care of this for me.

(ORSON *exits left 1, closing door.* SEBASTIAN *winks at audience and exits right 4.* VIOLA *enters right 3, dragging letter on string, and does short dance which ends with her jumping on the letter. She takes out a lock from her pants and locks her zipper. Then does dance cross to* OLIVIA's *door right 1.* OLIVIA *enters right 1, takes the letter on the string, flicks* VIOLA's *lock with it)*

OLIVIA *(Referring to the lock)*:
How long ya in fer?

(OLIVIA *gives raucous laugh at her own bad joke.* VIOLA *ignores her.* OLIVIA *notices a padlock key on the other end of the string, and delightedly shows it to* VIOLA)

VIOLA *(Panicked)*:
My key!!!

OLIVIA:

Ah! *(Triumphant)* I'll spring you about eight! (OLIVIA *exits right 1, closing door)*

VIOLA:

How will this fadge? My master loves her dearly,
And I (poor monster) fond as much on him;
As she (mistaken) seems to dote on me
What will become of this?

(VIOLA *does dance cross to* ORSON'S *door left 1. As she passes center: Envionment: change to warm yellow striped background on full set.* ORSON *enters left 1 and closes door.* VIOLA *not noticing him, does wild frug in her frustration. She finally sees him and embarrassedly recovers her composure.* ORSON *enters left 1. Opens and closes door)*

ORSON:

Success!

VIOLA:

Failure.

ORSON:

She loves me.

VIOLA:

[Forget it]!

Pause

ORSON:

You can tell me straight out. I can take it.

VIOLA:

Orson, face it.

ORSON:

Not even dinner?

VIOLA:

Never.

ORSON:

But you said one more letter would do it.

VIOLA:

She's never going to love you.

ORSON:

I don't believe it. You got the wrong girl, the wrong house.

VIOLA:

You're going to have to accept it sooner or later.

ORSON:

Later. Why later?

VIOLA:

Say there's a girl, and there could be, who loves you as
much as you love Olivia. Now, if you couldn't love her,
you would tell her; and she'd have to accept it, right?

ORSON (*Sullen*):

No woman's heart could hold such passion. Besides, they lack
retention.

VIOLA:

But I know . . .

ORSON:

What do you know?

VIOLA:

Too well what love women to men may owe.
In faith, they are as true of heart as we.
My father had a daughter lov'd a man,
As it might be perhaps, were I a woman,
I should love your lordship.

ORSON:

And what's her history?

VIOLA:

She never told her love,

She never told her love,
But let concealment like a worm in the bud
Feed on her damask cheek.

She sat like patience, like patience on a monument,
Smiling, smiling, smiling at grief.

ORSON:
What happened to your sister?

VIOLA:
I don't know yet.

ORSON:
Is she anything like you?

VIOLA:
Spittin' image.

ORSON:
She must be very attractive. . . . *(They stare at each other for long pause; then realizing)* . . . Charlie! I'll send another letter. No! I don't want to send another letter. Oh, hell! I don't seem to be able to do anything right. How about you? I mean, I'll bet you do it right, everything. Have you ever been in love, Charlie?

VIOLA:
Once.

ORSON:
What was she like?

VIOLA:
About your complexion.

ORSON:
Oh. Uh-huh . . .

VIOLA:
About your age.

ORSON:
It's a nice age.

VIOLA:

And a lot of your wonderful qualities.

ORSON:

Come to think of it, nobody ever sends me any letters. How'd it turn out? I mean you and the girl?

VIOLA:

I don't know yet.

ORSON:

Still hanging on, huh? Sorry. I mean for you. No, that's not nice. I guess I don't go about it right. If you want to know the truth, I don't do well with girls. I don't understand it. There's a lot of things about girls I don't understand. [ORSON *crosses and sits on bench*]

VIOLA (*Crossing to* ORSON *and kneeling in front of him; sings*):

When you love a girl, be very gentle.
Write her pretty sonnets, give her pretty things.
When you love a girl, be very gentle.
Whisper in her ear the words she likes to hear.

ORSON:

When I love a girl, I'll be very gentle.
I'll write her sonnets, I'll give her things.
When I love a girl, I'll be very gentle.
And if I can, I'll be her gentleman.

VIOLA:

When you love a girl, be very gentle.
Give her pretty presents tied with pretty strings.
When you love a girl, be very gentle.
Tell her that she's lovely, tell her she's your love.

ORSON:

When I love a girl, I'll be very gentle.
I'll give her presents tied with pretty strings.
When I love a girl, I'll be very gentle.

BOTH:

And all through life, she'll be my (your) gentle wife.

(ORSON *rises, pauses, looks back at* VIOLA *confused. Exits. Blackout, except for follow spot on* VIOLA)

JOHN WAYNE:
That man's falling for that boy!

BOGART:
That's your old problem. It's a girl.

JOHN WAYNE:
Yeh, but he don't know that.

BOGART:
Would it change anything if he did?

JOHN WAYNE:
Sure! It'd be decent.

BOGART:
No, just legal.

QUEEN ELIZABETH:
I say, "Pair anybody off with anything." The only crime I know is loneliness.

(Music underscoring starts)

SHAKESPEARE:
What is love? 'Tis not hereafter;
Present mirth hath present laughter;
What's to come is still unsure.
In delay there lies no plenty;
Then come kiss me, sweet and twenty:
Youth's a stuff will not endure.

VIOLA:
What do I know of me?
What do I know of you?
What do I know of rainbows after rain?
Where does the wind go after the storm?
Where does the sky meet the sea?

Where is that feeling friendly and warm
And when will it happen to me?

What do I know of life?
What do I know of love?
What are the signs that I'm supposed to see?

How will I tell them?
How will I feel?
How will I ever know?
When will there come one?
Where will someone be?

*(*APOCALYPSE *choral background offstage)*
What do I know of life?
What do I know of love?
How come I'm not the me I used to be?
Where is it happ'ning?
Where is it at?
When will I ever know?
What is the sum of,
What's to become of me?

(Blackout. VIOLA *exits. Music introduction.* SEBASTIAN *discovered center of top platform. Projection: Abstract slides of bright reds, yellows, and green. Environment for interior of* OLIVIA's *discotheque)*

SEBASTIAN:
Somethin's happ'nin', makes me want to fly.
Somethin's happ'nin', some new kind of high.

*(*SEBASTIAN *crosses to* OLIVIA's *door, jumps on bench up from door)*

Over and over and over and over
I'm goin' where I've never been.
Over and over and over and over
I've waited for this to begin.

*(*SEBASTIAN *knocks on* OLIVIA's *door.* APOCALYPSE *enter on platform)*

APOCALYPSE:
Make tracks, man! We've been lookin' for you!

SEBASTIAN (*Joining* APOCALYPSE *on platform*):
Go with it! Baby, I'm here!

SEBASTIAN & APOCALYPSE:
Somethin's happ'nin', makin' me feel good
Baby! Baby! Baby! Baby!

(OLIVIA *enters, leaving door open. She has* VIOLA's *padlock key*)

APOCALYPSE:
Somethin's happ'nin', gonna knock on wood

SEBASTIAN (*To* OLIVIA):
Eight o'clock and here's your mail.

APOCALYPSE:
Over and over and over and over and over
And over and over and over and over and
Over and over and over and over and over
And oh!

(As APOCALYPSE *sings the above,* OLIVIA *takes letter and with key unlocks padlock on* SEBASTIAN's *shirt, pulls zipper partway down, then turns to go back through door. She is stopped by whistle from* SEBASTIAN. SEBASTIAN *pulls zipper the rest of the way down.* OLIVIA *drops key on stage and exits*)

SEBASTIAN:
Somethin's happ'nin', happ'nin', happ'nin'

(SEBASTIAN *exits right 1*)

APOCALYPSE (*Crossing downstage to door.* MICHAEL *picks up key*):

Happ'nin', happ'nin', happ'nin', happ'nin',

(APOCALYPSE *cross upstage again to stage right on platform, with backs to audience as if to leave. Right 1 door closes*)

Somethin's happ'nin', baby! Baby!
Somethin's happ'nin'! Baby!

(*Music vamp continues.* VIOLA *enters, unseen by* APOCALYPSE, *in a rush to center stage from door left 1. Straightens out her shirt. Door is left open*)

VIOLA:
Sorry I took so long, fellas!

(APOCALYPSE, *in time with music tag, do a double-take toward* VIOLA, *thinking that she just left with* OLIVIA. *Lights build.* APOCALYPSE *cross downstage to* VIOLA)

MICHAEL (*Holding up key*):
Hey.

VIOLA:
My key! Where'd you get it?

MICHAEL:
Olivia dropped it. Here, this will get you back into Yale.

VIOLA:
Thanks. (*All ad-lib boos to* MICHAEL's *joke*) Boy, am I tired!

JOHN:
Why?

VIOLA:
I've been doing all of Orson's work for him.

MICHAEL (*Indicating* OLIVIA's *door*):
You couldn't have gotten much done.

JOHN:
Does he give you ten percent for that?

VIOLA (*Referring to the letters to* OLIVIA):
For playing post office?

MICHAEL:
Post office?

JOHN:
That's like spin the bottle.

MICHAEL:
Oh, that's quick.

(JOHN *gives quick kiss to* DANNY, *who resents it*)

VIOLA:
Come on, you guys. Tell me about old Orson. I mean, you've known him for a long time. What's his bag?

DANNY:
Would you believe brown paper?

VIOLA:
How long has this scene been going on with Olivia?

MICHAEL:
For Orson, about five years.

JOHN:
For Olivia, never.

VIOLA:
Poor Orson.

JOHN:
Poor Orson! He's an agent.

VIOLA:
You guys are kinda hard on him.

DANNY:
He hates us.

MICHAEL:
Yeah, because he thinks we take ninety percent of his salary.

VIOLA:
Well, I don't think he's such a bad guy.

MICHAEL:
Charlie, we know your story.

VIOLA:
You do?

MICHAEL:
You got no problem. You can move in on Orson whenever you like.

DANNY:
Sure, he needs a little shakin' up.

JOHN:
He can't find his bag because it's always over his head.

DANNY:
Orson's so busy trying to groove, he'll never know you're making the big move.

VIOLA:
Have you finks known about me all the time?

MICHAEL:
Sure, you think we're stupid?

VIOLA:
˙Will I lose my job?

DANNY:
Man, what do you think we are?

JOHN:
We'll keep your secret.

VIOLA:
You will?

JOHN:
Sure.

MICHAEL:
We know you're Olivia's mailman.

DANNY:
We know *Olivia!*

JOHN:
Olivia's yours, Charlie. Orson's in Limboville.

VIOLA:
Ahh! *(Switching octaves, from high to low)* Ah! Olivia's all mine? Wonderful!

STAGE MANAGER *(Enters left 1, leaving door open. He is carrying five "Hunca Munca" costumes and one pair of moccasins):*
Here are your freak suits for tonight, guys. You better try them on before they go out of style. *(He puts costumes on top of platform)*

DANNY:
Establishment!

MICHAEL:
Barf earner!

VIOLA:
Flower cruncher!

STAGE MANAGER:
Jerks!

MICHAEL:
Jerks! Oh! Delicious!(MICHAEL *faints into* JOHN's *arms)*

DANNY:
Mid-forties, Freudian implication . . .

MICHAEL:
Derivation—thirties!—from pud puller.

JOHN:
Biblically rooted . . . Old Testament . . . onanism!

MICHAEL:
Oh! Jerk! Jerk! Ooo! A collector's item.

DANNY:
Write it down.

STAGE MANAGER:
Your studs, links, and curlers are in the pockets.

JOHN:
Sartorial paranoid!

MICHAEL:
Hey! That's what I was going to call him. You've got ESP.
Hey, John's got ESP.

STAGE MANAGER:
ESP. I'm warning you guys. Don't bring that stuff in here.
(*He exits*)

JOHN:
He ought to try IBM. He's punchy.

DANNY:
Your studs, links and curlers are in the pockets.

(*This number is staged and choreographed in the style of
modern rock dances*)

VIOLA:
We're revolting from the age when lines were drawn
To separate the sexes.

ALL:
We're revolting from the age when all the men
Came from the state of Texas.

DANNY:
Men and women used to be so far apart in every way

That it's a mother wonder that there's still a mother
Human race today.

(VIOLA *and* APOCALYPSE *give the* STAGE MANAGER *the rasp-*
berries, through the door)

MICHAEL:
What's it all about

DANNY:
Makes me stomp and shout,

VIOLA:
Makes me want to move,

JOHN:
Makes me want to groove.

DANNY:
I'm so tightly trussed,

MICHAEL:
All this shakin' just

JOHN:
Makes me want to bust

VIOLA:
Right out of my body.

ALL:
Got a feel and the feel is feeling right.
Everybody is gonna fly tonight,
Do the things they don't allow.
We are the now generation.

Gotta move on in, make the band begin.
Waitin' for tonight, gotta look just right.

DANNY:
Got the latest gear,

MICHAEL:
Buttons up to here,

JOHN:
Ready to appear,

ALL:
We can't look shoddy.

VIOLA:
Let your hair down and shake out all your curls.
What's the difference, the boys all look like girls.

ALL:
Baby, you can take a bow, we are the now generation.

Many miniskirts, polka-dotted shirts,
What's the harm to be dressed from Carnaby?

DANNY:
How we love to dance

MICHAEL:
In bell-bottomed pants.

JOHN:
We can take a chance,

ALL:
We might get tangled.

VIOLA:
With our clothes on you can't tell us apart.
Just be careful you look before you start.

ALL:
You could get surprised and how!
We are the now generation.

Let me fill your cup, let me rev you up,
Baby, turn me on, au-go-go 'til dawn.

Lots of LSD, pot for you and me.
If you don't agree, you're too star-spangled.

Stuff your crewcuts and prim morality
Up your Stoneage conventionality.
Stay at home and milk a cow.
We are the now generation,
Our generation is now,
Our generation is now,
Our generation is here

(STAGE MANAGER appears in door left 1)

And now.

(*Music cut off.* APOCALYPSE *and* VIOLA *give* STAGE MANAGER *"the finger."* STAGE MANAGER *slams door shut*)

VIOLA (*Crossing up right to platform, with* MICHAEL):
    Hey, there are five freak suits. How come?

MICHAEL (*Handing* VIOLA *her costume*):
    Here, this one's yours. The extra one was for Fred before the poor bastard got drafted.

JOHN:
    I told him, "Fred," I said, "go north!" I told him, "You can see Niagara Falls on a box of shredded wheat—just get the hell across that border."

VIOLA:
    Wheeee!

MICHAEL (*Feigning cowardice*):
    I don't want to go to war!

JOHN (*Imitating World War I posters, pointing finger at* DANNY, *who is facing upstage*):
    Uncle Sam wants you!!!

DANNY (*Turning around and squinting eyes*):
Me, a Vietcong??? (*Pantomimes throwing grenade; pulling ring with teeth and throwing at the audience*)

(*Lights start down. Music underscoring starts.* APOCALYPSE *start changing into their costumes.* VIOLA *sees this; with costume in hand, she lets out small shriek and dashes out through door left 1, closing door behind her. As* VIOLA *leaves,* SEBASTIAN *enters right 1 door dressed in white undershorts, shirt, shoes and socks. His pants are over his arm.* SEBASTIAN *closes door as he enters*)

MICHAEL (*Seeing* SEBASTIAN):
Come on, man, you're not getting into your freak suit.

(SEBASTIAN *looks puzzled, does a take to audience, then willingly joins* APOCALYPSE *and begins changing into the costume they hand him. During the following slide sequence,* MICHAEL *takes off shirt and shoes, exits left 3, carrying his freak suit and* SEBASTIAN'S *boots.* JOHN *undresses down to his socks and undershorts, exits left 4 carrying clothes and freak suit.* DANNY *puts on red beret and exits left 2, carrying his freak suit and* SEBASTIAN'S *clothes.* SEBASTIAN *changes completely into freak suit and moccasins*)

QUEEN ELIZABETH:
Will, they're taking their clothes off on stage.

SHAKESPEARE:
So it would seem, madam.

SHIRLEY TEMPLE:
We must return to the old standards of public morality.

POPE:
This can never be given a good rating.

BOGART:
What about the Old Testament? There's some stuff in there I never saw in burlesque.

JOHN WAYNE:
Look at the red beret that guy's got on. Fruity.

(During the above line, DANNY is seen in red beret leaving the stage left 2. Lights should be enough to see APOCALYPSE undress)

BOGART:
Oh, yeah? What if the color was green?

JOHN WAYNE:
That's different! What's the theatre comin' to anyway? You know, now they're even using four-letter words right in public, on the stage.

QUEEN ELIZABETH:
Let's hear them!

(Lights restore. Projection: Soft, abstract pink and blue design. Environment for interior of OLIVIA's apartment)

SEBASTIAN (Sitting on lower platform):
What relish is in this? How runs the stream?
Or am I mad, or else this is a dream.
Let fancy still my sense in Lethe steep;
If it be thus to dream, still let me sleep.

(OLIVIA enters right 1, closing the door behind her)

Did you like my audition? (Suddenly realizing what he's said from OLIVIA's amused look) I meant my singing.

OLIVIA:
Take it easy, Charlie, you've already got the job. You're the best thing that ever happened to their group. My group, too.

(SEBASTIAN crosses to OLIVIA)

SEBASTIAN:
I can't believe all this is happening. You're not going to change your mind, are you? Look, I need this job. Really! And I'm clean, courteous, loyal . . .

OLIVIA:
Easy! I'm not going to change my mind.

SEBASTIAN:
Good! You know, when you get to know me *inside*(OLIVIA *smiles at this*), you'll find I'm quite a fellow. I'm very serious. I want to be a geologist.

OLIVIA:
A geologist!

SEBASTIAN:
I knew you'd think that was too square.

OLIVIA:
No, that's not true at all. Geology's close to "rock."

SEBASTIAN *(Sinks to floor)*:
Blaahh!

OLIVIA:
Well, Shakespeare did it.

SEBASTIAN:
And with no less shame. *(Pause)* You're an out-of-sight lady.

OLIVIA:
Thanks, Charlie.

SEBASTIAN:
My name is Sebastian.

OLIVIA:
Oh ... it's not Charlie? Strange. Oh, well. So you want to be a geologist! What are you doing about it? I mean, school and everything?

SEBASTIAN *(Rising)*:
I read every book I get a hold of. Collect samples. You see, Vi and I had been saving money ...

(Music underscoring: "Come Away Death")

OLIVIA (*Thinking there's another woman*):
  Vi?

SEBASTIAN:
  Vi was my sister.

OLIVIA (*Relieved, then realizing he said "was"*):
  Was?

SEBASTIAN:
  Yes.

OLIVIA (*Diplomatically*):
  You don't want to talk about it?

  (*Music out*)

SEBASTIAN:
  I'd rather not.

OLIVIA:
  You started to say you were saving money.

SEBASTIAN:
  Yes, for school. That's why I took up singing rock. So I could stash away the bread to be a geologist.

OLIVIA:
  You know, you're not going to believe this, but I wanted to be an archaeologist once.

SEBASTIAN:
  You're putting me on.

OLIVIA:
  I swear. One summer I went on a college expedition to diggings outside Cyrene, in Libya. You know where that is.

SEBASTIAN:
  No.

OLIVIA:

Oh, well, it's not important. I was given four square yards to excavate for my project. I dug all summer. I think I got the only four square yards in history where man has never set foot. One nice thing though, I was given a young Libyan boy to assist me. I spent most of the summer digging him. *(Realizing what she has just said,* OLIVIA *turns)*

SEBASTIAN *(Tactfully changing the subject to hide his disappointment)*:

Archaeology. Man, that's groovy. How'd you ever get into the discotheque racket?

OLIVIA:

Life always seems to give us another four square yards *(Realizing she's doing it again)* to dig somewhere.

SEBASTIAN *(Crossing to* OLIVIA*)*:

You and me'd make a good team. You could dig up the rocks and I could, like, identify them. What do you think?

OLIVIA:

Sounds heaven. *(*SEBASTIAN *gives her a short kiss)* Ah, that line again.

(They kiss again—longer)

SEBASTIAN:

You still haven't told me how you got from your four square yards in Libya to your discotheque off Third Avenue.

OLIVIA:

Well, after that summer I went *back* to Sarah Lawrence ... Did I tell you I had a minor in music? Well, I did. Anyway, Mother wanted me to be a cellist but old Daddy was an account executive at B. B. D. & O. and figured if the cello image wasn't too risky, the position I had to play it in was.

(Lights down. Both follow spots on SEBASTIAN. OLIVIA, *miming conversation, sits and she continues silent monologue)*

SEBASTIAN:
>This is the air; that is the glorious sun,
>This pearl she gave me, I do feel 't and see 't;
>And though 'tis wonder that enwraps me thus,
>Yet 'tis not madness. What a groovy lady.
>I'll bet she thinks, "He's a pleasant interlude—for a kid.
>Nice sense of humor, ambitious—for a kid." Goddammit,
>I'm nearly twenty. That's old—for a kid.

>*I finally made it! I shook myself free.*
>*No more wondering what became of me.*
>*I know where I'm going, no crocodile tears*
>*Solved the riddle, I'm in my middle years.*
>*The nights now are shorter tho, somewhat less gay.*
>*No more time to waste, I live each day*
>*And I happen to like it, so give a few cheers,*
>*Tune my fiddle, I'm in my middle years.*
>*It's sublime to live and love in my security.*
>*Old man time can't blame it on my immaturity.*
>*Look and see!*
>*I've got a few wrinkles. I wear them with pride.*
>*I've worked hard for them, I've nothing to hide.*
>*No more nights on the town.*
>*No more playing around.*
>*I've won my medal an' done all my pedalin',*
>*Ready for settlin' down.*
>*Hey diddle diddle! Here's to the middle years.*

(*Lights restore*)

OLIVIA:
>Sebastian, are you listening to me?

SEBASTIAN (*Caught daydreaming*):
>Yeah, every word.

OLIVIA:
>I asked you how old you were.

SEBASTIAN (*Wary*):

>You mean for a kid?

OLIVIA:
No, I mean for you.

SEBASTIAN:
In years?

OLIVIA:
If you make it looks, you've got to give me a handicap.

SEBASTIAN:
Do you have to poke it with a stick and give it a name?

(Starts to exit)

STAGE MANAGER: *(Enters left 2 with handful of forms)*

Hey, Disease. I've been looking for you. Fill these out, W4, Blue Cross, HIP. And don't play it cute like your freak friends. I don't want to know what war your name is, how many Famines you got for dependents or the city morgue for your address. Just your right Goddamn name.

(Exits right 2)

*(*SEBASTIAN *sits upstage of right door and begins reading forms)*

BALLOON:
"I asked you how old you were."

BALLOON:
"Big mouth."

BALLOON:
"Why did you have to ask that? Things were going great."

SEBASTIAN *(Reading forms with self-amusement)*:

Name, age, this number, that number, how many unions, how many diseases, how many years, first war, second war, Korea, present police action? It's a grand old flag. . . . Instead of your age, why don't they ask, "the number of people you love?"

BALLOON:
"Why did you have to mention that Libyan boy?

BALLOON:
"Olivia is a dirty old man."

BALLOON:
"Lady."

OLIVIA:
Right! *(She and* SEBASTIAN *look at each other at the sound of her voice)*

BALLOON:
"I asked you how old you were."

BALLOON:
"I asked you how old you were?"

BALLOON:
"I asked you how old you were?"

OLIVIA:
What you really meant was not, "How old are you, you marvelous, beautiful youth?", but, "Olivia, are you too old?" That's the horrible, terrible truth.

SEBASTIAN *(Handing her the forms)*:
Here. This'll tell you how "young" I am. *(Exits right 1. Leaves door open.* OLIVIA *looks at card. It is the cue for her song)*

OLIVIA:
He's twenty, I'm thirty. Does it matter?
When I'm forty, he'll be thirty. Does it matter?
Rules, labels, slots, categories
Lead the way to lonely purgatories.
What does it matter?

(She sets the forms down beside her on the bench)

I finally made it! I shook myself free!
No more wondering what became of me.
I know where I'm going, no crocodile tears
Solved the riddle, I'm in my middle years.
The nights now are shorter tho', somewhat less gay.
No more time to waste, I live each day.
And I happen to like it, so give a few cheers,
Tune my fiddle, I'm in my middle years.
It's sublime to live and love in my security.
Old man time can't blame it on my immaturity.
Look and see!

(SEBASTIAN *enters right, stands in doorway overhearing her*)

I've got a few wrinkles. I wear them with pride.
I've worked hard for them, I've nothing to hide.
No more nights on the town.
No more playing around.
I've won my medal an' done all my pedalin',
Ready for settlin' down.
Hi diddle diddle! Here's to my middle years.

SEBASTIAN:
I'm sorry. I got up tight about my age. I thought you were putting me down for being young or something. If you let me see you after work tonight, I'll age a little for you, I promise.

OLIVIA:
Okay. You age a little and I'll grow up.

(SEBASTIAN *exits right 2.* VIOLA *disgustedly enters left 3 with letter.* STAGE MANAGER *enters right 1*)

STAGE MANAGER:
Hey, Disease. Have you got those forms filled out yet?

VIOLA:
What forms?

STAGE MANAGER:
Come on, Goddammit! Do you guys always have to be such smart asses!

OLIVIA *(Giving him the forms* SEBASTIAN *had given her)*:
Here.

STAGE MANAGER *(To* VIOLA*)*:

You couldn't just give them to me. You had to make a whole
Goddamn production out of it. *(Starts to exit; reading forms)*
What's this? "Number of dependents?" "The world"?! What is
that! "The world"! You couldn't just say one, two or three?

VIOLA:
I don't have *any*.

STAGE MANAGER:
You couldn't say that?! The government isn't interested in
your Goddamn love movement! They want numbers, like one,
two, three, four, five . . . *(Exits right 1, closing door behind him)*

VIOLA:
What's his high?

OLIVIA:
Do I know?

VIOLA:
Here's another letter from Orson.

OLIVIA *(Mock excitement)*:
How very exciting.

VIOLA:
Shall I open it?

OLIVIA:
Please, my hands will shake.

VIOLA *(Not amused)*:

"I give you back your freedom
I cannot love you."

OLIVIA:
My Orson?

VIOLA *(Lighting up)*:
"Try to be resigned.
Make up your mind
That you'll have to find
Some other beau . . ."

OLIVIA *(Taking letter from Viola)*:
Let me see that?!

VIOLA:
He doesn't love you anymore!

OLIVIA:
Well, it's nothing to cheer about. It's like a big drop in A.T&T. *(VIOLA starts to exit left 2)* Hey, where're you off to?

VIOLA *(Crossing back to OLIVIA)*:
I'll be back in time for work.

OLIVIA *(Taking VIOLA's hand)*:
Okay. I'll see you up in my place afterward.

VIOLA *(Pulling hand away)*:
Look, Olivia. I'm not what you think I am. I mean, with me this job is going to be strictly business. And if you don't want to play it that way, then I'll quit. *(Exits left 3 at a run)*

(OLIVIA looks after her, does confused take toward audience and exits right 1, closing door behind her. Lights down)

ORSON *(Enters left 1 and leaves door open, carrying books under arm and reading one)*:
. . . "It is not uncommon that these latent desires appear, previously suppressed by fear of society's hostility . . . *(Looks around suspiciously and closes door)* and because the afflicted individual cannot include them in his own concepts of masculine behavior . . . " That's uncool! ". . . behavior which the same society has strictly regulated for him. The sudden appearance of these desires can cause great personality upheaval and mental anguish." *(One chord of crash from orchestra. ORSON switches books under his arms. Interrupts his own reading of second book)* I'm glad mother's dead! *(Continuing)* "Throughout history, civilizations have arisen in which the love

of one man for another has been an accepted part of the society in which it arose." *(Looks up with eyes)* "So much so that legend has grown up over the devotion of such lovers." *(Eyes look right and left)* "Every school child has read of Damon and Pythias, King David and . . . " King David?! ". . . and his friend Jonathan." *(Pause)* Yes, I read about them in Sunday school. *(Pause, then quietly)* Is that what they were doing?

(During this song, slides are projected over the entire set showing VIOLA *in beguiling poses. He sings)*

When you're young and in love,
When you're young and in love,
It's a beautiful thing.
You're a kid on a swing.
You feel higher than high.

When you're young and in love,
When you're young and in love,
Everybody's a king.
All the world starts to sing.
You can float in the sky.
You feel young though you're old.
You have powers untold.
You can make every commonplace thing
That you do seem a real work of art.

Every hour goes so fast,
Every breath seems your last.
This is merely the magical, mystical,
Musical song in your heart.

When you're young and in love,
When you're young and in love,
Every bell starts to ring, every season is spring,
Every bird is a dove,
When you're young and you're really in love.

*(*ORSON *fantasy sequence: During the following sequence, slide projections in silhouette of Romans, Greeks, Old Testament Hebrews, the American Western characters are accompanied by tableaux freezes in silhouette up center involving the* APOCALYPSE, VIOLA *and* SEBASTIAN. ORSON *reads from book)*

"In the Greek and Roman legions, lovers were known to be inseparable—living and dying together."

(*Projection: Slides with blue tint, the color of which is matched on the cyclorama upstage, show Greek and Roman warriors in battle. Freeze:* MICHAEL, JOHN, VIOLA *in "Hunca Munca" costumes on platforms in matching warrior tableau.* ORSON *walks excitedly upstage into that tableau*)

Charlie! This is it! (DANNY *enters left 3 on ramp and runs sword through* ORSON'S *back*) Ahh!

(*Blackout.* ORSON, *in follow spot, reads from a book*)

"However, the Senate did not encourage or sympathize with this practice." The Establishment again.

(*Projection: Roman Senate with red-orange tint, the color of which is matched on the cyclorama upstage. Freeze:* MICHAEL, JOHN, DANNY *in matching tableau.* ORSON *puts book down, takes bench and moves it away from wall, stands on it*)

Amo, amas, amat.
Amo, amas, amat.
Distinguised citizens of Rome! Love is a gas! It's where it's at! And if your own thing is against Establishment's barf concepts, you can drop out and groove with it. Right? Cato père! (JOHN *turns thumbs down*) *Cato fils!* (MICHAEL *turns thumbs down*) *Cicero!* (DANNY, *after pause, gives him the "up yours" third finger*) *Hmmn??*

(*Blackout. Projection: Greek students lamenting the death of their teacher in blue tint, the color of which is matched on the cyclorama upstage.* ORSON *staggers upstage, sits on lower platform, pantomimes cup of hemlock. To audience with "Old Fraternity" bravura*)

Hi, gang! The Senate's throwing the bash. It's a new kind of high called hemlock.

When you're young and in . . .

(ORSON *collapses in one beat and dies. Projection: Old Testament Hebrews in profile in green tint, the color of which is matched on the cyclorama upstage. Music under*)

VOICE OVER (VIOLA):
King David? King David?

(ORSON *sits up bewildered*)

ORSON:
Charlie?
This is merely the magical, mystical,
Musical song in your heart.

(ORSON *pantomimes playing harp. Blackout. Shadow of giant is cast on cyclorama*)

GOLIATH (*Offstage*):
Hey, you!

ORSON:
Who? Me?

GOLIATH (*Offstage*):

Yeah! Come on out and fight, you big fag!

(ORSON *takes out his handkerchief, pulls a button off his vest, makes a sling, and lets fly at upstage shadow. Shadow, hit in forehead, collapses out of sight. Blackout*)

JOHN WAYNE:
Get him on location in a Western and we'd straighten him out.

(ORSON *staggers as if being slapped by invisible hand*)

ORSON:
Pow! Pow! What the hell're you mad at me for, Wyatt? Come on, Marshall, you heard what he called me. What's one dead Philistine more or less?

*(Projection: Western hanging scene in sunset colors, which
are matched on upstage cyclorama. Freeze:* APOCALYPSE, SEBAS-
TIAN, *and* STAGE MANAGER *in matching tableau. Rope noose flies
in.* ORSON *backs up to lower platform with his hands behind
back as follow spot pins on his head)*

COWBOY *(Tape)*:
We don't want no sissy-type, dude-type, lady-type fellers in
these parts. Stand by to slap the team!

VIOLA *(Enters left 1, closing door behind her)*:
I never told my love,
I never told my love,
But let

ORSON *(Opening eyes slowly)*:
Charlie!

VIOLA:
Concealment

ORSON:
Charlie! You, too?

VIOLA *(She nods)*:
Like a worm

ORSON:
I was afraid to say anything.

VIOLA:
In the bud

ORSON:
But it's okay.

VIOLA:
Feed on my damask cheek.

ORSON:
There was King David and Jonathan, and a *whole lot* of
Greeks.

VIOLA:
I sat

ORSON *(Suddenly aware of cowboys)*:
Charlie, there's still time for you to get away.

VIOLA:
Like patience

ORSON:
They don't know it's you yet.

VIOLA:
Like patience

ORSON:
Please, Charlie, listen!

VIOLA:
On a monument,

ORSON:
You gotta run!

VIOLA:
Smiling,

ORSON *(Out the side of his mouth)*:
Charlie! Listen to me!

VIOLA:
Smiling,

ORSON *(Side of his mouth and high squeak)*:
Run!

VIOLA:
Smi-i-i-i . . .

ORSON:
Charlie! They're from *Marlboro* country!

(Blackout. ORSON *leaps off lower platform, falling on his behind. Lights restore.* VIOLA *rushes to him center and falls on her knees)*

VIOLA:
Orson! Orson! Are you all right!

ORSON:
Where am I?

VIOLA:
You fell off a step.

ORSON:
Is my neck broken?

VIOLA:
That's not what you fell on.

ORSON:
What about the rope burns!

VIOLA:
Orson, love, there aren't any.

ORSON:
You called me "love." Charlie, we've got to play this thing cool!

VIOLA:
Orson, I've got something to tell you. I didn't tell you the truth about myself.

ORSON:
I'll tell you. I didn't *know* the truth about myself. But it's okay, Charlie. If that's where it's at, we'll make it work.

VIOLA:
I would have told you sooner but at first I was afraid you'd fire me. And then back and forth, back and forth with all those love letters to Olivia . . .

ORSON (*Referring to* OLIVIA):
  That's when I was *confused*. Charlie, I'm glad you feel the same way.

VIOLA (*Putting her face to his hand*):
  Call me Viola.

ORSON (*Rising*):
  Charlie, that's not playing this thing very cool.

VIOLA (*Rising, amused*):
  Well, you can't call me Charlie.

ORSON:
  Give me time, I'm new at this!

VIOLA:
  New at what?

ORSON:
  Well, you don't have to believe this if you don't want to, but it's the truth. (VIOLA *moves in smiling.* ORSON *turns front to speak*) You're the first boy I ever loved.

VIOLA (*Small voice*):
  What?!!

ORSON:
  It's the truth. The first boy. I swear on my mother's . . .

VIOLA (*Holding up her hand and saying with delight*):
  But I'm a girl.

ORSON (*Embarrassed*):
  Charlie, it's too soon to talk about role-playing.

VIOLA:
  You mean you love me because I'm a boy?

ORSON:
  It was that or nothing. Charlie, you're . . . you're my . . . Him.

VIOLA:
Why, you ... You're a ...

ORSON:
Don't say it! For God's sake; I know what you're gonna say!

VIOLA:
You don't love me. You don't even know who I am. You're in love with a boy.

ORSON (*Now being afraid Charlie has changed his mind*):
I'm in love with you! The rest is somebody else's mistake.

VIOLA:
Yeah, mine!

ORSON:
But you said you felt the same way!

VIOLA:
I do; but for different reasons!

ORSON:
But if that's your thing, what the hell's the problem?

VIOLA (*Big anger*):
I'd be a big disappointment in bed!

ORSON (*Afraid of the lynch mob*):
For God's sake, Charlie! We could get arrested!

VIOLA:'
You're the one who's "arrested"! (VIOLA, *in tears, picks up* ORSON's *books and whams him in the gut and on the head.* ORSON *goes down. She exits in tears*)

ORSON (*Rises, picks up books*):
Charlie! I mean, Viola! I mean ... Oh my God! (*Exits after* VIOLA)

(APOCALYPSE *enter with* SEBASTIAN *onto platforms upstage. During this number the following visual effects are used together: a completely mad-hatter motion-picture film of bands marching, science-fiction characters, and assorted funny, totally unrelated scenes. The slide projections are polarized geometric shapes which seem to move in and out with the beat. An overhead slide projector covers the entire set with a moving liquid projection of colored, free-form shapes. The lighting is a kaleidoscope of colors. The total effect is one of a dimly lighted psychedelic happening. It takes place in* OLIVIA's *discotheque, where the* APOCALYPSE *are performing)*

APOCALYPSE & SEBASTIAN:
   Something new in cabarets,
   Flashing floors with lights ablaze,
   Crashing bores with eyes aglaze.
   Join the craze.
   Do the hunca munca.

   Lights go white to red to blue,
   Every color, ev'ry hue.
   Silver birds come into view.
   Me and you
   Do the hunca munca.

DANNY:
   Here's one dance that can't be angelic,
   Here's one dance that can't end up a relic.
   Furthermore, you'll find the floor
   Hypo, micro, psychedelic.

APOCALYPSE & SEBASTIAN:
   Soon you'll get the feeling of
   Crazy ceilings up above.
   Just the dance to turtle dove,
   Fall in love.
   Do the hunca munca.

(The dance section: This is a three-minute series of cross-overs involving the entire company in mimic situations and entanglements, including mistaken identity, unrequited love, and old-fashioned silent-movie antics. Throughout the number OLIVIA *and* ORSON *chase* VIOLA *and* SEBASTIAN *about the stage in*

an attempt to corner them. At one point, after a full company dance, OLIVIA *manages to trap* VIOLA, *tweak her cheeks and* VIOLA *says):*

VIOLA:
I'm really quitting now! You're all a bunch of sex maniacs! *(Exits right 1)*

*(*SEBASTIAN *enters right 2, crosses to* OLIVIA*)*

SEBASTIAN *(To* OLIVIA*):*
Are we still on for tonight?

OLIVIA *(To* SEBASTIAN*):*
Sex maniac! *(She slaps* SEBASTIAN *and exits left 1.* SEBASTIAN *follows her off, trying to placate her)*

(The number continues to its end with much door slamming, door opening, appearing and disappearing which culminates in a final full-company dance and reprise of number)

ALL:
Do the hunca munca.
Do the hunca munca.
Do the hunca munca.
Do the hunca munca.
Do the hunca munca.

(End film, projections; light change; company freeze on knees)

DIRKSEN:
"Oh Time, thou must untangle this, not I;
It's too hard a knot for me t'untie."
I remember that from a Christmas sticker.

(Full company exit to music except OLIVIA, *who sits on bench stage right, and* SEBASTIAN, *who sits on bench stage left, both in dim follow spot)*

SHIRLEY TEMPLE:
I think it's time for the moms and pops of America to take

big brother to the woodshed and remind him who is running things.

W. C. FIELDS:
And a little child shall lead them.

POPE:
Penitence is demandatory. Illicit coitus is being flaunted.

QUEEN ELIZABETH:
It certainly pays to head your own church.

SISTINE GOD:
How's she ever going to get by with disregard for a higher power?

BUDDHA:
She'll get by with a little help from her friends.

(*Another* BUDDHA *appears near* SEBASTIAN. *During the song,* BUDDHA *arms appear giving both* OLIVIA *and* SEBASTIAN *cards, which they read. When they have read the cards, projections appear over their heads*)

COPY:
Pride and twenty cents get you a ride on the subway.

OLIVIA:
Don't leave me, don't go away.
Please don't leave me, say that you'll stay.

SEBASTIAN & OLIVIA:
Believe me, you know it's true.

OLIVIA:
You need me.

SEBASTIAN:
And I need you.

BOTH:
Fill, please fill my heart

Until, until my heart is still.
We'll be together

(Environment change to warm, richly colored abstract)

Don't leave me, don't go away.
I love you, what more can I say?
Take (please take my heart) my heart
Or break (or break my heart) my heart
But don't leave me.

(They cross center toward each other but they never meet.
The moment is interrupted by):

ORSON *(Offstage right 1):*

Don't leave me, don't go away

(Enters right 1 leaving door open, lights build)

Please don't leave me, say that you'll stay.

(To SEBASTIAN*)*
Charlie!

SEBASTIAN:
My name is Sebastian.

ORSON:
I'll call you whatever you want—Charlie, Sebastian, Brune-
hilde! . . . (ORSON *falls to his knees, grabbing* SEBASTIAN'S *legs)*
I need you and you need me.
Fill my heart until my heart is still.
We'll be together . . .

*(*SEBASTIAN *frees himself of* ORSON, *pushing* ORSON *to the floor)*

SEBASTIAN:
He's really freaked out!! Get him out of here!! *(Exits)*

OLIVIA:
Orson! Have you lost your mind?!

ORSON:
Isn't it obvious?

OLIVIA:
Orson, it isn't acid!

ORSON:
No, it's bitter gall.

VIOLA (*Enters left 2 and crosses between* OLIVIA *and* ORSON. *To* OLIVIA):
I've come to give you back your clothes.

ORSON:
Charlie!

OLIVIA:
Cool it, Charlie. Orson's on a bum trip. He needs help.

VIOLA:
Help! He needs treatment!

ORSON (*Grabbing* VIOLA *by the wrist and caressing her*):
Don't leave me.

VIOLA (*To* OLIVIA):
See what I mean?

ORSON:
Don't go away.

OLIVIA (*Slapping* ORSON's *hands and freeing* VIOLA):
Orson! You cut that out! (OLIVIA *puts hand on* VIOLA's *shoulder, pulling her protectively toward her*)

VIOLA (*Slapping* OLIVIA's *hands and freeing herself*):
You cut that out!

ORSON (*To* OLIVIA):
I told you he loved me! Charlie! (*Grabs* VIOLA's *leg.* VIOLA *pushes him over backward*)

VIOLA:

I'm not Charlie! *(She takes off her vest-jacket and shirt and throws them at* ORSON. *She wears only a feminine bra. Sings)*

But look at me, look! You can see that I'm real.
I'm alive.

(Shouted)
I'm me!

ORSON *(Slow smile at* VIOLA'S *breasts)*:

Charlie?!

OLIVIA:
Sebastian?!

SEBASTIAN *(Enters right 1, leaves door open)*:

What's the ma . . . Vi!! Boy, am I glad to see you!

*(*SEBASTIAN *and* VIOLA *embrace)*

ORSON:
One face, one voice, one habit, and two persons?

SEBASTIAN:
I had a sister
Whom the blind waves and surges have devour'd
I should my tears let fall upon your cheek
And say "trice welcome, drowned Viola!"

OLIVIA *(Trying to stay calm)*:
Wait a minute. Wait a minute. Who delivered the notes from Orson?

VIOLA:
I did.

SEBASTIAN:
I did.

OLIVIA (*Starting over again*):

Well, which one ... with me ... ah ... (OLIVIA *gestures through the door where she and* SEBASTIAN *disappeared earlier.* SEBASTIAN *raises his hand.* OLIVIA *collapses against door with relief. Then recovering—*) I hoped it would turn out that way. (*To* ORSON) Alas, poor fool, how have they baffl'd thee!

ORSON:

Who's baffled? The fourth boy I hired and fell in love with wasn't a boy; he's a girl. But he's not a girl, he's twins. (SEBASTIAN *and* VIOLA *look at each other with affection*) And do I get my pick? (SEBASTIAN *and* VIOLA *look at each other with anger*) No, I don't get my pick! Because the boy doesn't like boys, and the girl doesn't like boys who like boys, and I never did like boys until she came along ... Oh, God! (*Turning to* VIOLA) Charlie, honest, I love you! Can't you see it's good? My love hasn't changed just because you have.

VIOLA:

But you really thought I was a boy!

ORSON:

I also really thought you were to be loved no matter what you were.

VIOLA:

You mean you love me just for me? No matter what I appear to be?

ORSON:

If you were a cricket, I'd snap your hind leg.

VIOLA (*Embracing* ORSON, *who is on his knees*):

Oh, Orson, I love you!

OLIVIA (*To* SEBASTIAN):
You don't mind me being older?

SEBASTIAN:
It's where I'm at. You don't mind me being younger?

OLIVIA:
  Listen, it's my bag.

VIOLA *(To* ORSON*)*:
  You don't mind me being a girl?

ORSON:
  I'll just go with it—you're my thing.

OLIVIA:
  Sebastian!

SEBASTIAN:
  Olivia!

VIOLA *(Who is embracing the kneeling* ORSON*)*:
  Orson!

ORSON:
  Charlie! *(He does take as he recognizes what he said, as lights go down)*

SHAKESPEARE:
  I had the same trouble with the ending.

*(*OLIVIA *and* SEBASTIAN *exit in character right 1 and close door.* ORSON *and* VIOLA *exit left 1 in character and close door.* APOCALYPSE *enter and climb steps, cross over ramp and down center during)*:

APOCALYPSE:
  Do your own thing,
  Pay no attention to people who look down on you.
  Do your own thing.
  It makes no difference who turns away and frowns at you.
  There'll come a day when the world will need you.
  There'll come a day when the world will need you.
  Tell it like it is, if it makes you happy.
  Why should you have to hide upon a shelf,
  Why shouldn't you be truthful to yourself?

You may change someday,
You may find another way
But for now, just for now:
Do your own thing,
Find your own dream,
Dig your own soul,
Or dig your own hole
And die.

(After the solo bows are completed and music ends, a full company Shakespearian tableau is formed as the lights go down, and):

SISTINE GOD *and* COPY:
"Hey, boy."

CHRIST *and* COPY:
"Yes, Father?"

SISTINE GOD *and* COPY:
"When are you going to get a haircut?"

(Blackout)

CURTAIN

HAIR

The American Tribal
Love-Rock Musical

Book and Lyrics by Gerome Ragni and James Rado

Music by Galt MacDermot

EDITOR'S NOTES

An epochal musical, *Hair* originally was produced by Joseph Papp at the New York Shakespeare Festival's Public Theatre (located in lower Manhattan) for a limited engagement of eight weeks. The "tribal love-rock musical" was greeted with loud hosannas by critics and public alike, not only as a significant stride forward in the art of musical theatre, but also as stirring entertainment.

Unwilling to let his hirsute hit expire, Mr. Papp (in association with Michael Butler) moved it to Cheetah, a large Broadway discotheque, for another run, limited only because the building was about to be torn down.

Undaunted by its gypsyesque preliminary engagements, *Hair* was subsequently revised by the authors and composer and restaged for Broadway by Tom O'Horgan, opening at the Biltmore Theatre on April 29, 1968. It immediately became one of the most successful musicals in Broadway history. With an eventual world gross of $80 million (it was performed in virtually every conceivable country) and eleven original cast record albums (in as many languages), *Hair* became the archetypal musical of the sixties, the love song of the flower-children generation. With its freewheeling story line and barbed comments on sex, drugs, military service, money, religion, and other contemporary concerns, its vibrant and often memorable rock score, and a sprinkling of nudity, it shattered Broadway conventions and ran for 1,750 performances while fourteen other companies played concurrently in various parts of the United States.

Even the most conservative of critics doffed their hats to the "rock 'n' rebellion" musical. Brooks Atkinson, dean of theatre journalists, avowed that *"Hair* is the freshest and most spontaneous show I've seen." Clive Barnes of *The New York Times* described it as "so likable, so new, so fresh and so unassuming, even in its pretensions. It is the first Broadway musical in some time to have the authentic voice of today rather than the day before yesterday."

Richard Watts, Jr. reported in the *New York Post: "Hair* has surprising if perhaps unintentional charm; its high spirits are contagious, and its young zestfulness makes it difficult to resist." Others rated it as "a remarkable experience" and "one of the most important developments in modern American theatre. . . . It is a frenetic, non-stop celebration of love, pot, rock and the generation on the near side of the gap. It also is relentlessly pro-people and anti-computer and glorious fun!"

A London edition of the musical opened at the Shaftesbury Theatre on September 27, 1968, and the event prompted dramatist and critic Frank Marcus to jubilantly note in the *Sunday Telegraph*: "At long last the London theatre has burst into flame. When I emerged from the theatre, dazed, shattered and delighted, smothered in confetti, flowers and balloons, the cast and some of the audience were dancing frantically on the stage. For all I know they may be dancing still. This show is in every sense of the word, sensational." *Hair* ran for 1,997 performances before folding its West End–based tribal tents.

Co-authors of the book and lyrics, Gerome Ragni and James Rado are both actors and on more than one occasion have appeared in the same production, as they did in *Hair*, and with several Off-Broadway theatre companies.

Mr. Ragni, a native of Canada, studied at Georgetown University and made his Broadway debut in the record-breaking production of *Hamlet* which starred Richard Burton. A former member of the Open Theatre and Café La Mama, he next returned to Off-Broadway for a role in *Hang Down Your Head and Die*, and later, in the long-running comedy, *The Knack*.

In 1972 Mr. Ragni was represented on Broadway as the sole author of the book and lyrics (with music once again by Galt MacDermot) for the short-lived *Dude*.

Mr. Rado, whose hometown is Washington, D.C., graduated from understudy in the Henry Fonda vehicle, *Generation*, to one of the principals in *A Lion in Winter*. He also appeared in the New York and Chicago companies of *The Knack* and subsequently understudied Albert Finney in the title role of *Luther*.

In addition to winning international acclaim for his *Hair* score, Galt MacDermot composed the music for *Two Gentlemen of Verona* which appears earlier in this volume.

Prior to his eventful debut as a theatre composer, Mr. MacDermot was variously a writer of rock and jazz songs, a piano player for dance bands, and a church organist. *Hair* was his first show. Subsequently, he composed music for productions of *Hamlet, Twelfth Night, The Tale of Cymbeline,* and a series of modern works, most notably, the background scores for the Tony Award–winning *Sticks and Bones* and Tennessee Williams's *Vieux Carré.*

A film version of *Hair,* directed by Milos Forman, is scheduled for release in 1978.

PRODUCTION NOTES

Hair originally was presented by the New York Shakespeare Festival (Joseph Papp, Producer) at the Anspacher Theatre, New York, on October 17, 1967. The cast was as follows:

Dionne	*Jonelle Allen*
"Dad"	*Ed Crowley*
Claude	*Walker Daniels*
Woof	*Steve Dean*
Jeanie	*Sally Eaton*
"Mom"	*Marijane Maricle*
Sheila	*Jill O'Hara*
Crissy	*Shelley Plimpton*
Berger	*Gerome Ragni*
Hud	*Arnold Wilkerson*
Susan	*Susan Batson*
Linda	*Linda Compton*
Suzannah	*Suzannah Evans*
Louise	*Jane Levin*
Alma	*Alma Robinson*
Charlie	*Warren Burton*
Thommie	*Thommie Bush*
Bill	*William Herter*
Paul	*Paul Jabara*
Bob	*Bob Johnson*
Jim	*Edward Murphy, Jr.*

Directed by *Gerald Freedman*
Scenery Designed by *Ming Cho Lee*
Costumes Designed by *Theoni V. Aldredge*
Lighting by *Martin Aronstein*
Musical Director: *John Morris*
Associate Producer: *Bernard Gersten*

Hair opened on Broadway on April 29, 1968. It was presented by Michael Butler in the Natoma Production, at the Biltmore Theatre, with the following cast:

Ron	*Ronald Dyson*
Claude	*James Rado*
Berger	*Gerome Ragni*
Woof	*Steve Curry*
Hud	*Lamont Washington*
Mother	*Sally Eaton*
	Jonathan Kramer
	Paul Jabara
Father	*Robert I. Rubinsky*
	Suzannah Norstrand
	Lamont Washington
Jeanie	*Sally Eaton*
Dionne	*Melba Moore*
Sheila	*Lynn Kellogg*
Crissy	*Shelley Plimpton*
Tourist Couple	*Jonathan Kramer*
	Robert I. Rubinsky
Box Office	*Steve Gamet*
General Grant	*Paul Jabara*
Young Recruit	*Jonathan Kramer*
Parents	*Diane Keaton*
	Robert I. Rubinsky
The Tribe	*Donnie Burks*
	Lorri Davis
	Leata Galloway
	Steve Gamet
	Walter Harris
	Diane Keaton
	Hiram Keller
	Marjorie LiPari
	Emmaretta Marks
	Natalie Mosco
	Suzannah Norstrand
	Robert I. Rubinsky

Directed by *Tom O'Horgan*
Scenery Designed by *Robin Wagner*
Dance Director: *Julie Arenal*
Musical Director: *Galt MacDermot*
Costumes: *Nancy Potts*
Lighting: *Jules Fisher*
Sound: *Robert Kiernan*
Executive Producer: *Bertrand Castelli*

MUSICAL NUMBERS

ACT ONE

Aquarius	The Company
Introductions:	
1. *Manchester*	Claude
2. *Manhattan*	Berger
3. *Colored Spade*	Hud
4. *Sodomy*	Woof
Ain't Got No	Claude, Berger, Woof, Hud, and Company
I Got Life	Claude, Mom
Air	Jeanie, Crissy, Dionne
Initials	The Company
Going Down	Berger and Company
Hair	Claude, Berger, and Company
My Conviction	Mom
Dead End	Sheila, Claude, Berger
Don't Put It Down	Berger, Woof
Frank Mills	Crissy
Hare Krishna	The Company
Where Do I Go	Claude and Company

ACT TWO

Electric Blues	The Leather Bag
Easy to Be Hard	Sheila, Berger, and The Leather Bag
Manchester (Reprise)	Claude and Company
White Boys	Dionne and Group
Black Boys	Jeanie, Crissy, and Another Girl
Walking in Space	The Company
Prisoners in Niggertown	The Company
Walking in Space (Reprise)	The Company
Good Morning, Starshine	Claude, Berger, Sheila, and Company
The Bed	The Company
Exanaplanetooch	Claude
Climax	Sheila
Sentimental Ending	The Company

The Present.

New York City, mostly the East Village.

The bare stage, totally exposed, no wing masking and, if possible, the entire proscenium arch stripped of any curtain, thus exposing the fly area, the grid, etc. The brick walls, the radiator pipes, the stage ropes, the light-pipes, all lights, are visible, as well as the three flag drops—perhaps some costumes might be hung on light-pipes and flown.

The floor is raked slightly and should be made to simulate dirt.

There are two permanent set pieces on the raked stage. They are:
1. *Totem Pole—stage right center—a large, authentic, beautiful American Indian totem pole.*
2. *A Crucifix-Tree—stage left center—a metal, modern sculpture Crucifix, with a rather abstract Jesus on it. The Crucifix also resembles a tree: the main cross branch, other smaller branches. Jesus is electrified with tiny twinkling lights in his eyes and on his body. At times, of course, the tree is climbed.*

The stagehands, the stage managers, etc., will be visible in the wings (though the wings are not brightly lit).

In short, all of the elements of this production are contained within the stage area from the outset and are manipulated in full view of the audience as the play progresses.

Exterior scenes make use of the dirt floor. For the interior scenes, Oriental rugs will be rolled out by THE TRIBE *themselves. In fact,* THE TRIBE *will do most of the set changes, as simple as they are.*

In summary, the set:
1. *Bare, exposed stage*
2. *Dirt, raked floor*

3. *Totem Pole and Crucifix-Tree*
4. *Drops to be flown in*
     a. *American flag—from 1776*
     b. *Another American flag—1776*
     c. *American flag—1967*

THE SOUND *will be rock music. It is very important that an excellent sound system be used that can regulate the balances of voice and musical instrumentation. The lyrics must be heard and for this reason all solo singers will probably have to wear chest mikes. Standard floor mikes will be used on occasion, as well, perhaps even in dialogue exchange for a specific effect. An engineer should be employed to control the balance through a master panel at the rear of the theatre.*

THE CAST:

*The cast numbers approximately twenty-five. There are ten principals. Two of them—*MOM *and* DAD*—are about forty-five years old. They play six or seven different roles each, weaving through the play as the representatives of "the older generation." The rest of the cast is comprised of seventeen- to twenty-five-year-olds. All the boys have very long hair.*

*In addition, we will use huge puppets—ten feet tall, made in the form of policemen—(*TRIBE *inside, manipulating them)—to hover in background at appropriate moments, as well as in the aisles. When not in use, they hang on hooks on the walls.*

THE TRIBE:

THE KIDS *should be approached, directorially, as a "tribe."*

Marshall McLuhan describes today's world as a "global village." And today's youth is involved in group-tribal activity. So Hair should be a group-tribal activity. An extension of what's happening. A coming-together for a common reason: a search for a way of life that makes sense to the young, that allows the growth of their new vision, however defined or undefined that may be; to find an alternative to the unacceptable standards, goals, and morals of the older generation, the establishment. (No matter that their task may never be accomplished, or that it may.) It's what's happening now. The tribes are forming, establishing their own way of life, their own morality, ideology, their own mode of dress, behavior; and the use of drugs, by the way, has a distinct parallel in ancient cultures, in tribal spiritual tradition, both East and West.

THE KIDS *are a tribe. At the same time, for the purpose of* Hair, *they know they are on a stage in a theater, performing for an audience, demonstrating their way of life, in a sense, telling a story, in order to persuade those who watch of their intentions, to perhaps gain greater understanding, support, and tolerance, and thus perhaps expand their horizons of active participation toward a better, saner, peace-full, love-full world. They are trying to turn on the audience.*

The entire opening of the show, for example, from the moment the audience enters the theater, is THE TRIBE *preparing for the ceremony, the ritual, the war dance (the peace dance), the play—*Hair.

Note should be taken of the spiritual theme running through the play; outer space, astrology, the earth, the heavens, interplanetary travel, mysticism, as seen in the songs "Aquarius," "Walking in Space," "Good Morning Starshine," and "Exanaplanetooch," especially.

Also take note of the ever-present threat of the outside world on THE TRIBE, *as expressed through the presence of the large police puppets, the projections on the walls of FBI, CIA, dark mysterious men, and* MOM *and* DAD *at times.*

Act One

The audience enters the theater. THE TRIBE *is already on stage, informal, dressing, putting on war paint, peace paint, dressed as American Indians: headbands, beads, the guys in loincloths, moccasins, beaded dresses, etc. A small improvised tent is being pitched in the background. Some of* THE TRIBE *wear blankets. Possible use of tribal masks, colored greasepaints used freely on faces. Rhythms drummed on old tin pots. Occasional Indian yelps. Rising and subsiding drum rhythms from the band. Surrounding the stage are all the props that will be used during the course of the evening: stacks of newspapers, rolled-up rugs, metal oil drums, old mattresses, toy props that are used during the war scene, an umbrella with "Love" painted on it in bright colors, sticks, poles, banners, balloons, flags, homemade improvised staffs with feathers on the ends of them, etc. The atmosphere of a primitive American Indian camp at twilight. All looks quite primitive, tribal, and perhaps could be mistaken for another century were it not for the twinkling Jesus on the Crucifix. This is the* ELECTRIC TRIBE. *Bare feet, sandals, saris, loincloths, beads, old military uniforms, band uniforms, psychedelic design, incense, flowers, oriental rugs, candles, all combine to illustrate the emergence of a new-ancient culture among the youth.*

No overture.

Twilight in the Indian camp. Drumming from tin pots, bottles, spoons, paper bags, metal objects, etc., and the band. Rhythm building. THE TRIBE *is gathering.*

SOLO VOICE:
> When the moon is in the seventh house
> And Jupiter aligns with Mars
> Then peace will guide the planets
> And love will steer the stars
> This is the dawning of the Age of Aquarius
> The Age of Aquarius

THE TRIBE:
Aquarius
Aquarius

SOLO VOICE:
Harmony and understanding
Sympathy and trust abounding
No more falsehoods or derisions
Golden living dreams of visions
Mystic crystal revelation
And the mind's true liberation

THE TRIBE:
Aquarius
Aquarius

SOLO VOICE:
When the moon is in the seventh house
And Jupiter aligns with Mars
Then peace will guide the planets
And love will steer the stars
This is the dawning of the Age of Aquarius
The Age of Aquarius

THE TRIBE:
Aquarius
Aquarius

Aquarius
Aquarius

CLAUDE (*North Country accent*): My name is Claude. Claude Hooper. Claude Hooper Bukowski. I'm human being number 1005963297 dash J, Area Code 609; maybe you've seen me around. Just another number. The most beautiful beast in the forest. I come from Manchester, England.

Manchester England England
Across the Atlantic Sea
And I'm a genius genius
I believe in Gawd
And I believe that Gawd

Believes in Claude
That's me that's me
Now that I've dropped out
Why is life dreary dreary
Answer my weary query
Timothy Leary dearie

CLAUDE *and* BERGER:
Manchester England England
Across the Atlantic Sea
And I'm a genius genius
I believe in Gawd
And I believe that Gawd believes in Claude
That's me that's he
That's me that's he
That's me that's he
That's me

BERGER (Indian war whoop):
Woo Woo Woo Woo Woo Woo Woo Woo
Manhattan beggar
Manhattan gypsy
Manhattan Indian

I'm a whole new thing
I'm a lot of wild
Ev'ryday of the week
I'm society's freak
I'm a flower child

Manhattan tomtom
Manhattan tattoo
Manhattan tomahawk

I'm a whole new thing
A mutated breed
I'm a penniless head
Won't you gimme some bread
To feed my need

Hashish
Cocaine

Heroin
Opium
LSD
DMT
STP, BMT, A&P, IRT, APC, alcohol,
Cigarettes, rubber cement, Scotch
Tape, saffron, shoe polish,
Morning glory seeds, cough syrup,
Nutmeg, Ann Page, Dexedrine,
Benzedrine, Methedrine, TWA,
S-E-X and Y-O-U. WOW!

My name is George Berger. But I don't dig George, so just call me Bananaberger. I know you people think right off, oh, look, dear, isn't he a cute one, what is it a boy or a girl? (*To a woman in the first row*) Hey, lady, can you spare a handout, something for a poor young psychedelic teddy bear like me? To keep my chromosomes dancing.

HUD: (*Dressed like a medicine man*) Comes the eclipse. I cover the white moon. I don't exist.

BERGER: More on Vietnam in a moment.

HUD:
Walla walla
Gooba gooba

CLAUDE (*As interpreter*): Hud is mean. Hud is bad.

HUD:
Walla walla
Booga booga

CLAUDE: Hud whips women. Hud is happy.

HUD:
Walla walla
Goona goona
I'm a
Colored Spade
A Pickaninny
Jungle Bunny Jigaboo

Nigger Coon and Cotton Picker
Mau Mau and Ubangi-lipped Swamp Guinea

I'm
Uncle Tom and Aunt Jemima
Voodoo zombie Little Black Sambo
Resident of Harlem
And President of
the United States of Love

WOOF: And if you ask him to dinner, feed him:

HUD:

Watermelon
Hominy Grits
Alligator ribs
An' Shortnin' Bread

CLAUDE, BERGER, WOOF:
  And if you don't watch out

(HUD *taps*)

  The Boogie Man will shout
(HUD *taps*)

HUD:
  Boooooooooooooo!

(*Stops tapping. Catholic Latin incantation by* THE TRIBE.
BERGER *swings smoking Catholic incense chalice*)
WOOF (*Holding out an imaginary bit of something*): This is the
  body and blood of Jesus Christ and I'm going to eat you. (*He
  eats it, crosses himself, kneels, raising his right hand*) I swear
  to tell you the truth, the whole truth, and nothing but the
  truth so help me God, in the name of the Father, the Son,
  and the Holy Ghost, Amen.

Sodomy
Fellatio

Cunnilingus
Pederasty

Father
Why do these words
Sound so nasty

Masturbation can be fun . . .

I'm Catholic, my name is Woof, and I refuse to join the
YMCA or sleep there overnight. They advertise it as a
Christian organization, but all they have in the lobby are
Protestant Pansies. Pee Pee.
(Drums under)
HUD: I'm the Imperial Wizard of the KKK.
WOOF: I'm brainwashed people. Jesus Saves.
BERGER: I'm the Aluminum Coxman and you'll eat me up up
up.
CLAUDE: I'm Aquarius—destined for greatness or madness.

HUD:
I'm black I'm black

WOOF:
I'm pink I'm pink

BERGER:
I'm Rinso white

CLAUDE:
I'm in . . . vi . . . si . . . ble

(CLAUDE, BERGER, WOOF, HUD *join hands and start "humming"
a chord. The rhythm from the band under this. The chord
grows in volume, moves up in pitch, increases in intensity;* THE
TRIBE *gradually joins in; the rhythm from the band becomes
more rapid and driving; the crescendo reaches its peak as the
"Culpepper Minute Men" flag lowers rapidly behind the four
guys. The flag: it is large, covers practically all the stage. It is a
replica of an authentic American flag dating from approximately 1776. On it is a huge rattlesnake, coiled, ready to strike.
Above it reads: "The Culpepper Minute Men." In the middle*

reads: "Liberty or Death." At the bottom reads: "Don't Tread on Me." THE TRIBE *tapers off the chord rapidly as* CLAUDE, BERGER, WOOF, *and* HUD *go into "Ain't Got No")*

	ANSWERS
	DIVIDED AMONG
WOOF:	OTHER THREE:
Ain't got no home	*So*
Ain't got no shoes	*Poor*
Ain't got no money	*Honey*
Ain't got no class	*Common*
Ain't got no scarf	
Ain't got no gloves	*Cold*
Ain't got no bed	*Beat*
Ain't got no pot	*Busted*
Ain't got no faith	*Catholic*

(THE TRIBE *panhandles the audience*)

HUD:	OTHER THREE:
Ain't got no Mother	*Orphan*
Ain't got no culture	*Man*
Ain't got no friends	*Lucky*
Ain't got no schoolin'	*Dumb*
Ain't got no shine	
Ain't got no underwear	*Bag*
Ain't got no soap	*Dirty*
Ain't got no A-train	
Ain't got no mind	*Lost it*

(CLAUDE *has put on steel-rimmed reading glasses, takes out of his back pocket an air-mail edition of* The [London] Times, *moves downstage and kneels, spreading newspaper on floor, reading it. Stacks of newspapers all over stage.* MOM *comes downstage and begins dancing around* CLAUDE *to a "Thirties-type melody," undressing as she dances, down to her slip and stocking feet, placing her clothes on the chair.* CLAUDE *takes no note of her, continues reading. She continues the seduction)*

CLAUDE (*Exorcism of the newspaper, affecting North Country English accent, Yoga lotus position, incense, pot smoking*): "Hello there ... ever thought how you're living smack bang in the middle of the Stone Age? This, folks, is the Psychedelic Stone Age. Without doubt, the most exciting time this weary, whirling, square globe has seen for generations. And it's *your* age . . . you are living it, you are psyching it, you are stoning it . . ."

(He tears up pieces of newspaper)

MOM: I'm beat . . .

CLAUDE: "It's the age of electronic dinosaurs and cybernetic Indians and the *Daily News*, the age where it's more fun than ever to be young . . ."

MOM: Did you see about that job today?

CLAUDE: "An age where it's more fun than ever to be stoned."

(CLAUDE tears up newspaper violently)

MOM *(Sarcastic, but still the seductress)*: Mountains of paper all over this house . . . your clippings, your magazines, your newspapers . . .

CLAUDE *(Cool British, reading from another newspaper)*: Got to keep up with the *Times* tra la . . .

(Tears out an article very neatly)

MOM: Tear, tear, tear, you are nothing but tissue paper . . .

(Music stops abruptly, as CLAUDE, *in a mock rage, attacks* MOM, *still with English accent)*

CLAUDE: You save S&H Green Stamps and King Korn Stamps and bloody Plaid Stamps and boxtops and Betty Crocker Coupons and Cut Rite and Kelloggs and soap coupons and Co-Op and God-knows-what-coupons. *(Pointing accusatory finger)* I've seen you pasting one regular King Korn Stamp in each thirty spaces on this page and pasting five *Big* Ten King Korn Stamps here and licking one *Super Bonus* King Korn Stamp for each fifty blocks on this page. You cut out, rip open, paste on, and save, and I am your lover, and I demand my civil rights, and there is . . .

MOM: Stop that! You stop that right now. We work hard for a living. Start being an American. Find a job. The trouble with you is you're not an American. All these Bolshevik ideas. It's disgusting. Look at yourself.

CLAUDE:

Manchester England England
Across the Atlantic Sea
And I'm a genius genius

I believe in Gawd
And I believe that Gawd believes in Claude
That's me that's me

But I don't know how long me old man's gonna put up with
that, do I?

MOM: He told me he's not giving you any more money.

CLAUDE: Oh, I've got to get out of this flat and start Liverpoolin'
it up with me mates.

MOM: What are you going to do with your life? Besides
disheveled . . . what do you want to be?

CLAUDE: Kate Smith.

MOM: Start facing reality . . .

CLAUDE: Which one?

MOM: Your father and I love you.

CLAUDE: I was born right here in dirty, slummy, mucky, polluted
Flushing.

MOM: Look at those trousers.

CLAUDE: I'm Aquarius and destined for greatness or madness.

MOM: So's your father. Don't shame us, Claude.

CLAUDE: Out onto the Technicolor streets with me daffodils . . .

MOM: The Army . . .

CLAUDE: . . . me daffodils . . .

MOM: . . . The Army'll make a man of you . . .

CLAUDE: . . . tambourining it up and everyone lookin' at electronic me.

MOM: The Army.

CLAUDE: Stand aside, sergeant.

MOM: Or the Navy.

CLAUDE: I'm sleeping out tonight.

MOM: This is where it's at, honey, not out there . . .

CLAUDE: Carry on . . .

MOM: You will change your trousers before you leave this *home*
. . . and take off my beads.

CLAUDE: Mother, it's embarrassing . . . the audience . . .

MOM (*To audience*): Hello, there. This is not a reservation,
Tonto!

CLAUDE: This is 1968, dearie, not 1948.

MOM: 1968! What have you got, 1968, may I ask? What have
you got, 1968, that makes you so damn superior and gives me
such a headache?

CLAUDE: Well, if you really want to know, 1948 . . .

I got life, Mother
I got laughs, Sister
I got freedom, Brother
I got good times, Man

I got crazy ways, Daughter
I got Million-Dollar Charm, Cousin
I got headaches and toothaches
And bad times, too
Like you

(MOM *now has tambourine and accompanies* CLAUDE)

I got my hair
I got my head
I got brains
I got my ears

I got my eyes
I got my nose
I got my mouth
I got my teeth

I got my tongue
I got my chin
I got my neck
I got my tits

I got my heart
I got my soul
I got my back
I got my ass

I got my arms
I got my hands
I got my fingers
Got my legs

I got my feet
I got my toes

I got my liver
Got my blood

I got life, Mother
I got laughs, Sister
I got headaches and toothaches
And bad times, too
Like you

I got my hair
I got my head
I got my brains
I got my ears

I got my eyes
I got my nose
I got my mouth
I got my teeth

I got my tongue
I got my chin
I got my neck
I got my tits

I got my heart
I got my soul
I got my back
I got my ass

I got my arms
I got my hands
I got my fingers
Got my legs

I got my feet
I got my toes
I got my liver
Got my blood

	COMMENTS BY THE TRIBE:
I got my guts	*Mashkalumba!*
I got my	*Tell 'em, white man*
muscles	*Maharishi Yogi*
I got life	*Let it all hang out*
life life	*Tell it like it is*
life life	*Hallelujah*
	Hallelujah
	Tell him, Mom.

MOM: And you got a lot of nerve, baby.

CLAUDE:

And I'm gonna spread it around
the world, Brother
And I'm gonna spread it around
the world, Sister
And I'm gonna spread it around
the world, Mother
So everybody knows
What I got

MOM *and* TRIBE:
Amen.
Amen.

(MOM *exits.* CLAUDE *runs back to game*)

CLAUDE:

Ain't go no smokes	*Shit*
Ain't got no job	*Lazy*
Ain't got no work	
Ain't got no coins	
Ain't got no pennies	*Hustler*
Ain't got no girl	*Horny*
Ain't got no ticket	
Ain't got no token	*Walk*
Ain't got no God	*Good*

BERGER:

Ain't got no father	*Dead*
Ain't got no T.V.	*Honest*

Ain't got no pizza	*Starvin'*
Ain't got no Gallo	*Nervous*
Ain't got no sleep	*High*
Ain't got no rhythm	*White*
Ain't got no books	*Lovely*
Ain't got no socks	*Nasty*
Ain't got no sex	*Ugly*

(BERGER *sits in chair*)

DAD *(Very pleasant)*: Well, Berger.

BERGER: *(Rising)* Yes, sir.

DAD: Sit down, Mr. Berger. (BERGER *sits*) Do you know why I called you in here today, Mr. Berger?

BERGER: I think so, yes.

DAD: We're getting to be well-acquainted, aren't we? You're a bad example for us here, Berger. And I must add you're not the only one. We've done everything to help you, persuade you, encourage you, and you've done nothing for yourself. You continue to make us promises and do nothing about it.

BERGER: Is that all, sir? Can I go now?

DAD: It's a shame, Mr. Berger. I don't understand all this.

BERGER: I hate your school.

DAD: You're such a bright boy and a good student.

BERGER: Screw *your* logic and reason. I'm tired of your *brainwash* education.

DAD: Mr. Berger, you may dematriculate in the front office!

BERGER: *(Rises and goes, turning at door, rather English)* Mr. MacNamara, this is 1968 not 1967. So long, love. Super . . . super . . . super . . . super . . .

(He exits, standing facing audience down left. DAD, *in a fury, picks up microphone to school intercom system, amplifying his voice.* BERGER *stands outside in the hall listening, motionless. Three bells ring—ding, ding, ding)*

DAD: Attention. Attention. This is your principal, Mr. Mac-Namara. *(Ding, ding, ding)* All right, now, what is this school becoming? A costume party? Some kind of a giant festival dizzyland? Some students in this school have been ignoring PS 183's Personal Appearance Code, upsetting the morale of their classmates, distracting their fellow students, and I know the teachers feel their teaching is adversely affected in the presence of these apparitions. Well . . . one of your rebellious beatnik leaders has just been expelled by me. And let this be an ultimatum to the rest of you. This is World War III.

THE TRIBE:
Help!

Ain't got no home	*So*
Ain't got no shoes	*Poor*
Ain't got no money	*Honey*
Ain't got no class	*Common*
Ain't got no scarf	
Ain't got no gloves	*Cold*
Ain't got no bed	*Beat*
Ain't got no pot	*Busted*
Ain't got no faith	*Catholic*

DAD (*With whip and gun*): Mr. Berger.
BERGER (*Growling like a lion*): Yes, sir.
DAD: Be seated.
BERGER: The girls love my look, they flock to me.
   (*All* THE TRIBE, *as lions, flock to* BERGER)
DAD: We've become well-acquainted.
BERGER: I'm busy.
DAD: Bright boy.
BERGER: No, thanks.
DAD: Fine student.
BERGER: Thanks, love.
DAD: Are you hopeless?
BERGER: Watch me!
DAD: We've tried.
BERGER (*The last line as a lion*): Channel 13.
DAD: I'm hip.
BERGER: Mr. MacNamara.
DAD: Mr. Berger, we do not send our chemistry teachers on trips.
   Your hair, your dress . . .
BERGER (*Now a cheerleader*): Macy's Bargain Basement.
THE TRIBE (*Responding to the cheer, in* BERGER's *rhythm*):
   Macy's Bargain Basement.
DAD: But this, Mr. Berger.
BERGER (*Cheerleader*): Call me Doctor Spock.
THE TRIBE: Call me Doctor Spock.

DAD: The last monstrous straw.

BERGER: Another chance?

DAD: Sorry.

BERGER (*Cheerleader*): Oh, the social stigma.

THE TRIBE: Oh, the social stigma.

DAD: Further remarks?

BERGER (*Cheerleader*): This is 1968, not 1967.

THE TRIBE: This is 1968, not 1967.

DAD (*As a Nazi*): You may dematriculate in the front office, Mr. Berger.

BERGER (*"Heil Hitler"*): Mr. MacNamara.

THE TRIBE (*"Heil Hitler"*): Mr. MacNamara.

DAD (*To audience*): General Hershey says draft 'em!

BERGER: Hell, No, We Won't Go!

THE TRIBE:
   Hell, No, We Won't Go
   Hell, No, We Won't Go

DAD: President Johnson says call up the reserves.

THE TRIBE:
   Hell, No, We Won't Go
   Hell, No, We Won't Go
   Hell, No, We Won't Go
   Hell, No, We Won't Go

DAD: Governor Reagan says turn the schools into concentration camps.

BERGER: Brainwash the masses!

THE TRIBE:
   What do we think is really great?
   To bomb lynch and segregate
   What do we think is really great?
   To bomb lynch and segregate

DAD: Pope Paul says Stop the Peace Demonstrators!

THE TRIBE:
   No No No No No
   No No No No No

No No No No No
No No No No No

Black White Yellow Red
Copulate in a King-Size Bed
Black White Yellow Red
Copulate in a King-Size Bed

Hell, No, We Won't Go
Hell, No, We Won't Go
Hell, No, We Won't Go
Hell, No, We Won't Go

What Do We Want	*No No No No No*
Peace	*No No No No No*
When Do We Want It	*No No No No No*
Now	*No No No No No*

What Do We Want	*No No No No No*
Freedom	*No No No No No*
When Do We Want It	*No No No No No*
Now	*No No No No No*

Peace Now
Freedom Now
Peace Now
Freedom Now
Peace Now
Freedom Now

Ain't got no grass	*Can't take no trip*
Ain't got no acid	*Can't blow my mind*
Ain't got no clothes	*You're full of puss*
Ain't got no pad	*You're full of piss*
Ain't got no apples	*We got balls*
Ain't got no knife	*Can't cut you up*
Ain't got no guns	*We got bananas*
Ain't got no garbage	*White trash*

CLAUDE (*Who has been burning a piece of paper during the above*):

Ain't got no draft card   Burned it

THE TRIBE:
Burned it burned it burned it burned it

("Burned It" overlaps the following)

Ain't got no earth
Ain't got no fun
Ain't got no bike
Ain't got no pimples
Ain't got no trees
Ain't got no air
Ain't got no water
City
Banjo
Toothpicks
Shoelaces
Teachers
Football
Telephone
Records
Doctor
Brother
Sister
Uniforms
Machine guns
Airplanes
Air Force
Germs
M-1, bang bang bang
M-2, bang bang bang

(In unison)

A Bombs
H Bombs
P Bombs
Q Bombs
Chinese Checks
Hindus

Bindus
Italianos
Polacks
Germans
Youse
Jews
Up and downs
On 'ems and in 'ems

(Shouting to the audience now, out of rhythm, overlapping each other, not in unison)

Vietnam, Johnson, high school, sex, coffee, books, food, scissors, magazines, news, cigarettes, cancer, LSD, 007, Supermans, Batmans, Castros, Subways, Con Edisons, Hollywood, Napalm, Tuesday Weld, Burton-Taylor, Pop art, Pop off, popcorn, popsicle, Andy Warpop, pop paper, pop up, Popeye, poppers, lipstick, dresses, combs, glasses, leather, sandals, harmonicas, England, Outer Space, astronauts, Jesus, air, air, air, air, air, air, air, air . . .

(CLAUDE, BERGER, WOOF, HUD *are gasping for air, as* JEANIE, CRISSY, *and* DIONNE *come forward)*

JEANIE:
Welcome, sulfur dioxide
Hello, carbon monoxide
The air the air
Is everywhere

Breathe deep
While you sleep
Breathe deep

Bless you, alcohol bloodstream
Save me, nicotine lung steam

Incense incense
Is in the air

Breathe deep
While you sleep
Breathe deep

Cataclysmic ectoplasm
Fallout atomic orgasm

Vapor and fume
At the stone of my tomb

Breathing like
A sullen perfume

Eating at
The stone of my tomb

Welcome, sulfur dioxide
Hello, carbon monoxide

The air the air
Is everywhere

Breathe deep
While you sleep
Breathe deep

(Cough)

Deep

(Cough)

Deep deep deep

(Cough)

I wired my parents for money . . . I told them I was stranded.
They said: Stay stranded.
DIONNE: That's Jeanie.
JEANIE: I live with a whole bunch of people on Teeny Bopper
Island . . .

DIONNE: She loves Claude.

JEANIE: Third Street and Avenue C. Claude is my acid. Claude is my trip. Methedrine's a bad scene. And Claude loves me.

(ANGELA, CRISSY, *and* DIONNE *shake their heads behind her back. They exit. The Culpepper Minute Men flag is pulled back and we are in The Intergalactic Bathtub—there is a sign which designates this tribal hangout.*

As a yellow bathtub and Oriental rug are being rolled out, the kids sing and dance)

[Note: MOM *and* DAD *sit at an upstage table perhaps, facing the action on the stage, and react as an extension of the audience*]

THE TRIBE:
LBJ took the IRT
Down to 4th Street USA

When he got there what did he see
The youth of America on LSD

LBJ	*IRT*
USA	*LSD*
LSD	*LBJ*
FBI	*CIA*
FBI	*CIA*
LSD	*LBJ*

(BERGER *enters*)

WOOF (*Reading a nudist pornography magazine*): Berger!

BERGER: Woof!

HUD: Berger!

BERGER: Hud! (*English accent*) Claude here yet?

HUD: No.

(BERGER *jumps. Takes his key from his pocket*)

BERGER (*The height of cool*): He entered. He locked the door. He checked out the scene. He put his right hand on his left breast and stretched his left arm high above his head, waving to his blue-eyed soul brothers with a smile. A hush came over the room—(*Italian accent*) Ladies and gentlemen, listen, when I drop-a dead, when-a my heart-a go pzzzzzzzzt, like-a this, I want to be buried in a bronze-a casket, beautiful-a bronze, no clothes, nothing, put-a me down stomach first, like-a this, everybody come-a see me, they come-a kiss-a my ass.

He put out his hand and said: "Lay me five, man, I'm free like a cockroach."

WOOF (*Skinning* BERGER's *hand*): I'm screwed up like a nudist.

BERGER: Blowing his cool, he said . . . (*Now he bursts with excitement*) Woof, Woof, baby, Hud . . . I finally got out. Out. Out.

WOOF: Out of who?

BERGER:
Me and Lucifer
Lucifer and me

Just like the angel that fell
Banished forever to Hell
Today have I been expelled
From high school Heaven

Elevator going down
Going down
Going down

Everybody going down
Going down
Going down

This is my doom, my humiliation
October, not June, and it's summer vacation
Such a disgrace, how can I face the nation
Why should this pain bring me such strange elation

Escalator going down
Going down
Going down

Everybody going down
Going down
Going down

Emancipation Proclamation
Oh, Dr. Lincoln, my head needs shrinkin'
Lu lu lu lu lu lu lu lu lu lu lu lu Lucifer and me
Doomed from here to eternity
Baa baa baa

Growing up going down
Going down
Going down

Growing up going down
Going down
Going down

Forgive me if I don't cry
It's like the Fourth of July
Thank God that angels can fly
From high school heaven

Everybody going down
Going down
Going down

Thank God that angels can fly
From high school heaven

Everybody going down
Going down
Going down

Thank God that angels can fly
From high school heaven

(Amos 'n' Andy dialect)

Waiter, waiter.

HUD (Very British): Oh, yes, sir. You rang, sir? What is the master's pleasure this time?

BERGER (Pointing to various objects all over the stage): I'll have one of those and one of those and that and that and that over

there and this over here and that way over there and one of
those one of those that and that and . . . YOU!

(BERGER *empties small bottle of pills on the table*)

HUD (*Still British*): Oh, yes, sir. Three cups of blood.

BERGER: And make it fast.

HUD: You see the color of my skin. It's white, sir. And you
remember that. It's white, white, white. I'm no slave of yours.
I'm white. (*Goes to get three cups of coffee*)

WOOF (*Upper British accent*):
Digger Digger
Dirty Nigger
Digger Nigger
Pull the Trigger
Nigger Nigger
Grows it Bigger

HUD: Oh, yes, sir, and don't you forget it.

(*Behind the next* THE TRIBE *sings softly*)

THE TRIBE:
Everybody going up
Going up
Going up

Everybody going up
Going up
Going up
Etc.

BERGER (*Dividing the pills into three piles*): One for Billy
Graham, one for Prince Philip, and one for Joe Louis. One
for Cardinal Spellman, one for Rabbi Schultz, one for
Muhammad Ali. One for Shirley Temple, one for Ronald
Reagan, and one for Miss Rheingold.

(WOOF *starts to drink*)

BERGER: Uh-uh-uh-uh-uh-uh! Not yet hophead. (*Bronx Jewish
accent*) My daughter. Let me tell you about my daughter.
She sees flying saucers and monsters and all sorts of these
things. And now she's floating around in that San Francisco
somewhere . . . and all because of these pills.

ONE OF THE TRIBE: Oy!

BERGER *(He toasts)*: Up PS 183.

HUD: Blood in your eye.

BERGER: Hud, can I pitch my tent here tonight?

HUD: Feel free.

WOOF: I gotta kick this drug bag. It's a bad scene.

BERGER: I don't care if you hate me for telling you this, but you've got bad breath.

WOOF: Can I sleep with you tonight, Berger?

BERGER: Sure. Come on in. And, Woof, don't tell Claude about school; let me tell him. *(To audience—very square)* High School Dropouts: Dial OR 7-7390 for our Free Booklet telling how you can get your diploma learning at home-a. This is a recording.

(CLAUDE *enters*)

CLAUDE: This is Claude's day.

BERGER: Claudio! (CLAUDE *does not move*) Wait wait wait . . . don't tell me.

(CLAUDE *and* BERGER *and* WOOF *and* HUD *nod heads simultaneously*)

WOOF: No kidding.

BERGER: Aw, Claude, that's death, man . . .

HUD: Tough luck, baby . . .

CLAUDE: I've thought it over . . . I'll tell them I'm a faggot and hide out in Toronto.

(CLAUDE *picks up battery-powered megaphone, speaks into it, reading from his notebooks, first pantomiming taking a drag from a stick of marijuana*)

"Ode to a Stick"

Poem

by Pfc Claude Hooper Bukowski

(Electronic beeps, blurps, bells, and tinkles in background)

Pick up my glowworm

(Another drag)

My little magic fellow

My little block of gold

My little blue flame

My little cloud in the sky

My little poison ivy

My little nonconformist

My little American bird

My little magic flower

My little electricity blowhole
My little white erection
My little garden of heaven
My little high above the tree castle
My little village far below
My little rug of grass
My little sunny balloon farm
My little growing on the hills
My little daybreak crumbles away
My little weird weed
My little Sunday breeze
My little raft of wood
My little naked tree
My little streak across the sky
My little special sunset
My little raindrop bed
My little whisper to the world
My little beautiful thing
My little swallow me
My little wrinkled old man
My little Lord of the Rings
(*Another drag*)
Pick up my glowworm.

BERGER: The doctors dug your body, huh.

CLAUDE: They're hot for my ding-dong.

BERGER: Didn't you tell them you're going to Pratt next year?

CLAUDE (*English*): They're queer for me gear. They flipped. Next year means shit. I'm not going in. I'll eat it first. I'm not.

WOOF: Eat what?

CLAUDE: My draft card.

BERGER: I thought you burned it.

CLAUDE: That was my driver's license.

WOOF: Eat it on CBS Television.

CLAUDE: Berger, help me. How am I gonna get out of going?

BERGER: Dance bare-assed down Forty-second Street.

WOOF: Tell them you're a closet queen.

HUD: Shave your armpits.

CLAUDE: C'mon—what am I gonna do?

BERGER (*English*): Do you think homosexuality is here to stay, love?

CLAUDE: Yes, dear, until something better comes along.

BERGER: Take me with you. Tell them I'm your girlfriend and you can't sleep without me.

HUD: Bet the induction officer your cock is bigger than his.

BERGER: Tell them your mother volunteered to fight in your place.

WOOF: Do they know she's a Viet Cong?

HUD: Uncle Sambo Wants You!

CLAUDE *(To audience)*: I want to be over here doing the things they're defending over there.

(Starts to burn a card)

BERGER: Become a nun.

HUD: Wet the bed, baby.

CLAUDE: They're not gonna cut it off.

BERGER *(Reading the burning card in: CLAUDE's hand)*: Mr. Claude Hooper Bukowski—New York Public Library.

CLAUDE: Berger, help me, no kidding around . . . if they draft me, I'll get killed or a leg shot off or something . . . I know it . . . they're not gonna get me . . .

BERGER: Oh, yes, they are. You will go, and you will get killed and rape and loot; you will do exactly what THEY tell you to do.

CLAUDE: It's not funny, Berg . . . I'm not going . . . it took me years to get it like this, and I'm not gonna let them do it.

BERGER: Five years in prison at hard labor.

CLAUDE: I don't want to die.

THE TRIBE: Ahhh!

("The Caissons Go Rolling Along")
Lift your skirt point your toe
Volunteer for the USO
Bake cookies and pies for our guys

BERGER, WOOF, HUD:
 Lift your skirt point your toe
 Volunteer for the USO
 Bake cookies and pies for our guys

(BERGER asks woman in the audience for lipstick)

("Anchors Aweigh")
Your legs—Shave the hair off

Your eyebrows—Pluck 'em
Refuse to take your underwear off
And if they make you pucker your lips up and puck 'em

("The Marine Hymn")
You'll forget your Ruby Tuesday,
You'll forget Michelle Your Belle
As for Lovely Rita Meter Maid

(BERGER *puts lipstick on* CLAUDE)

Well, she can go to Hell
Even Mother Sweet cannot compete
With the neatest piece we've seen
Claudine Hooper Bukowski
She's the Queen of the United States Marines
Nervous Nellie

(MOM *and* DAD, *who have gotten up from the back table, approach the young men.* MOM *is dominant;* DAD *has a camera and a pad and pencil and takes notes*)

MOM (*To* CLAUDE): Young man, excuse me. May I introduce myself. (*She hands* CLAUDE *a Kleenex. He removes his lipstick*) Here's my card. I did overhear just a wee portion of your conversation, and I would like to ask you a question, if you wouldn't mind.

CLAUDE: Sure, of course, what is it?

MOM: Well . . . (*She giggles*) . . . this may sound a bit naïve . . . foolish . . . oh, my, I don't know why I feel so embarrassed . . . I . . . being a visitor from another generation like myself . . .

CLAUDE: Cool it. (*She fans herself, using her hand*) What would you like to know?

MOM: Well . . . why? . . . I mean . . . why? Why? (*She climbs up on chair* CLAUDE *is sitting in, straddling him*) Why? Why?

(BERGER *places another poster against the counter: "Ronald Reagan Is a Lesbian"*)

CLAUDE: You mean this?

(*Holds up a strand of his own hair, while putting his arms around* MOM's *legs; outrageous orgiastic actions*)

MOM (*Rubbing her hands through* CLAUDE's *hair*): Yes . . . why

that? I mean, is it because you're a . . . oh, dear . . . Are you?
. . . please forgive me . . . are you . . . a . . . Hippie?

(*She caresses* CLAUDE *passionately as the stage falls apart.
Glitter dust is thrown by* THE TRIBE, *bells, horns, rattles, great
reaction to "the magic word"*)

BERGER: Is the Pope Catholic?

DAD (*A timid soul, but he sits on the floor, grabs hold of*
CLAUDE's *leg and begins pushing trouser leg up*): Who are
your heroes?

(WOOF *displays a poster he has made: "Jesus Was a
Catholic"*)

BERGER: Medusa.

(*He embraces* MOM *who kisses him*)

DAD (*Rubbing* CLAUDE's *leg while grabbing for his wife*): Aa-ha!

HUD: Wonder Woman.

WOOF (*Trying to climb up on the chair, too*): Prince Valiant.

DAD: Aa-ha!

BERGER: Orphanie Annie.

CLAUDE: Vernica Lake.

DAD: Oh-ho!

HUD (*Who does not have long hair, of course, joins the throng
of intertwined bodies*): It's very simple . . . you ask me why?
Like I like the feel of the silky strands on my ears and the
back of my neck and on my shoulders. Goose-bump time—
know what I mean?

MOM: That's very interesting. (*To* DAD) You see, he does it for
the sensual experience.

(*Now caressing* HUD *passionately*)

That's why . . .	HUD (*To* DAD):
That's why	
That's why	You dig my Dixie Peach?
That's why	
That's why	DAD:
That's why	I dig your Dixie Peach!
(*Poster: "Hair"*)	

CLAUDE (*Breaks up the orgy with the start of his singing . . . or
perhaps the orgy could continue into song*):

She asks me why

Don't ask me!

I'm just a hairy guy
I'm hairy noon and night
Hair that's a fright

I'm hairy high and low
Don't ask me why—Don't know

It's not for lack of bread
Like the Grateful Dead

Darlin'
Give me a head with hair
Long beautiful hair
Shining gleaming streaming
Flaxen waxen

Give me down-to-there hair
Shoulder-length or longer
As long as God can grow it
Flow it
Show it

Hair Hair
Hair Hair Hair
Hair Hair Hair

Flow it
Show it
Long as God can grow it
My hair

Let it fly in the breeze
And get caught in the trees
Give a home to the fleas
In my hair

A home for fleas
A hive for bees
A nest for birds
There ain't no words
For the beauty the splendor
The wonder of my

Hair Hair
Hair Hair Hair
Hair Hair Hair

Flow it
Show it
Long as God can grow it
My hair

I want it long straight curly fuzzy
Snaggy shaggy ratty matty
Oily greasy fleecy
Shining gleaming streaming
Flaxen waxen
Knotted polka-dotted
Twisted beaded braided
Powdered flowered and confettied
Bangled tangled spangled and spaghettied

Oh, say you can see my eyes
If you can
Then my hair's too short

Down to here
Down to there
Down to where
It stops by itself

Doo Doo Doo Doo Doo Doo Doo Doo Doo Doo
Doo Doo Doo Doo Doo Doo Doo Doo Doo Doo

They'll be ga-ga at the go-go
When they see me in my toga
My toga made of blond brilliantined
Biblical hair

My hair like Jesus wore it
Hallelujah, I adore it

Hallelujah, Mary loved her son
Why don't my mother love me

Hair Hair
Hair Hair Hair
Hair Hair Hair

Flow it
Show it
Long as God can grow it
My hair

(MOM *ecstatically embraces the* BOYS, *this time with warm, motherly affection.* DAD *shakes all their hands*)

MOM: Oooooo, these boys love to dress up like this . . . I love them . . . I love all of you . . . I wish every mother and father would make a speech to their teenagers: "Be free . . . no guilt . . . be whoever you are . . . do whatever you want . . . just so you don't hurt anyone . . . I am your friend." Can we get a picture of you?

(BERGER *gives* MOM *his key*)

BOYS: Sure.

MOM: Hubert!

CLAUDE: BE MANIPULATED!

ONE OF THE TRIBE:
I wanna be in pictures . . .
That's why I'm here, to be in pictures . . .

WOOF (*In a whisper to* BERGER): See him? That's you two years from now.

BERGER (*To* WOOF): See her? That's you one year from now. (*To* MOM *aloud*) Love your dress, call me Thursday.

MOM: Thank you. Ready, Hubert? (*The four guys line up for a picture—*DAD *uses Polaroid Swinger camera*) Get the best. YES, dear. Don't go past it. YES!

(BERGER *puts his hand on* CLAUDE's *crotch as* DAD *focuses. Neither* DAD *nor* MOM *sees this*)

CLAUDE: We're the Grope Group!

(DAD *snaps the picture*)

MOM: Thank you. Thank you one and all.

(*To audience*)

I would just like to say that it is my conviction
That longer hair and other flamboyant affectations

Of appearance are nothing more
Than the male's emergence from his drab camouflage
Into the gaudy plumage
Which is the birthright of his sex

There is a peculiar notion that elegant plumage
And fine feathers are not proper for the man
When actually that is the way things are
In most species

(THE TRIBE *holds out their hands for money*)
Good-bye, all you sweet little flowerpots.
(DAD *and* MOM *exit*)
THE TRIBE: Fuck you, Margaret Mead.
(As if saying, most cheerily: "Thank you, Margaret Mead")
HUD: Scene One: Sheila's Entrance.
CLAUDE (*To audience*): Fasten your jockstraps!
BERGER: She is flying in at an altitude of 10,000 rubles.
(SHEILA *enters carrying purse, packages, cardboard posters*)
SHEILA: Bergerbaby, I thought that was you.
WOOF (*He does a kazoo flourish*): It's Joan of Arc. (*He gives another kazoo toot*)

SHEILA:

Sheila Franklin
Second semester
NYU
And she's a protester

(Dropping her belongings)
Hi, Hud. (HUD *runs to* SHEILA, *kisses her entire body as she talks to audience*) I'll probably major in social psychology garbage. Or I might flunk out or quit. My mother and father and older sister and her husband and baby live in Port Chester. I live in the East Village with a sweet painter, Andrew ... who moved in after I had an affair with that one ... (*She throws a daffodil at* BERGER, *who raises his hand*) ... and I'm much happier. (*Breaking from embrace with* HUD *and speaking to* BERGER) Is that cool enough for you? (*To audience*) I'm very social-injustice conscious.

She loves protests in the park
Like he said: she's Joan of Arc
Voices and all
Sheila Franklin

CLAUDE, WOOF, HUD:

Sheila Franklin

SHEILA *(Running to* WOOF, *hugging him)*: Runaway Woof, the flower child.

WOOF *(As* SHEILA *is hugging him—to* BERGER*)*: Bananaberger, Sheila's back, baby.

HUD: Scene Two: Sheila and Berger.

BERGER: This Indian land—buzz off.

CLAUDE: When did you get in? I thought you were picketing in D.C.

BERGER: *Protesting!!!*

SHEILA: Spreading the groovy revolution.

WOOF *(Throws his arm around* BERGER's *neck)*: Let's go over to the park, man, and scare some tourists.

SHEILA *(To audience)*: Isn't love beautiful?

BERGER: Hello, Sheila.

SHEILA: Hello, Claude.

(Note: BERGER *is being pleasant, genuinely, to* SHEILA; SHEILA *is the one who is resentful and refuses to say "Hello, Berger")*

CLAUDE: Hello, Sheila.

BERGER: Hello, Sheila.

CLAUDE: Hello, Sheila.

(Pause)

SHEILA: Hello, Claude.

WOOF: C'mon, man, let's split.

SHEILA: Guess what, Claude? From President Johnson's bedroom window, Eartha Kitt waved to Sheila Franklin!

BERGER: Disgrace!

CLAUDE *(To* HUD*)*: Another cup of blood for *(Pointing to* SHEILA*)* LBJ.

SHEILA *(Looking at* BERGER*)*: Thanks, Aquarius.

HUD *(Reading from a magazine)*: "The draft is white people sending black people to make war on yellow people to defend the land they stole from red people."

CLAUDE: We missed you, Sheila.

SHEILA: Did you really?

CLAUDE: Didn't we miss her, Berger?

BERGER: Yeah! We did.

SHEILA (*Speaks to* BERGER *for first time, handing him poster material*): Berger has to help Sheila make posters.
(*She returns to* CLAUDE)

BERGER: We're always making posters, Miss Poster. What're the posters for this time?

SHEILA: For the end of the show, stupid. (*To* CLAUDE) Did Berger miss Sheila?

BERGER: Claude missed Sheila.

HUD: Tomorrow morning on the front steps at City Hall there will be a huge suck-in for peace. Bring your blankets and something to suck.

WOOF: What did she get you this time?

SHEILA (*Holding up yellow satin shirt to* CLAUDE): Sheila brought back Berger a beautiful yellow satin shirt. Take that filthy rag off. (*Throws shirt to* BERGER) Claude, help me make these posters.
(*Taking posters from* BERGER *to* CLAUDE)

BERGER: Oooooooooo, Sheila! My eyes cannot behold such beauty . . .

SHEILA (*To* BERGER): You dig, delicious?
(BERGER *takes off his shirt*)

WOOF: A body's a wonderful thing.

SHEILA (*Scratches* BERGER's *back*): Give me some skin, baby.

HUD: Scene Three: Sheila's Rape!
(CLAUDE *tears holes in paper napkin, opens it, pastes it on his face as a mask*)

BERGER: Ooooo, Sheila, you shouldn't have . . . I'm turned on, flipped out, switched on . . . you really shouldn't have done it. It's too boss, a groove, a gas. Send me to Saigon, it's the grassy end . . . it's just superlative . . .

SHEILA: Berger, stop it . . . you like it?

BERGER (*Suddenly very angry*): Don't tell me to stop. You always do that. You don't allow me to have any friends, you're jealous, suspicious, you use the double standard, you test me, spy on me, you nag, nag, nag, you won't allow me to be myself, you follow me, you're always picking a fight, and then you expect me to love you . . . well, I can't have sex that way . . . sex! That's the last thing I'd want . . .

SHEILA: Berger, you're so crazy, I adore you. Please put it on.

BERGER: It's super-goosey-gassy. I'm turny on-ey, I'm flipey outey, stoney switchey oney, I'm freakey outey, hungey-upey, I'm hung, I'm hung, I'm hung, I'm hung, I'm hung, I'm hung, I'm hung . . . (*During this next, he grabs* WOOF *and has him get on top of* SHEILA, *screwing her*) . . . head like a freaked-out Frankenstein, belt buckle ajar, write "Fugs" on the wall, I'm buzzin' out on glue you, stand back banana, airplane, rocket, pencil, smoke stack, I'm hung on the sides, over the ears, down my leg and straight down my back, open the door, pull it out . . . my shirt collar . . . I'm hung . . . everybody groove and stare . . . no underwear . . . I'm hung . . . (BERGER *collapses onto* WOOF's *sleeping bag, as though he has just expended himself in an orgasm*) Woof, it's sex, not a stomach ache.

[*Note:* BERGER *has just fucked* SHEILA *in public. Or rather raped her in public.* BERGER *has had his orgasm. She was fighting him off and reacts to his attack*]

HUD: Scene Four: Claude loves Sheila.

CLAUDE (*Removing napkin-mask from his face, as though nothing had happened*): Sheila, I wrote a great part for you in my movie.

SHEILA: Huh?

CLAUDE: I wrote a great part for you in my movie.

SHEILA: Huh?

CLAUDE: Yes, I did.

SHEILA (*In shock*): We have to make posters. We have to make posters.

(*Poster in Background: "Legalize Abortion"*)

CLAUDE: It's about a chick hung up on this straight cat . . . no, it isn't. . . . It's about this girl in love with this square guy . . . but she gets mixed up with somebody like Berger . . . searching for her self-identity, you know, alienated youth in a totally committed society and all that shit. . . . Here . . . See: "Sheila: nineteen years old, waist-length, straight, mouse-blond hair, unkempt, somewhat unclean, very bright, the least dressy of all the girls, but pretty underneath it all. Involved in protest marches and a student at NYU."

SHEILA: Let me see that. (*She takes script and reads*) "Berger? Eighteen years old, long dark hair, bright, funny, wild, but serious underneath it all. Claude's best friend. Woof! Hud!" Your movie's about us!

CLAUDE: I told you. Here, read this scene with me. (*Reading*)

"Medium long shot: Sheila and Claude entering the bar."
(*To* SHEILA *with North Country English accent*) "Don't you
ever get lonely?"

SHEILA: "Of course I do, but I don't dwell on it, do I?"

CLAUDE: "What would you like to drink?"

SHEILA: "Just coffee."

CLAUDE: "I'll have a Guinness, please. I'm sorry, Sheila.
Shouldn't have been so careless . . . all my fault."

SHEILA: "I just hope I'm not knocked up. I don't want to have a
baby, do I?"

CLAUDE: "I wonder if you would say the same thing if it were
Berger's baby."

SHEILA: Claude, I don't understand why you're writing this
about me!

CLAUDE: "You still love Berger and you're having my baby."

SHEILA: "Oh, Claude, please let's not start again. I can't take it."
Oh, Claude, please with this. I really *can't* take it.

CLAUDE (*Hitting the table hard*): "All right, I don't care what
you do. Get rid of it if that's what you want."

SHEILA: Claude, excuse me, please, before I throw up. You've
got a sick mind. Write a poster! (CLAUDE *takes his script and a
poster and sits in bathtub. Turning to Berger*) You really like
the shirt?

BERGER: Why don't you give it to Claude? It'll look better on
him.

WOOF: Give it to me.

SHEILA: I'm trying to control myself. Sometimes you go just too
far.

BERGER: What do you want from my life? Just leave me alone.

SHEILA: Cool it, baby. Groove on a poster.

BERGER: Sheila.

SHEILA: Creative time! I didn't know I could still get to you.

BERGER: Sheila, who's gonna leave? You or me?

SHEILA: Why're you so uptight, groovy?

WOOF (*To* CLAUDE): He got kicked out of school.

CLAUDE: What?

BERGER: Woof!

WOOF: He got kicked out of school!

SHEILA: What do you mean . . . he got . . . he got . . .

BERGER: Burn the schools to the ground, men. Graffiti the
blackboards.

SHEILA: When did it happen? . . . This is terrible.

BERGER: This morning and it's a groovy day. I switch off, move me to Suburbia. I surrender. Carpet me wall-to-wall. (*To* CLAUDE, *climbing into bathtub*) Move over. I'm Vietnam bait, Claudio.

WOOF: If I hear this Vietnam one more time, I'm leaving this theater.

SHEILA: He got kicked out?

CLAUDE: High school drop-outs should drop dead.

SHEILA: Wait a minute . . . wait a minute.

WOOF: Sheila, do you know any groovy miniskirts?

SHEILA: Shut up, Quasimodo!

BERGER: Don't get your balls in an uproar, Sheila. School never did anything for my twentieth-century computer.

CLAUDE: Shit, I'm a patriot, but I'm a patriot for the whole damn world.

BERGER: Education squashes my growth.

CLAUDE: I'm not going to die for my country.

SHEILA: Well, then, die for something else.

CLAUDE: I'd rather live and rot in jail a few years.

SHEILA: Claude, tell them you don't want to kill people. Tell them you're against killing people.

CLAUDE: Oh, that this too, too solid flesh would melt.

BERGER: Back to Miss Poster's posters.

WOOF: Let's blow, Berg.

SHEILA: He's irresponsible. He's insensitive. He lies.

BERGER: Let's blow our minds on these, Toulouse.

SHEILA: He's neurotic. He's a pothead. Let the stupid Army get him.

CLAUDE: Let the stupid Army get *him?* What about me?

SHEILA: He's an uncommitted, hedonistic jerk.

BERGER: How many do we need, Miss NYU?

SHEILA: He's paranoid.

BERGER: I thought we saved the signs from before.

CLAUDE: Sheila, how about a flick tonight or something, and we can really talk about Berger.

BERGER: What should I say?

SHEILA: Talk about Berger in a movie?

CLAUDE: Come to the movies with me, Sheila.

SHEILA: I've got a date with the park police.

BERGER: What do you dig in that Death Body, Sheila, man? She puts you down bad.

CLAUDE: What does she dig in your Death Body, man?

BERGER: Whatever it is, I'd like to chop it off.

SHEILA: I had plans for you.

BERGER: Sheila, be a good fly. Buzz off.

(HUD *enters with* DIONNE, *bringing two cups of coffee*)

HUD: Blood for Sheila, Watusi Katanga.

SHEILA: I gotta split.

BERGER: Drink it and come together.

SHEILA (*To* BERGER): You and me.

CLAUDE (*To* SHEILA): You and me.

WOOF (*To* BERGER): You and me.

HUD (*To* DIONNE): Walla walla. Gooba gooba.

BERGER: Do you know what Sheila the Sex Swamp likes to do in bed? She loves to . . .

HUD: Miobie Manatoga.

SHEILA: Berg, oh, George Berger . . . I just want to be your friend . . .

HUD: Walla walla . . . voodoo waba . . .

DIONNE: Stop that, Hud . . . stop putting us down all the time. Bwana bwana.

BERGER: We're finished . . . we've had it . . . I don't see you anymore.

SHEILA: You're like everything you're against.

BERGER: I never did see you.

HUD: Boogie Woogie.

DIONNE: Don't talk that way.

SHEILA: You talk about freedom . . .

BERGER: I'm off limits to you.

CLAUDE: Let's go see *Whips and Satin* on Forty-second Street.

HUD: Bad scene. Bad scene.

SHEILA: Don't put up a wall.

CLAUDE: Come to the flicks.

BERGER: Forbidden. This way out.

SHEILA: No bicycling. No skating. No littering. No loitering. No spitting. No smoking. No eating. No tipping. No talking. No singing. No browsing. No breathing. No loving.

Dead End
Don't Walk
Keep Out
Red Light
Red Light

Steep Cliff
Beware
Mad Dog
Blind Man
Blind Man

Warning—Land Mine
High-Voltage Line
Don't Make A Pass
Keep Off The Grass

Detour
Wet Paint
Hands Off
Dead End
Dead End

Sharp Curve
Steep Hill
Danger
One-Way
One-Way

Emer—
Gency
Exit
Only
Only

Warning—Markers Hidden
Loitering Forbidden
All Trespassers Will Be Shot
Claude Loves Sheila—He Better Love Her Not

Wet Paint
Hands Off
Keep Out
Dead End
Dead End

SHEILA: ALL:
    Dead End   *Dead End*
    Don't Walk
    Keep Out
    Red Light   *Keep Out*
    Red Light   *Keep Out*

    Steep Cliff   *Stop Sign*
    Beware
    Mad Dog
    Blind Man   *Turn Off*
    Blind Man   *Turn Off*

                  Warning—Land Mine
                  High-Voltage Line
                  Don't Make A Pass
                  Keep Off The Grass

    Detour   *Detour*
    Wet Paint
    Hands Off
    Dead End   *Do Not*
    Dead End   *Enter*

    Sharp Curve   *No Turns*
    Steep Hill
    Danger
    One-Way   *Dead End*
    One-Way   *Dead End*

    Emer-   *Keep Out*
    Gency
    Exit
    Only   *Wet Paint*
    Only   *Blind Man*

                  Warning—Markers Hidden
                  Loitering Forbidden
                  All Trespassers Will Be Shot
                  Claude Loves Sheila—
                      He Better Love Her Not

Wet Paint	*Hands Off*
Hands Off	
Keep Out	
Dead End	*Dead End*
Dead End	*Dead End*
	Men Working
Dead End	
	Men Working
Dead End	
	No Standing
Dead End	
	No Parking
Dead End	
	No Smoking
Dead End	
	No Joking
Dead End	
Dead End	
My Friend	

(*Blackout. Lights up on* BERGER *and* WOOF *with an old, battle-torn American flag*)

WOOF *and* BERGER (*Both high*):

Om mane padme om
Om mane padme om
Om mane padme om
Shanti Shanti Shanti

WOOF:

Folding the flag means taking care of the nation.
Folding the flag means putting it to bed for the night.
I fell through a hole in the flag.
I got lost in the folds of the flag.

WOOF *and* BERGER:

Don't put it down
Best one around
Crazy for the red blue and white
Crazy for the red blue and white

You look at me
What do you see
Crazy for the white red and blue
Crazy for the white red and blue

Cause I look different
You think I'm subversive
Crazy for the blue white and red
Crazy for the blue white and red

My heart beats true
For the red white and blue
Crazy for the blue white and red
Crazy for the blue white and red
  And yellow fringe

Crazy for the blue white red
  And yellow

BERGER: C'mon watch us burn it at the Be-In!

(BERGER *and* WOOF *exit.* CLAUDE *stands next to lowered Waverly Theater marquee.* MOM, *carrying stool, speaking as she enters*)

MOM IN BOX-OFFICE: Waverly Theater . . . *The Assassination and Hallucination of the Marat de Sade* directed by the Inmates of the Asylum of Charenton starring Peter Brook at 8:15 and 11:10 together with *The Gorilla Queen* performed live by the Judson Memorial Church at ten o'clock. This is a recording and thanks for calling the Waverly. (*Hangs up—to* CLAUDE) Move on, you. You can't stand here if you don't buy a ticket.

CLAUDE (*To audience*):
  The flesh failures

  We starve-look at one another
    Short of breath
  Walking proudly in our winter
    Coats
  Wearing smells from
    Laboratories
  Facing a dying nation of moving
    Paper fantasy

Listening for the new told lies
With supreme visions of lonely
    Tunes

Somewhere inside something there
    Is a rush of greatness
Who knows what stands in front
    Of our lives

I fashion my future on films in
    Space
Silence tells me secretly . . .
    Everything

Singing my space songs on a
    Spiderweb sitar
Life is around you and in you
Answer for Timothy Leary dearie

Let the sunshine in

(Pause)

MOM: How many, please?
CLAUDE: I'm waiting for Sheila.
    (JEANIE *and* CRISSY *enter.* JEANIE *is in her sari,* CRISSY *in her Be-In outfit*)
JEANIE: Let the beatniks through, please. Excuse me, sir, did you see a mooky-lookin' blond guy *cruisin'* around here?
CLAUDE: Hi, Jeanie.
JEANIE: Why didn't you call me?
CLAUDE: I been busy looking for a job.
JEANIE: What's the matter, you embarrassed? We had a good time, didn't we?
CLAUDE: I had to take my physical for the Army.
JEANIE: What are you doing here? Waiting for somebody?
CLAUDE: No, no, I'm going to the movies.
MOM: How many, please? The feature's about to begin.
JEANIE: Want some company? I've got my own bread.
CLAUDE: No, I'm meeting Berger.

JEANIE: Like my new button? Psychedelicize South Korea.

MOM: Move on, you! You can't stand here if you don't buy a ticket.

CLAUDE: I gotta go.

MOM: How many, please?

CLAUDE: Just one.

JEANIE: Claude, I just saw Sheila. She can't make it. She won't be able to meet you. She'll be at the Be-In if you want to see her.

CLAUDE: I'd like a refund, please.

MOM *(Now very sweet)*: Sorry, we don't give refunds.

CLAUDE: But I changed my mind, Rosie. I just bought the ticket.

MOM: Sorry, we have our rules.

CLAUDE: I already saw this film.

MOM: You'll have to see the manager.

CLAUDE *(To* MOM*)*: Forget it!

JEANIE: Come with the beatniks to the Be-In, Claude.

CLAUDE: Forget it . . . I'm going to the movies. Tell Sheila you didn't see me.

JEANIE: Watch the FAGS don't get you.

CLAUDE: Drop dead. *(Exits)*

JEANIE: He loves me. (THE TRIBE *enters through the audience and passes out leaflets announcing the Be-In simultaneous with* JEANIE's *speech)* Dig it, people, I'm tripped, high, zonked, stoned, right here, right now in this theater. I've had every drug going except some jungle vines somewhere. I have a right to put anything I want in my body. What's going on inside all those little *Daily News* heads? Anybody who says pot is bad is full of shit. This is my living room and I'm gonna say something I always wanted to say, "Alan Burke Sucks."

THE TRIBE: Come to the Be-In. See the Hippies get busted by the New York City Police. See them smoke marijuana, the killer weed. Bring your own pot. Tourists . . . See the Hippies. See the Land of the Underground Movies. See the freak show. See them . . . The gypsy tribes . . . Watch the beatniks . . . See them get arrested . . . See the Potheads get busted by the Federal Bureau of Narcotics. See . . . see the Hippie Phenomenon.

JEANIE *(To* CRISSY*)*: Well, are you going to stay here, or are you going to the Be-In like a human being?

CRISSY: I'm gonna wait.

JEANIE: You've got no face, Crissy, no face.

CRISSY:

I met a boy called Frank Mills
On September twelfth right here
    In front of the Waverly
But unfortunately I lost his
    Address

He was last seen with his friend,
    A drummer
He resembled George Harrison of
    The Beatles
But he wears his hair tied in a
    Small bow at the back

I love him
But it embarrasses me to walk
    Down the street with him
He lives in Brooklyn somewhere
And wears this white crash
    Helmet

He has gold chains on his
    Leather jacket
And on the back is written the
    Names
Mary and Mom and Hell's Angels

I would gratefully appreciate it
If you see him tell him I'm in the
    Park with my girlfriend
And please

Tell him Angela and I
Don't want the two dollars
    Back . . .
Just him

(The Be-In . . . The sound of bells from offstage, from the
back of the theater, from the aisles. Ankle, wrist, hand bells.
THE TRIBE enters from all directions with their bells, carrying
candles and incense, enveloping the audience, first with the

slight, insistent rhythm, moving into "Hare Krishna," the rhythms building throughout the scene. A peace-pipe is passed around. Flowers, fruit and raisins, and nuts, given out. Flowers and incense to the audience.

DAD *and* MOM *begin their participation in the scene at its outskirts, employing their rational, establishment, middle-class viewpoints and logic against the music of the Be-In—the music which never ceases)*

THE TRIBE:

Hare Krishna Hare Krishna
Krishna Krishna Hare Hare

Hare Rama Hare Rama
Rama Rama Hare Hare

(This repeats several times, as kids envelop the stage, and under it comes the chant)

Love Love
Love Love
Love Love
Love Love

Drop Out
Drop Out
Drop Out
Drop Out

Be In
Be In
Be In
Be In

Hare Krishna Hare Krishna
Krishna Krishna Hare Hare

Hare Rama Hare Rama
Rama Rama Hare Hare

Beads Flowers Freedom Happiness
Beads Flowers Freedom Happiness
Beads Flowers Freedom Happiness
Beads Flowers Freedom Happiness

Smoke Smoke Smoke
Smoke Smoke Smoke
Take Trips
Get High
Laugh Joke and Good-Bye

Beat Drum and Old Tin Pot
I'm High on You-Know-What

Beat Drum and Old Tin Pot
I'm High on You-Know-What

High High High High
Way Way Up Here
Ionosphere

Love Love Love Love Love
Love Love Love Love Love

Hare Krishna Hare Krishna
Krishna Krishna Hare Hare

Hare Rama Hare Rama
Rama Rama Hare Rama

Love Love Love Love
Love Love Love Love
Love Sex Love Sex
Love Sex Love Sex

Hare Krishna Hare Krishna
Krishna Krishna Hare Hare
Etc.
Etc.

MOM: We had another generation before you who went to war, went to colleges, worked for a salary . . . you're a disgrace to this country . . . you are certainly mixed up, all of you . . . just bringing attention to yourselves.

ANNOUNCER-MAN (*Neutral, religious, manly*):

Keep America strong.

Make America stronger.

May God bring our nation victory.

DAD: We're fighting a war. Use atomic weapons and win it, for Crissake. Get China now, before they get us, and have faith in God and Nation and the Military-Industrial Complex.

ANNOUNCER-FEMALE (*Factual, unemotional, matter-of-fact*): A demonstration to end United States involvement in Vietnam will be held on Saturday at one P.M. We're going to meet at Times Square and march around the world.

MOM: Oh, you're all so naïve about the power structure of our civilization. The subtleties, the intricacies, the complexities . . . you don't know what's really going on . . . the *top-secret truth* about what's really happening in Red China.

ANNOUNCER-MAN (*Unctuously*): The LSD Research Group sponsors a series of psychedelic lectures and celebrations on various aspects of the effect of LSD—"The Death of the Mind." How should you give a person LSD? Who regards LSD as dangerous? Tickets five dollars at the door. Or by appointment in advance. At the Planetarium Subway Station. Or call PO 3-3333-3333.

DAD: You parents should care more about *sex* and stop worrying about the drugs. Drugs are innocent compared to the violence mixed up with *sex*. Did you realize this? It is time to deal with this sex mess. Sex isn't love or even pleasure anymore . . . They preach love . . . narcotic love.

MOM: What does a nineteen-year-old kid know?

THE TRIBE:

Mari Juana Mari Juana
Juana Juana Mari Mari

Mari Juana Mari Juana
Juana Juana Mari Mari

(THE TRIBE *responds to* DAD *and* MOM'*s invectives only with more song, stronger rhythm, and by bedecking* DAD *and* MOM *with flowers, beads, loading their arms with gifts, fruit, etc.)*

MOM: You kids don't appreciate the maturity and wisdom that age brings. *(To audience)* My son wears a black armband . . . he's an antiwar with an armband. His father can't even walk down the street.

DAD *(Almost to himself)*: My son doesn't like me. He doesn't like me.

MOM: We have got to help these young people. How did they get off the track? This is serious, lady.

DAD: I can't even go into my son's room. My son has no shame. He leaves everything right out in the open where I can see it.

MOM: He is our son, dear, and we are his mummy and daddy.

(DAD and MOM as a result become more incensed, enraged, angry, moving closer and closer to the center of the Be-In all the while)

DAD *(Now walking among THE TRIBE, looking around at them and getting very upset)*: What's happening to our bedrock foundation of baths and underarm deodorant? How do they eat? Where do they sleep? Why do they have to be dressed like this?

MOM *(Walking among THE TRIBE)*: Flower power, putting on, turning on, blowing the mind . . . what language do you speak?

DAD: In two months my son will be in Vietnam and is going to be killed, and I'm proud of him.

MOM: Physical contact with any of these animals would repulse me. *(To audience)* I say, support our fighting, short-haired men in Vietnam.

DAD *(Intensely frustrated at not being able to penetrate THE TRIBE's concern with the Be-In, and shouting)*: I'd like to see one of your Daffodil Crowd in front of a machine gun.

MOM *(Shouting above their chants)*: Ship these Peaceniks to the Vietnam meat-grinder.

THE TRIBE:

Hare Krishna Hare Krishna
Krishna Krishna Hare Hare

Hare Rama Hare Rama
Rama Rama Hare Hare

(This chant continues as a new chant develops behind it and overtakes it)

Strip
Strip
Strip
Strip
Strip
Strip
Strip
Strip Strip
Strip Strip
Strip Strip
Strip Strip
Strip Strip Strip
Strip Strip Strip
Strip Strip Strip
Strip Strip Strip
Strip Strip Strip
Strip Strip Strip

(This chant predominates now with the ferocious intensity of the drums. BERGER *has removed all his clothes by this time and is seen totally naked for a brief moment by the audience. He is then surrounded by* THE TRIBE, *but the* POLICE-PUPPETS *have seen him and close in for an arrest.* THE TRIBE *forms a protective wall against the* POLICE *and sings)*

THE TRIBE:

We love cops
We love cops
We love cops
We love cops

Hare Krishna   *We love cops*
Hare Krishna   *We love cops*
Krishna Krishna   *We love cops*
Hare Hare   *We love cops*
                   We love cops

Hare Rama
Hare Rama

Rama Rama
Hare Hare

(*A large flag is held aloft on two poles. It dates from about 1776. It has a green pine tree in its center on a yellow field. A rattlesnake twines about the tree trunk. Below it reads: "Don't Tread on Me." Above the tree it reads: "An Appeal to Heaven." Violent drumming on oil drums, as* SHEILA *comes forward holding a flaming Maxwell House coffee can in her right hand above her head. She strikes a Statue of Liberty pose*)
THE TRIBE: Democracy's Daughter!
(*In her other hand,* SHEILA *holds a bunch of daffodils. One by one, each guy comes forward, lighting their draft cards, dropping the remains into the can. As each card is burned,* THE TRIBE *cheers.* SHEILA *gives each guy a daffodil in exchange.* CLAUDE *is last; he approaches the can, hesitates a moment, holds his card above it, it catches fire, and he pulls it back quickly, extinguishing the flame.*

SHEILA *puts the flaming can center stage;* THE TRIBE *sits around it, as if it were their campfire, huddling in blankets, as the drums die away rapidly.*

CLAUDE *stands apart and sings*)

CLAUDE:

Where do I go
Follow the river
Where do I go
Follow the gulls

Where is the something
Where is the someone
That tells me why
I live and die

Where do I go
Follow the children
Where do I go
Follow their smiles

Is there an answer
In their sweet faces

That tells me why
I live and die

> *Follow the wind song*
> *Follow the thunder*
> *Follow the lightning in*
>   *Young lovers' eyes*

> *Down to the gutter*
> *Up to the glitter*
> *Into the city where the*
>   *Truth lies*

Where do I go
Follow my heartbeat
Where do I go
Follow my hand

Where will they lead me
And will I ever
Discover why
I live and die

THE TRIBE:

Where do I go
Follow the children
Where do I go
Follow their smiles

Is there an answer
In their sweet faces
That tells me why
I live and die

> *Follow the wind song*
> *Follow the thunder*
> *Follow the lightning in*
>   *Young lovers' eyes*

> *Down to the gutter*
> *Up to the glitter*

Into the city where the
   Truth lies

CLAUDE:

> *Where do I go*
> *Follow my heartbeat*
> *Where do I go*
> *Follow my hand*
>
> *Where will they lead me*
> *And will I ever*
> *Discover why*
> *I live and die*

THE TRIBE:

> *Why*

CLAUDE:

> *I live and die*

THE TRIBE:

> *Why*

CLAUDE:

> *I live and die*

Note: At the end of the intermission, just before Act Two begins, CRISSY puts two old seventy-eight-rpm records on an antique windup victrola. The songs: "Anything Goes," followed by "White Cliffs of Dover"; this going into "Electric Blues."

Act Two

Band on stage now. This is the Intergalactic Bathtub electrified. Moving light projections.

The sound from the band is full and furious. The band is THE LEATHER BAG—*four guys dressed in leather outfits—perhaps black, brown, and white in color. Electric wiring everywhere, from amplifiers, guitars, hand mikes, and even from the leather costumes—wires from backs, heads, fingers, hands, feet, crotches.*

THE TRIBE *dances.*

Note: All the kids wear military uniforms, mismatching, etc.

THE LEATHER BAG:

> We're all encased in sonic armor
> Beltin' it out through chrome grenades
> Miles and miles of Medusan chord
> The electronic sonic boom
>
> It's what's happening, Baby
> It's where it's at, Daddy
>
> They chain ya and brainwash ya
> When you least suspect it
> They feed ya Mass Media
> The age is electric
>
> I got the electric blues
> I got the electric blues
> I got the electric blues
> I got the electric blues

> Thwump . . .   Old-
>   Rackety . . .   Fashion
>   Whomp   Melody
> Rock . . . Folk Rock . . .
>   Rhythm and Blues

444 |

Electrons   *Old-*
   Explodin' . . .   *Fashion*
   Rackety-Clack   *Melody*
Thwump . . . Whoomp . . .
   Whump

Plugged In . . .   *Old-*
   Turned On   *Fashion*
Rackety . . . Shomp . . .   *Melody*
   Rock
Rock . . . Folk Rock . . .
   Rhythm and Blues
Thwump . . .
   Rackety-Clack
Whoomp . . . Whump . . .
   Poof
Caved In . . . Caved In
   . . . Yes, Caved In

Lyrics shatter like broken glass
In the sonic boom
Lyrics shatter like broken glass
Electronic doom

I got the electric blues
I got the electric blues
I got the electric blues
I got the electric blues

(The tempo slows, the music softens)

Tell me who do you love, Man?
Tell me what, Man?
Tell me what's it you love, Man?

An old-fashion melody

Tell me what's it that moves you?
Tell me what's it that grooves you?

An old-fashion melody

But old songs leave you dead
We sell our souls for bread

(Back to the beat and the fury)

We're all encased in sonic armor
Beltin' it out through chrome grenades
Miles and miles of Medusan chord
The electronic sonic boom

It's what's happening, Baby
It's where it's at, Daddy

They chain ya and brainwash ya
When you least suspect it
They feed ya Mass Media
The age is electric

I got the electric blues
I got the electric blues
I got the electric blues
I got the electric blues

Thwump . . . Rackety . . . 　*Whomp*	*Old-* *Fashion* *Melody*
Rock . . . Folk Rock . . . 　*Rhythm and Blues*	
Electronics 　*Explodin' . . .* 　*Rackety-Clack*	*Old-* *Fashion* *Melody*
Thwump . . . Whoomp . . . 　*Whump*	
Plugged In . . . 　*Turned On*	*Old-* *Fashion* *Melody*
Rackety . . . Shoomp . . . 　*Rock*	
Rock . . . Folk Rock . . . 　*Rhythm and Blues*	
Thwump . . . 　*Rackety-Clack*	
Whoomp . . . Whump . . . 　*Poof*	

Caved In . . . Caved In
    . . . Yes, Caved In

Lyrics shatter	*(Shouting)*
Like	*Amplifiers higher*
Broken glass	*Turn 'em up higher*
In the sonic	*Amplifiers higher*
Boom	*Turn 'em up higher*
Lyrics shatter	*Higher higher*
Like	*Louder Louder*
Broken Glass	*Fire Fire*
Electronic	
Doom	

(The amplifiers, the mikes, the power systems explode, but THE LEATHER BAG *goes on singing and playing, no sound coming out,* THE TRIBE *continues dancing to no music. The words are mouthed)*

I got the	*(*THE TRIBE *dances,*
Electric blues	*screaming out every*
I got the	*time* THE LEATHER BAG
Electric blues	*sings "I got the Elec-*
I got the	*tric Blues")*
Electric blues	
I got the	
Electric blues	

*(*THE TRIBE *clears the dance floor, leaving* SHEILA *and* BERGER *dancing to a soft snare from the drummer. They dance awhile before speaking)*

BERGER *(Speaking and singing as they dance; to audience)*: Claude Hooper Bukowski leaves us tomorrow morning.

SHEILA *(To* BERGER*)*: I *like* Claude. But that's as far as I can take it.

BERGER: Claude has been drafted.

SHEILA: Claude's going to play soldier.

BERGER *(To audience)*: Tonight is for him. Sheila's gonna do Claude a favor tonight.

SHEILA: Oh, no, I'm not.

BERGER *(To audience)*: The greatest going-away gift we can give our friend.

SHEILA: What am I, the tribal sacrifice?
(*A group starts singing with the band in the background.* SHEILA *and* BERGER *dance throughout*)

GROUP:

> *How can people be so heartless?*
> *How can people be so cruel?*

BERGER: Sheila, you have to do this for Claude.

GROUP:

> *Easy to be hard*
> *Easy to be cold*

SHEILA: Do *this? This* is a four-letter word.

GROUP:

> *How can people have no feelings?*

BERGER: Please. (*Tries to kiss her*)

GROUP:

> *How can they ignore their friends*

BERGER: I'll be good to you. (*Tries to embrace her*)

GROUP:

> *Easy to be proud*

SHEILA (*Breaking away from* BERGER): No!

GROUP:

> *Easy to say no*

BERGER (*Backed by the* GROUP):

Especially people who care about strangers
Who care about evil and social injustice
Do you only care about the bleeding crowd
How about a needing friend

SHEILA *and* GROUP:

How can people be so heartless
How can people be so cruel

GROUP:

Easy to give in
Easy to help out

How can people have no feelings
You know I'm hung up on you

BERGER: I'll make a deal with you.

SHEILA: Sheila's the faithful kind.

BERGER: You do it tonight with Claude; I'll do it tomorrow night with you.

SHEILA: A Berger barter!

BERGER: Sheila, we got this big going-away scene planned for Claude. If you do this for Claude, it'll make it perfect. He loves you, love.

SHEILA: Claude is a boy for going. It takes a man to say no.

BERGER: Okay, Sheila. That's it. We're finished. It's over. We've had it.

(BERGER *starts walking off angrily*)

GROUP:

Easy to be hard
Easy to be cold
Easy to be proud
Easy to say no

(BERGER *exits*)

SHEILA: So long, love.

(CLAUDE *enters*, SHEILA *exits*. THE TRIBE *greets* CLAUDE *with wild enthusiasm.* CLAUDE *wears a white, floor-length Indian linen gown, gold-embroidered. He carries a small overnight bag and throws up into the air various gifts he has brought for* THE TRIBE: *some colored shirts, a Buddha, necklaces, etc., all of them his personal belongings)*

HUD: It's Lord Buckingham!

CLAUDE:

> *Manchester England England*
> *Across the Atlantic Sea*
> *And I'm a genius genius*
> *I believe in Gawd*
> *And I believe that Gawd believes in Claude*
> *That's me that's me*

(THE TRIBE *dances around* CLAUDE *singing "Too much, too much" softly behind the next dialogue)*

HUD:	THE TRIBE:
Claude, baby, how ya' doin', man?	*Too Much Too Much* *Too Much Too Much* *Super Goosey Gasey*
CLAUDE: I'm cooling it, ding dong.	*Super Goosey Gasey* *Too Much Too Much* *Too Much Too Much* *Etc.*

HUD: This your night.

JEANIE: Oh, poor baby.

WOOF: Claude, I'm disappointed in you. I thought you said they wouldn't get you.

YOUNG MAN: You chickened out.

CLAUDE: Yeah, I'm chickenshit.

WOOF: Ah, you should've burned it and got your picture in the papers.

CLAUDE: I'm no hero . . . starting right now.

JEANIE: Claude, *that sari*, where did you get *that sari!* Barney's Boys' Town?

CLAUDE: Where's Berger?

YOUNG MAN: Clip, clip, clip . . . tomorrow morning. *(Pantomiming cutting* CLAUDE's *hair)*

WOOF: Oh, leave the poor soldier boy alone.

CLAUDE: It's bad enough without you guys bugging me.

(DIONNE *on bandstand with two other Negro girls. She signals to the band*)

DIONNE: Fellas, oh, fellas!

(*The band plays a fanfare and the three girls turn to face the audience. They impersonate the Supremes. One wears a high-fashion blond wig; all in high heels and sexy-cheap sequin dresses*)

I want you to meet PFC Booo-Booo-Booo-kowski.

DIONNE *and* TWO GIRLS (*Playing with* CLAUDE):

White boys are so pretty
Skin as smooth as milk
White boys are so pretty
Hair like Chinese silk

White boys give me goose bumps
White boys give me chills
When they touch my shoulder
That's the touch that kills

> *My Mother calls 'em lilies*
> *I call 'em piccadillies*
> *My Daddy warns me to stay away*
> *I say come on out and play*

White boys are so groovy
White boys are so tough
Every time they're near me
Just can't get enough

White, White, White, White, White, White, White, White
White Boys

(JEANIE *pins large button on* CLAUDE's *lapel: "Support Our Boys in Vietnam"*)

White boys are so pretty
White boys are so sweet

White boys drive me crazy
Drive me indiscreet

(CLAUDE *dances*)

White boys are so sexy
Legs so long and lean
Love those sprayed-on trousers
Love the love machine

> *My Brother calls 'em rubble*
> *They're my kind of trouble*
> *My Daddy warns me "No No No"*
> *But I say "White Boys Go Go Go"*

(HUD *joins* CLAUDE *dancing*)

White boys are so lovely
Beautiful as girls
Love to run my fingers
And toes thru all their curls
White White White White White White White White
White Boys

(HUD *takes over dancing as* JEANIE, CRISSY, *and* ANGELA *sing to him*)

JEANIE, CRISSY, ANGELA:

Black boys are delicious
Chocolate-flavored love

Licorice lips like candy
Keep my cocoa handy

I have such a sweet tooth
When it comes to love

> *Once I tried a diet*
> *Of quiet, rest, no sweets*

> *But I went nearly crazy*
> *And I went clearly crazy*

Because I really craved for
My chocolate-flavored treats

Black boys are nutritious
Black boys fill me up

Black boys are so damn yummy
They satisfy my tummy

I have such a sweet tooth
When it comes to love
Black Black Black Black Black Black Black Black
Black Boys

(Joined by DIONNE's *trio)*

White Boys
Black Boys
White Boys
Black Boys

Mixed Media . . .

CLAUDE: Hey, Woof, from my bedroom to your bedroom. *(Hands* WOOF *rolled-up photo)*
WOOF *(Unrolls photo)*: Oh, Claude, I love it. Hey, Claude, it's beautiful. Hey, everybody, look what Claude gave me. . . . I love you. Oh, I love you. I'm in love with you. I can't help it. You're terrific . . . I'm in love with this guy, see. I like his looks to begin with. Anybody would. Besides he has a certain spectacular quality. I love him, I can't help it. I'm not a homosexual or anything like that . . . but I'd go to bed with him . . . and make great love to you. . . . He's the sun and I'm the earth. He's infinite. He's got this beautiful head. He's Leo the Lion, the only guy I'd ever go to bed with.

Mick Jagger—Mick . . . Mickey . . . My
Mick . . . My Mickey Mick . . .

Mickey my Mickey Mick
My Mickey Jag Mickey Jag
Micky Mick my Mickey Mick
My Micky Jag Jag

Mickey Mick Mick
Mickey Mick Mick
Mick Mick my Jagger

BERGER (*Entering, followed by* SHEILA): Hud, let's lock up.
HUD: Right.
   (*The band has stopped playing,* THE TRIBE *now speaks in low voices, as if expecting something to happen.* HUD *switches off the lights. For a moment the stage is in darkness, but candles are lit.* HUD *locks the door*)
SHEILA (*Breaking the silence—to audience*): I'm so tired . . . I hope this doesn't take long.
CLAUDE: What did you say?
BERGER (*Wearing dark goggles, passing out sticks of marijuana to* THE TRIBE. *As he stops by each, he has a line*): Forty-four and one-hundred-percent pure.
SHEILA: Oh . . . your movie . . . I see you're taking it with you . . .
CLAUDE: My baby . . .
BERGER: Separates the men from the boys.
SHEILA: How's it coming?
BERGER: No sticky mess.
CLAUDE: I'm almost finished with it . . .
BERGER: Jet to Miami—come on down.
SHEILA: Finished with what?
CLAUDE: My movie . . .
BERGER: That heavenly flavor.
SHEILA: Oh, yeah, how's it coming? What's Berger doing?
BERGER: Relieve headache pain fast, fast, fast.
CLAUDE: He's passing out the pot.
BERGER: Relief is just a swallow away.
CLAUDE: It's groovy for food and sex.
BERGER: Shrinks hemorrhoids.
SHEILA: All you want to do is ball.
CLAUDE: I beg your pardon.
BERGER (*Bringing the pot to* SHEILA *and* CLAUDE): Only one calorie.
SHEILA (*Sarcastically to* CLAUDE): Have a good trip!
BERGER (*Nicely to* CLAUDE): Yeah, bon voyage!
CLAUDE (*To* BERGER): Bless you, sweet child of God.
BERGER (*To audience*): I got my job through the *Village Voice*.
CLAUDE (*To* THE TRIBE): Pick up your glowworms.
   (THE TRIBE *all lights up. There is no talking now. No music.*

All is silent, but for the sound of THE TRIBE *inhaling. This should be a rather significant moment. The drummer quietly begins a rocking rhythm with a snare drum and brush)*

THE TRIBE:

> *Doors locked*
> *Doors locked*
> *Blinds pulled*
> *Blinds pulled*
> *Lights low*
> *Lights low*
> *Flames high*
> *Flames high*
>
> *My body*
> *My body*
> *My body*
> *My body*
> *My body*
> *My body*
>
> *My body*
> *Is walking in space*
> *My soul is in orbit*
> *With God, face to face*
>
> *Floating, flipping*
> *Flying, tripping*
>
> *Tripping from Pottsville to Mainline*
> *Tripping from Mainline to Moonville*
>
> *On a rocket to the fourth dimension*
> *Total self-awareness the intention*
>
> *My mind is clear as country air*
> *I feel my flesh, all colors mesh*
>
> *Red-black*
> *Blue-brown*
> *Yellow-crimson*

Green-orange
Purple-pink
Violet-white
White-white
White
White

All the clouds are cumuloft
Walking in space
Oh my God, Your skin is soft
I love your face

How dare they try to end this beauty
How dare they try to end this beauty

To keep us under foot
They bury us in soot

Pretending it's a chore
To ship us off to war

In this dive
We rediscover sensation
In this dive
We rediscover sensation

Walking in space
We find the purpose of peace

The beauty of life
You can no longer hide

Our eyes are open
Our eyes are open
Our eyes are open
Our eyes are open
Wide Wide Wide

(*Lights down on stage during last part of this song. Spot on* CLAUDE. *The following is his trip*)

GI 1 (HUD): All right, my pretty boys. Prepare to bail out. Bail out, soldier boys. I said, skydive.

GI 2 (WOOF): I'm not even twenty-one yet and they've got me jumping out of airplanes.

GI 1 (HUD): Hello, White Man.

GI 2 (WOOF): Hello, Yellow Man, down there. I'm gonna get you.

GI 1 (HUD) *(Taking* WOOF's *hand)*: Black and white go nice together, don't they?

GI 3: We're unfrocked paratroopers.

GI 4: Home of Macrobiotics and Sanpaku.

GI 5: It just proves what I always said. There just aren't that many places to go anymore.

GI 6: The machine age is overexposing me.

GI 7: My father is sure a jerk.

GI 8 (CLAUDE): Gee, just like the movies.

GI 9: I don't want to be anything, and I certainly don't want to be a housewife with kids.

GI 10: Don't worry, you won't.

ALL THE TRIBE: I'm hanging loose.

(THE TRIBE *runs off as* BERGER *impersonating* GEORGE WASH-INGTON, *enters. He wears a powdered wig askew, carries a battle-worn American flag, leads a bedragged troop of men)*

GEORGE *(Marching on)*: Hut two three four. Hut two three four. Jump to it, lads. Kill the Redcoats. Into the Delaware, men. Grab your muskets. For God, for Country, for Crown, for Freedom, for Liberation, for Mother . . .

MESSENGER (WOOF) *(Running on)*: General Washington, General Washington, your Highness . . . news from the front. The word is retreat. Threat of attack.

(GEORGE WASHINGTON *hands powdered wig and flag to* MES-SENGER *and flees as* INDIANS *in loincloths with tomahawks and war paint attack)*

INDIAN 1: White Man DIE!

INDIAN 2: Crazy Horse say, White Man DIE!

INDIAN 3: Cochise say, White Man DIE!

INDIAN 1: Geronimo say, White Man DIE!

INDIAN 2: Sitting Bull say, White Man DIE!

INDIAN 3: Little Beaver say, White Man DIE!

INDIAN 1: This INDIAN land. Oh, Manitou, Great Spirit, White Man steal our land. White Man must die.

INDIAN 2: Many moons since Roanoke. Once again White man comes. Queen Bess and John Smith from England make peace. Take Papoose Pocahontas. Wahunsunacook kill white man.

(The INDIANS *exit in a war dance of victory.* GEORGE WASH-INGTON'*s men lie still on stage in a massacre. A bugle sounds reveille. The man playing the bugle appears wearing a Civil War Rebel uniform)*

U. S. GRANT *(Heavy Southern drawl)*: Friends, I want you to meet a great friend of yours . . . General Grant. I have arrived. I say, General Grant is here. Hey, wake up. Come on, you guys . . . get up . . . *(He shakes the men and they gradually revive and get up)* . . . wake up . . . come on. We have to push on to Raleigh. *(The men fall into formation)* Roll Call: Abraham Lincoln. *(He takes a swig of whiskey)*

ABRAHAM LINCOLN: "P"-resent, sir.

U. S. GRANT: John W. Booth.

JOHN W. BOOTH *(Shakespearean actor)*: Evah-prrresent, sire. *(Brandishing small pistol)*

U. S. GRANT: Calvin Coolidge.

CALVIN COOLIDGE: Voh-dee-oh-doe, sir.

U. S. GRANT: Clark Gable.

CLARK GABLE (WOOF): Yup.

U. S. GRANT: Scarlett O'Hara.

SCARLETT *(Southern accent)*: Here I am.

U. S. GRANT *(Going to kiss her)*: Why, Scarlett, honey! . . . Teddy.

TEDDY ROOSEVELT (HUD): Right. I'm ready, giddy-up.

U. S. GRANT: Colonel Custer.

COLONEL CUSTER (JEANIE): At last.

U. S. GRANT: Claude Bukowski.

CLAUDE: He couldn't make it.

U. S. GRANT: Well, men, let's be gone. Heads up . . . shoulders back . . . onward, Christian soldiers, to Appomattox. Forward, March.

(They dance a minuet, but are attacked from behind by a group of Negroes. Some modern day, with switchblades. Some Africans with blowguns and spears, dressed as natives in feathers, etc., some dirty, poor slaves. African drums in background. The Negroes confront the whites)

AFRICAN WITCH DOCTOR *(Carrying spear)*:

Walla walla
Goona goona
Miobie
Manatoga
Gooba Gooba
Voodoo Waba

LE ROI JONES (HUD) (*Carries a banner "Black Power" and a switchblade knife*): I cut yo' up. I hate you and your white mothers. I hope you all die and rot. You're all for shit.
(*The Negroes attack and kill the white soldiers*)

SLAVE (*Standing over the dead bodies, with his foot on Abraham Lincoln's chest, very happy*): Yes, I'm finished on y'all's farm land. With yo' boll weevils and all, and pluckin' y'alls chickens, fryin' mother's oats in grease. I'm free now, thanks to yo', Massa Lincoln, emancipator of the slave. Yeah! Emancimotherfuckin'-pator of the slave.
(*The Negroes sing together*)

THE NEGROES:

Happy birthday, Abie baby
Happy birthday to you . . .

(*Suddenly the stage becomes a battlefield. War sound effects up loud. Plus electronic music in the background. They exit in fright. Four* BUDDHIST MONKS *enter in long saffron robes, kneeling down front. The first* MONK *pours gasoline over himself from a can*)

BUDDHIST MONK 1: Use high octane and feel the tiger in your tank.
(*He lights a wad of flash paper, dies an agonizing death, lies in a heap on the stage*)

BUDDHIST MONK 2: Everyone should be Buddha.

BUDDHIST MONK 3: We are all one.

BUDDHIST MONK 4: No more war toys.

BUDDHIST MONK 2: Hustling is an honest profession.
(*Three Catholic* NUNS *enter behind praying* BUDDHISTS)

THE NUNS: Hail, Mary, full of Grace, blessed is the Fruit of the Loom. (*They strangle the* BUDDHISTS *with their rosary beads*) Holy Mary, Mother of God, pray for us sinners, now and at the hour of our death . . .
(*Three* ASTRONAUTS *enter behind the* NUNS, *killing them with ray guns. Three* CHINESE *enter behind the* ASTRONAUTS, *carrying machine guns, killing the* ASTRONAUTS. *Four American* INDIANS *with war yelps, kill the* CHINESE *with tomahawks. Two* GREEN BERETS *with machine guns kill the* INDIANS *and each other. All the bodies lie in a heap as a strobe light flashes on. The killing scene goes into reverse now, all the bodies coming back to life, exiting backward and reentering at a faster pace to go through*

the exact killing ritual two more times, each time at a still-faster pace. At the end, all the sound and strobe lights off, leaving the bodies in a silent, motionless heap.

One by one the bodies rise in slow motion, as others sing)

THE TRIBE *(Perhaps prerecorded):*

Ripped open by metal explosion
Caught in barbed wire
Fireball
Bullet shock
Bayonet electricity
Shrapneled
Throbbing meat
Electronic Data Processing
Black uniforms
Bare feet
Carbines
Mail-order rifles
Shoot the muscles
256 Vietcong captured
256 Vietcong captured

(Live—the whole TRIBE *singing)*

Prisoners in Niggertown
It's a dirty little war
Three five zero zero
Take weapons up and begin to kill
Watch the long long armies drifting home

(Into a joyous march)

Prisoners in Niggertown
It's a dirty little war
Three five zero zero
Take weapons up and begin to kill
Watch the long long armies drifting home

(Settling back down on the floor, as at the beginning of "Walking in Space")

How dare they try to end
  This beauty
How dare they try to end
  This beauty

Walking in space
We find the purpose of peace
The beauty of life
  You can no longer hide

Our eyes are open
Our eyes are open
Our eyes are open
Our eyes are open

(*Lights down, spot on* CLAUDE *as at beginning of war sequence*)

Wide
Wide
Wide

(*Stage in darkness but for spot on* CLAUDE *with his eyes closed. He opens his eyes, stands slowly, not knowing where he is for a moment*)

CLAUDE: Berger . . . George.
  (*All* THE TRIBE *on stage prostrate, as if asleep*)
BERGER (*Sits up*): I'm zonked.
  (CLAUDE *rushes over to* BERGER, *sits next to him, looks at* BERGER, THE TRIBE, *and the audience*)
CLAUDE: What a piece of work is man. How noble in reason, how infinite in faculties, in form and moving how express and admirable, in action how like an angel.
BERGER: In apprehension how like a god . . .
BERGER *and* CLAUDE (*Together*): The beauty of the world, the paragon of animals.
CLAUDE: I have of late—but wherefore I know not—lost all my mirth . . . this goodly frame, the earth, seems to me a sterile promontory, this most excellent canopy, the air, look you, this brave o'er-hanging firmament, this majestical roof fretted with golden fire, why, it appears no other thing to me than a foul and pestilent congregation of vapours.

BERGER: Claude . . .

CLAUDE: What?

BERGER: I feel lonely already, Claude.

(They look at each other for a moment, BERGER *moves to* CLAUDE, *puts his arm around* CLAUDE. CLAUDE *makes no response)*

CLAUDE: Start facing reality . . . sometimes I think I'm going crazy . . . out of mind . . . maybe cancer on the brain or something . . .

BERGER: Maybe the Army is the best place for you . . . let them keep you, sleep you, feed you. I'm putting you on, Claude.

CLAUDE: I'm not going into the Army tomorrow!

BERGER: I know.

CLAUDE: Let's go to Mexico, George.

BERGER: I told you the *boogey man* would get you.

CLAUDE: I want to eat mushrooms and sleep in the sun.

BERGER: Okay. Let's go. I'll go with you.

CLAUDE: I know where it's at.

BERGER: You know where it's at.

CLAUDE: You know where it's at.

BERGER: I know where it's at.

CLAUDE: I can't live like this anymore. I'm not happy. It's too difficult—I can't open myself up like that. I can't make this moment-to-moment living on the streets.

BERGER: I dig it.

CLAUDE: I don't.

BERGER: Putting on his peace paint he said: On with the groovy revolution.

CLAUDE: I don't want to be a dentist or a lawyer or a bum or an IBM machine. I don't want to be a rock 'n' roll hero or a movie star. I just want to have lots of money.

BERGER: I'm gonna go to India . . . float around . . . live in little huts in Beirut . . . feed the poor Indians in a little village somewhere . . . like Albert Schweitzer . . . bake bread. I'm gonna stay high forever. They'll never get me. I'm gonna stay high forever.

CLAUDE: I'll tell you the thing I'd really like to be . . . invisible. I don't need drugs. An invisible man, and I could fly and see into people's minds and know what they're thinking . . . I could do anything, go anywhere, and be happy . . . not tied down to a stupid job or anybody. And I could perform miracles. That's the only thing I'd like to do or be on this dirt.

BERGER: Then you're the King of Wands.

CLAUDE: Shazam! (*He tries to fly*) Oh, my God, it's one o'clock. I have to be at the station at eight-thirty.

BERGER: Claude, they've sucked you in.

CLAUDE: They've fucked me.

BERGER: I hate the fuckin' world, don't you?

CLAUDE: I hate the fuckin' world, I hate the fuckin' winter, I hate these fuckin' streets.

BERGER: I wish the fuck it would snow at least.

CLAUDE: I wish it was the biggest fucking snowstorm. Blizzards, come down in sheets, mountains, rivers, oceans, forests, rabbits, cover everything in beautiful, white, holy snow, and I could hide out a hermit and hang on a cross and eat cornflakes.

BERGER: A fucking blizzard.

CLAUDE: Oh, fuck.

BERGER: Oh, fuckey, fuck, fuck.

CLAUDE (*To audience*): I was in the shower this morning, and I reached down and I couldn't find it . . . it fell off and washed down the drain.

BERGER: Anybody see it, anybody see this little thing? Sheila, did you see it? Claude lost this little thing, about this big . . . (*He goes to* SHEILA *and helps her up*) Sheila, how come you're so groovy-looking tonight? You've got fab eyes.

SHEILA (*Shaking him off*): Come off it, Iceberger.

CLAUDE (*Coming over*): Sheila, you're not mad at me, are you?

SHEILA: No, why should I be mad?

CLAUDE: Well, let's all go someplace . . . get coffee . . .

WOOF: I'm tired, I'm going home . . .

BERGER: We're going up to Sheila's pad. Aren't we, Sheila?

(*Focus now centers on* WOOF, JEANIE, CRISSY, CHARLIE, SHARON. *As each talks, he helps the other up*)

WOOF: Jeanie, you want to come with me?

JEANIE: Disappear, Shrimpboats.

(*She walks away*)

WOOF: Okay. How about you, Crissy? You wanna come?

CRISSY: No, not tonight, I'm comin' with Charlie, ain't I, Charlie?

CHARLIE: I don't care. (*To* SHARON) Is it all right, Sharon, if Crissy comes with us?

SHARON: We slept together last week. I'd rather sleep alone together.

CRISSY: What about me?

WOOF *(To* CRISSY*)*: How about me?

CRISSY: Too little, tobacco breath.

CHARLIE *(To* CRISSY*)*: Look, I don't care . . . *(To* SHARON*)* It's all the same thing, isn't it?

(CRISSY *and* SHARON *both walk away from* CHARLIE, CRISSY *moving over to* DIONNE)

WOOF: See ya', Charlie. *(Moves away)* I'm going home to finish the Bible.

CHARLIE *(Standing alone)*: Hey, wait a minute . . .

(CHARLIE *follows* SHARON *upstage.•Focus shifts to other side of stage—*DENNIS, BOB, DICK)

DENNIS *(To* DICK*)*: Just come over to my pad, baby . . .

DICK: Eat your own sperm.

BOB: Let's go down to the docks for cocks.

DICK: Aw, go get married!

WOOF: Everybody, if we all sleep together, it'll be nice and warm . . .

(Focus shifts to JEANIE, DIONNE, *and* CRISSY)

JEANIE *(To* DIONNE*)*: I don't want to sleep with *that.*

DIONNE *(To* CRISSY*)*: All right, then, you sleep with it.

CRISSY: Me? Never happen.

WOOF: Hey, Helen, I'll walk you home, Helen.

HELEN: Walk to Hoboken?

(Focus now to include CLAUDE, BERGER, SHEILA, DIONNE, WOOF)

JEANIE *(Moving to* CLAUDE*)*: I'll sleep with *you* if you want me to. Do you?

CLAUDE: Boring . . . *(Turning to* SHEILA*)* Sheila, I'd like to go to bed with you.

SHEILA: Why?

CLAUDE: Because I like you.

LOUISE *(Skinny girl)*: Woof, I'd like to take a bath with you.

WOOF: Ahhhh! I'm Catholic!

BERGER *(Organizing* CLAUDE, SHEILA, HUD, DIONNE, WOOF*)*: C'mon, C'mon . . .

WOOF: Sheila, will you marry me?

JEANIE: I wanna go, too.

(She tags along)

HUD: Oh . . . we're gonna go Ubangi . . .

BERGER:	DIONNE:
To Sheila's pad . . .	Bang bang.
	Gang bang.
JEANIE:	Bang gang.

Go, go, Ubangi . . .   Bugaloo-a-boo-boo.
WOOF: Yeah, yeah, c'mon, everybody, bang bang . . .
SHEILA *(Looking at the sky)*:

Good morning, Starshine
The earth says hello
You twinkle above us
We twinkle below

(DIONNE *joins* SHEILA)

DIONNE *and* SHEILA *(Looking at the sky)*:
Good morning, Starshine
You lead us along
My love and me
As we sing our
Early morning singing song

Gliddy Glup Gloopy
Nibby Nabby Noopy
La La—Lo Lo

CLAUDE, BERGER, WOOF, HUD:
Sabba Sibby Sabba
Nooby Aba Naba
Le Le—Lo Lo

Tooby Ooby Wala
Nooby Aba Naba

Early morning
Singing song

Good morning, Starshine
The earth says hello
You twinkle above us
We twinkle below

Good morning, Starshine
You lead us along
My love and me
As we sing our
Early morning singing song

Gliddy Glup Gloopy
Nibby Nabby Noopy
La La—Lo Lo

ALL:
Tooby Ooby Wala
Nooby Aba Naba

Early morning
Singing song

Singing a song
Humming a song
Singing a song
Loving a song
Laughing a song
Sing the song
Sing the song
Song Song Song Sing
Sing Sing Sing Song

MAN: Shut up, down there! We want to get some sleep! Scum bags!

BERGER *(Climbing partway up the Crucifix-Tree)*: Behold, he said, with a wave toward the harbor, see the magnificent ocean ... Italy, Spain, Switzerland, Russia, and, yes, Claude's England.

HUD *(Reading from a* National Enquirer): "Learn How Twenty-seven Die in Acid."

SHEILA: Sheila's hands, George's feet, and Claude's poor little brain matter more than the whole sweep of those damned constellations.

WOMAN: Shut up! We're trying to sleep. We have to go to work in the morning, Flag Burners!

CLAUDE: Cosmic Fart!

BERGER *(Shouting)*: I ride into Infinitude on the top of Manhateeny Island.

SHEILA: God has hands like mine and feet like yours and Claude's brain.

HUD: "Youth Threatens to Drop LSD in New York City Reservoir."

BERGER: Save me God from Infinity.

HUD: GM gets rich, GI's die.

SHEILA: Without God, we'd be no more than bacteria breeding on a pebble in space.

BERGER: Blah! to the immensity of space.

HUD: "Man Gives Address as Heaven Six Hours Before Plane Crashes."

MAN *and* WOMAN *(From up above)*: Shut up, down there, for God's sake, we want to get some sleep, etc.

CLAUDE *(Shouting at* MAN *and* WOMAN*)*: I am the Son of God . . .

MAN: Oh, yeah, New York is a rat's ass.

WOMAN *(Correcting him)*: New York is a Winter Festival. Blah!

CLAUDE *(Quietly)*: I am the Son of God.

BERGER *(Shouting)*: Blah! to the electric universe.

CLAUDE: I will vanish and be forgotten.

(Quiet reprise: "Good Morning, Starshine")

SHEILA *(Looking at the sky)*:
Look at the moon
Look at the moon
Look at the moon
Look at the moon
Look at the moon
Look at the moon
Look at the moon

Good morning, Starshine
The earth says hello
You twinkle above us
We twinkle below

DIONNE *and* JEANIE *(Joining* SHEILA*)*:
Good morning, Starshine
You lead us along
My love and me
As we sing
Our early morning singing song

Gliddy Glup Gloopy
Nibby Nabby Noopy
La La La Lo Lo

CLAUDE, BERGER, WOOF, HUD *(Joining in)*:
  Sabba Sibby Sabba
  Nooby Aba Naba
  Le Le Lo Lo

  Tooby Ooby Wala
  Nooby Aba Naba

  Early morning singing song

(All THE TRIBE *joins on a repeat of this lyric.*
  As they sing, the relationships of the principals should be very
evident: DIONNE *and* HUD *together;* JEANIE *and* WOOF, *each*
separate, almost outsiders, but each with so much love to give;
SHEILA *very aware of the situation now, still very much hung up*
on BERGER, *yet liking* CLAUDE; CLAUDE *in love with* SHEILA, *but of*
course having no idea of what is in store for him, very aware he
will soon be leaving all this; BERGER *realizing how close it is to*
CLAUDE's *departure and trying to be happy-go-lucky in spite of*
his feelings.
  Some of THE TRIBE *are bringing in the mattresses from off)*
THE TRIBE: Look what we found!
(This song starts as a chant)

  UUUUUUUUUUUUUUUUU The Bed
  AAAAAAAAAAAAAAAAA The Bed
  UUUUUUUUUUUUUUUUGH The Bed
  Oh the bed
  MMMMMMM The Bed
  I love the bed

(During the following they manipulate the mattresses, put on
psychedelic sheets, pillows, flower petals, and end by placing
CLAUDE *and* SHEILA *on the bed side by side)*

  You can lie in bed
  You can lay in bed
  You can die in bed
  You can pray in bed

  You can live in bed
  You can laugh in bed

You can give your heart
Or break your heart
  In half in bed

You can tease in bed
You can please in bed
You can squeeze in bed
You can freeze in bed

You can sneeze in bed
Catch the fleas in bed
All of these
Plus eat crackers and cheese
  In bed

  Oh, the bed is a thing
  Of feather and spring
  Of wire and wood
  Invention so good

  Oh, the bed comes complete
  With pillow and sheet
  With blanket electric
  And breath antiseptic

  Let there be sheets
  Let there be beds
  Foam rubber pillows
  Under our heads

  Let there be sighs
  Filling the room
  Scanty pajamas
  By Fruit of the Loom

You can eat in bed
You can beat in bed
Be in heat in bed
Have a treat in bed

You can rock in bed
You can roll in bed

Find your cock in bed
Lose your soul in bed

You can lose in bed
You can win in bed
But never never never never
Never never never never
Never never never
Never can you sin in bed

Never sin in bed

(*As the song ends,* THE TRIBE *has placed* CLAUDE *and* SHEILA *side by side on the bed and they exit—or stand forming walls of the room.*
Hold on the image of CLAUDE *and* SHEILA *side by side on the bed, then*)
SHEILA (*Getting up, running to door*): Berger . . . Berger.
CLAUDE: Oh, did Berger go? . . . I'll go, too. (*Starting to get up*)
SHEILA: No, you can stay.
CLAUDE: Stay?
SHEILA: Stay for coffee.
CLAUDE: Okay, coffee!

(SHEILA *goes off to make coffee,* CLAUDE *stands on bed, takes bow out of his hair, combs hair, as* JEANIE *runs on, tackling* CLAUDE, *they fall on the bed*)
JEANIE: Claude, what time does your train leave?
CLAUDE: Jeanie . . . you left!
JEANIE: Oh . . . I won't be able to make the train, Claude. I'm gonna get killed when I get home . . . so, can I say good-bye now?

(JEANIE *is on top of* CLAUDE *as* SHEILA *enters holding two burning sticks of incense*)
SHEILA: Hi, Jeanie.
JEANIE: Hi, Sheila.
CLAUDE: Beat it, Jeanie.
JEANIE: Yeah, yeah, yeah . . . aw, Claude, I just love you, that's all. Don't mind me.
CLAUDE: Jeanie, please.
JEANIE: I'm going, don't worry. (*Getting up from the bed*) Claude, I want you to have a great time, Claude. You're a great guy. You're sweet.

CLAUDE: You're sweet too, Jeanie. Beat it.

JEANIE: So long, love.

(She exits. Long pause as CLAUDE *and* SHEILA *take in their situation)*

SHEILA: You're standing on my bed.

CLAUDE *(Not moving)*: Thank you. It's beautiful.

SHEILA: Well?

CLAUDE: Well?

*(*SHEILA *sits on bed, lotus position, holding two burning sticks of incense)*

SHEILA: My pad is the crossroads of a thousand private lives. Why don't you sit down?

CLAUDE *(Sitting)*: He sits.

SHEILA: Do you want some incense?

CLAUDE *(Taking a stick)*: No.

SHEILA: Well?

CLAUDE: Well?

SHEILA: Relax!

CLAUDE *(Falling back on the bed)*: He relaxes.

SHEILA: Where did Berger go?

CLAUDE: Why don't *you* relax?

SHEILA: Claude, I'm the hippest . . .

CLAUDE: Don't you love me?

SHEILA: . . . I know your problem.

CLAUDE *(Sitting up)*: Have pity on your poor war baby.

*(*CLAUDE *touches* SHEILA*'s arm)*

SHEILA *(Violent reaction—She gets up from the bed.)*: I'll scream bloody murder if you touch me, Daddy Warbucks!

CLAUDE: What?

SHEILA: . . . You lay a pinky on my *titty* and they'll hear about it all over the *city.*

CLAUDE: Oh, you're a Liverpool poet.

SHEILA: I'm sorry, Claude . . . I can't do it . . . I'm so upset . . . I'm so mixed up . . .

CLAUDE: I'm not asking you to do anything.

SHEILA: It's not you who's asking.

CLAUDE: I'm not gonna bite you . . . unless you ask me to . . .

SHEILA: I'm sorry, Berger.

*(*CLAUDE *hears her mistake)*

CLAUDE: Sheila . . . I'd like to tell you something that I've never told to anyone else. Not even Berger. But I don't know if you're strong enough to take it.

SHEILA: What do you mean?

CLAUDE: Sit down.

SHEILA *(Sitting on floor, next to bed)*: She sits.

CLAUDE: Now, please, Sheila, you must believe me, and promise me you won't get frightened or anything.

SHEILA: I don't know what you're talking about. What do you mean?

CLAUDE: Well, you see, Sheila . . . I come from another planet.

SHEILA: Oh, yeah? I'm leaving . . .

(Getting up to move away, CLAUDE *grabs her hand)*

CLAUDE: Yeah, it's true. Just look at my eyes. I have been sent to Earth on a mission. There are many others here like me. We're observing you.

SHEILA: Another scene from your Walt Disney movie?

CLAUDE: Believe me, it's true . . . please don't make fun of me. I'm from another planet in another galaxy.

SHEILA: What's your planet called?

CLAUDE: What's it called?

SHEILA: What's it called?

CLAUDE: Explanezanetooch.

SHEILA: What?

CLAUDE: Exanaplanetooch.

SHEILA: Nice name.

CLAUDE: You believe me?

SHEILA: Of course.

CLAUDE: Can I tell you about it?

SHEILA: Of course, I'm dying to hear about it.

CLAUDE: No, I don't think I can . . . I shouldn't have told you . . . you don't believe me . . .

SHEILA: I believe you, believe me, I believe you . . . I always knew there was something strange about you . . . you come from another planet . . .

CLAUDE:

Exanaplanetooch
A planet in another galaxy
Exanaplanetooch
A place where all the people
  Look like me

A planet where the air is pure
The river waters crystal bright

The sky is green
And in the night
Twelve golden moons
Provide the light

The buildings in the cities
Shaped like hills
Made of black and green
And blue and yellow glass
With rivers running through
  Them
Crystal bright

Swim in the water
Drink from the rivers
Total beauty total health
Ev'ryman's an artist
  And a scientist-philosopher
No government and no police
No wars no crime no hate
Just happiness and love

Fulfillment of each man's
  Potential
And ambition
With ever-widening horizons

Exanaplanetooch
A planet in another galaxy
Exanaplanetooch
Would you like to go back
  With me

(*Music continues under*)
Sheila, I'm not going into the Army tomorrow. My people are
sending a space ship for me, and I'm going back to my home.
Will you come with me?
SHEILA: It would be exciting, wouldn't it? (*Crawling toward*
CLAUDE) Exanaplanetooch
CLAUDE: Exanaplanetooch
SHEILA: I'll leave a note for my parents.
CLAUDE *and* SHEILA: Exanaplanetooch

(They go down on the bed together, CLAUDE on top of SHEILA, kissing her.
Lights fade. Spotlight on them throbs a little and goes out.
In the blackout, the bed is carried off, as we hear THE GIRLS' voices:)

THE GIRLS:
  Sentimental ending
  Sentimental ending
  Sentimental ending
  Sentimental ending
  etc.

  (Spotlight up on SHEILA)

SHEILA:
  I reached it
  He reached it
  You reached it
  We all reached the climax

  I loved it
  He loved it
  You loved it
  We all loved the climax

  Fasten your seatbelts
  Hang on uptight
  Approaching for landing
  And everything turns out
    Delightfully right

  I've had it
  He's had it
  You've had it
  We've all had the climax

  This is the turning point

  Funny
  But by the end
  Bitter and serious and deadly

(Lights up behind SHEILA *as* THE GUYS *file in at attention, in full Army battle dress, steel helmets, back packs, etc. They join* SHEILA)

THE GUYS:
  I've had it

SHEILA:
  I've had it

THE GUYS:
  He's had it

SHEILA:
  He's had it

THE GUYS:
  You've had it

SHEILA:
  You've had it

THE GUYS *and* SHEILA:
  We've all had the climax
  The climax
  The climax

SHEILA:
  This is the turning point

*(*SHEILA *exits. Lights up full)*
THE SOLDIERS *(Viciously exaggerated and rapid military maneuvers)*: Right Face. Left Face. In-Place March. About Face. Parade Rest. Attention. Left Face. Right Face. Double-Time March, etc.
(They freeze at attention. MOM *and* DAD *enter, carrying a man's suit on a hanger with a mask. This represents their son. They stand center, both looking at the suit of clothes which* DAD *holds between them)*
MOM *(Kissing the mask)*: Momma loves you.
DAD *(Goes to kiss mask, but pulls back, shakes arm of suitcoat)*: I've waited a long time for this day.

MOM (*Kisses mask*): Now write me a letter tonight.

DAD (*Starts to kiss, pulls back, shakes the empty sleeve*): You don't know how proud I am of you, son, today.

MOM (*Kisses mask*): Give us a kiss. (*Kisses mask*)

DAD (*Shakes the empty sleeve and puts money into coat pocket*): Be a man.

(*They walk him over to* THE GUYS *and hand suit to one of* THE GUYS. MOM *and* DAD *stand to one side.*

BERGER *enters, calling to* SHEILA)

BERGER: Sheila . . . Sheila . . . over here . . .

(SHEILA *enters from opposite direction. She wears* CLAUDE's *white sari with a sash.* BERGER *hugs her affectionately. She makes no response. He backs away, reacting to this and really seeing for the first time that* SHEILA *is wearing* CLAUDE's *sari*)

BERGER: Sheila, we thought you were gonna miss the train.

WOOF: Where's Claude?

BERGER: Yeah, where is he?

SHEILA: He's here. He's here. He's embarrassed.

BERGER: Embarrassed? About what?

SHEILA: You'll see.

BERGER: Listen, the train's leaving.

DAD: All aboard! (*Someone imitates a train whistle*)

SHEILA (*Calling off*): Claude . . .

(CLAUDE *approaching, not yet in view*)

BERGER: Claude, what did you do to yourself?

(CLAUDE *enters, almost in shock; he wears a dark sweater, dark slacks, a navy knit stocking cap, carries his bag and the movie script*)

CLAUDE: Berger . . . I feel like I died.

BERGER: What happened, Claudio?

CLAUDE: I . . . I . . .

SHEILA: I cut his hair off . . . he asked me to . . .

CLAUDE: I didn't want them to get it. Here, George, I want you to have it.

(*He hands* BERGER *a paper sack, his shorn hair inside*)

BERGER (*Looking at package*): Oh, Claude . . . Claude . . .

CLAUDE: Keep it for me. Maybe I can have a wig made when I get out.

BERGER: Claude . . . I . . .

CLAUDE: Don't anybody say anything . . .

DAD (*Transformed into a sergeant*): Irish.

SOLDIER 1: Present, sir.

DAD: Italian.

SOLDIER 2: Present, sir.

DAD: Jew.

SOLDIER 3: Here, sir.

DAD: German.

SOLDIER 4: Present, sir.

DAD: English.

SOLDIER 5: Yo! sir.

DAD: Puerto Rican.

SOLDIER 6: Present, sir.

DAD: Polish. *(No response)* Claude Bukowski. *(No response)*
. Claude Bukowski.

CLAUDE *(Joins the file of men, then answers)*: Present, sir.

DAD: Left Face.

(The SOLDIERS*—"the train"—do a left face)*

MOM: Where's a taxi? . . . Service is terrible . . . I want to get
home . . .

DAD *(No longer the sergeant)*: I guess maybe we have to take the
subway . . .

MOM: Oh, I'm so tired . . .

DAD: Let's take the subway . . .

MOM: *You* take the subway. When I get home, I'm going to
soak in that tub . . .

(The SOLDIER-TRAIN *begins to move in an ominous, funeral*
march tempo)

THE TRIBE:
Sentimental ending
Sentimental ending
Sentimental ending
Sentimental ending
Sentimental ending
  Ripped open by metal explosion
Sentimental ending
  Caught in barbed wire
Sentimental ending
  Fireball
  Bullet shock
Sentimental ending
  Bayonet electricity

Sentimental ending
  Shrapneled
  Throbbing meat
Sentimental ending
  Electronic Data Processing
Sentimental ending
  Black uniforms
  Bare feet
  Carbines
Sentimental ending
  Mail-Order rifles
  Shoot the muscles
  256 Vietcong captured
Sentimental ending
Sentimental ending
Sentimental ending
Sentimental ending

(The Train circles the stage in the funeral march tempo as the "Sentimental Ending" rhythm accelerates in contrast. The Train exits, leaving BERGER, SHEILA, *and* WOOF. BERGER *goes to* SHEILA, *takes her hand. She looks at him and leaves.* BERGER *stands motionless, holding the bag of* CLAUDE's *hair, as* WOOF *comes over to join him.* WOOF *grabs hold of his yellow satin shirt. Lights fade. "Sentimental Ending" at a furious pace in background, as if a train is racing away)*

Curtain

TOMMY

A Rock Opera

By Pete Townshend

and The Who

EDITOR'S NOTES

Tommy is unquestionably a landmark in the glittering history of international rock music. Written and composed by The Who's Pete Townshend, with a few songs tossed in for good measure by two other members of the group, John Entwistle and Keith Moon, it was the very first "rock opera." When it was released on records in 1969, it was hailed on both sides of the Atlantic. According to critics of the day, no musical creation as ambitious as *Tommy* had ever been heard prior to its conception and realization. The idea of a popular rock group taking a single, continuous theme and following it through one and a half hours of recording certainly was innovative. As one journalist wrote: "Apart from its qualities as an exciting, moving and tuneful story, *Tommy* is a milestone in advancing the idea of rock music as another medium for expressing thought and philosophical concepts. By combining the classical form of the opera with the musical form of contemporary rock, it may well lead to a new area of musical expression."

Millions of copies of the album sold throughout the world. Such was its enormous appeal that a second version was released in 1972, performed by the London Symphony Orchestra and utilizing such soloists as Ringo Starr, Richard Harris, and Rod Stewart. In the wake of its recording fame, *The Who* performed the work on concert stages and theatres in England and the United States.

In 1975 *Tommy* was brought to the screen with The Who (Pete Townshend, John Entwistle, Keith Moon, and Roger Daltrey—the last in the title role), Ann-Margret, Oliver Reed, Elton John, Jack Nicholson, and Tina Turner. Described as "rock's most acclaimed stab at opera," it was pronounced by *Variety* as "spectacular in nearly every way." The tale of the traumatized deaf, dumb, and blind boy who, in search of a miracle cure, discovers that he has a fantastic way with pinball machines and, eventually, after miraculously regaining his senses, is hailed as the new messiah, was filmed without a spoken word of dialogue. Every line of dialogue was sung; and where there were no words, the action was backed entirely by instrumental music and dramatic sound effects orchestrated into the score.

By now, almost everyone is familiar with the celebrated British rock group known as The Who. After scoring in local areas around London, they came to international attention while appearing at Soho's famous Marquee Club and soon became the bellwether of contemporary music and performing. As mentioned earlier, *Tommy* was the first "rock opera" ever written and recorded; in June 1970, The Who broke another precedent by becoming the first rock group ever to appear at the Metropolitan Opera House, which offered two performances of *Tommy*.

While much debate has ensued as to whether *Tommy* rightfully deserves the title of opera, one Met spokesman put it rather aptly: "It's a story told with music and words. It uses the methods and the means of opera. It's opera in a new language." As composer-librettist Pete Townshend observed: "Rock is a reflection of changes of ideas. Rock is going in a certain direction and I think it's a good direction."

The tremendous success of *Tommy* in its various manifestations, on records, in concert halls, theatres, and motion pictures, inspired subsequent "rock operas," most notably, *Jesus Christ Superstar* which appears earlier in this volume.

SYNOPSIS

Tommy is born toward the close of World War I. At the age of three he witnesses the unexpected return of his father (wrongly reported missing in the war) and the murder of his mother's lover. Tommy's mother beats and brainwashes the child. She tries to drive out the memory of the scene to erase it from the child's mind.

She succeeds in shutting down Tommy's power of speech, hearing and sight altogether. They are psychologically blocked out; for all practical purposes, he is deaf, dumb, and blind. From now on his education will be possible only through his sense of touch and through his own powers of imagination. Tommy's parents never give up hope for a cure for the boy and visit a number of unscrupulous peddlers like the "hawker" who sings of the praises of his gypsy wife and her miraculous powers. Tommy lives the life of an incurable, backward child. Son and parents long to communicate with each other—but in vain. Left on his own with his unpleasant Cousin Kevin, Tommy is bullied mercilessly. As he is dumb, there is no risk of comeback.

The gypsy appears with her famous medicine. She is motivated by pure malice. She administers LSD to the boy. In the "Underture," Tommy's experiences are portrayed instrumentally. Tommy's parents are out for the evening, leaving him in care of his Uncle Ernie, who willfully molests the boy. Tommy's lack of conditioning or preconceived ideas protects him from any psychological ill effects. Tommy's only remaining sense is that of touch. Shooting pinballs, done as a hobby, he masters the game completely. He becomes National Pinball Champion.

An eminent doctor diagnoses Tommy's condition as an illusion—a purely psychological block. Tommy seems to communicate or see only when he is gazing at his own reflection in the mirror.

Tommy's mother tries uselessly to get through to him by pleading and persuasion.

Finally she passes from threats to action. She breaks the mirror, and with this the boy's inner block. As the mirror splinters, Tommy's world opens up.

Tommy realizes the enormous powers that he now has and becomes aware of his destiny as a great popular religious leader.

The fame of the National Pinball Champion's miracle cure builds his following. His religious concerts sell out. His fans are in the millions.

Tommy gives his message to his followers: "I'm free, I'm free, and freedom tastes of reality. I'm free, I'm free, I'm waiting for you to follow me." Vast holiday camps are constructed as temples for the new religion as enthusiasm sweeps through the country. Uncle Ernie welcomes new converts to the camp. Some years have passed now as we hear Tommy making his stock speech of welcome to new arrivals. But the religious discipline of his holiday camps becomes too harsh and unfeeling to hold his followers. Riots break out; the religion is discredited. Tommy's camps are reduced to ruins. Once more Tommy is completely isolated and unable to communicate.

MUSICAL NUMBERS

Overture
It's a Boy!
You Didn't Hear It (1921)
Amazing Journey
Sparks
Christmas
Cousin Kevin
The Acid Queen
Underture
Do You Think It's All Right?
Fiddle About
Pinball Wizard
There's a Doctor
Go to the Mirror!
Tommy, Can You Hear Me?
Smash the Mirror
Sensation
Miracle Cure
Sally Simpson
I'm Free
Welcome
Tommy's Holiday Camp
We're Not Gonna Take It!
See Me, Feel Me

Overture

Captain Walker
Didn't come home
His unborn child,
Will never know him
Believe him missing
With a number of men
Don't expect
To see him again.

It's A Boy

NURSE:
   It's a boy, Mrs. Walker, it's a boy.
   It's a boy, Mrs. Walker, it's a boy.

CHORUS:
   A son! A son! A son!

You Didn't Hear It (1921)

LOVER:
   I've got a feeling twenty-one
   Is going to be a good year.
   Especially if you and me
   See it in together.

FATHER:
   So you think twenty-one is going to be a good year.
   It could be good for me and her,
   But you and her—no, never!
   I had no reason to be over optimistic,
   But somehow when you smiled
   I could brave bad weather

MOTHER:
> *What about the boy?*
> *What about the boy?*
> *What about the boy?*
> *He saw it all!*

MOTHER & FATHER:
> *You didn't hear it*
> *You didn't see it.*
> *You won't say nothing to no one*
> *Ever in your life.*
> *You never heard it*
> *Oh, how absurd it*
> *All seems without any proof.*
> *You didn't hear it*
> *You didn't see it*
> *You never heard it not a word of it.*
> *You won't say nothing to no one*
> *Never tell a soul*
> *What you know is the Truth.*

Amazing Journey

NARRATOR:
> *Deaf, dumb and blind boy*
> *He's in a quiet vibration land*
> *Strange as it seems his musical dreams*
> *Ain't quite so bad.*
>
> *Ten years old*
> *With thoughts as bold as thought can be*
> *Loving life and becoming wise*
> *In simplicity.*
>
> *Sickness will surely take the mind*
> *Where minds can't usually go.*
> *Come on the amazing journey*
> *And learn all you should know.*

A vague haze of delirium
Creeps up on me.
All at once a tall stranger I suddenly see.
He's dressed in a silver-sparked
Glittering gown
And His golden beard flows
Nearly down to the ground.

Nothing to say and nothing to hear
And nothing to see.
Each sensation makes a note in my symphony.

Sickness will surely take the mind
Where minds can't usually go.
Come on the amazing journey
And learn all you should know.

His eyes are the eyes that
Transmit all they know.
Sparkle warm crystalline glances to show
That he is your leader
And he is your guide
On the amazing journey together you'll ride.

Sparks (Instrumental Number)

Christmas

FATHER:
  Did you ever see the faces of children
  They get so excited.
  Waking up on Christmas morning
  Hours before the winter sun's ignited.
  They believe in dreams and all they mean
  Including heaven's generosity.

Peeping round the door
To see what parcels are for free
In curiosity.

And Tommy doesn't know what day it is.
Doesn't know who Jesus was or what praying is.
How can he be saved
From the eternal grave?

Surrounded by his friends he sits so silently.
And unaware of everything.
Playing poxy pinball
Picks his nose and smiles and
Pokes his tongue at everything.
I believe in love
But how can men who've never seen
Light be enlightened.
Only if he's cured
Will his spirit's future level ever heighten.

And Tommy doesn't know what day it is.
Doesn't know who Jesus was or what praying is.
How can he be saved
From the eternal grave?
Tommy, can you hear me?

Tommy, can you hear me?
Tommy, can you hear me?
How can he be saved?

TOMMY:
See me, feel me
Touch me, heal me.
See me, feel me
Touch me, heal me!

Tommy, can you hear me?
Tommy, can you hear me?
Tommy, can you hear me?
How can he be saved?

Cousin Kevin

COUSIN KEVIN:
We're on our own, cousin,
All alone, cousin.
Let's think of a game to play
Now the grownups have all gone away.
You won't be much fun
Being blind deaf and dumb
But I've no one to play with today.
D'you know how to play hide and seek?
To find me it would take you a week,
But tied to that chair you won't go anywhere
There's a lot I can do to a freak.
How would you feel if I turned on the bath,
Ducked your head under and started to laugh?
What would you do if I shut you outside,
To stand in the rain
And catch cold so you died?

I'm the school bully!
The classroom cheat.
The nastiest playfriend,
You could ever meet.
I'll stick pins in your fingers
And tread on your feet . . .

Maybe a cigarette burn on your arm
Would change your expression to one of alarm,
I'll drag you around by a lock of your hair
Or give you a push at the top of the stairs . . .

I'm the school bully!
The classroom cheat.
The nastiest playfriend,
You could ever meet.
I'll put glass in your dinner
And spikes in your seat . . .

The Acid Queen

GYPSY:

If your child ain't all he should be now
This girl will put him right.
I'll show him what he could be now
Just give me one night.
I'm the Gypsy—the Acid Queen.
Pay before we start.
I'm the Gypsy—the Acid Queen.
I'll tear your soul apart.

Give us a room and close the door
Leave us for a while.
Your boy won't be a boy no more
Young, but not a child.
I'm the Gypsy—the Acid Queen.
Pay before we start.
I'm the Gypsy—the Acid Queen.
I'll tear your soul apart.

Gather your wits and hold on fast,
Your mind must learn to roam.
Just as the Gypsy Queen must do
You're gonna hit the road.

My work is done—now look at him
He's never been more alive.
His head it shakes his fingers clutch.
Watch his body writhe
I'm the Gypsy—the Acid Queen.
Pay before we start.
I'm the Gypsy—I'm guaranteed.
To break your little heart.

Underture (Instrumental Number)

Do You Think It's All Right?

MOTHER:
> Do you think it's all right,
> To leave the boy with Uncle Ernie?
> Do you think it's all right;
> He's had a few too many tonight!
> D'you think it's all right?

FATHER:
> I think it's all right, yes I think it's all right.

Fiddle About

UNCLE ERNIE:
> I'm your wicked Uncle Ernie
> I'm glad you won't see or hear me
> As I fiddle about
> Fiddle about
> Fiddle about!
>
> Your mother left me here to mind you
> Now I'm doing what I want to
> Fiddling about
> Fiddling about
> Fiddle about!
>
> Down with the bedclothes
> Up with the nightshirt!
> Fiddle about

Fiddle about
Fiddle about!

You won't shout as I fiddle about
Fiddle about
Fiddle about
Fiddle about!
Fiddle, fiddle, fiddle.

Pinball Wizard

LOCAL LAD:
  Ever since I was a young boy,
  I've played the silver ball.
  From Soho down to Brighton
  I must have played them all.
  But I ain't seen anything like him
  In any amusement hall . . .
  That deaf dumb and blind kid
  Sure plays a mean pinball!

  He stands like a statue,
  Becomes part of the machine.
  Feeling all the bumpers
  Always playing clean.
  He plays by intuition,
  The digit counters fall.
  That deaf dumb and blind kid
  Sure plays a mean pinball!

  He's a pinball wizard
  There has to be a twist.
  A pinball wizard,
  S'got such a supple wrist.

  'How do you think he does it? I don't know!
  What makes him so good?'

He ain't got no distractions
Can't hear those buzzers and bells,
Don't see lights a flashin'
Plays by sense of smell.
Always has a replay,
'n' never tilts at all . . .
That deaf dumb and blind kid
Sure plays a mean pinball.

I thought I was
The Bally table king.
But I just handed
My pinball crown to him.

Even my usual table
He can beat my best.
His disciples lead him in
And he just does the rest.
He's got crazy flipper fingers
Never seen him fall . . .
That deaf dumb and blind kid
Sure plays a mean pinball!!!!!

There's A Doctor

FATHER:

There's a doctor I've found
Could bring us all joy!
There's a doctor I've found could cure the boy!
There's a doctor I've found could cure the boy!

There's a man I've found could remove his sorrow,
He lives in this town let's see him tomorrow,
He lives in this town let's see him tomorrow!

Go to the Mirror!

DOCTOR:

>He seems to be completely unreceptive.
>The tests I gave him showed no sense at all.
>His eyes react to light the dials detect it.
>He hears but cannot answer to your call.

TOMMY:

>See me, feel me, touch me, heal me.
>See me, feel me, touch me, heal me.

DOCTOR:

>There is no chance no untried operation.
>All hope lies with him and none with me.
>Imagine though the shock from isolation.
>When he suddenly can hear and speak and see.

TOMMY:

>See me, feel me, touch me, heal me.
>See me, feel me, touch me, heal me.

DOCTOR:

>His eyes can hear
>His ears can see his lips speak
>All the time the needles flick and rock.
>No machine can give the kind of stimulation,
>Needed to remove his inner block.

>Go to the mirror, boy!
>Go to the mirror, boy!

FATHER:

>I often wonder what he's feeling.
>Has he ever heard a word I've said?
>Look at him now in the mirror dreaming
>What is happening in his head?

TOMMY:
> Listening to you I get the music.
> Gazing at you I get the heat
> Following you I climb the mountain
> I get excitement at your feet!
>
> Right behind you I see the millions
> On you I see the glory.
> From you I get the opinions
> From you I get the story.

FATHER:
> What is happening in his head
> Ooooh I wish I knew, I wish I knew.

Tommy, Can You Hear Me?

FATHER:
> Tommy, can you hear me?
> Can you feel me near you?

MOTHER:
> Tommy, can you feel me?
> Can I help to cheer you.

Smash the Mirror

MOTHER:
> You don't answer my call
> With even a nod or a twitch
> But you gaze at your own reflection!
> You don't seem to see me
> But I think you can see yourself.
> How can the mirror affect you?

Can you hear me
Or do I surmise?
That you fear me can you feel my temper
Rise.

Do you hear or fear or
Do I smash the mirror.
Do you hear or fear or
Do I smash the mirror? Smash!

Sensation

TOMMY:

I overwhelm as I approach you
Make your lungs hold breath inside!
Lovers break caresses for me
Love enhanced when I've gone by.

You'll feel me coming,
A new vibration
From afar you'll see me
I'm a sensation.

They worship me and all I touch
Hazy eyed they catch my glance,
Pleasant shudders shake their senses
My warm momentum throws their stance.

You'll feel me coming,
A new vibration
From afar you'll see me
I'm a sensation.

I leave a trail of rooted people
Mesmerised by just the sight,
The few I touched now are disciples
Love as One I Am the Light . . .

Soon you'll see me can't you feel me
I'm coming ...
Send your troubles dancing he knows the answer
I'm coming ...
I'm a sensation.

Miracle Cure

NEWSBOY:
   Extra! Extra!
   Read all about it.
   Pinball Wizard in a miracle cure!
   Extra Extra read all about it
   EXTRA!

Sally Simpson

NARRATOR:
   Outside the house Mr. Simpson announced
   That Sally couldn't go to the meeting.
   He went on cleaning his blue Rolls Royce
   And she ran inside weeping.
   She got to her room and tears splashed the picture
   Of the new Messiah.
   She picked up a book of her father's life
   And threw it on the fire!

   She knew from the start
   Deep down in her heart
   That she and Tommy were worlds apart,
   But her mother said, "Never mind, your part ...
   Is to be what you'll be."

   The theme of the sermon was come unto me,
   Love will find a way,

So Sally decided to ignore her dad,
And sneak out anyway!
She spent all afternoon getting ready,
And decided she'd try to touch him,
Maybe he'd see that she was free
And talk to her this Sunday.

She knew from the start
Deep down in her heart
That she and Tommy were worlds apart,
But her mother said, "Never mind, your part . . .
Is to be what you'll be."

She arrived at six and the place was swinging
To gospel music by nine.
Group after group appeared on the stage
And Sally just sat there crying.
She bit her nails looking pretty as a picture
Right in the very front row
And then a DJ wearing a blazer with a badge
Ran on and said, "Here we go!"

The crowd went crazy
As Tommy hit the stage!
Little Sally got lost as the police bossed
The crowd back in a rage!

But soon the atmosphere was cooler
As Tommy gave a lesson.
Sally just had to let him know she loved him
And leapt up on the rostrum!
She ran across the stage to the spotlit figure
And touched him on the face
Tommy whirled around as a uniformed man,
Threw her off the stage.

She knew from the start
Deep down in her heart
That she and Tommy were worlds apart,
But her mother said, "Never mind, your part . . .
Is to be what you'll be."

Her cheek hit a chair and blood trickled down,
Mingling with her tears.
Tommy carried on preaching
And his voice filled Sally's ear
She caught his eye she had to try
But couldn't see through the lights
Her face was gashed and the ambulance men
Had to carry her out that night.

The crowd went crazy
As Tommy left the stage!
Little Sally was lost for the price of a touch
And a gash across her face! OOoooh.

Sixteen stitches put her right and her Dad said,
"Don't say I didn't warn yer."
Sally got married to a rock musician
She met in California
Tommy always talks about the day
The disciples all went wild!
Sally still carries a scar on her cheek
To remind her of his smile.

She knew from the start
Deep down in her heart
That she and Tommy were worlds apart,
But her mother said, "Never mind, your part . . .
Is to be what you'll be."

I'm Free

TOMMY:

I'M FREE—I'm free,
And freedom tastes of reality,
I'm free—I'm free,
AN' I'm waiting for you to follow me.

If I told you what it takes
To reach the highest high,

You'd laugh and say 'nothing's that simple'
But you've been told many times before
Messiahs pointed to the door
And no one had the guts to leave the temple!

I'm free—I'm free
And freedom tastes of reality
I'm free—I'm free
And I'm waiting for you to follow me.

CHORUS:
How can we follow?
How can we follow?

Welcome

TOMMY:
Come to my house
Be one of the comfortable people.
Come to this house
We're drinking all night
Never sleeping.

Milkman come in!
And you baker,
Little old lady welcome
And you shoemaker

Come to this house!
Into this house.

Come to this house
Be one of us.
Make this your house
Be one of us.

You can help
To collect some more in

Young and old people
Let's get them all in!

Come to this house!
Into this house.

Ask along that man who's wearing a carnation.
Bring every single person
From Victoria Station.
Go into that hospital
Bring nurses and patients.
Everybody go home and fetch their relations!

Come to this house
Be one of the comfortable people.
Lovely bright home
Drinking all night never sleeping.

We need more room
Build an extension
A colorful palace
Spare no expense!

Welcome to this house
Be one of us.
Come into this house
Be one of us.
Come to our house
Come to this house!

Tommy's Holiday Camp

UNCLE ERNIE:
   I'm your Uncle Ernie,
   And I welcome you to Tommy's Holiday Camp!
   The camp with a difference,

Never mind the weather,
When you come to Tommy's, the holiday's forever!

Camp with a difference, never mind the weather,
When you come to Tommy's, the holiday's forever!
WELCOME!!!

We're Not Gonna Take It

TOMMY:
> *Welcome to the camp*
> *I guess you all know why we're here*
> *My name is Tom and I became aware this year.*
> *If you want to follow me*
> *You've got to play pinball.*
> *So put in your earplugs*
> *Put on your shades*
> *And you know where to put the cork!*
>
> *Hey, you, gettin' drunk*
> *So sorry, I've got you sussed.*
> *Hey, you, smokin' mother nature,*
> *You missed the bus.*
> *Hey, hung up old Mister Normal*
> *Don't try to gain my trust.*
> *Cos you ain't gonna follow me*
> *Any of those ways*
> *Although you think you must!*

CHORUS:
> *We're not gonna take it.*
> *We're not gonna take it.*
> *We're not gonna take it,*
> *Never did and never will,*
> *We don't have to take it.*
> *Gonna break it!*
> *Gonna shake it!*
> *Let's forget it better still!*

TOMMY:

> Now you can't hear me,
> Your ears are truly sealed.
> You can't speak either,
> Your mouth is filled.
> You can't see nothing
> And pinball completes the scene.
> Here comes Uncle Ernie
> To guide you to
> Your very own machine.

CHORUS:

> We're not gonna take it!
> We're not gonna take it!
> We're not gonna take it,
> Never did and never will
> Don't want no religion
> And as far as we can tell
> We ain't gonna take you
> Never did and never will
> We're not gonna take you!
> We forsake you!
> Gonna rape you!
> Let's forget you better still!

> We forsake you
> Gonna rape you
> Let's forget you . . . better still.

See Me, Feel Me

TOMMY:

> See me, feel me, touch me, heal me.
> See me, feel me, touch me, heal me.

> Listening to you I get the music.
> Gazing at you I get the heat
> Following you I climb the mountain

I get excitement at your feet!
Right behind you I see the millions
On you I see the glory.
From you I get opinions
From you I get the story.

PROMENADE

Book and Lyrics by María Irene Fornés

Music by Al Carmines

EDITOR'S NOTES

One of the major delights of the 1969-70 New York theatre season was the María Irene Fornés–Al Carmines rock musical, *Promenade*, which satirized our world as seen through the eyes of a pair of convicts.

Within hours after the opening-night curtain had fallen, Clive Barnes transmitted to readers of *The New York Times* that "*Promenade* is a joy from start to finish. Wickedly amusing, joyously blithe. A triumph!"

Marilyn Stasio of *Cue* termed it "thoroughly enchanting, as uninhibited as a daydream . . . with a kind of manic exuberance so exultantly good-natured it would take a rigid soul indeed to resist it." Jack Kroll of *Newsweek* called it "a sequined shower of Firbankian philosophy" while critic Martin Gottfried found it "far and away superior to anything that has been seen in New York in the past few years."

According to Michael Smith of the *Village Voice*, "the core experience of *Promenade* is its exquisite and delicious humor," which also categorizes most of Miss Fornés's other works for the theatre. Her individualistic style perhaps was best described by Richard Gilman in his introduction to a collection of the author's plays:

> While directing Miss Fornés' *The Successful Life of 3* for the Open Theatre in 1965, I felt in need of some principle of performance and presentation that would do justice to her imagination and dramatic powers. And so I queried myself about just what kind of imagination she had and about her particular strengths as a playwright, and I thought I knew. She was "absurd" (the term was still new enough for you to think it told you something) blessed with a sense of the incongruities and discontinuities of language, zany, fruitfully illogical and tuned in to social inanity as a kind of radical parodist.

María Irene Fornés was born in Havana, Cuba, and emigrated to the United States with her family when she was fifteen. While studying painting in night school, she engaged in a variety of jobs, including typing, translating, and waiting on tables.

After a brief term of study with Hans Hoffman at the Provincetown School, Miss Fornés went to Paris, where she lived for three years. In 1960 she started writing plays, which have since been presented all over Europe and the United States. Performances of her work have been given by the Actors Workshop in San Francisco, the Firehouse Theatre in Minneapolis, and many New York groups including the Open Theatre, the Judson Poets' Theatre, La Mama Experimental Theatre Club, and the New Dramatists, as well as in such theatrical centers as London, Amsterdam, Stockholm, and at the Festival of Two Worlds in Spoleto, Italy.

Miss Fornés received an Off-Broadway Obie Award for distinguished writing, and has been recipient of a John Hay Whitney Fellowship, a Rockefeller Grant, a Yale-ABC Fellowship in Film Writing, and a residence fellowship of the Centro Mexicano de Escritores.

The author's other plays include *A Vietnamese Wedding; The Red Burning Light; Dr. Kheal; Molly's Dream; Tango Palace;* and *The Successful Life of 3.* Her most recent work, *Fefu and Her Friends,* which she also directed, opened to acclaim at the American Place Theatre, New York, in January 1978.

The multi-talented Al Carmines has functioned in the theatre as composer, lyricist, director, producer, and performer. As if this were not quite sufficient, he is also pastor of the Washington Square Methodist Church in New York City, where many of his works were first produced.

Among the many operas, cantatas, musical comedies, and operettas for which he composed the scores (and frequently wrote the lyrics and librettos as well) are *The Way of the Cross; The Cup of Trembling; The Family Reunion; Home Movies; In Circles* (an opera based on Gertrude Stein's *A Circular Play); The Duel,* and *Sacred and Profane Love.*

Mr. Carmines has also appeared in leading cabarets and on numerous concert stages.

PRODUCTION NOTES

Promenade was first performed by the Judson Poets' Theatre at the Judson Memorial Church, New York, on April 9, 1965. The cast was as follows:

105	*David Vaughn*
106	*George Bartenieff*
Jailer	*Michael Elias*
Miss I	*Gretel Cummings*
Miss O	*Crystal Field*
Miss U	*Joan Fairlee*
Mr. R	*John Toland*
Mr. S	*Christopher Jones*
Mr. T	*Christopher Ross*
Servant	*Sheila Roy*
Miss Cake	*Florence Tarlow*
Waiter	*Howard Roy*
Chinaman	*Frank Emerson*
Warden	*William Pardue*
Mother	*Jerri Banks*

Directed by *Lawrence Kornfeld*
Scenery by *Malcolm Spooner*
Costumes by *Miss Fornés* and *Ellen Levene*
Lighting by *Kathy Lewis*
Musical Direction by *Mr. Carmines*

An expanded version of *Promenade* was the inaugural production at the Promenade Theatre, New York, opening on June 4, 1969. The cast was as follows:

105	*Ty McConnell*
106	*Gilbert Price*
Jailer	*Pierre Epstein*
Servant	*Madeline Kahn*
Miss I	*Margot Albert*
Miss O	*Carrie Wilson*

Miss U	*Alice Playten*
Mr. R	*Marc Allen III*
Mr. S	*Glenn Kezer*
Mr. T	*Michael Davis*
Waiter	*Edmund Gaynes*
Rosita (Miss Cake)	*Florence Tarlow*
Dishwasher	*Art Ostrin*
Mayor	*George S. Irving*
Mother	*Shannon Bolin*

Produced by *Edgar Lansbury* and *Joseph Beruh*
Directed by *Lawrence Kornfeld*
Scenery by *Rouben Ter-Arutunian*
Costumes by *Willa Kim*
Lighting by *Jules Fisher*
Orchestrations by *Eddie Sauter*
Musical Direction by *Mr. Carmines*
Orchestra Conducted by *Susan Romann*

MUSICAL NUMBERS

ACT ONE

Scene 1: The Cell
Promenade Theme	Orchestra
Dig, Dig, Dig	105 and 106

Scene 2: The Banquet Room
Unrequited Love	Misses I, O, U; Messrs. R, S, T; Servant; Waiter; 105; 106
Isn't That Clear?	Mr. S. with Ensemble
Don't Eat It	Ensemble
Four	Misses I, O, U; Messrs. R, S, T, Servant, Waiter, 105, 106, Dishwasher
Chicken Is He	Rosita
The Moment Has Passed	Miss O
Apres Vous I	105, 106, Jailer
Bliss	Servant, 105, 106 and Ensemble

Scene 3: The Street
Thank You	Dishwasher
The Clothes Make The Man	Servant, 105, 106

Scene 4: The Park
The Cigarette Song	Servant, with 105, 106
Two Little Angels	Mother, with 105, 106
The Passing Of Time	105, 106
Capricious and Fickle	Miss U
Crown Me	Servant, with 105, 106

ACT TWO

Scene 1: The Battlefield
Mr. Phelps	Waiter
Madeline	Waiter
Spring Beauties	Ensemble
Apres Vous (Reprise)	Ensemble
A Poor Man	105 and 106
Why Not	Dishwasher & Servant, with Mother, Waiter, 105, 106

Scene 2: The Drawing Room
The Finger Song	Mr. R with Ensemble

Little Fool	Mr. T with Ensemble
Czardas	Servant, Miss I (Viola)
The Laughing Song	Ensemble
A Mother's Love	Mother
Scene 3: The Cell	
I Saw A Man	Mother
All Is Well In The City	105, 106 and Ensemble

CHARACTERS

105
106
JAILER
SERVANT
MISS I
MISS O
MISS U
MR. R
MR. S
MR. T
MISS CAKE
WAITER
DISHWASHER
DRIVER
INJURED MAN
MOTHER
SOLDIER I
SOLDIER II

The roles of WAITER, DRIVER and SOLDIER I are to be played by one actor. So are the roles of DISHWASHER, INJURED MAN and SOLDIER II.

Act One

SCENE 1

The Cell. 105 and 106 dig and sing. The JAILER *enters. He is out of breath. he sits and dries his forehead.*

105 and 106:
  Dig, dig, dig
  A hole to be free.
  Dig a hole, dig a hole,
  A hole to be free.

JAILER: It's been a hard day.

105 and 106:
  Dig, dig, dig.

JAILER: Screwing all day.

105 and 106:
  A hole to be free.

JAILER: Can't let the ladies visit the inmates unless they pay dues.

105 and 106:
  Dig a hole, dig a hole,
  A hole to be free.

JAILER: Oh, it's been a hard day. 34's wife, 48's daughter, 108's widow.

105 and 106:
  Fly the coop.
  Break the wall.
  See the sun.

JAILER: Well, better get back to the ladies. Just came up for some air . . . What are you two doing there?

105 and 106:
Dig a hole, dig a hole,
A hole to be free.

JAILER: Hm. You look like you're digging. Well, I better get back to the widow before she finds out her old man's dead.

105 and 106:
Unacquainted with evil we are
This shelter protects us from wrong.
To discover the appearance of sin
We must go where the dog takes a leak.

JAILER: So long, boys , . . By the way, if you want to get visitors just let me know. (*The* JAILER *laughs loudly as he walks away*) I can arrange it for you.

105 and 106:
The hole is dug.
Here we go.

(*105 and 106 disappear through the hole*)

SCENE 2

The Banquet. There are LADIES *and* GENTLEMEN *in evening clothes around the table. The* SERVANT *sweeps. The* WAITER *serves the* GUESTS. *105 and 106 enter. They put on top hats and tails. They sit at the table and eat.*
MR. R: Speech . . . speech . . .
MR. S: Let's play croquet . . .
MR. R: Speeches and music . . .
MR. T: Let's call Mr. Lipschitz . . .
MR. S: No speeches . . . No speeches . . .
MR. R: Let's have a song . . .
(*105 and 106 clear their throats*)
MISS O: Mr. T, was that you I saw on the corner of Fifth and Tenth?

MR. T: Perhaps.

MISS O: With Mrs. Schumann and her newly clipped poodle?

MR. T: Oh, no, it wasn't I. Friday night I was out of town.

MISS O: Ah! And how did you know it was Friday night I saw you on the corner of Fifth?

(They all laugh)

MR. T: Well, I must confess. The lady loves me.

(They all laugh)

MISS U: She shows good taste.

MR. R: Then, introduce us. She'll surely fall for me.

(The LADIES *giggle.* MR. R *writes in a notebook)* Mrs. Schumann . . . lady of taste. . . . Bring dog biscuit. *(To* MR. T*)* What is her address?

MR. T: Tch-Tch.

MISS I: Oh, Mr. R, what perspicacity.

MISS O: Are you sure that's what you mean?

*(*MISS I *looks a little embarrassed)*

MR. S: Let's have a song.

(105 and 106 stand and get ready to sing)

MISS O: And who are these? Dear me.

(105 and 106 realize they have been indiscreet. They sit back at the table and pretend not to hear the others)

MISS I: They must be friends of Mr. S.

MISS U: My dear. You go right to the point. . . .

MISS I: Mr. S does frequent rather unearthly places, doesn't he?

MR. T: What do you mean?

MISS I: I mean the lower depths.

MR. T: Oh, yes.

MR. S: If I am sometimes in the company of this and that, my dear, it's only because I like to study life. . . . I am what you might call a student of life. . . . This . . . and that.

MISS U: Oh, how incredibly personal you are, Mr. S. Have I not always said you have the artist in you?

MR. S: I am neither more than I seem to be, nor more than I am, and no less, also.

SERVANT *(Mimicking in a low voice)*: And no less . . . also.

MR. R: Miss I . . .

MISS I: Yes?

MR. R: Last Saturday I waited for a certain lady who never arrived.

MISS I: You did?

MR. R: Yes.

MISS I: Oh, she couldn't come. She spent all afternoon walking up and down a certain street where a gentleman (*Referring to* MR. T) who shall remain nameless lives. She was hoping to have an accidental meeting . . . a sort of unexpected encounter with him. But he never left his house . . . nor did he enter it.

(MISS O *and* MISS U *giggle. The* SERVANT *is bored by the* LADIES' *and* GENTLEMEN's *repartee. Through the following speeches she pantomimes their gestures)*

MR. T: He didn't, madam . . . he didn't. He saw the lady from his window and she did indeed walk up and down his street. But he couldn't receive her . . . his heart was torn. You see, he received a letter from the one he loves (*Referring to* MISS U) telling him his love was unrequited. He spent all afternoon sitting by his window plucking petals from flowers, and the answer always was . . . she loves me not.

MISS O: And who is this he speaks of?

MISS U: She is not free to love. Her heart belongs to he (*Referring to* MR. S) whose glance drives her to a frenzy, and whose mere presence brings color to her cheeks.

MR. S: The man who puts you in such a state has eyes only for O. Oh, Miss O.

MISS I: Oh! What tension! A name has been mentioned.

MISS U: And what have you to say to that, O?

MISS O: I regret I cannot speak since Mr. S has mentioned me by name. But do you wonder why O shuns you when you are so indiscreet? (*Taking a step toward* R) And besides, she loves R. (R *takes a step toward* I) (I *takes a step toward* T) (T *takes a step toward* U) (U *takes a step toward* S) (S *takes a step toward* O) (O *takes a step toward* R)

MISS U:

You were there when I was not.
I was there when you were not.
Don't love me, sweetheart,
Or I might stop loving you.

Unrequited love,
Unrequited love.

MISS O:

> *Passionate lips are sweet.*
> *But oh, how much sweeter*
> *Are lips that refuse.*
> *Don't love me, sweetheart,*
> *Or I might stop loving you.*

MISS I:

> *Inviting lips,*
> *Alluring lips*
> *Which shape the word no*
> *No no no no no no.*
> *Don't love me, sweetheart,*
> *Or I might stop loving you.*

MR. R:

> *You know nothing of life,*
> *You know nothing of love*
> *Till you have tasted*
> *Of unrequited love.*
> *Don't love me, sweetheart,*
> *Or I might stop loving you.*

ALL:

> *Unrequited love,*
> *Unrequited love.*
> *There is no love*
> *Like unrequited love.*

MISS I: Oh! We sang that well.

MR. R: He who scrubs the pot finds it most shiny.

MR. S *(To* MR. R*)*: And he who soils it, turns up his nose. Mr. R, you were flat.

MISS I: *Touché!*

MISS U: What a marvelous mind.

MR. S: Just frank.

SERVANT *(Mimicking)*: Just frank.

> *(They all look at the* SERVANT, *shocked)*

MISS I: Mr. S, it's up to you to think of a rejoinder.

MR. S: Dear me, I'm speechless. Wait! Listen to my answer. *(He improvises the following:)*

My frankness, my dear,
My wit, my veneer,
Are something you should revere.

LADIES: A rhyme! A rhyme!

MR. S:

Instead, you just think it queer.
Your unprosperous status
Produces a dubious,
Fallacious, and tedious
Outlook on life.

(The SERVANT *makes a face at him)*

You do not know what we're about
We do not know what you're about
Or care to know.

(The SERVANT *lowers her head)*

It's sad your career
Depends on our whim.
On with your work, my dear,
Or you'll get thin.
You see, even if you're here,
And we're also here,
You are not near.
Isn't that clear?

MISS U: Oh, Mr. S, how well you rhyme.
MR. S: Not difficult, dear. Just keep the ending of the word in
mind . . . it will come.
MISS U: *Incendo, incendis, incendit, incendimos, incenditis,*
incendunt.
MR. S: No, dear, the ending, not the beginning.
MISS U: But, Mr. S, how can one tell how a word will end?
MR. S: Foresight.
(The WAITER *brings in a giant cake to the accompaniment of*
musical fanfare. The DISHWASHER *follows)*
MR. T: Oh look! Look! Look! The cake is here.
MR. S: Oh look! Look! Look! It's time for dessert.

LADIES:
> *Don't eat it,*
> *Don't eat it.*
> *Wait until midnight.*

GENTLEMEN:
> *Put it on the table,*
> *Put it on the table.*

MISS U: Phooey. . . . It smells of garlic.

GENTLEMEN:
> *It's not to be eaten,*
> *It's not to be eaten.*

(MISS CAKE *steps out of the cake. They all applaud and cheer*)

LADIES:
> *Don't eat her,*
> *Don't eat her.*
> *Wait until midnight.*

GENTLEMEN:
> *Put her on the table,*
> *Put her on the table.*

LADIES:
> *She's not to be eaten,*
> *She's not to be eaten.*

MISS I: What is she for?
DISHWASHER: To look at.
> (*The* JAILER's *head appears through the door*)
MR. S: And to touch.
MR. R: Only to touch.
DISHWASHER: And to look at.
MISS I: May the ladies touch, too?
MR. R: No, not the ladies, only the gentlemen.
MISS O: I want to be naked, too.

MR. R:
  Only one,
  Only one
  Naked lady.

MISS O *(Taking off her dress)*:
  Two . . . two. . . .
  I want to be naked, too.

MR. R:
  Only one,
  Only one
  Naked lady.
  All right,
  Two naked ladies.

MISS O:
  Thank you,
  Thank you, sir.

GENTLEMEN:
  Only two,
  Only two
  Naked ladies.

MISS I *(Taking off her dress)*:
  Three . . . three. . . .
  I want to be naked, too.

GENTLEMEN:
  Only two,
  Only two
  Naked ladies.
  All right,
  Three naked ladies.

MISS I:
  Thank you,
  Thank you, sir.

GENTLEMEN:
> *Only three,*
> *Only three*
> *Naked ladies.*

MISS U *(Taking off her dress)*:
> *Four . . . four. . . .*
> *I want to be naked, too.*

GENTLEMEN:
> *Only three,*
> *Only three*
> *Naked ladies.*
> *All right,*
> *Four naked ladies.*

MISS U:
> *Thank you,*
> *Thank you, sir.*

ALL:
> *Only four,*
> *Only four*
> *Naked ladies.*
> *Four . . . four . . .*
> *Four naked ladies.*

LADIES:
> *Thank you,*
> *Thank you, sir.*

MISS I: *Mademoiselle, comment vous appelez-vous?*
MISS CAKE: *Moi, je m'appelle La Rose de Shanghai.*
MISS U: *Est-ce que vous êtes française?*
MISS CAKE: *Pas au'jourd'hui.*

> *Let the fruit ripen on the tree*
> *For if not the meat will harden.*
> *I'm the peach of the west.*
> *Chicken is he who does not love me.*

> *I come from a country named America*

MR. R: You do?
MISS CAKE: I do.

Chicken is he who does not love me;
For there's more to the cake than the icing.
A morsel I'm not, I'm a feast,
And this not every man knows.
Remember all the times
You thought you got a bargain?

MISS U: I do.

MISS CAKE:
And it cost you more than it was worth?

MISS I: Aha!

MISS CAKE:
That's what we're here for,
To learn one thing or another;
For on art alone one cannot live.
Chicken is he who does not love me.

Tell me you adore me, and I'll let you go.

ALL: We adore you.

MISS CAKE:
I'm the peach of the west, you know,
And a bit of a rebel, just a bit.
And chicken is he, chicken are you all.
I'm not a morsel, I'm a feast,
I'm not a morsel, I'm a feast,
I'm not a morsel, I'm a feast.

MR. R: A toast. . . . A toast. . . .
MR. S: To the ladies. . . . To the ladies. . . .
(They all dance)

ALL:
Only four,
Only four

Naked ladies.
Four . . . four . . .
Four naked ladies.

LADIES:
   Thank you,
   Thank you, sir.

(*The* JAILER *enters*)
JAILER: Everybody's under arrest.
(105 *and* 106 *freeze in an effort to conceal themselves*)
MR. S: No, we're not under arrest, we're frolicking.
MISS I: Oh, what fun!
JAILER: Everybody's under arrest. I'm looking for two prisoners
   escaped from the penitentiary. And everybody's under arrest
   until I find them.
MR. T: Oh, silly man, don't you see we're having fun. Oh joy, joy,
   joy.
(*The* LADIES *and* GENTLEMEN *start sitting around the table*)
JAILER (*Suspiciously*): And why is everybody naked?
MR. S: Only the ladies are naked. The men are in full dress.
(*The* JAILER *looks around*)
JAILER: True . . . true. . . .
(*He goes after* MISS U. MISS U *takes a few little steps away from*
him)
MISS U (*Pressing her nostrils with her fingers and striking a*
   cherubic arabesque): Oh.
JAILER: Well, I may not smell of roses, but when there's a job to
   do, I do it. I'm looking for those prisoners and nothing can
   detract me from my search. (MISS I *walks past him. He follows*
   her) I sense complicity here. (*Looking closely at her buttocks*)
   Fingerprints, perhaps . . . (*He touches her buttocks;* MISS U
   slaps his hand. To MISS O): Madam, as an officer of the law I
   must conduct a search.
MISS O: Oh, stop bringing the street into our lives. You're
   common.
JAILER (*To* MISS CAKE): Speaking of common, madam, I've seen
   you. You look familiar.
(MISS CAKE *hits the* JAILER *on the head. He crawls under the*
table)
MISS O (*To* MR. R): Let us be irrational.
(MR. R *walks away. She addresses herself to* 105 *and* 106)

Let's you and me embrace.

(105 and 106 are not sure which one she means. They both start moving and bump against each other, bow to each other, offer the way to each other and so on. They finally reach her with open arms)

The moment has passed.

You have, perhaps, made me feel something,
But the moment has passed.
And what is done cannot be undone.
Once a moment passes, it never comes again.

I once had a man who loved me well.
His mouth was smaller than his eye.
But I loved him just the same.
Yes, I loved him just the same.

He said he would kill for me.
And I said, "like, for instance, whom?"
And he said, "like, for instance, you,
Like for instance you."

Sometimes it hurts more than others.
Sometimes it hurts less.
Sometimes it's just the same.
Sometimes it's really just the same.

But never mind that.
No, never mind that.
God gave understanding just to confuse us,
And it's always the same anyway.
It's always the same anyway.

If it's in your path to hurt me,
By all means, do.
But, I beg you, don't go out of your way
Don't go out of your way to do so.

You don't know what to make of me.
But I know what to make of you.

I have nothing to lose,
Or not much, anyway.
But never mind that.
God gave understanding just to confuse us,
And it's always the same anyway.

You have, perhaps, made me feel something,
But the moment has passed.
And what is done cannot be undone.
Once a moment passes, it never comes again.

(MISS O *joins the rest at the table*)
MR. T (*Offering* MISS I *a smelling potion*): Have a little philter-
   philtre.
(MR. R *holds a bunch of grapes over* MISS U's *mouth while he*
eats a leg of turkey)
MISS U: Oh, how good these grapes are. . . . To the left, Mr. R . . .
   a little to the left. . . .
MISS I: Pass the syrup, Mr. S. . . . You pour it. I like the way you
   pour . . . profusely, Mr. S . . . let it flow. Ahhh.
(*The* JAILER *kisses* MISS U's *foot.* MR. R *leans over and eats*
grapes from the same bunch as MISS I. *The* SERVANT *and the*
WAITER *wait on the* GUESTS. MR. R *and* MR. S *offer grapes to* MISS
CAKE. *She looks at one and then the other*)
MISS CAKE: I seem to be undecided. I'll take both, one from each.
(*She opens her mouth. They each push the bottom grape of*
their bunches in her mouth with the tip of their fingers. She
closes her mouth and they pull the bunch off)
MR. R and MR. S: Ahhh . . .
(*They all begin to yawn and feel drowsy*)
MISS I: Ahh, I feel a breeze.
(MR. S *blows in her direction*)
MISS O: Sleep, sweet sleep.
MISS U (*In a sleepy manner*): I'd like another taste.
MISS I: Have you tasted the melon, Mr. T? It's sweet and
   ripe. . . .
MR. T: Mommommmom. . . .
(MR. S *burps. They start snoring. 105 and 106 survey the*
room)
105: Can you bear this bliss?
106: Yes!

105: The source of satisfaction is wealth. Isn't it?
106: It is.

(105 *and* 106 *start stealing jewels from the* LADIES *and* GENTLEMEN. *The* JAILER *notices them and starts walking toward them stealthily.* 105 *and* 106 *move furtively around the room. The* JAILER *follows them*)

106 (*Making a gallant gesture*): Après vous.
JAILER (*Repeating the gesture*): Pas du tout.
106 (*Repeating the gesture*): Je vous en prie.
JAILER (*Repeating the gesture*): Mon plaisir.
105 and 106 (*Repeating the gesture*): Le nôtre.

JAILER, 105 and 106:
> Après vous.
> Après vous.
> Pas du tout.
> Je vous en prie.
> Mon plaisir.
> Le nôtre.
> Permettez-moi.
> Notre plaisir.
> Le mien.
> A votre service.
> Au votre.
> Au votre.
> L'age avant la beauté.

(*The* SERVANT *kicks the* JAILER *out the door.* 105 *and* 106 *kiss her and resume stealing. They sing while they take the* MEN's *wallets and watches, the* LADIES' *jewelry, the candlesticks, the silverware, the tablecloth and the chandelier. They put everything in their sacks*)

105:
> Can you bear this bliss?

106:
> No.

105:
> Can you bear this bliss?

106:
Yes.

105 and 106:
Eating is a blessing.
Money is a joy.
Drinking is a pleasure,
And riches a delight.

SERVANT:
We've come to one conclusion
That's readily discerned:
A lot of satisfaction
Does away with discontent.

Doesn't it?
A lot of satisfaction
Produces happiness.
And the source of satisfaction
Is wealth.
Isn't it?
All that man possesses
Displaces discontent.

SERVANT: What? What? What? What? What?

105 and 106:
Diamonds and cakes,
Macaroons and furs
Dispel discontent.
Chandeliers and wine,
Porcelain and lace
Efface discontent.

(106 *takes a jewel from* MISS CAKE)
MISS CAKE (*Taking it back*): Oh, no, you don't!

105, 106 and SERVANT:
Silverware and hats,
Embroideries and salt,
Flower pots and yachts,
Cinnamon and bells,

And awnings
And cushions,
And satins,
And rings,
And castles,
And crackers,
And things,
Things,
Things,
Things,

(105, 106 *and the* SERVANT *exit as they continue singing*)

Things,
Things . . .

(*The* LADIES *and* GENTLEMEN *begin to stir*)
MISS O: Ah! We have been robbed!
MR. T: Where is my pearl stickpin?
MISS I: Oh, where, where, where?
MR. R: Where is my fur *porte-monnaie*?
MISS U: Where is my ruby tooth?
MR. S: Where is my monogram?
ALL: Where? Where? Where? Where? (*As they exit*) Where?
Where? Where? Where?

SCENE 3

The Street. 105, 106, *and the* SERVANT *enter arm in arm doing*
a dance step.
105: Did you really like that party?
(*They stop dancing*)
106: Yes . . . I liked it.
105: I liked it, too. . . .
106: You did?
105: Yes. . . .
106 (*To the* SERVANT): Did you?
(*She thinks a moment. They resume the dance step and*
circle the stage)
SERVANT: You know?
(*They stop dancing*)
106: What?

SERVANT: To discover what everyone has always known is not
    important.
106: No, it isn't.
    (105 *and* 106 *take a step as if to resume the dance*)
SERVANT: However . . .
105: What?
SERVANT: I have just discovered what life is all about.
105: You have?
SERVANT: I have.

> *To walk down the street*
> *With a mean look in my face,*
> *A cigarette in my right hand*
> *A toothpick in my left;*
> *To alternate between the cigarette*
> *And the toothpick,*
> *Ah! That's life.*
>
> *Yes, I have learned from life.*
> *Every day I've learned some more.*
> *Every blow has been of use.*
> *Every joy has been a lesson.*
> *Yes, I have learned from life.*
> *What surprises me*
> *Is that life*
> *Has not learned from me.*

Why? . . . Well. . . . That would be hard to explain. . . . If I
could give you a kiss, perhaps you'd understand.

(*The* SERVANT *gives each a kiss*)

You still don't understand? . . . No?

> *Well, then,*
> *Because I'm placid as a cow,*
> *As lucid as glass,*
> *As frank as a bald head,*
> *As faithful as a dog.*

(*They start exiting doing the same dance step*)

You see what I mean?

(105 and 106 express doubt with their faces and nod. They exit. The MOTHER *enters. She walks slowly across the stage. When she reaches mid-stage she turns to the audience)*

MOTHER: Have you seen my babies? *(Pause)* No? . . . All right.

(She exits. There is the sound of a car, brakes, and a crash. The INJURED MAN *is hurled on stage. The car is heard starting and taking off at high speed. 105, 106 and the* SERVANT *enter. They look the* INJURED MAN *over. They pull the top of their sack open and give it to the* SERVANT *to hold. 106 takes the* INJURED MAN*'s wallet, watch, ring, shoes, and jacket, and passes them to 105 who puts them in the sack. They start tiptoeing away)*

INJURED MAN: Ohh . . .

(105, 106 and the SERVANT *stop short)*
Ohhh . . . ohhh . . .
105 *(Still without moving)*: What was that?
INJURED MAN: Ohhh . . .
(105, 106 and the SERVANT *tiptoe to the* INJURED MAN. *105 picks up the* INJURED MAN*'s arm)*
Ohhh . . .
(105 drops the arm. There is a short pause. He picks up the other arm)
Ohhh . . .
(105 drops the arm)
Ohhh . . .
105: He aches.
(They look at each other. They look at the INJURED MAN. *The* DRIVER *enters)*
DRIVER: I came back.
INJURED MAN: Ohh. Ohh.
DRIVER: To the scene of the crime.
INJURED MAN: Ohh. Ohh.
DRIVER: I'm a hit-and-run driver.
INJURED MAN: Ohh. Ohh.
DRIVER: I'll kill myself if you die.

INJURED MAN: Ohh. Ohh. I'm cold.

(*The* JAILER *enters*)

JAILER: Have you seen two prisoners escaped from the penitentiary? One tall. The other just a little taller? (105 *and* 106 *lie
as injured*) They wear prisoners' uniforms with the number
105 and 106 on the front and on the back of their jacks.

(105 *and* 106 *take off their jackets and put them on the*
INJURED MAN. *The number* 105 *is visible on his chest and* 106 *on
his back*)

INJURED MAN:
Thank you,
Thank you.
You're so nice,
You're so nice.
Thank you,
Thank you.
You're so nice,
You're so nice,
You're so nice.
Thank you,
Oh, thank you.

JAILER (*Pointing to the* INJURED MAN): That's one of them! Get
up, 105. (*The* JAILER *hits the* INJURED MAN *on the stomach.
The* INJURED MAN *bends over. The number* 106 *is visible on
his back*) There's the other. Get up, 106. That's them all
right. Get up.

DRIVER: Leave him alone. You're kicking the injured man.

JAILER: What do you mean? That's 105 and 106.

DRIVER: Does that look like two people to you? That's the
injured man.

(105 *and* 106 *begin to shiver*)

INJURED MAN: My friends are cold, too. Someone must have
stolen their clothes.

DRIVER: I'll take the clothes off my back to give to your friends.
If you die I'll kill myself. (*The* DRIVER *gives his jacket and
vest to* 105 *and* 106. *He shivers*) Now I'm cold.

INJURED MAN (*Giving one of the jackets to the* DRIVER): I have
enough for two.

JAILER: Which reminds me of this little woman I used to have.
She used to take her clothes off all the time. That was the

only thing I liked about her ... hey! There you are, 105 and 106. *(Taking the* DRIVER *and the* INJURED MAN *by the collar)* Don't tell me you're just one. I see you as plain as day. One and two. I can count. Don't tell me I can't count.

(He exits with the DRIVER *and the* INJURED MAN*)*

SERVANT:
Neither probe nor ignore
That the clothes make the man.
Isn't it true that costumes
Change the course of life?

Who can marry a gigolo?
Can you?
Can you?
I can't.

Who can love a businessman?
Can you?
Can you?
I can't.

Who can pity a cop?
Who can reason with a clown?
Who can dance with a priest?
Can you?
Can you?
I can't.

105, 106 and SERVANT:
You see, a costume
Can change your life.
Be one and all.
Be each and all.
Transvest,
Impersonate,
'Cause costumes
Change the course
Of life.

(The JAILER *re-enters, carrying the prisoners' jackets by the collar)*

JAILER: I'm taking these two prisoners back to jail.
(He shrugs his shoulders and exits)

105, 106 and SERVANT:
Who can argue with a jailer?
Can you?
Can you?
I can't.

Be one and all.
Be each and all.
Transvest,
Impersonate,
'Cause costumes
Change the course
Of life.

(They exit)

SCENE 4

*The Park. 105 and 106 sit on a bench. They each knit one
end of a single scarf. The* SERVANT *sits between them. The*
MOTHER *enters.*

MOTHER: I've lost my babies. I've been looking for them for
years and I can't find them. Have you seen them?
106: No.
MOTHER: You haven't seen my babies, have you?
SERVANT: No.
MOTHER: They aren't very pretty, but they have beautiful eyes. I
lost my babies right here. Have you seen them?
105 and 106: No.

MOTHER:
Have you seen my babies?
I've been looking for them for years,
And I can't find them.

Have you seen them?
Have you seen them?
Have you seen them?

Have you seen two little angels?
Have you? With skin soft like feathers
In diapers still.

Have you seen them?
Have you seen them?
Have you seen them?

Have you seen those sweet angels?
Have you seen them . . .

(The MOTHER *looks closely at* 105 *and* 106)

No . . . My babies were pretty. These are not my babies. *(She
looks again)* No. These are big, ugly and old. Mine were this
big. *(She indicates the size of an infant)* And pretty. . . . 'Bye.
105 and 106: 'Bye.
(The MOTHER *exits)*
106: Hmm. Big, ugly and old . . .
105: Well, we could be younger.
(The MOTHER *re-enters and watches* 105 *and* 106 *from behind
the bushes)*
106: True.
105: We could be prettier.
106: Not true.
105: We could be smaller.
106: Don't want to be.

105 and 106:
  It's to age
  That we owe
  What we are.

  In fact we're grateful
  For the passing of time.
  It's only fitting
  We should be grateful
  For the passing of time.
  'Cause
  Without growth
  We'd not be
  What we are.

MOTHER: What are you?

(They pose for her. They point to themselves from head to toe. They do a turn. They do a tap step)

105 and 106:
We are
All that we are.
From head to toe.

Once it's thoroughly thought through
We should realize
It's only appropriate
We should be attracted
To the passing of time,
Attracted to the passing of time.
'Cause it's to age
That we owe what we are.
And without it
We'd not be
What we are.

MOTHER: It's distressing to get old.

106: Well, you are bound to get older . . .

105: If you're going to be alive.

(The LADIES *and* GENTLEMEN *walk in, led by* MR. S, *who scans the floor for footprints. They walk by* 105, 106 *and the* SERVANT *without noticing them)*

MR. S: They went this way. Follow me. I took a course in trails, tracks and clues. *(He discovers* MISS U*'s foot)* Oh, what pretty feet you have, Miss U.

MISS U: I do?

MR. T: Feet? Where? Oh . . .

MR. S: Dainty.

MR. T: Hm. Delicious. *(Lifting her skirt)* Let's see your ankle, Miss U. Oh, it's pretty.

MISS U: Mr. R, wouldn't you like to admire my feet? Each toe has a personality all its own.

MR. R: Oh, I've seen them.

MISS U: You cad! *(To* MR. S *and* MR. T*)* Who am I?

MR. S and MR. T: The queen!

MISS U: And what are my virtues?

*(*MR. S *and* MR. T *lift her up on their shoulders)*

MR. S and MR. T: You are flighty! You are fickle! And you are
  wicked!
MISS U: That's right.
  (*They put her down.* MISS U *walks to* MR. R. *He turns his back
  to her*)

  You rascal!

  Capricious as I am, and fickle,
  In spite of my renowned restlessness,
  In spite of my noted changeability;
  My versatility, my spirit of adventure,
  One day because of your winning ways
  I gave you all I had.
  And you in your typical fashion,
  Conceited, flippant, and complacent,
  Just threw it all away,
  Just threw it all away.
  You heel! You cad!
  You treated me the way I treated others.
  You scoundrel!
  How dare you bring shame to my life? Shame ... shame.

  One day, because of your amorous claims,
  I learned that pleasure
  Does not need fabrication;
  That true love catches you by surprise.
  But you, confirmed egotist,
  You were just playing games.

  You insisted on re-enacting
  A moment from your past;
  Either a moment that you lived
  Or a moment that you imagined.
  You heel! You were just playing games. Shame ... shame. ...

  I am conceited, flippant and deceitful,
  And I am flighty, frivolous, and vain.
  And you, scoundrel,
  You treated me the way I treated others.
  Just who do you think you are?

In spite of my reputation
As a lady without heart
I gave my heart to you.
You heel . . .
And here I am.
I've lost my heart to you.

Unaccustomed as I am
To asking a man for his favor,
I'm asking you,
Come . . . come . . . come . . .
I'm helpless without you.

(MR. R *walks to* MISS U. *They kiss. Immediately after,* MR. R *touches* MISS I's *face and blows her a kiss.* MISS U *punches* MR. R *in the stomach.* MR. R *falls.* MR. T *and* MR. S *carry him off followed by* MISS O, MISS I, MISS U, *and the* MOTHER)

SERVANT: Ahhhh. Riches made them dumb.
105: Who?
SERVANT: All of them. Mr. R, Mr. S, Mr. T, Miss I, Miss O, Miss U.
105: Really?
SERVANT: Yes, money made them dumb.
106: Did it? How dumb?
SERVANT: Very dumb. Money makes you dumb.
106: Naw . . .
SERVANT: Yes! . . . I'll show you.

(*She puts on a bracelet, a necklace and a brooch. She imitates the speech of the* LADIES *and* GENTLEMEN)

If someone scrubs the pot. Perhaps it will get shiny. I'm neither this, nor that. Only exactly what I think I am. That is, if you think I'm frank, frank, frank.

(*She reaches for more jewels.* 105 *and* 106 *begin to dress her. They drape a lace tablecloth around her, hang the silverware around her waist and put the rest of the jewelry on her. At the end of the song they put the chandelier on her head as a crown*)

Is it time yet to be naked?
Oh, no no no no no, oh, no.
It might be a little indiscreet

To take off my clothes before three.
Aah . . . aah . . . aah . . .

It is now time to get dressed.
Dress, dress, dress, dress, dress me.
It is time to put on my clothes.
Aah . . . aah . . . aah . . .

In my life I've made some errors.
Errors one and two and three,
Four, five, six,
Seven, eight, nine, ten.
Wonderful errors. Marvelous errors.
From a to z.

I used to be an ordinary girl
With a delicate soul.
Now I'm just ordinary.
Where did my soul go?
Aah . . . aah . . . aah
Where did it go?
Where did my soul go?

Someone has mentioned my name.
But who is it he speaks of?
You see I'm neither this nor that,
Neither this nor that.
And I'm not free to love.

Someone has mentioned my name
But I'm neither this nor that.
And I've forgotten who I am,
I've forgotten who I am
But I can, I can, I can rhyme,
Yme,* yme, yme, yme, yme,
I can, I can, I can rhyme,
Yme, yme, yme, yme, yme.

Why have you not crowned me yet.
I'm neither this nor that

* Pronounced ime.

But I can rhyme.
I can rhyme
Yme, yme, yme, yme, yme.

(They crown her)

I can rhyme
Yme, yme, yme, yme, yme.
You see what I mean?

105: Not really.
(106 *shakes his head*)
SERVANT (*In an attempt to convince them*):

Yme yme yme yme yme yme
Rhyme.

It's also bad for your health. (She sneezes)

106: Are you rich, dear? You seem to have a cold.
SERVANT: I used to be poor. Very, very poor. But now, I'm very, very, very, very rich. (*She sneezes*)
105: You are?
SERVANT: Yes.
106: Watch out you don't lose your brains. Remember, riches make you dumb. Ho ho ho.
105: And you are even beginning to imagine things. Ho ho.

106:
Riches make you dumb.

105:
Yme, yme, yme, rhyme.

SERVANT:
I can rhyme.

(105 *places the sack on the floor next to the* SERVANT, *while* 106 *picks her up and stands her on the sack. Now she is part of their loot. The* JAILER *watches from a corner. They pull the sack over the* SERVANT's *head, carry her on their shoulders and exit*)

Act Two

SCENE 1

The Battlefield. There is the sound of bombs. The lights flash on and off. SOLDIERS I *and* II *lie on the floor. Their heads, arms, and torsos are wrapped in bandages.* 105 *and* 106 *run across the stage. They still carry the* SERVANT. *The* JAILER *follows them. He stops when he sees the* SOLDIERS.

JAILER: There you are, 105 and 106, you're digging. Your disguise does not deceive me. I'd recognize you miles away. I'm a smart man, and your tricks are puerile. *(Bomb)* I think I'll watch from afar. This time they're playing with dynamite and a man can get hurt with that. *(Bomb. He exits)*

SOLDIER I: John . . .

SOLDIER II: What?

SOLDIER I: Did you get drafted?

SOLDIER II: Drafted!

SOLDIER I: Did you volunteer?

SOLDIER II: For what?

SOLDIER I: To get the bombs dropped on you.

SOLDIER II: No, I didn't.

SOLDIER I: How did they get you?

SOLDIER II: I was going home from work when someone said: "Hey, soldier!" and I made the mistake to look.

SOLDIER I: You volunteered then.

SOLDIER II: Why?

SOLDIER I: Because you looked.

SOLDIER II: Gosh! I shouldn't have looked.

SOLDIER I: Well, they get you anyway, whether you look or not.

SOLDIER II: How did they get you?

SOLDIER I: I got drafted. When the man said "Hey, soldier," I kept walking. But he hit me on the head, told me to drop my pants, spread my cheeks, threw me on a barber chair, and here I am. . . . They didn't even let me face the mirror.

SOLDIER II: That's tough.

SOLDIER I: John, we used to have a good time, didn't we?

SOLDIER II: Yes, remember the time we got in trouble by the fountain?

SOLDIER I: *You* got in trouble.

SOLDIER II: I was a little drunk. And there was a cop standing in the corner. And I said to him "Hey, flatfoot.". . . Ha ha ha ha ha. . . . It was a nice evening.

SOLDIER I: John . . .

SOLDIER II: What?

SOLDIER I: Do you think we're going to win the war?

SOLDIER II: We might.

SOLDIER I: How can we? We don't even have guns.

SOLDIER II: Only bandages.

SOLDIER I: What can we do with bandages?

SOLDIER II: Just wait till we get hit, I guess.

(*A bomb falls. At the same time* 105 *and* 106 *are hurled on stage. Their heads and torsos are wrapped in bandages.* SOLDIERS I *and* II *fall to the ground. Another bomb falls.* 105 *and* 106 *huddle up to the* SOLDIERS. *They are silent and motionless for a while*)

SOLDIER I: John . . .

SOLDIER II: What?

SOLDIER I: Are you alive?

SOLDIER II: Yes. I'm just wounded. . . . And you?

SOLDIER I: Just wounded. . . . (*Pause*) John . . .

SOLDIER II: What? (SOLDIER I *points to* 105 *and* 106. SOLDIER II *turns his head cautiously*) Who are they?

SOLDIER I (*Pointing to* SOLDIER II, *himself and all around*): Same thing . . . enlisted . . . (*To* 105 *and* 106) How did they get you?

106: We were walking down the street and we heard someone say, "Hey, soldier."

SOLDIER I: And you looked.

SOLDIER II: You shouldn't have looked.

SOLDIER I: Well, they get you anyway. I didn't look, but they hit me on the head, threw me on the barber chair, and here I am . . . waiting for the bombs . . . (*Pause*) John . . .

SOLDIER II: What?

SOLDIER I: In case I don't make it, drop this in the mail, will you?

SOLDIER II: What is it?

SOLDIER I: A letter. Can't you see it's a letter?

SOLDIER II: What does it say?

(SOLDIER I *takes the letter out of the envelope and sings*)

SOLDIER I:
Sidney N. Phelps, Director.
Dining, sleeping, and parlor car,

Penn Central, Long Island City,
New York, one one one o one.

Mr. Phelps,
On Tuesday, March seventeenth,
On board The Boston Colonial
Of the Penn Central Railroad
I had the worst hamburger
I ever had;
Served to me on dining car
Four four seven four four.
Mr. Phelps, I've had
Bad hamburgers before,
But that was the worst
I ever had.

SOLDIER II: That's awful. I'll mail it for you.

(*He reaches for the letter but is distracted by the* MAYOR *and* MISS CAKE'*s entrance. He carries a picnic basket. She wears a shawl. They walk through serenely and gallantly*)

MAYOR: My rose, is it too cool for you?

MISS CAKE: No, it's rather balmy. And besides, I'm wearing my wrap.

MAYOR: It's so nice of you to come with me to review the troops.

MISS CAKE: Don't mention it.

(*The* SOLDIERS, 105 *and* 106 *watch them exit.* SOLDIER II *reaches for the letter again*)

SOLDIER I: I don't really want it mailed.

SOLDIER II: Why not?

SOLDIER I: I don't care about the hamburger.

SOLDIER II: You don't?

SOLDIER I: No.

SOLDIER II: Why did you write the letter?

SOLDIER I: I was angry . . . at Madeline.

SOLDIER II: You wrote a letter about a hamburger because you were angry at Madeline?

SOLDIER I: Yes.

When Madeline told me it was all off
I took The Boston Colonial,
And as the train pulled off
I looked to see if my Madeline was there,
But she wasn't.

Oh, Madeline. Oh, Madeline
Why weren't you there?
Why weren't you there?

(Bomb. The MOTHER *enters)*

MOTHER: Have you seen my babies? *(The* SOLDIERS, 105 *and* 106 *shake their heads)* They were round and tender.... They only spoke two words ... poles apart.... Let me see if I can remember.... North-South.... No, that's not it.... Well, take any two words and say they were it. Have you seen them? *(They shake their heads)* They had small teeth. Like little grains of rice. And just two ... in front.... You haven't seen them?

(They shake their heads. The MOTHER *exits singing "Two Little Angels" sotto-voce. The* MAYOR *and* MISS CAKE *enter)*

MAYOR: Ah, there you are. I seem to have bypassed you. *(To* MISS CAKE) Here is the platoon, my lily. We bypassed them.

MISS CAKE: Yes.... This is where they are ... and were.

(The SERVANT *enters, running. She carries the loot bag. The* JAILER *follows her. They circle the* SOLDIERS *twice. The* JAILER *changes direction and grabs the* SERVANT *as she runs toward him. She throws the loot bag up in the air.* 106 *catches it and throws it to* 105 *as the* JAILER *goes toward him)*

MAYOR: Oh, what's happening? Why all the running? *(The bag goes from hand to hand until it falls in the* MAYOR's *hands)* Oh, a donation for the orphanage ... from the troops. How timely. I was just thinking I need a new team of horses ... for my new carriage. *(He starts giving the bag to the* JAILER) Here, take this to my house. Never mind, I'll do it myself. *(He gives the* JAILER *the picnic basket)* Take this. Go find a nice spot for the picnic, with flowers and a view. And take my damsel to it. Make sure it's a shady spot. The sun makes her blush.

MISS CAKE: Flush.

JAILER: Flush sounds better. I'm sure this lady never blushed.

(The SERVANT *tries to take the bag from the* MAYOR. *He threatens her with the back of his hand. The* LADIES *and* GENTLEMEN *enter in the manner of people at a garden party)*

MAYOR: What now? Review the troops. Att-en-tion. There you are ... standing at attention. Fine bunch. They jump at my command. *(They all jump slightly)* Ha ha. That's the spirit. Let's see ... *(Referring to* MISS I) That's a nice posture, sergeant. (*Giving her a slap on the back*) Good boy . . . good boy. Splendid, get his name. (*To* MISS O) That's a nice uniform, officer, where did you have it made? Shipshape. (*He kisses* MISS O *on both cheeks*) You can't tell the men from the women nowadays. But it doesn't matter . . . it does not matter as long as they can shoot. Shoot. Shoot. Nothing wrong with you boys. (*Looking at* MISS U) Hm, that's a good cannon ball. Yes, shipshape. Everything's in good form. Lucky stiffs. Shoot. Shoot. (*Bomb*) Ooops. Don't shoot your captain now. Shoot to the side. Ha ha. Yes, sir, pretty field you have here, roses and fireworks. Lucky stiffs, you can have a picnic any time you want . . . Look at those guns. Great guns. Rifles. That's what you call them. (*Bomb*) Ooops. What's that noise? I didn't know it was the Fourth of July. . . . Neither did I. Hm. I'm sure I brought someone with me. Where is my damsel?

MISS CAKE: Yooo hoooo. I'm here.

MAYOR: There you are of course.

(*The* MAYOR *goes to* MISS CAKE)

MISS U: Rompous-mompus-gambol-mumble!

(*The music for "Spring is Here" starts*)

MAYOR: Hmmm. I smell chocolate pudding. . . . Where is it?

(*He stands abruptly and runs after the* SERVANT)

LADIES: Mompus-mumble-rompous-gambol!

(*The* JAILER *and the* MAYOR *bump against each other. They start dancing together.* MISS CAKE *dances on the tablecloth. The* LADIES *and* GENTLEMEN *start undoing the* SOLDIER's *head bandages*)

LADIES and GENTLEMEN: Spring is here!

LADIES:
Ahaa ahaa ahaa
Arbutus are here,
And spring beauties.
Ohoo ohoo ohoo
It's springtime,
And hepaticas are blooming.

(*The* LADIES *and* GENTLEMEN *dance around the* SOLDIERS *using their head bandages as ribbons around a Maypole*)

LADIES and GENTLEMEN:
I see a bride,
Oohoohoo hoohoohoo
I see a bride in white.
Oohoohoo hoohoohoo

SOLDIER I: Oh, please don't.

LADIES and GENTLEMEN:
I see a lady,
I see two,
I see a groom behind a tree.
Oohoohoo hoohoohoo

SOLDIER I: Don't do that.
(Simultaneously with:)
SOLDIER II: Please don't.

LADIES and GENTLEMEN:
Come out, come out
Wherever you are.
Come out, come out
Wherever you are.

LADIES: Those who give will get of nature's bounty through the
year.
SOLDIER I and SOLDIER II: Oh.
(The MOTHER *starts hitting the* DANCERS*)*
MOTHER: Leave them alone . . .

LADIES and GENTLEMEN:
I see a bride,
Oohoohoo hoohoohoo.
I see a bride in white,
Oohoohoo hoohoohoo.

MOTHER: Leave them alone. Let go.

LADIES and GENTLEMEN:
I see a lady,
I see two.
I see a groom

Behind a tree,
Oohoohoo hoohoohoo.

Apples,
Peaches,
Pumpkin pie.
I see you,
I see you,
Anyone I see is it.

LADIES: Look down a well reflected in a mirror. And you'll see your future spouse's face.
SOLDIER I: Oh, Madeline.

LADIES:	GENTLEMEN:
Ready or not here I come.	*Come out, come out*
Ready or not here I come.	*Come out, come out*

SOLDIER I:
I looked to see if my Madeline
Was there.
But she wasn't.
Oh, Madeline, Madeline, Madeline.
Why weren't you there?

LADIES and GENTLEMEN: O, what a fierce and fiery fiesta.

SERVANT, 105, 106:	LADIES, GENTLEMEN:
Riches made them dumb	*I see a lady*
Riches made them dumb	*I see two.*

MOTHER: Let them go.
MAYOR: Come to my house everyone. I have plenty of wine, and you people are a jolly bunch.
(The DANCERS exit as they sing the following:)

DANCERS:
Après vous,
Après vous,
Pas du tout.
Je vous en prie.
Mon plaisir.

Le nôtre.
Permettez-moi.
Nôtre plaisir.
Le mien.
A votre service.
Au votre.
Au votre.
L'age avant la beauté.

(*The* MOTHER, 105, 106 *and the* SERVANT *go to the* SOLDIERS. *The* MOTHER *and the* SERVANT *hold them in their arms while* 105 *and* 106 *take off their bandages*)

MOTHER: Here. I have something you'll like. (*She looks in her pockets*) Oh, I forgot to bring it. (*She looks again*) I always have something in my pockets. Well, I'll tell you a story . . . There was a man . . . a very wise man who wanted to conquer pain. He tried and tried but he couldn't find a way. . . . One day he went fishing just to distract himself from this thought that occupied his mind. . . . He caught one fish and then another . . . and as he sat there waiting for the next fish to bite, he suddenly said, "I got it! You conquer pain the way you catch a fish. When pain bites you don't look away. You pull it toward you. And when it's right on top of you, and it starts flapping, and almost knocking you down, that's when you have it conquered, because it's out of the water." Yes, that's what he said.

105 and 106:
When I was born I opened my eyes,
And when I looked around I closed them;
And when I saw how people get kicked in the head,
And kicked in the belly, and kicked in the groin,
I closed them.
My eyes are closed but I'm carefree.
Ho ho ho, ho ho ho, I'm carefree.

105:
A poor man has fifty problems every day,
Fifty problems upon opening his eyes,
Fifty problems every minute of the day.
And life is sour.
One thing a poor man has,

That a rich man doesn't have,
Is fifty problems every day.

When a wound is open
And the guts are hanging out,
It hurts.
And it hurts as much
When a man's life
Is dark and narrow.

A poor man doesn't know
Where his pain comes from.
There is a dark wall,
And a closed door,
And a dirty old room,
And he doesn't know how he got there.

A poor man's life is sour
And he doesn't know
Who made it so.

106:

A poor man has to do what he's told.
He doesn't know just why he does it.
He just has to do what he's told.

Do the dirty work.
Get off the street.
It's you who has to fight the war.

He gets kicked in the head,
And kicked in the belly,
And kicked in the groin.

I know what madness is.
It's not-knowing how another man feels.
A madman has never been
In another man's shoes.

Madness is lack of compassion,
And there's little compassion
In the world.

It's only stupid things
That make a madman feel sure:
Money, power, adulation;
Never just being alive,
Having two feet on the ground,
And having heart to give.

105 and 106:
When I was born I opened my eyes,
And when I looked around I closed them;
And when I saw how people get kicked in the head,
And kicked in the belly, and kicked in the groin,
I closed them.
My eyes are closed but I'm carefree.
Ho ho ho, ho ho ho, I'm carefree.

(The SOLDIERS *feel their healed bodies)*

SOLDIER II: I feel better.
SOLDIER I: I do, too.
SOLDIER II: Let's go to the Mayor's party.
MOTHER: I don't want to go to the Mayor's party.
SOLDIER II: Why not?
MOTHER: I don't like him.
   (SOLDIER II *beckons the* SERVANT. *She shakes her head)*
SOLDIER II *(To 105 and 106):* There'll be wine there.
   (They shake their heads. He goes to SOLDIER I *and punches him lightly.* SOLDIER I *shakes his head. The music to "Why Not" starts.* SOLDIER II *starts dancing. He turns to the* MOTHER*)*
Come . . .
   (He leads the MOTHER *in a simple dance)*

SOLDIER I, II, the SERVANT and the MOTHER:
La la la
La la la
La la la
La la la

(He beckons the SERVANT *once more)*

SERVANT:
Why not? Why not?
Let's go and have some fun

Why not?
If we can dance and have some fun;
If there's free wine.
We're a jolly bunch.

(The MOTHER *and* SOLDIER II *start exiting doing the same dance step.* SOLDIER I *and the* SERVANT *join them)*

SOLDIER I, II, the SERVANT and the MOTHER:
Why not? Why not?
Why not?
Why not!

(105 and 106 follow them. They are downcast)

SCENE 2

The MAYOR's *drawing room. The* MAYOR *sits on a high chair. A stethoscope hangs from his neck. The* JAILER *and* MISS CAKE *stand by his sides. The rest enter in the order they left the previous scene.*

MAYOR: Welcome . . . Welcome . . . I am about to entertain. Whoever is not amused will be sent to the common cell.

JAILER: Hear, hear. The show is about to start.

MAYOR: Have any of you ever heard the story of the rabbit and the turtle?

ALL: Yes.

MAYOR: You see, it goes like this: There was once a rabbit who said to the turtle: "Run fast. Run fast, or I'll win the race." "I'll run slowly," said the turtle, "and win the race." "If that is the case, I'll take a rest," said the rabbit. "Who are you to give me advantages?" said the turtle. And so on . . . and so on . . . and so on. Whoever doesn't laugh will be sent to the common cell. *(They all laugh reluctantly)* Good. Now the party's over. Let me see what time it is. *(Looking at his watch)* Too late! Everybody's under arrest for keeping me up so late. Wait, you've been reprieved. My watch stopped. It must be earlier than I thought. Or later. Amuse yourselves. I give the best parties in town. I don't? Who said that? I must be hearing things again. No one would dare say I don't give the best parties in town. Now, who has some mighty good entertainment?

(MR. R, MR. S *and* MR. T *walk to the center in a vaudevillian manner*)

MR. R: This is my son. (*Apologetically*) He needs a haircut.

MR. S: What he needs is a new face.

(MR. R, MR. S *and* MR. T *laugh heartily*)

MAYOR: Pretty dull. Pretty dull. I have seen better entertainment than that. You better do something funny, or I'll tell you another story.

(MR. R *steps forward*)

MR. R:

Whenever my fingers went like this,
I said: "Hell, my fingers always go like that."
Until one day somebody said to me:
"How original it is that your fingers go like that."

Since then, every time my fingers go like this,
I say: "Look at my fingers go like that.
How original it is that my fingers go like this."
One of these days I'll sell them.

(*They applaud*)

MAYOR: That's nothing! I wouldn't buy your fingers if you paid me. Why, I remember the days when I could do all kinds of things with my fingers and my mother used to say to me, "Why Jennifer, you're being salacious." Ha ha. (*They all laugh reluctantly*) Who's next?

(MR. T *takes out a song sheet. He gets the key from the piano and sings:*)

MR. T:

It is true, I told you I would love you
And I never did.
But remember, I'm forgetful,
Little fool.
Longings are like vapor.
They go as they come.
And remember, little fool,
I'm forgetful.

Both my wife's and my mistress' name is Kate.
One day, while I made love to Kate, my wife,
I thought of my sweet mistress Kate.

In a moment of passion and confusion,
I said: "Kate, dear Kate, oh, Kate."
My wife, hearing me speak my mistress's name,
Said harsh words to me, and put me on the street.
Is that fair, I ask you, is that fair?

It is true, I told you I would love you,
And I never did.
But remember, I'm forgetful,
Little fool.

ALL:

Longings are like vapor.
They go as they come.

MR. T:

And remember, little fool,
I'm forgetful.

(They all applaud. The SERVANT *does a dance to the accompaniment of the "Czardas." Others play instruments, do head stands, kazatskis, and different tricks according to the actor's ability)*

MAYOR: No good. No good. That's common and ordinary. I'm a poet and a scholar. Let's hear some poetry.

105: Miss Cake?

MISS CAKE: Yes, Mr. 105.

105: What do you aim at in your work?

MISS CAKE: Magic.

106: Do you always achieve it?

MISS CAKE: Yes. Once in a while.

106: You don't mean always, then.

MISS CAKE: Yes, I do.

105: Explain.

MISS CAKE: In mathematical terms, if the impossible is ever achieved, it becomes always. That is how eternity is conceived.

MAYOR: That makes sense. But it's not poetry. Go back to your cake. Now, this is poetry.

A petunia is a flower like a begonia.
You fry begonia like you fry sausage.
Sausage and battery is a crime.

Monkeys crime trees.
Tree is a crowd.
The cock crowd and made a noise.
You have a noise on your face, also two eyes.
The opposite of ayes is nays.
A horse nays and has a colt.
You go to bed with a colt,
And wake up with double petunia.

Whoever doesn't laugh will be sent to the common cell.
(*All except* 105 *and* 106 *sing the* "Laughing Song." *The* MAYOR *uses his stethoscope to make sure they are all laughing. At the end of the song he reaches* 105 *and* 106. *To the* JAILER:
Take them away.
(*As the* JAILER *takes* 105 *and* 106 *away, the* MOTHER *takes a few steps toward them*)
MOTHER: Don't take my children away.

Does anyone understand a mother's love?
Except a mother?
Does a father understand a mother's love?
Except a good father?
Does anyone understand a mother's love?
Except a son, or a grandfather, or an uncle?

ALL: Everyone.

MOTHER (*Recitative*):
Then do you know that one autumn afternoon
My children disappeared and that that very
Autumn afternoon my life ended?

(*The* JAILER *re-enters with* 105 *and* 106)
JAILER: I went the wrong way. That's the kitchen. (*He walks in the opposite direction*)
MOTHER: Oh . . . I must kill myself.
(*The* MOTHER *pantomimes reaching for a knife and stabbing herself. She falls to the ground*)
MAYOR: Marvelous . . . marvelous. That's good entertainment. Do it again. (*The* MOTHER *stands and repeats the same motions*) Marvelous. Now the party is over. Let me see what time it is. Too late! Everybody's under arrest for keeping me

up so late. Good night. That was mighty good entertainment. The old lady's on the ball. *(The* JAILER *takes everyone to jail. The* MAYOR *waves)* I must remember that.

(He tries to remember the MOTHER'*s movements. The lights fade)*

SCENE 3

The Cell. It is empty. There is the sound of voices. All except the MAYOR *enter.*

JAILER: The ladies are to come with me to the next cell ... one at a time. It's too crowded here.

MISS O: Yes, it's too crowded here. I am not having fun.

MR. T: Don't push, Miss I. There is no place to go. *(To* MR. S*)* You are stepping on my toe.

MR. S: Who said that being arrested could be fun?

MISS I: Well, it's not all that it's made up to be. It's a bore.

MISS U: I like it.

MR. R: She likes it. Why do you like it?

MISS U: It's different.

MR. R: You're sticking your elbow in my back, Miss O.

MISS O: I can't help it. I'm being pushed.

MR. R: Well, don't bend your arm. Keep it straight.

(MISS O *straightens her arm)*

MR. S: Oops. Who did that?

MR. T: I'm going home. Make way.

MISS O: Me, too.

JAILER: You can't go home. You're under arrest.

(MR. T *and* MISS O *exit through the hole)*

MR. S: Little man, step aside.

(The JAILER *steps aside. All except the* MOTHER, *the* SERVANT, 105 *and* 106 *begin to exit)*

MR. R: Let's call Mr. Lipschitz.

MR. S: Let's play croquet. At night you don't know if the ball went under the wicket.

MISS O: Oh, let's play it on my lawn. I don't even have a set.

MISS I: Fickle ...

(The JAILER *exits through the door and locks it)*

JAILER: Well, whoever is left is under arrest.

(He exits)

SERVANT: Sure. *(Pause)* Well ... I'll go now....

MOTHER: Where will you go?

SERVANT: I don't know . . . I'll go for a walk.
MOTHER: Will you be all right?
SERVANT: Yes, it's almost morning. The city is quiet now.
MOTHER: Be careful.
SERVANT: I'll be careful. *(To 105 and 106)* Good night, friends.
105 and 106: Good night.
SERVANT: I'll be seeing you.
105 and 106: Would you like us to go with you?
SERVANT: No. I . . . It's okay. I'd like to be alone . . . and think.
105 and 106: We'll see you soon. . . .
SERVANT: Real soon.

(The door opens for her. She steps out of the cell and turns to wave. They wave back. She exits)

MOTHER: Well, it's time to go to sleep now.
105 and 106: Yes.
MOTHER: Did you have a good time, my children?
105 and 106: Yes.
MOTHER: Did you find evil?
105 and 106: No.
MOTHER: Good night, then. Sleep well. You'll find it some other time.
105 and 106: Good night.

(The MOTHER rocks them to sleep)

MOTHER:

I saw a man lying in the street,
Asleep and drunk,
He had not washed his face.
He held his coat closed with a safety pin
And I thought, and I thought
Thank God, I'm better than he is.
Yes, thank God, I'm better than he.

I have to live with my own truth,
I have to live with it.
You live with your own truth,
I cannot live with it.
I have to live with my own truth,
Whether you like it or not,
Whether you like it or not.

There are many poor people in the world,
Whether you like it or not.
There are many poor people in the world.
But I'm not one of them.
I'm not one of them.
Someone's been stealing my apples
But I'm not one of them,
I'm not one of them.

I know everything.
Half of it I really know,
The rest I make up,
The rest I make up.
Some things I'm sure of,
Of other things I'm too sure,
And of others I'm not sure at all.
People believe everything they hear,
Not what they see, not what they see.
People believe everything they hear;
But me, I see everything.
Yes, I see everything.

The saddest day of my life was the day
That I pitied a despicable man.
And I've been sad ever since,
Yes, I've been sad ever since.
I'd like to go where a human being
Is not a strange thing,
Is not a strange thing.

When I go, no one will water my plants.
When I go, no one will water my plants.
No one ... no one ... no one ...

Yes, my children, you'll find evil ... some other time. . . .
Good night.
(She exits)

105 and 106: Good night.

All is well in the city.
People do what they want.

They can go to the park.
They can sleep all they want.
And for those who have no cake,
There's plenty of bread.

STANLEY RICHARDS

Since the publication of his first collection in 1968, Stanley Richards has become one of our leading editors and play anthologists, earning rare encomiums from the nation's press (the *Writers Guild of America News* described him as "easily the best anthologist of plays in America"), and the admiration of a multitude of devoted readers.

Mr. Richards has edited the following anthologies and series: *America on Stage: Ten Great Plays of American History; Best Plays of the Sixties; Great Musicals of the American Theatre: Volume One; Great Musicals of the American Theatre: Volume Two; Best Mystery and Suspense Plays of the Modern Theatre; 10 Classic Mystery and Suspense Plays of the Modern Theatre* (the latter six, Fireside Theatre–Literary Guild selections); *The Tony Winners; Twenty One-Act Plays; Best Short Plays of the World Theatre: 1968–1973; Best Short Plays of the World Theatre: 1958–1967; Modern Short Comedies from Broadway and London; Canada on Stage;* and, since 1968, *The Best Short Plays* annuals.

An established playwright as well, Mr. Richards has written twenty-five plays, twelve of which (including *Through a Glass, Darkly; Tunnel of Love; August Heat; Sun Deck; O Distant Land;* and *District of Columbia*) were originally published in earlier volumes of *The Best One-Act Plays* and *The Best Short Plays.*

Journey to Bahia, which Mr. Richards adapted from a prize-winning Brazilian play and film, *O Pagador de Promessas*, premiered at the Berkshire Playhouse, Massachusetts, and later was produced in Washington, D.C., under the auspices of the Brazilian Ambassador and the Brazilian-American Cultural Institute. The play also had a successful engagement Off-Broadway and subsequently was performed in a Spanish translation at Lincoln Center. During the summer of 1975, the play was presented at the Edinburgh International Festival, after a tour of several British cities.

Mr. Richards' plays have been translated for production and

publication abroad into Portuguese, Afrikaans, Dutch, Tagalog, French, German, Korean, Italian and Spanish.

He also has been the New York theatre critic for *Players Magazine* and a frequent contributor to *Playbill, Theatre Arts, The Theatre* and *Actors' Equity Magazine,* among other periodicals.

As an American Theatre Specialist, Mr. Richards was awarded three successive grants by the U.S. Department of State's International Cultural Exchange Program to teach playwriting and directing in Chile and Brazil. He taught playwriting in Canada for over ten years and was Visiting Professor of Drama at the University of Guelph, Ontario. He has produced and directed plays and has lectured extensively on theatre at universities in the United States, Canada and South America.

Mr. Richards, a New York City resident, is now at work on two new play anthologies.